LYRA GRAECA

I

—As the hyacinth which the shepherd tramples
on the hill
Lies upon the ground and lying bloometh
purple still.

SAPPHO

FROM A FIFTH CENTURY KYLIX
BY SOTADES IN THE BRITISH MUSEUM

LYRA GRAECA

BEING THE REMAINS OF ALL THE GREEK LYRIC POETS FROM EUMELUS TO TIMOTHEUS EXCEPTING PINDAR

NEWLY EDITED AND TRANSLATED BY

J. M. EDMONDS

LATE FELLOW OF JESUS COLLEGE CAMBRIDGE

IN THREE VOLUMES

VOLUME I

INCLUDING

TERPANDER ALCMAN SAPPHO AND ALCAEUS

LONDON : WILLIAM HEINEMANN

NEW YORK : G. P. PUTNAM'S SONS

MCMXXII

1922

ΜΑΘΗΤΡΙΑΙΣ
ΣΥΜΜΑΘΗΤΗΣ

PREFACE

SINCE the appearance of the fourth edition of Theodor Bergk's *Poetae Lyrici Graeci*, in which they form the third volume, the Lyric Fragments, or as they are more accurately called, the Melic Fragments, have not been published complete. The last forty years, thanks mainly to the work of the Egypt Exploration Fund and similar societies, have added very notably to our slender store, and a new edition has been long overdue. My book will, I hope, go some way to supply the want. It is complete in the sense that its sole omissions are fragments which have only palaeographical value, and it contains all that is really necessary by way of exegesis. In all places where the text adopted would otherwise be misleading I have given critical notes, save only where I have already discussed the reading in one or other of the classical periodicals. Many scholars—and to say this is not to depreciate a great work; for such things depend on the point of view—must have found Bergk lacking in two respects. First, when so little is known of these great figures of antiquity, all that little has value for us if they are to seem things of flesh and blood and not the mere subjects of a lesson in translation. With the single exception of Sappho's, the Fragments alone are not enough. I have therefore included, unlike Bergk, the chief passages of ancient literature which throw light on the life and personality of the poets and their literary reputation in antiquity—not making an exception of Sappho; for the clear-drawn self-

portrait she gives us in her Fragments is so precious that its very frame is of surpassing interest. To these 'Lives' I have added the ancient accounts of such early poet-musicians as Olympus and Thaletas, partly to serve in some sort as an introduction to the subject, and partly in order to avoid creating the impression that only the poets of whom some work is extant are of any importance to the student of Greek poetry. Secondly, if these mere quotations are to have more than linguistic interest, in nine cases out of ten they want explanation, and in at least five of those nine the explanation may be had from the context in which they are found. Bergk appears to have regarded the contexts as a necessary evil, and has not only relegated them to the footnotes but has made them less useful than they might have been by cutting them as short as he possibly could. I have thought it better to give full contexts in the body of the page, printing them, however, in small type so that the reader may the more easily omit them if he will.

A feature peculiar to this edition is the inclusion of a considerable number of restorations made *exempli gratia* of passages preserved only in paraphrase. These restorations, as well as those of the new Fragments, are mainly my own. The reader should clearly understand that in many cases where he finds square brackets, and all where he finds '*e.g.*,' or '*e.g.*' and a vertical line, he is dealing with restorations which, though they are far from being mere guesses, are only approximations to the truth. Similar warnings are sometimes conveyed by dots and pointed brackets. A dot placed beneath a letter means that that letter is a possible interpretation of the traces,

a pointed bracket indicates that the letters within it are not or cannot have been in the MS. The emendations and restorations for which I believe myself to be responsible are marked *E* in the notes. All restorations have been checked where possible by a palaeographical method explained and exemplified in various articles in the periodicals. Briefly, it consists of the tracing of letter-groups from photographs of the extant portions of the papyrus or vellum MS. Suggestions are rejected which, when traced out by this method, are shown, with all reasonable allowance made for variation in the size of the letters and the spaces between them, to exceed or fall short of the requirements of the gap; and where the gap is bounded on the left by an imaginary marginal line, all suggestions are made to correspond—again with all reasonable allowance made—in what I may call for convenience 'written length.' Scholars who have not tried this method will be surprised, when they do, at the way in which it reduces the possibilities. One instance must suffice. In the first lines of Alcaeus 27, the letters Δ of *παί]δων*, AI of *πρώ]τα̣*, TO before *γάρ*, and IC of *ἄλλ]αις*, come immediately under one another. Metre requires *two* supplementary syllables in lines 1 and 2, *three* in line 3, and *one* in line 4. All these supplements must correspond in written length not only with one another but with any suggestions made for the four subsequent lines, and when they are made the result must be not only a passage satisfactory in metre, grammar, dialect and sentiment, but something which Alcaeus might have written. I should add here that so far as I have found it practicable my work on the new Fragments is based

on the actual MSS.; where I have used only photographs the results should be taken as still requiring corroboration. The latter cases are indicated in the footnotes.

The arrangement of the Fragments follows, where this can be inferred, the arrangement of the editions current in the later antiquity; but it must not be understood as certainly reproducing it. Cross-references to the numerations of Bergk and Hiller-Crusius will be found on page 431. I have added a separate index of the ancient authors, including those to whom we are indebted for most of our knowledge of these poets and their works. Among the modern writers who have collected, emended, and interpreted the Fragments, next to Bergk[1] and those on whom he drew—Ahrens, Bekker, Benseler, Bentley, Blomfield,[2] Boissonade, Brunck, Cobet, Cramer, Gaisford, Hartung, Hecker, Hermann, Keil, Kock, Matthiae, Meineke, O. Müller, Nauck, Neue, Porson, Reiske, Schneidewin,[3] Schweighäuser,[4] Seidler, Ursinus, Volger, Voss, Welcker, Wolf—I owe most to E. P. Grenfell, A. S. Hunt, Kaibel and U. von Wilamowitz-Moellendorff. My obligations to these, as to other recent and living scholars, are indicated in the notes. I must here record my thanks to the Director of the British Museum for permission to reproduce the Sotades vase, and to the Council of the Egypt Exploration Fund for allowing me to print the Oxyrhynchus Fragments; to D. Bassi, J. Harrower, W. Schubart, and the Directors of the Bibliothèque Nationale and of Graz University, for supplying me with photographs of papyri and other MSS. in their care. And I gratefully acknowledge the help and

[1] *B* [2] Blf. [3] Schn. [4] Schw.

encouragement I have received from Mrs. Adam, H. I. Bell, S. G. Campbell, A. B. Cook, R. D. Hicks, H. Rackham and A. J. B. Wace.

An account of the MS. tradition when the authors concerned run into the sixties is a formidable affair, and would be beyond the scope of this book. For the most important, the scholar will find much of what he requires in O. Hoffmann's *Griechische Dialekte* and in the introduction to A. C. Pearson's *Fragments of Sophocles*. The earlier history of the text has been ably worked out by Wilamowitz in the works mentioned in the Bibliography. But it should be borne in mind that statements on the Aeolic metres and dialect published before 1914 may need modification. I cannot hope that the many references in this book are quite exhaustive, modern, and correct. But I have done my best to make them so. A few not quite obvious errors, of which the worst is *Alexandrides* for *Anaxandrides* on pp. 100 and 101, will be found corrected in the Indexes. In the translation of Sappho *fr.* 35 the proverb should be in square brackets. The omitted fragments of merely palaeographical value will be found in the Papyrus Collections—*Oxyrhynchus, Berliner Klassikertexte, Halle, Società Italiana*. It will perhaps be useful to the reader to know that Volume II, which is already in the press, includes Stesichorus, Ibycus, Anacreon, and Simonides, and that Volume III., which is in preparation, will include Corinna, Bacchylides, Timotheus, the Scolia, the Folk-Songs, the Anacreontea, and the Adespota, with an account of Greek Lyric Poetry.

J. M. E.

CAMBRIDGE,
December 22, 1921.

PREFACE

encouragement I have received from Mrs. Adam, H. I. Bell, S. G. Campbell, A. B. Cook, R. D. Hicks, R. Rackham and A. J. B. Wace.

An account of the MS. tradition of the authors concerned in the text is a formidable affair, and would be beyond the scope of this book. For the most important, the scholar will find much of what he requires in O. Hoffmann's *Griechische Dialekte* and in the introduction to A. C. Pearson's *Fragments of Sophocles*. The earlier history of the text has been ably worked out by Wilamowitz in the works mentioned in the Bibliography. But it should be borne in mind that statements on the Aeolic metres and dialect published before 1914 may need modification. I cannot hope that the many references in this book are quite exhaustive, modern, and correct. But I have done my best to make them so. A few not quite obvious errors, of which the worst is *Alexandria* for *Alexandrides* on pp. 388 and 191, will be found corrected in the Indexes. In the translation of Sappho *fr.* 52 the proverb should be in square brackets. The omitted fragments of merely palaeographical value will be found in the Papyrus Collections—*Oxyrhynchus, Berliner Klassikertexte, Halle, Società Italiana*. It will perhaps be useful to the reader to know that Volume II, which is already in the press, includes Stesichorus, Ibycus, Anacreon, and Simonides, and that Volume III, which is in preparation, will include Corinna, Bacchylides, Timotheus, the Scolia, the Folk-Songs, the Anacreontea, and the Adespota, with an account of Greek Lyric Poetry.

J. M. E.

Cambridge,
December 20, 1921.

CONTENTS

[1] For early poets such as Orpheus see note on page 10

CONTENTS

SELECT BIBLIOGRAPHY

Theodor Bergk *Poetae Lyrici Graeci* Leipzig 1882 vol. III (reprinted without correction 1914); text with contexts and Latin notes

G. S. Farnell *Greek Lyric Poetry* London 1891; select text with introductions and notes

O. Hoffmann *Die Griechischen Dialekte in ihrem historischen Zusammenhange mit der wichtigsten ihrer Quellen* Göttingen 1891–8; select text of certain authors with contexts and critical notes (used with inscriptions, etc. to illustrate the dialects)

H. Weir Smyth *Greek Melic Poets* London 1900; select text with introductions, notes, and bibliography

E. Hiller and O. Crusius *Anthologia Lyrica sive Lyricorum Graecorum veterum praeter Pindarum reliquiae potiores* Leipzig 1903; select text with a few critical notes; contains no new fragments

---

U. von Wilamowitz-Moellendorff (1) *Textgeschichte der griechischen Lyriker* Berlin 1900; history of the text, (2) *Sappho und Simonides* Berlin 1913; various articles on certain of the Lyric Poets and their works, (3) *Griechische Verskunst* Berlin 1921; a study of Greek Metre[1]

A. C. Pearson *The Fragments of Sophocles* Cambridge 1917 introduction; on the 'sources' and their MSS

J. W. Mackail *Lectures on Greek Poetry* London 1910

See also *Oxyrhynchus Papyri* I (1898) and X (1914), Pauly-Wissowa *Realencyklopädie* under *Alcman*, *Sappho*,[1] *Alcaeus*, etc., J. Sitzler in Bursian (Kroll), *Jahresbericht über die Fortschritte der klassischen Altertumswissenschaft* 1900, 1907, 1919, and various articles by the editor of this edition in the *Classical Review*, *Classical Quarterly*, and *Cambridge Philological Society's Proceedings* from 1909 to 1922

[1] These reached me too late for me to profit by them in preparing my first volume

LYRA GRAECA

ΠΙΝΔΑΡΕ Μουσάων ἱερὸν στόμα, καὶ λάλε Σειρὴν
ΒΑΚΧΥΛΙΔΗ, ΣΑΠΦΟΥΣ τ' Αἰολίδες χάριτες,
γράμμα τ' ἈΝΑΚΡΕΙΟΝΤΟΣ, Ὁμηρικὸν ὅς τ' ἀπὸ ῥεῦμα
ἔσπασας οἰκείοις ΣΤΗΣΙΧΟΡ' ἐν καμάτοις,
ἥ τε ΣΙΜΩΝΙΔΕΩ γλυκερὴ σελίς, ἡδύ τε Πειθοῦς
ἼΒΥΚΕ καὶ παίδων ἄνθος ἀμησάμενε,
καὶ ξίφος ἈΛΚΑΙΟΙΟ τὸ πολλάκις αἷμα τυράννων
ἔσπεισεν πάτρης θέσμια ῥυόμενον,
θηλυμελεῖς τ' ἈΛΚΜΑΝΟΣ ἀηδόνες, ἵλατε, πάσης
ἀρχὴν οἳ λυρικῆς καὶ πέρας ἐστάσατε.[1]

---

[1] *Anth. Pal.* 9. 184 line 4 Jahn καπέτοις 'irrigation-ditches' perhaps rightly line 10 Mein: mss ἐσπάσατε

That holy mouth of the Muses PINDAR, that sweetly prattling Siren BACCHYLIDES, those Aeolian Graces of SAPPHO; the book ANACREON wrote, STESICHORUS whose work was fed from the stream of Homer; the delicious scroll of SIMONIDES, IBYCUS gatherer of the bloom of Persuasion and of lads, the sword ALCAEUS used, to shed tyrant blood and save his country's rights, the maiden-tunèd nightingales of ALCMAN; I pray you all be gracious unto me, ye that have established the beginning and the ending of all lyric song.[1]

---

[1] *Palatine Anthology:* probably the motto for a book of selections from the Nine Lyric Poets; cf. 9. 571 (p. 165)

ΟΛΥΜΠΟΥ

Βίος

Plut. *Mus.* 5 Ἀλέξανδρος δ' ἐν τῇ Συναγωγῇ τῶν Περὶ Φρυγίας κρούματα Ὄλυμπον ἔφη πρῶτον εἰς τοὺς Ἕλληνας κομίσαι, ἔτι δὲ καὶ τοὺς Ἰδαίους Δακτύλους· Ὕαγνιν δὲ πρῶτον αὐλῆσαι, εἶτα τὸν τούτου υἱὸν Μαρσύαν, εἶτ' Ὄλυμπον.

Ibid. 7 [π. αὐλῳδικῶν νόμων]· λέγεται γὰρ τὸν προειρημένον Ὄλυμπον, αὐλητὴν ὄντα τῶν ἐκ Φρυγίας, ποιῆσαι νόμον αὐλητικὸν εἰς Ἀπόλλωνα τὸν καλούμενον Πολυκέφαλον· εἶναι δὲ τὸν Ὄλυμπον τοῦτόν φασιν <ἔνιοι>[1] ἕνα τῶν ἀπὸ τοῦ πρώτου Ὀλύμπου τοῦ Μαρσύου πεποιηκότος εἰς τοὺς θεοὺς τοὺς νόμους· οὗτος γὰρ παιδικὰ γενόμενος Μαρσύου καὶ τὴν αὔλησιν μαθὼν παρ' αὐτοῦ τοὺς νόμους τοὺς ἁρμονικοὺς ἐξήνεγκεν εἰς τὴν Ἑλλάδα, οἷς νῦν χρῶνται οἱ Ἕλληνες ἐν ταῖς ἑορταῖς τῶν θεῶν. ἄλλοι δὲ Κράτητος εἶναί φασι τὸν Πολυκέφαλον νόμον, γενομένου μαθητοῦ Ὀλύμπου. ὁ δὲ Πρατίνας Ὀλύμπου φησὶν εἶναι τοῦ νεωτέρου τὸν νόμον

[1] *E*

---

[1] in ancient times there was some confusion between the elder and younger musicians of this name. Both seem to have been musicians pure and simple, but are included here

OLYMPUS

LIFE[1]

Plutarch *On Music*: Alexander in his *Collections on Phrygia* declares that instrumental music was introduced into Greece by Olympus and by the Idaean Dactyls or Priests of Cybelè. The first flute-player according to him was Hyagnis, who was followed by his son Marsyas, who was succeeded by Olympus.

The Same: [on lyre-sung 'nomes']: We are told that the Olympus of whom we spoke just now, a flute-player from Phrygia, composed a flute-nome[2] to Apollo which is known as the Many-Headed. This Olympus, however, is said by some authorities to have been a descendant of the first Olympus, son of Marsyas, who composed the nomes to the Gods.—This earlier Olympus was in his boyhood a favourite of Marsyas, and learning flute-playing of him, introduced the musical nomes[2] into Greece, where they are now used at the festivals of the Gods.—According to another account, however, the Many-Headed nome is the work of Crates 'a pupil of Olympus,' though Pratinas declares it to be the work of Olympus the Second. The Harmatian

because the development of Greek lyric poetry is hardly separable in its early stages from that of Greek music
[2] *i.e.* a certain type of air for the flute alone, not for flute and voice as above

τοῦτον, τὸν δὲ καλούμενον Ἁρμάτιον νόμον λέγεται ποιῆσαι ὁ πρῶτος Ὄλυμπος, ὁ Μαρσύου μαθητής. . . . ὅτι δ' ἐστὶν Ὀλύμπου ὁ Ἁρμάτιος νόμος, ἐκ τῆς Γλαύκου Ἀναγραφῆς τῆς ὑπὲρ τῶν Ἀρχαίων Ποιητῶν μάθοι ἄν τις . . . ἄλλοι δέ τινες ὑπὸ Μυσῶν εὑρῆσθαι τοῦτον τὸν νόμον· γεγονέναι γάρ τινας ἀρχαίους αὐλητὰς Μυσούς.

Plut. *Mus.* 11 Ὄλυμπος δὲ ὡς Ἀριστόξενός φησιν, ὑπολαμβάνεται ὑπὸ τῶν μουσικῶν τοῦ ἐναρμονίου γένους εὑρετὴς γεγενῆσθαι· τὰ γὰρ πρὸ ἐκείνου πάντα διάτονα καὶ χρωματικὰ ἦν. ὑπονοοῦσι δὲ τὴν εὕρεσιν τοιαύτην τινὰ γενέσθαι· ἀναστρεφόμενον τὸν Ὄλυμπον ἐν τῷ διατόνῳ καὶ διαβιβάζοντα τὸ μέλος πολλάκις ἐπὶ τὴν διάτονον παρυπάτην, τότε μὲν ἀπὸ τῆς παραμέσης, τότε δ' ἀπὸ τῆς μέσης, καὶ παραβαίνοντα τὴν διάτονον λιχανὸν καταμαθεῖν τὸ κάλλος τοῦ ἤθους, καὶ οὕτω τὸ ἐκ τῆς ἀναλογίας συνεστηκὸς σύστημα θαυμάσαντα καὶ ἀποδεξάμενον ἐν τούτῳ ποιεῖν ἐπὶ τοῦ Δωρίου τόνου· οὔτε γὰρ τῶν τοῦ διατόνου ἰδίων οὔτε τῶν τοῦ χρώματος ἅπτεσθαι, ἀλλ' ἤδη τῶν τῆς ἁρμονίας. εἶναι δ' αὐτῷ τὰ πρῶτα τῶν ἐναρμονίων τοιαῦτα . . . φαίνεται δ' Ὄλυμπος αὐξήσας μουσικὴν τῷ ἀγένητόν τι καὶ ἀγνοούμενον ὑπὸ τῶν ἔμπροσθεν εἰσαγαγεῖν, καὶ ἀρχηγὸς γενέσθαι τῆς Ἑλληνικῆς καὶ καλῆς μουσικῆς.

Ibid. 15 Ὄλυμπον γὰρ πρῶτον Ἀριστόξενος ἐν τῷ πρώτῳ περὶ Μουσικῆς ἐπὶ τῷ Πύθωνί φησιν ἐπικήδειον αὐλῆσαι Λυδιστί.

Ibid. 29 καὶ αὐτὸν δὲ τὸν Ὄλυμπον ἐκεῖνον, ᾧ δὴ τὴν ἀρχὴν τῆς Ἑλληνικῆς τε καὶ νομικῆς μου-

nome, as it is called, is reputed the work of the first Olympus, the pupil of Marsyas . . . and this view is supported by Glaucus in his *Account of the Ancient Poets*. . . . It is held, however, by some writers that the Harmatian nome was a Mysian invention, Mysia having produced flute-players in ancient times.

Plutarch *On Music*: According to Aristoxenus, musicians ascribe the invention of the Enharmonic scale (EE′FABB′CE)[1] to Olympus. Before his time the only scales had been the Diatonic and the Chromatic. The invention is supposed to have come about thus: In descending in the Diatonic scale his melody frequently passed from B or from A to F, omitting G. Realising the beauty of this effect, Olympus in his astonishment accepted the principle for the whole system, and composed in it in the Dorian 'mode,' rejecting all intervals peculiar to the Diatonic or Chromatic scales and concerning himself directly with the mode. Such was the origin of his Enharmonic scale. . . . It is clear that Olympus made a real advance in music by introducing an entire novelty, and was the father of good music in Greece.

The Same: We are told by Aristoxenus in the first Book of his *Treatise on Music* that the first flute-player to use the Lydian mode was Olympus in his Lament for the serpent Python.

The Same: The Olympus who is reputed the originator of art-music in Greece, is considered to

[1] the dash indicates a quarter-tone

σης ἀπυδιδόασι, τό τε τῆς ἁρμονίας γένος ἐξευρεῖν φασι, καὶ τῶν ῥυθμῶν τόν τε προσοδιακὸν ἐν ᾧ ὁ τοῦ Ἀρέως νόμος, καὶ τὸν χορεῖον ᾧ πολλῷ κέχρηται ἐν τοῖς Μητρῴοις· ἔνιοι δὲ καὶ τὸν βακχεῖον Ὄλυμπον οἴονται εὑρηκέναι. δηλοῖ δ' ἕκαστον τῶν ἀρχαίων μελῶν ὅτι ταῦθ' οὕτως ἔχει.

Plut. *Mus.* 33 οἷον Ὀλύμπῳ τὸ ἐναρμόνιον γένος ἐπὶ Φρυγίου τόνου τεθὲν παίωνι ἐπιβάτῳ μιχθέν· τοῦτο γὰρ τῆς ἀρχῆς τὸ ἦθος ἐγέννησεν ἐπὶ τῷ τῆς Ἀθηνᾶς νόμῳ· προσληφθείσης γὰρ μελοποιΐας καὶ ῥυθμοποιΐας τεχνικῶς δὲ μεταληφθέντος τοῦ ῥυθμοῦ μόνον αὐτοῦ καὶ γενομένου τροχαίου ἀντὶ παίωνος, συνέστη τὸ Ὀλύμπου ἐναρμόνιον γένος.

Ibid. 18 καὶ οἱ παλαιοὶ δὲ πάντες οὐκ ἀπείρως ἔχοντες πασῶν τῶν ἁρμονιῶν ἐνίαις ἐχρήσαντο· οὐ γὰρ ἡ ἄγνοια τῆς τοιαύτης στενοχωρίας καὶ ὀλιγοχορδίας αὐτοῖς αἰτία γεγένηται· οὐδὲ δι' ἄγνοιαν οἱ περὶ Ὄλυμπον καὶ Τέρπανδρον καὶ οἱ ἀκολουθήσαντες τῇ τούτων προαιρέσει περιεῖλον τὴν πολυχορδίαν τε καὶ ποικιλίαν. μαρτυρεῖ γοῦν τὰ Ὀλύμπου τε καὶ Τερπάνδρου ποιήματα καὶ τῶν τούτοις ὁμοιοτρόπων πάντων. ὀλιγόχορδα [1] γὰρ ὄντα καὶ ἁπλᾶ διαφέρει τῶν ποικίλων καὶ πολυχόρδων, ὡς μηδένα δύνασθαι μιμήσασθαι τὸν Ὀλύμπου τρόπον, ὑστερίζειν δὲ τούτου τοὺς ἐν τῷ πολυχόρδῳ τε καὶ πολυτρόπῳ καταγιγνομένους.

[1] Volkmann: mss τρίχορδα

have invented not only the Enharmonic scale but the two rhythms known as the Prosodiac (– – ‿), which is that of the Nome of Ares, and the Choree (‿ ‿ ‿) which occurs so frequently in the tunes used in the worship of Cybelè. The Bacchius (‿ – –) also is sometimes ascribed to him.[1] These statements are borne out by each of the ancient melodies.

Plutarch *On Music*: Take for instance the Enharmonic scale employed by Olympus with the Phrygian mode and the Epibatic Paeon,[2] the combination which gives its character to the opening of the Nome to Athena. Both melody and rhythm make their contribution, the metre being merely changed in a cunning way so as to become as it were trochaic instead of paeonic, and the effect is completed by the use of the Enharmonic scale of Olympus.

The Same: Moreover, although the ancient poets used only some of the 'modes,' they knew them all. It is not through ignorance that they confine themselves to employing so few strings,[3] or that composers like Olympus and Terpander and their followers denied themselves the use of many strings and the variety which that entails. This is clear both from the works of Olympus and Terpander and those of the composers who belong to the same school. Though they are quite simple and written only for a few strings, they so far excel the elaborate works written for many, that the style of Olympus remains inimitable and the exponents of the opposite principle have to take the second place.

[1] see also Plut. *Mus.* 10 (on Thaletas p. 37)   [2] perh. the '3rd Paeon' (‿ ‿ – ‿) called δρόμιος or 'running'
[3] or 'notes'; the Greek word is intended to include the stops of the flute; so also below

Arist. *Pol.* 8. 5 [π. μουσικῆς]· τοῦτο δ' ἂν εἴη δῆλον, εἰ ποιοί τινες τὰ ἤθη γιγνόμεθα δι' αὐτῆς. ἀλλὰ μὴν ὅτι γιγνόμεθα ποιοί τινες, φανερὸν διὰ πολλῶν τῶν ἑτέρων, οὐχ ἥκιστα δὲ καὶ διὰ τῶν Ὀλύμπου μελῶν. ταῦτα γὰρ ὁμολογουμένως ποιεῖ τὰς ψυχὰς ἐνθουσιαστικάς, ὁ δ' ἐνθουσιασμὸς τοῦ περὶ τὴν ψυχὴν ἤθους πάθος ἐστίν.

Suid. Ὄλυμπος· Φρύξ, νεώτερος, αὐλητὴς γεγονὼς ἐπὶ Μίδου τοῦ Γορδίου.

Hesych. Ὀλύμπου νόμος· τῶν αὐλητικῶν τις.

Ar. *Eq.* 7 ΔΗ. ὦ κακόδαιμον, πῶς ἔχεις;
ΝΙ. κακῶς καθάπερ σύ.
ΔΗ. δεῦρο δὴ πρόσελθ', ἵνα
ξυναυλίαν κλαύσωμεν Οὐλύμπου νόμον.
ΔΗ. ΝΙ. μὺ μῦ μὺ μῦ μὺ μῦ μὺ μῦ μὺ μῦ μὺ μῦ.

Sch. ad loc. . . . ὁ δὲ Ὄλυμπος μουσικὸς ἦν, Μαρσύου μαθητής. ἔγραψε δὲ αὐλητικοὺς καὶ θρηνητικοὺς νόμους.

Vide Apollod. 1. 4. 2, Plut. *Mus.* 10, Eur. *I. A.* 577, Plat. *Symp.* 315 c, *Ion* 533 b, *Laws* 3. 677 b, *Min.* 318 b, Luc. *adv. ind.* 5, Strab. 10. 470, 12. 578,

---

Among their earliest lyric poets the Greeks numbered Olen, Linus, Pamphos, Orpheus, Chrysothemis, Philammon, Thamyris, Eumolpus, and Musaeus. Works ascribed to some of these were extant in antiquity. See,

LIFE OF OLYMPUS

Aristotle *Politics*: [on music]: This would be clear if we could show that music affects our characters. And we can, by many instances, notably that of the musical compositions of Olympus, which admittedly carry us away, an effect which is a condition of the character of the soul.

Suidas *Lexicon*: Olympus: A Phrygian, the younger of the name, a flute-player who flourished in the time of Midas [1] son of Gordias.

Hesychius *Glossary*: Nome of Olympus: One of the composers for the flute.

Aristophanes *Knights*:
DEMOSTHENES. My poor old mate, how d'ye feel?
NICIAS. Bad, as bad as you do.
DEM. Then come here, and
'let's pipe Olympus' nome of woe in concert.'
[*They hum a few bars.*]

Scholiast on the passage: Olympus was a musician, a pupil of Marsyas. He wrote dirge-nomes for the flute.

[1] died B.C. 693.

Ael. *V. H.* 13. 20, Ov. *Met.* 6. 393, Plin. *N. H.* 36. 5. 4, Hyg. *F.* 165, 273, Paus. 10. 30. 9.

---

for instance, Hdt. 4. 35, 7. 6, *Plato* Crat. 402 *b*, Rep. 364 *e*, *Arist.* H.A. 563 *a* 18, *Paus.* 1. 14. 3, 22. 7, 7. 21. 9, 9. 27. 2, 29. 7 *f*, 10. 7. 2, *Clem. Al.* Str. 1. 21. 131, *Procl. ap. Phot.* Bibl. 320.

ΕΥΜΗΛΟΥ

Βίος

Paus. 2. 1. 1. ἡ δὲ Κορινθία χώρα, μοῖρα οὖσα τῆς Ἀργείας ἀπὸ Κορίνθου τὸ ὄνομα ἔσχηκε. Διὸς δὲ εἶναι Κόρινθον οὐδένα οἶδα εἰπόντα πω σπουδῇ, πλὴν Κορινθίων τῶν πολλῶν. Εὔμηλος δὲ ὁ Ἀμφιλύτου τῶν Βακχιδῶν καλουμένων, ὃς καὶ τὰ ἔπη λέγεται ποιῆσαι, φησὶν ἐν τῇ Κορινθίᾳ Συγγραφῇ, εἰ δὴ Εὐμήλου γε ἡ συγγραφή, Ἐφύραν Ὠκεανοῦ θυγατέρα οἰκῆσαι πρῶτον ἐν τῇ γῇ ταύτῃ . . .

Sch. Ap. Rh. 1. 146 [Αἰτωλὶς Λήδη]· . . . Γλαύκου δὲ αὐτὴν τοῦ Σισύφου ἐκ πατρὸς ἐν Κορινθιακοῖς λέγει Εὔμηλος καὶ Παντειδυίας μητρός.

Sch. Pind. *O.* 13. 74 διδάσκει δὲ τοῦτο Εὔμηλός τις ποιητὴς ἱστορικός . . .

Clem. Al. *Str.* 6. 267 τὰ δὲ Ἡσιόδου μετήλλαξαν εἰς πεζὸν λόγον καὶ ὡς ἴδια ἐξήνεγκαν Εὔμηλός τε καὶ Ἀκουσίλαος οἱ ἱστοριογράφοι.

Ibid. 1. 151 ἀλλὰ καὶ ὁ τὴν Εὐρωπίαν ποιήσας ἱστορεῖ τὸ ἐν Δελφοῖς ἄγαλμα Ἀπόλλωνος κίονα εἶναι διὰ τῶνδε . . .

Sch. *Il.* 6. 131 τῆς ἱστορίας πολλοὶ ἐμνήσθησαν, προηγουμένως δὲ ὁ τὴν Εὐρωπίαν πεποιηκὼς Εὔμηλος.

Paus. 9. 5. 8 ὁ δὲ τὰ ἔπη τὰ ἐς Εὐρώπην ποιήσας φησὶν Ἀμφίονα χρήσασθαι λύρᾳ πρῶτον Ἑρμοῦ διδάξαντος.

Ath. 7. 277 d . . . ὁ τὴν Τιτανομαχίαν ποιήσας,

EUMELUS

LIFE

Pausanias *Description of Greece*: The district of Corinth, which is part of the district of Argos, has its name from Corinthus, who to the best of my belief is seriously called a son of Zeus only by the local if loud authority of the inhabitants. Eumēlus son of Amphilytus of what is known as the house of the Bacchids, the reputed author of the epic poem (*Corinthiaca*), declares in the *Corinthian History*, if indeed his title to this is not false, that this country was first settled by Ephyra daughter of Oceanus . . .

Scholiast on Apollonius of Rhodes *Argonautica* [Aetolian Leda]: . . . She is made the daughter of Sisyphus and Panteiduia by Eumelus in the *Corinthiaca*.

Scholiast on Pindar: . . . We are told this by an historical poet called Eumelus.

Clement of Alexandria *Miscellanies*: What Hesiod wrote was put into prose and published as their own by the historians Eumelus and Acusilaüs.

The Same: Moreover the statue of Apollo at Delphi is shown to have been a pillar by the words of the poet of the *Europia* . . .

Scholiast on the *Iliad*: This account (of Dionysus) is given by many authors, but occurs first in Eumelus the poet of the *Europia*.

Pausanias *Description of Greece*: According to the author of the poem on Europa, the first player on the lyre was Amphion, who was taught by Hermes.

Athenaeus *Doctors at Dinner*: The poet of the

εἴτ' Εὔμηλός ἐστιν ὁ Κορίνθιος ἢ Ἀρκτῖνος ἢ ὅστις δήποτε χαίρει ὀνομαζόμενος.

Euseb. Ol. 4. 4 Eumelus poeta qui *Bugoniam* composuit et *Europiam* cognoscebatur.

Clem. Al. *Str.* 1. 144 Εὔμηλος δὲ ὁ Κορίνθιος . . . ἐπιβεβληκέναι Ἀρχίᾳ τῷ Συρακούσας κτίσαντι.

Vide *Frag.* 1, Clem. Al. *Str.* 6. 264, Paus. 2. 3. 10, 2. 2, Apollod. 3. 8. 2, 9. 1, 11. 1, Sch. Ap. Rh. 2. 948, 3. 1371, 4. 1212, Tz. ad Lyc. 480, ad Hes. *Op.* 1.

ΕΥΜΗΛΟΥ

1 Προσόδιον εἰς Δῆλον

Paus. 4. 4. 1 [π. Μεσσηνίων]· ἐπὶ δὲ Φίντα τοῦ Συβότα πρῶτον Μεσσήνιοι[1] τῷ Ἀπόλλωνι ἐς Δῆλον θυσίαν καὶ ἀνδρῶν χορὸν ἀποστέλλουσι. τὸ δέ σφισιν ᾆσμα προσόδιον ἐς τὸν θεὸν ἐδίδαξεν Εὔμηλος· εἶναί τε ὡς ἀληθῶς Εὐμήλου νομίζεται μόνα τὰ ἔπη ταῦτα.

Ibid. 4. 33. 3 [π. Ἰθώμης]· ἄγουσι δὲ (Μεσσήνιοι) καὶ ἑορτὴν ἐπέτειον Ἰθωμαῖα· τὸ δὲ ἀρχαῖον καὶ ἀγῶνα ἐτίθεσαν μουσικῆς· τεκμαίρεσθαι δέ ἐστιν ἄλλοις τε καὶ Εὐμήλου τοῖς ἔπεσιν. ἐποίησε γοῦν καὶ τάδε ἐν τῷ προσοδίῳ τῷ ἐς Δῆλον·

τῷ γὰρ Ἰθωμάτᾳ καταθύμιος ἔπλετο Μοῖσα
ἁ καθαρὰν <κίθαριν> καὶ ἐλεύθερα σάμβαλ' ἔχοισα.[2]

2

Ibid. 5. 19. 10 [π. λάρνακος τῆς Κυψέλου]· τὰ ἐπιγράμματα δὲ τὰ ἐπ' αὐτῆς τάχα μέν που καὶ ἄλλος τις ἂν εἴη πεποιηκώς, τῆς δὲ ὑπονοίας τὸ πολὺ ἐς Εὔμηλον τὸν Κορίνθιον εἶχεν ἡμῖν, ἄλλων τε ἕνεκα καὶ τοῦ προσοδίου μάλιστα ὃ ἐποίησεν ἐς Δῆλον.

[1] mss insert τότε   [2] *B* : mss ἁ καθαρὰ καὶ

---

[1] traditional date 734 or 757   [2] cf. Ibid. 2. 1. 1 : ref. to

EUMELUS

Titanomachy, Eumelus of Corinth, Arctinus, or whoever the good man may be . . .

Eusebius *Chronicle*: Fourth year of the Fourth Olympiad (B.C. 761): Flourished Eumelus, the poet of the *Bugonia* and the *Europia*.

Clement of Alexandria *Miscellanies*: Eumelus of Corinth . . . was contemporary with Archias the founder of Syracuse.[1]

---

p. 23, Laur. Lyd. *Mens.* 4. 48, and for fragments of these epics Kinkel *Epic. Gr. Frag.* p. 185.

EUMELUS

1 Processional to Delos

Pausanias *Description of Greece* [on Messenia]: In the reign of Phintas son of Sybotas the Messenians first sent a sacrifice and a male chorus to Apollo at Delos. Their trainer in the processional song to the God was Eumelus, and the epic lines they sang are believed to be the only genuine work of Eumelus now extant.

The Same [on Ithōmè]: The Messenians hold a yearly festival (of Zeus Ithomatas) called the Ithomaea. In ancient times they had a musical contest too, as is testified, among other things, by the lines of Eumelus, who wrote in his *Processional to Delos*:

For he of Ithome taketh delight in a Muse that hath a pure lyre and weareth the sandals of freedom.[2]

2

The Same [on the Chest of Cypselus]: The inscriptions upon the chest may, of course, be the work of some other man, but my impressions on the whole point to Eumelus of Corinth, particularly in view of his *Processional to Delos*.[3]

Messenia's struggles with Sparta c. 725? [3] the dates are against P.'s view

ΤΕΡΠΑΝΔΡΟΥ

Βίος

Ath. 14. 635 d ἀγνοεῖ δ' ὁ Ποσειδώνιος ὅτι ἀρχαῖον ἐστιν ὄργανον ἡ μάγαδις σαφῶς Πινδάρου λέγοντος τὸν Τέρπανδρον ἀντίφθογγον εὑρεῖν τῇ παρὰ Λυδοῖς πηκτίδι τὸν βάρβιτον (*fr.* 125)· 'Τόν ῥα Τέρπανδρός ποθ' ὁ Λέσβιος εὗρε, | πρῶτος ἐν δείπνοισι Λυδῶν | ψαλμὸν ἀντίφθογγον ὑψηλᾶς ἀκουῶν πηκτίδος.' πηκτὶς δὲ καὶ μάγαδις ταὐτόν . . . ὅτι δὲ καὶ Τέρπανδρος ἀρχαιότερος Ἀνακρέοντος δῆλον ἐκ τούτων· τὰ Κάρνεια πρῶτος πάντων Τέρπανδρος νικᾷ, ὡς Ἑλλάνικος ἱστορεῖ ἔν τε τοῖς ἐμμέτροις Καρνεονίκαις κἀν τοῖς καταλογάδην. ἐγένετο δὲ ἡ θέσις τῶν Καρνείων κατὰ τὴν ἕκτην καὶ εἰκοστὴν Ὀλυμπιάδα, ὡς Σωσίβιός φησιν ἐν τῷ Περὶ Χρόνων. Ἱερώνυμος δ' ἐν τῷ Περὶ Κιθαρῳδῶν, ὅπερ ἐστὶ πέμπτον Περὶ Ποιητῶν, κατὰ Λυκοῦργον τὸν νομοθέτην τὸν Τέρπανδρόν φησι γενέσθαι, ὃς ὑπὸ πάντων συμφώνως ἱστορεῖται μετὰ Ἰφίτου τοῦ Ἠλείου τὴν πρώτην ἀριθμεῖσαν τῶν Ὀλυμπίων θέσιν διαθεῖναι.

Mar. Par. 34 ἀφ' οὗ Τέρπανδρος ὁ Δερδένεος ὁ Λέσβιος τοὺς νόμους . . .[1] καὶ τὴν ἔμπροσθε

[1] for the gap of about 30 letters (partly filled by Selden's transcript) see Jacoby *Marm. Par.*

TERPANDER

Life

Athenaeus *Doctors at Dinner*: When Poseidonius says this, he does not realise that the *magadis* is an ancient instrument, because Pindar plainly states that Terpander invented the *barbitos* or lyre to respond [1] to the Lydian *pectis* or lute, in the words 'Which Lesbian Terpander invented of old to vibrate in answer to the low-pitched lute at the feasts of the Lydians;' and the *pectis* and the *magadis* are the same . . . It is clear that Terpander was earlier than Anacreon from the following considerations. According to Hellanicus both in his metrical and in his formal lists of Victors at the Carneian Festival, the first recorded name is Terpander's; and we know from Sosibius' *Chronology* that the festival was founded in the 26th Olympiad (B.C. 676–673), while Hieronymus' tract *On Singers to the Lyre*, which forms the fifth Book of his *Treatise on the Poets*, assigns him to the time of the lawgiver Lycurgus, who is admitted on all hands to have arranged with Iphitus of Elis the first Olympic Games reckoned in the list (B.C. 776).

Parian Chronicle: From the time when the Lesbian Terpander son of Derdenes . . . the 'nomes' . . .

[1] *i. e.* to accompany it an octave higher? (ὑπάτη lit. 'highest' was according to our reckoning the lowest note in a Greek 'mode')

μουσικὴν μετέστησεν ἔτη ΗΗΗ𐅄ΔΔΔΙ ἄρχοντος Ἀθήνησιν Δρωπίδου.

Eus.: Ol. 33. 2: Terpander citharoedus insignis habetur.

Tim. *Pers.* 234 πρῶτος ποικιλόμουσον Ὀρφεὺς χέλυν ἐτέκνωσεν
υἱὸς Καλλιόπας Πιερίας ἔπι.
Τέρπανδρος δ' ἐπὶ τῷ δέκα
ζεῦξε μοῦσαν ἐν ᾠδαῖς·
Λέσβος δ' Αἰολία νιν Ἀν-
τίσσᾳ γείνατο κλεινόν·
νῦν δὲ Τιμόθεος μέτροις
ῥυθμοῖς τ' ἑνδεκακρουμάτοις
κίθαριν ἐξανατέλλει.

Arist. *Probl.* 19. 32 διὰ τί διὰ πασῶν καλεῖται ἀλλ' οὐ κατὰ τὸν ἀριθμὸν δι' ὀκτώ, ὥσπερ καὶ διὰ τεττάρων καὶ διὰ πέντε; ἢ ὅτι ἑπτὰ ἦσαν αἱ χορδαὶ τὸ ἀρχαῖον, εἶτ' ἐξελὼν τὴν τρίτην Τέρπανδρος τὴν νήτην προσέθηκε, καὶ ἐπὶ τούτου ἐκλήθη διὰ πασῶν ἀλλ' οὐ δι' ὀκτώ· δι' ἑπτὰ γὰρ ἦν.

Plut. *Mus.* 28 οἱ γὰρ ἱστορήσαντες τὰ τοιαῦτα Τερπάνδρῳ μὲν τήν τε Δώριον νήτην προσετίθεσαν, οὐ χρησαμένων αὐτῇ τῶν ἔμπροσθεν κατὰ τὸ μέλος.

Ibid. 30 [π. Τιμοθέου]· οὗτος γὰρ ἑπταφθόγγου τῆς λύρας ὑπαρχούσης ἕως εἰς Ἀριστοκλείδην, τὸν Τερπάνδρειον τόνον [1] διέρριψεν εἰς πλείονας φθόγγους.[2]

Suid. Τέρπανδρος· Ἀρναῖος, ἢ Λέσβιος ἀπὸ Ἀντίσσης, ἢ Κυμαῖος· οἱ δὲ καὶ ἀπόγονον Ἡσιόδου ἀνέγραψαν· ἄλλοι δὲ Ὁμήρου, Βοίου

and changed the style of music 381 years, in the archonship of Dropides at Athens (B.C. 645).

Eusebius *Chronicle*: Olympiad 33. 2 (B.C. 647) Flourished Terpander the singer to the lyre.

Timotheus *Persae*: In the beginning did Orpheus son of Calliopè beget the motley-musicked shell on Mount Pieria, and after him came the famous Terpander, born of Aeolian Lesbos at Antissa, and yoked the Muse unto poems ten. And lo! now Timotheus giveth the lyre new life with times and measures of eleven strings.

Aristotle *Problems*: Why is the octave described as *diapason* or 'at an interval of all,' rather than numerically 'at an interval of eight,' as we say 'at an interval of four' or 'of five'? Is it because the strings were in old times seven, and Terpander removed the 'third' when he added the *netè* or 'highest,' thus keeping the total seven and not increasing it to eight?[1]

Plutarch *on Music*: The musical historians attributed the Dorian *nete* or octave-note to Terpander, musicians before him not having employed it.

The Same [on Timotheus]: Down to the time of Aristocleides the lyre had had seven strings. Timotheus divided the Terpandrean mode into a greater number of notes.[2]

Suidas *Lexicon*: Terpander: Variously described as of Arnè, a Lesbian of Antissa, and of Cymè[3]; according to some authorities a descendant of Hesiod, or again of Homer, with the pedigree

[1] cf. *fr.* 5 [2] the reading is doubtful [3] Diodorus in Tzetzes *Chil.* 1. 16 calls him a Methymnaean

---

[1] Westphal -*E*: mss ἕως εἰς Τέρπανδρον τὸν Ἀντισσαῖον
[2] cf. *fr.* 5

λέγοντες αὐτὸν τοῦ Φωκέως, τοῦ Εὐρυφῶντος, τοῦ Ὁμήρου· λυρικός, ὃς πρῶτος ἑπτάχορδον ἐποίησε τὴν λύραν καὶ νόμους λυρικοὺς πρῶτος ἔγραψεν, εἰ καί τινες Φιλάμμωνα θέλουσι γεγραφέναι.

Plut. *Mus.* 18.

Ibid. 3 Ἡρακλείδης δ' ἐν τῇ Συναγωγῇ τῶν ἐν Μουσικῇ τὴν κιθαρῳδίαν καὶ τὴν κιθαρῳδικὴν ποίησιν πρῶτόν φησιν Ἀμφίονα ἐπινοῆσαι τὸν Διὸς καὶ Ἀντιόπης, τοῦ πατρὸς δηλονότι διδάξαντος αὐτόν. πιστοῦται δὲ τοῦτο ἐκ τῆς ἀναγραφῆς τῆς ἐν Σικυῶνι ἀποκειμένης, δι' ἧς τάς τε ἱερείας τὰς ἐν Ἄργει καὶ τοὺς ποιητὰς καὶ τοὺς μουσικοὺς ὀνομάζει. κατὰ δὲ τὴν αὐτὴν ἡλικίαν καὶ Λίνον . . . λέγει καὶ Ἄνθην . . . καὶ Πίερον . . .· ἀλλὰ καὶ Φιλάμμωνα . . .· Θάμυριν δὲ . . . καὶ Δημόδοκον . . . καὶ Φήμιον . . . οὐ λελυμένην δ' εἶναι τῶν προειρημένων τὴν τῶν ποιημάτων λέξιν καὶ μέτρον οὐκ ἔχουσαν, ἀλλὰ καθάπερ Στησιχόρου τε καὶ τῶν ἀρχαίων μελοποιῶν, οἳ ποιοῦντες ἔπη, τούτοις μέλη περιετίθεσαν· καὶ γὰρ τὸν Τέρπανδρον ἔφη κιθαρῳδικῶν ποιητὴν ὄντα νόμων, κατὰ νόμον[1] ἕκαστον τοῖς ἔπεσι τοῖς ἑαυτοῦ καὶ τοῖς Ὁμήρου μέλη περιτιθέντα ᾄδειν ἐν τοῖς ἀγῶσιν· ἀποφῆναι δὲ τοῦτον λέγει ὀνόματα πρῶτον τοῦς κιθαρωδικοῖς νόμοις· ὁμοίως δὲ Τερπάνδρῳ Κλονᾶν, τὸν πρῶτον συστησάμενον τοὺς αὐλῳδικοὺς νόμους καὶ τὰ προσόδια, ἐλεγείων τε καὶ ἐπῶν ποιητὴν γεγονέναι . . . οἱ δὲ νόμοι οἱ κατὰ τούτους, ἀγαθὲ Ὀνησίκρατες, αὐλῳδικοὶ ἦσαν . . . οἱ δὲ τῆς κιθαρῳδίας νόμοι πρότερον πολλῷ χρόνῳ τῶν αὐλῳδικῶν κατεστάθησαν ἐπὶ Τερ-

Homer—Euryphon—Boeus of Phocis—Terpander; a lyric poet who invented the lyre of seven strings and, *pace* those who ascribe this to Philammon, was the first writer of lyric 'nomes.'

Plutarch *on Music* [see on Olympus p. 8].

The Same: According to Heracleides' *Collections on the Musicians*, the art of singing to the lyre and the kind of poetry which belongs to it were the invention of Amphion son of Zeus and Antiopè, who presumably was taught by his father. His authority is the register preserved at Sicyon, from which he derives his lists of the priestesses at Argos, the poets, and the musicians. Of the same generation, according to him, were Linus . . ., Anthen . . ., Pierus . . ., Philammon . . ., Thamyris . . ., Demodocus . . ., and Phemius. . . . These poets' writings were not in prose, but resembled those of Stesichorus and the old lyric poets who wrote epic lines and set them to music. Even Terpander, he declares, whose *forte* was the citharoedic or lyre-sung nome, and to whom he ascribes the naming of these nomes, in every one of them set his own or Homer's epic lines to music for singing at the Games. In the same way Clonas, the first composer of flute-sung nomes and the originator of processional songs, used elegiac and epic verse. . . . The nomes of these flute-poets, my excellent Onesicrates, were sung to the flute, and are these. . . . The lyre-sung nomes, which were established much earlier, namely in the time

---

[1] *B* προοίμιον

πάνδρου· ἐκεῖνος γοῦν τοὺς κιθαρῳδικοὺς πρῶτος[1] ὠνόμασε, Βοιώτιόν τινα καὶ Αἰόλιον Τροχαῖόν τε καὶ Ὀξὺν Κηπίωνά τε καὶ Τερπάνδρειον καλῶν, ἀλλὰ μὴν καὶ Τετραοίδιον. πεποίηται δὲ τῷ Τερπάνδρῳ καὶ προοίμια κιθαρῳδικὰ ἐν ἔπεσιν. ὅτι δ' οἱ κιθαρῳδικοὶ νόμοι οἱ πάλαι ἐξ ἐπῶν συνίσταντο, Τιμόθεος ἐδήλωσε· τοὺς γοῦν πρώτους νόμους ἐν ἔπεσι διαμιγνύων διθυραμβικὴν λέξιν ᾖδεν, ὅπως μὴ εὐθὺς φανῇ παρανομῶν εἰς τὴν ἀρχαίαν μουσικήν. ἔοικε δὲ κατὰ τὴν τέχνην τὴν κιθαρῳδικὴν ὁ Τέρπανδρος διενηνοχέναι· τὰ Πύθια γὰρ τετράκις ἑξῆς νενικηκὼς ἀναγέγραπται. καὶ τοῖς χρόνοις δὲ σφόδρα παλαιός ἐστι· πρεσβύτερον γοῦν αὐτὸν Ἀρχιλόχου ἀποφαίνει Γλαῦκος ὁ ἐξ Ἰταλίας ἐν συγγράμματί τινι, τῷ Περὶ τῶν Ἀρχαίων Ποιητῶν τε καὶ Μουσικῶν· φησὶ γὰρ αὐτὸν δεύτερον γενέσθαι μετὰ τοὺς πρώτους ποιήσαντας αὐλητικήν.[2]

Ἀλέξανδρος δ' ἐν τῇ Συναγωγῇ τῶν περὶ Φρυγίας κρούματα Ὄλυμπον ἔφη πρῶτον εἰς τοὺς Ἕλληνας κομίσαι, ἔτι δὲ καὶ τοὺς Ἰδαίους Δακτύλους· Ὕαγνιν δὲ πρῶτον αὐλῆσαι, εἶτα τὸν τούτου υἱὸν Μαρσύαν, εἶτ' Ὄλυμπον· ἐζηλωκέναι δὲ τὸν Τέρπανδρον Ὁμήρου μὲν τὰ ἔπη, Ὀρφέως δὲ τὰ μέλη. ὁ δ' Ὀρφεὺς οὐδένα φαίνεται μεμιμημένος· . . . τινὰς δὲ τῶν νόμων τῶν κιθαρῳδικῶν τῶν ὑπὸ Τερπάνδρου πεποιημένων Φιλάμμωνά φασι τὸν ἀρχαῖον τὸν Δελφὸν συστήσασθαι.

τὸ δ' ὅλον ἡ μὲν κατὰ Τέρπανδρον κιθαρῳδία καὶ μέχρι τῆς Φρύνιδος ἡλικίας παντελῶς ἁπλῆ τις οὖσα διετέλει· οὐ γὰρ ἐξῆν τὸ παλαιὸν οὕτω

of Terpander, were first named by him, and are these: Boeotian, Aeolian, Trochaic, High-pitched, Cepion, Terpandrean, and Four-song. Terpander also wrote lyric Preludes in epic metre; and it becomes clear that the ancient lyre-sung nomes were composed of epic lines, if we consider that Timotheus, when he employed the dithyrambic style, interspersed his earlier nomes with them, in order to avoid the appearance of breaking the rules of the ancient music. There is reason to believe that Terpander was supreme in the art of the lyre-song. It is recorded that he won the prize at the Pythian Games four times running; and the period at which he lived must have been very early, because Glaucus the Italian in his *History of the Ancient Poets and Musicians* puts him before Archilochus, making him only a very little later than the first composers for the flute.

Alexander, in his *Collections on Phrygia*, declares that instrumental music was introduced into Greece by Olympus, and also by the Idaean Dactyls or Priests of Cybelè, and that while the first flute-player was Hyagnis, who was followed by his son Marsyas, who was succeeded by Olympus, Terpander (the lyrist) emulated in his verse Homer and in his music Orpheus, who appears to have been entirely original. . . . It is said that some of the citharoedic or lyre-sung nomes thought to be the work of Terpander were really composed by the ancient Delphian composer Philammon.

In fine, lyric song continued from Terpander's time to that of Phrynis to be wholly simple. Poets were not permitted in those days to compose for the lyre

---

[1] mss πρότερος [2] Westphal: mss αὐλῳδίαν

ποιεῖσθαι τὰς κιθαρῳδίας ὡς νῦν οὐδὲ μεταφέρειν τὰς ἁρμονίας καὶ τοὺς ῥυθμούς· ἐν γὰρ τοῖς νόμοις ἑκάστῳ διετήρουν τὴν οἰκείαν τάσιν· διὸ καὶ ταύτην ἐπωνυμίαν εἶχον· νόμοι γὰρ προσηγορεύθ ησαν, ἐπειδὴ οὐκ ἐξῆν παραβῆναι ὡς ἐβούλοντο[1] καθ' ἕκαστον νενομισμένον εἶδος τῆς τάσεως. τὰ γὰρ πρὸς τοὺς θεοὺς ἀφοσιωσάμενοι ἐξέβαινον εὐθὺς ἐπί τε τὴν Ὁμήρου καὶ τῶν ἄλλων ποίησιν· δῆλον δὲ τοῦτ' ἐστὶ διὰ τῶν Τερπάνδρου προοιμίων. ἐποιήθη δὲ καὶ τὸ σχῆμα τῆς κιθάρας πρῶτον κατὰ Κηπίωνα τὸν Τερπάνδρου μαθητήν· ἐκλήθη δ' Ἀσιὰς διὰ τὸ κεχρῆσθαι τοὺς Λεσβίους αὐτῇ κιθαρῳδοὺς πρὸς τῇ Ἀσίᾳ κατοικοῦντας. τελευταῖον δὲ Περίκλειτόν φασι κιθαρῳδὸν νικῆσαι ἐν Λακεδαίμονι Κάρνεια τὸ γένος ὄντα Λέσβιον· τούτου δὲ τελευτήσαντος, τέλος λαβεῖν Λεσβίοις τὸ συνεχὲς τῆς κατὰ τὴν κιθαρῳδίαν διαδοχῆς.

Suid. νόμος· ὁ κιθαρῳδικὸς τρόπος τῆς μελῳδίας, ἁρμονίαν ἔχων τακτὴν καὶ ῥυθμὸν ὡρισμένον. ἦσαν δὲ ἑπτὰ οἱ ὑπὸ Τερπάνδρου· ὧν εἷς ὄρθιος, τετραοίδιος,[2] ὀξύς.

Ibid. Μόσχος· . . . τὸ δὲ Βοιώτιον οὕτω καλούμενον εὗρε Τέρπανδρος, ὥσπερ καὶ τὸ Φρύγιον.

Ibid. ὄρθιον νόμον καὶ τροχαῖον· τοὺς δύο νόμους ἀπὸ τῶν ῥυθμῶν ὠνόμασε Τέρπανδρος. ἀνατετάμενοι ἦσαν καὶ εὔτονοι . . .

Plut. *Mus.* 28 ἔτι δέ, καθάπερ Πίνδαρός φησι, καὶ τῶν σκολιῶν μελῶν Τέρπανδρος εὑρετὴς ἦν.

[1] Westphal : mss ὡς βούλονται after θεοὺς [2] mss τετράδιος

as they do now with frequent change of mode or rhythm. They maintained in the nomes the scale proper to each, which indeed is the reason of that name, these compositions being called 'nomes' or 'laws' because it was not permitted to go beyond the proper scale. As soon as the composer had done his duty by the Gods, he passed on to the poetry of Homer and other epic poets. This is proved by the Preludes of Terpander. As for the form of the lyre, that was established in the time of Cepion the pupil of Terpander; and it was called 'Asian' because it was used in Lesbos which is adjacent to Asia. The last Lesbian lyrist to win the prize at the Spartan Carneia was Pericleitus. His death put an end to the continuous succession of Lesbian singers to the lyre.

Suidas *Lexicon*: Nome: The lyric style of song-music composed according to strict rules of mode and rhythm. There were seven nomes composed by Terpander, the Orthian, the Four-song, the High-pitched . . .[1]

The Same: The Boeotian (tune), as it is called, and the Phrygian were invented by Terpander.

The Same: Orthian and Trochaic Nomes: The two nomes so called from their rhythms by Terpander. They were high-pitched and of a vigorous character . . .

Plutarch *on Music*: Further, Pindar tells us that Terpander was the inventor of scolia or drinking-songs.

[1] the list is incomplete, and the High-pitched was probably identical with the Orthian; cf. also Suid. and Hesych. s. ὄρθιος νόμος, Hdt. 1. 24

Plut. *Mus.* 12 ἔστι δέ τις καὶ περὶ τῶν ῥυθμῶν λόγος· γένη γάρ τινα καὶ εἴδη ῥυθμῶν προσεξευρέθη, ἀλλὰ μὴν καὶ μελοποιιῶν τε καὶ ῥυθμοποιιῶν.[1] πρώτη[2] μὲν γὰρ ἡ Τερπάνδρου καινοτομία καλόν τινα τρόπον εἰς τὴν μουσικὴν εἰσήγαγε· Πολύμναστος δὲ μετὰ τοῦ Τερπανδρείου τρόπου καινῷ[3] ἐχρήσατο, καὶ αὐτὸς μέντοι ἐχόμενος τοῦ καλοῦ τύπου.

Ibid. 9 ἡ μὲν οὖν πρώτη κατάστασις τῶν περὶ τὴν μουσικὴν ἐν τῇ Σπάρτῃ Τερπάνδρου καταστήσαντος γεγένηται.

Ibid. 42 ὅτι δὲ καὶ ταῖς εὐνομωτάταις τῶν πόλεων ἐπιμελὲς γεγένηται φροντίδα ποιεῖσθαι τῆς γενναίας μουσικῆς, πολλὰ μὲν καὶ ἄλλα μαρτύρια παραθέσθαι ἔστι· Τέρπανδρον δ' ἄν τις παραλάβοι τὸν τὴν γενομένην ποτὲ παρὰ Λακεδαιμονίοις στάσιν καταλύσαντα.

Ael. *V.H.* 12. 50 Λακεδαιμόνιοι μουσικῆς ἀπείρως εἶχον· ἔμελε γὰρ αὐτοῖς γυμνασίων καὶ ὅπλων· εἰ δέ ποτε ἐδεήθησαν τῆς ἐκ Μουσῶν ἐπικουρίας ἢ νοσήσαντες ἢ παραφρονήσαντες ἢ ἄλλο τι τοιοῦτον δημοσίᾳ παθόντες, μετεπέμποντο ξένους ἄνδρας οἷον ἰατροὺς ἢ καθαρτὰς κατὰ πυθόχρηστον. μετεπέμψαντό γε μὴν Τέρπανδρον καὶ Θάλητα καὶ Τυρταῖον καὶ τὸν Κυδωνιάτην Νυμφαῖον καὶ Ἀλκμᾶνα.[4]

Suid. μετὰ Λέσβιον ᾠδόν· παροιμία λεγομένη ἐπὶ τῶν τὰ δεύτερα φερομένων. οἱ γὰρ Λακεδαιμόνιοι τοὺς Λεσβίους κιθαρῳδοὺς πρώτους προσεκαλοῦντο. ἀκαταστατούσης γὰρ τῆς πόλεως αὐτῶν, χρησμὸς ἐγένετο τὸν Λέσβιον ᾠδὸν μεταπέμπεσθαι· οἱ δ' ἐξ Ἀντίσσης Τέρπανδρον ἐφ'

Plutarch *on Music*: Something also should be said about rhythms. For there have been innovations in the form or kind of rhythms, and indeed of methods of metre and rhythm. Terpander first broke new ground by introducing into music a beautiful style of rhythm called after him the Terpandrean. Polymnastus who followed him employed a new rhythm as well as his, but preserved throughout the same beautiful style . . .

The Same: The first establishment of music at Sparta was due to Terpander.

The Same: Many circumstances could be cited to show that good music has been a matter for concern to the best-regulated states, and not least among these the quelling of a sedition at Sparta by Terpander.

Aelian *Historical Miscellanies*: The Spartans, whose bent was for bodily exercises and feats of arms, had no skill in music. Yet if ever they required the aid of the Muses on occasion of general sickness of body or mind or any like public affliction, their custom was to send for foreigners, at the bidding of the Delphic oracle, to act as healers or purifiers. For instance they summoned Terpander, Thales, Tyrtaeus, Nymphaeus of Cydonia, and Alcman.

Suidas *Lexicon*: Next to the poet of Lesbos: Said proverbially of persons who come off second best. The singers to the lyre first called in by the Spartans were of Lesbos. When their city was torn by faction there was an oracle delivered that they should fetch the poet of Lesbos, and accordingly they sent for Terpander of Antissa, who was living in exile at

---

[1] mss *μελοποιῶν τε καὶ ῥυθμοποιῶν* [2] mss *προτέρα*
[3] *E*- Westphal: mss accus. and *καὶ ᾧ* [4] cf. Philod. *Mus.* xx (on Stes. 71)

αἵματι φεύγοντα μεταπεμψάμενοι ἤκουον αὐτοῦ ἐν τοῖς συσσιτίοις καὶ κατεστάλησαν.—ὅτι οἱ Λακεδαιμόνιοι στασιάζοντες μετεπέμψαντο ἐκ Λέσβου τὸν μουσικὸν Τέρπανδρον, ὃς ἥρμοσεν αὐτῶν τὰς ψυχὰς καὶ τὴν στάσιν ἔπαυσεν. εἴποτε οὖν μετὰ ταῦτα μουσικοῦ τινος ἤκουον οἱ Λακεδαιμόνιοι, ἔλεγον 'Μετὰ Λέσβιον ᾠδόν.' <μέμνηται τῆς παροιμίας ταύτης Κρατῖνος ἐν Χείρωνι.>[1]

Ael. Dion. ap. Eust. *Il.* 1. 129 καὶ Ἀριστοτέλης ἐν τῇ Λακεδαιμονίων Πολιτείᾳ τὸ 'Μετὰ Λέσβιον ᾠδόν' τὸν Τέρπανδρόν φησι δηλοῦν, ἐκαλοῦντο δέ φασιν εἰς τὴν ἐκείνου τιμὴν πρῶτον μὲν ἀπόγονοι αὐτοῦ, εἶτα εἴ τις ἄλλος παρείη Λέσβιος, εἶθ' οὕτως οἱ λοιποὶ μετὰ Λέσβιον ᾠδόν, τὸν ἁπλῶς δηλαδὴ Λέσβιον.

Anth. Pal. 9. 488 Τρυφῶνος εἰς Τέρπην κιθαρῳδὸν . . .

Τέρπης εὐφόρμιγγα κρέκων σκιάδεσσιν ἀοιδὰν
 κάτθαν' ἀνοστήσας ἐν Λακεδαιμονίαις,
οὐκ ἄορι πληγεὶς οὐδ' ἐν βέλει ἀλλ' ἐνὶ σύκῳ
 χείλεα. φεῦ· προφάσεων οὐκ ἀπορεῖ θάνατος.

Plut *Lyc.* 28 διὸ καί φασιν ὕστερον ἐν τῇ Θηβαίων εἰς τὴν Λακωνικὴν στρατείᾳ τοὺς ἁλισκομένους Εἵλωτας κελευομένους ᾄδειν τὰ Τερπάνδρου καὶ Ἀλκμᾶνος καὶ Σπένδοντος τοῦ Λάκωνος παραιτεῖσθαι φάσκοντας οὐκ ἐθέλειν τοὺς δεσποσύνους.

Vide Clem. Al. *Str.* 1. 16. 78, Plut. *Mus.* 28, Themist. *Or.* 26. 316, Eucl. *Intr. Harm.* 19, Philod. *Mus.* 30.

[1] Zenobius

Sparta because of a murder, and listening to his music at their public dinners, ceased their factious strife. Another account is this: The Spartans at a time of internecine struggles sent to Lesbos for the musician Terpander, who restored harmony to their minds and put an end to the strife of parties; and so whenever after that time the Spartans listened to a musician, the saying went 'Next to the poet of Lesbos.' This proverb is mentioned by Cratinus in his *Cheiron.*

Aelius Dionysius quoted by Eustathius: Aristotle in his *Constitution of Sparta* declares that in the saying 'Next to the poet of Lesbos' the reference is to Terpander, and it is said that the Spartans used to summon to take his place of honour [1] first his descendants, then any Lesbian poet present, and the rest as they came, 'after the poet of Lesbos,' that is after any poet that came from Lesbos.

Palatine Anthology: Tryphon on the lyrist Terpes [2] . . . :

When in the Spartan Place of Meeting Terpes was singing a song to the thrumming of his sweet lyre, he perished never to return, not by a sword, nor yet an arrow, but by the casting of a fig between his lips. Alas! Death suffers from no lack of pretexts.

Plutarch *Life of Lycurgus*: Thus it is said that later during the Theban invasion of Laconia the Helot prisoners refused to sing at the bidding of their captors the songs of Terpander or Alcman or Spendon the Laconian, on the plea that their masters never allowed it.

[1] Hesych. s. μετὰ Λέσβ. 'called first before the judges of the musical contests' [2] apparently an abbreviation of Terpander, cf. Suid. s. γλυκὺ μέλι

ΤΕΡΠΑΝΔΡΟΥ

1 εἰς Δία

Clem. Al. *Str.* 6. 784 ἡ τοίνυν ἁρμονία τοῦ βαρβάρου ψαλτηρίου, τὸ σεμνὸν ἐμφαίνουσα τοῦ μέλους, ἀρχαιοτάτη τυγχάνουσα, ὑπόδειγμα Τερπάνδρῳ μάλιστα γίνεται πρὸς ἁρμονίαν τὴν Δώριον ὑμνοῦντι τὸν Δία ὧδέ πως·

Ζεῦ, πάντων ἀρχά,
πάντων ἁγῆτορ,
Ζεῦ, σοὶ πέμπω
ταύταν ὕμνων ἀρχάν.[1]

2 εἰς Ἀπόλλωνα

Suid. ἀμφιανακτίζειν· ᾄδειν τὸν Τερπάνδρου νόμον τὸν καλούμενον ὄρθιον, οὗ τὸ προοίμιον ταύτην τὴν ἀρχὴν εἶχεν·

Ἀμφί μοι αὖτε Ϝάναχθ' ἑκατήβολον ἀειδ', ὦ
φρήν.[2]

3 εἰς Ἀπόλλωνα καὶ Μούσας

Keil *An. Gram.* 6. 6 [π. σπονδείου]· σπονδεῖος δ' ἐκλήθη ἀπὸ τοῦ ῥυθμοῦ τοῦ ἐν ταῖς σπονδαῖς ἐπαυλομένου τε καὶ ἐπᾳδομένου, οἷον·

Σπένδωμεν ταῖς Μνάμας
παισὶν Μώσαις
καὶ τῷ Μωσάρχῳ
Λατοῦς υἱεῖ.

[1] ἁγῆτορ : mss ἀγήτωρ, ἁγήτωρ [2] αὖτε Herm : mss αὖτις, αὐτὸν, αὖ τὸν ἄειδ' ὦ Crus : mss ᾀδέτω, ἀειδέτω, ἀοιδέτω

TERPANDER

1 To Zeus

Clement of Alexandria *Miscellanies*: So the mode or scale of the barbarian psaltery (of David), displaying solemnity as it does and being very ancient, furnishes an example or foreshadowing of Terpander thus singing the praise of Zeus in the Dorian mode:

Zeus, the beginning of all, the leader of all; Zeus, to thee I bring this gift for a beginning of hymns.[1]

2 To Apollo

Suidas *Lexicon*: ἀμφιανακτίζειν: to sing the Nome of Terpander called the Orthian or High-pitched, of which the prelude begins:

Of the Far-flinging Lord come sing me, O my soul.[2]

3[3] To Apollo and the Muses

Keil *Grammatical Extracts* [on the Spondee]: This rhythm is so called from that of the songs sung to the flute at σπονδαί or 'libations,' such as:

Let us pour to the Daughters of Memory and their Lord the Son of Leto.

[1] the solemnity is partly due to the absence of short syllables if the words are really T.'s the meaning of 'all' is prob. not cosmogonic cf. Ars. 261; Apostol. 3. 29 c [2] cf. Suid. ad loc. Sch. Ar. *Nub.* 595 (ἐκ τῶν Τερπάνδρου προοιμίων), Hesych. ἀμφὶ ἄνακτα· ἀρχὴ κιθαρῳδικοῦ νόμου [3] ascription doubtful

4 εἰς Διοσκούρους

Dion. Hal. *Comp.* 17 [π. ῥυθμῶν]· ὁ δ' ἐξ ἁπασῶν μακρῶν, μολοττὸν δ' αὐτὸν οἱ μετρικοὶ καλοῦσιν, ὑψηλός τε καὶ ἀξιωματικός ἐστι καὶ διαβεβηκὼς ἐπὶ πολύ· παραδεῖγμα δὲ αὐτοῦ τοιόνδε·

Ὦ Ζηνὸς καὶ Λήδας κάλλιστοι σωτῆρες

5

Strab. 13. 618 [π. Μηθύμνης]· οὗτος μὲν οὖν (ὁ Ἀρίων) κιθαρῳδός· καὶ Τέρπανδρον δὲ τῆς αὐτῆς μουσικῆς τεχνίτην γεγονέναι φασὶν καὶ τῆς αὐτῆς νήσου, τὸν πρῶτον ἀντὶ τῆς τετραχόρδου λύρας ἑπταχόρδῳ χρησάμενον, καθάπερ καὶ ἐν τοῖς ἀναφερομένοις ἔπεσιν εἰς αὐτὸν λέγεται·

ἡμεῖς τοι τετράγηρυν ἀποστέρξαντες ἀοιδὰν[1]
ἑπτατόνῳ φόρμιγγι νέους κελαδήσομεν ὕμνους.

6

Plut. *Lycurg.* 21 ὅλως δὲ ἄν τις ἐπιστήσας τοῖς Λακωνικοῖς ποιήμασιν ὧν ἔτι καθ' ἡμᾶς ἔνια διεσώθη,[2] καὶ τοὺς ἐμβατηρίους ῥυθμοὺς ἀναλαβὼν οἷς ἐχρῶντο πρὸς τὸν αὐλὸν ἐπάγοντες τοῖς πολεμίοις, οὐ κακῶς ἡγήσαιτο καὶ τὸν Τέρπανδρον καὶ τὸν Πίνδαρον τὴν ἀνδρείαν τῇ μουσικῇ συνάπτειν. ὁ μὲν γὰρ οὕτως πεποίηκε περὶ τῶν Λακεδαιμονίων·

ἔνθ' αἰχμά τε νέων θάλλει καὶ Μῶσα λίγεια
καὶ Δίκα εὐρυάγυια καλῶν ἐπιτάρροθος ἔργων.

7

Joh. Lyd. *Mens.* 72 Τέρπανδρός γε μὴν ὁ Λέσβιος Νύσσαν λέγει τετιθηνηκέναι τὸν Διόνυσον τὸν ὑπὸ τινῶν Σαβάζιον ὀνομαζόμενον, ἐκ Διὸς καὶ Περσεφόνης γενόμενον, εἶτα ὑπὸ τῶν Τιτάνων σπαραχθέντα.

[1] so Eucl: Strab. σοὶ δ' ἡμεῖς and ἀποστρέψ. [2] mss διεσώζετο

TERPANDER

4[1] To the Dioscuri

Dionysius of Halicarnassus *Composition* [on rhythms]: The rhythm which consists entirely of long syllables—called *molossus* by the writers on metre—is elevated and dignified and takes long strides; and this is an example of it:

O [Sons] of Zeus and Leda; saviours most beautiful.

5

Strabo *Geography* [on Methymna]: Arion was a singer to the lyre; and according to tradition the same branch of music had an exponent in a native of the same island, Terpander, who was the first to use a lyre with seven strings instead of four, as is recorded in the epic lines ascribed to him:

To thee we will play new hymns upon a lyre of seven strings, and will love the four-voiced lay no more.[2]

6

Plutarch *Life of Lycurgus*: Indeed if the reader will consider the Laconian poetry of which some is still extant and the march-rhythms the Spartans used to the tune of the flute when they went into battle, he will conclude that both Terpander and Pindar have good reason to connect valour with music as the former does where he says of Sparta:

Where bloom both the spear of the young men and the clear sweet Muse, and eke that aider unto noble deeds, Justice that goeth in broad streets . . .[3]

7

Johannes Lydus *On the Months*: According to Terpander of Lesbos, Dionysus, who is sometimes called Sabazius, was nursed by Nyssa; he was the son of Zeus and Persephone and was eventually torn in pieces by the Titans.[4]

[1] ascription doubtful [2] cf. Eucl. *Intr. Harm.* 19, Cram. *A.P.* 1. 56. 10; Clem. Al. *Str.* 6. 814, Poll. 4. 66 [3] cf. Arr. *Tact.* fin. [4] cf. Inscr. Theatr. Dion. Keil *Philol.* 23 608

ΘΑΛΗΤΑ ἢ ΘΑΛΗΤΟΣ

Βίος

Diog. L. 1. 1. 11 γεγόνασι δὲ καὶ ἄλλοι Θαλαῖ, καθά φησι Δημήτριος ὁ Μάγνης ἐν τοῖς Ὁμωνύμοις, πέντε. ὧν . . . τρίτος ἀρχαῖος πάνυ κατὰ Ἡσίοδον καὶ Ὅμηρον καὶ Λυκοῦργον.

Plut. *Lyc.* 4 ἕνα δὲ τῶν νομιζομένων ἐκεῖ σοφῶν καὶ πολιτικῶν χάριτι καὶ φιλίᾳ πείσας ἀπέστειλεν εἰς τὴν Σπάρτην, Θάλητα, ποιητὴν μὲν δοκοῦντα λυρικῶν μελῶν καὶ πρόσχημα τὴν τέχνην ταύτην πεποιημένον, ἔργῳ δὲ ἅπερ οἱ κράτιστοι τῶν νομοθετῶν διαπραττόμενον. λόγοι γὰρ ἦσαν αἱ ᾠδαὶ πρὸς εὐπείθειαν καὶ ὁμονοίαν ἀνακλητικοὶ διὰ μελῶν ἅμα καὶ ῥυθμῶν πολὺ τὸ κόσμιον ἐχόντων καὶ καταστατικόν . . .

Eph. ap. Str. 10. 48 [π. Κρητῶν]· ὡς δ' αὔτως καὶ τοῖς ῥυθμοῖς Κρητικοῖς χρῆσθαι κατὰ τὰς ᾠδὰς συντονωτάτοις οὖσιν, οὓς Θάλητα ἀνευρεῖν, ᾧ καὶ τοὺς παιάνας καὶ τὰς ἄλλας τὰς ἐπιχωρίας ᾠδὰς ἀνατιθέασι καὶ πολλὰ τῶν νομίμων.

Paus. 1. 14. 4 Θαλῆς δὲ ὁ Λακεδαιμονίοις τὴν νόσον παύσας . . . Θαλῆτα δ' εἶναί φησι Γορτύνιον Πολύμναστος Κολοφώνιος ἔπη Λακεδαιμονίοις ἐς αὐτὸν ποιήσας.

Ael. *V.H.* 12. 50

Plut. *Mus.* 9 ἡ μὲν οὖν πρώτη κατάστασις τῶν περὶ τὴν μουσικὴν ἐν τῇ Σπάρτῃ Τερπάνδρου

---

[1] cf. Strabo 10. 482

THALETAS OR THALES

LIFE

Diogenes Laertius *Life of Thales the Philosopher*: According to Demetrius of Magnesia in his *Men of the Same Name*, there have been five others of this name, of whom . . . the third belongs to very ancient times, namely those of Hesiod, Homer, and Lycurgus.[1]

Plutarch *Life of Lycurgus*: One of the men who had a name in Crete for wisdom and statesmanship Lycurgus prevailed on by favour and friendship to go to Sparta. This was Thales, who was ostensibly a composer of songs for the lyre but did the work of a lawgiver of the best sort. For his songs were exhortations to lawabidingness and concord made by means of melodies and rhythms themselves marked by order and tranquillity.

Ephorus quoted by Strabo *Geography* [on the Cretans]: Similarly the rhythms they use in their songs are Cretan, the grave and severe rhythms invented by Thales, to whom moreover they ascribe the Paeans and other native songs as well as many of their customs.

Pausanias *Description of Greece*: Thales who stayed the plague at Sparta . . . was a native of Gortyn according to Polymnastus of Colophon, who composed some epic lines on him for the Spartans.

Aelian *Historical Miscellanies* [see above on Terpander, p. 27].

Plutarch *On Music*: The first establishment of music at Sparta was due to Terpander. The second

καταστήσαντος γεγένηται· τῆς δευτέρας δὲ Θαλήτας τε ὁ Γορτύνιος καὶ Ξενόδαμος . . . καὶ Ξενόκριτος . . . καὶ Πολύμναστος . . . καὶ Σακάδας . . . μάλιστα αἰτίαν ἔχουσιν ἡγεμόνες γενέσθαι . . . τούτων γὰρ εἰσηγησαμένων τὰ περὶ τὰς Γυμνοπαιδίας τὰς ἐν Λακεδαίμονι λέγεται κατασταθῆναι . . . ἦσαν δ' οἱ περὶ Θαλήταν τε καὶ Ξενόδαμον καὶ Ξενόκριτον ποιηταὶ παιάνων . . .

Plut. *Mus.* 42 ὅτι δὲ καὶ ταῖς εὐνομωτάταις τῶν πόλεων ἐπιμελὲς γεγένηται φροντίδα ποιεῖσθαι τῆς γενναίας μουσικῆς, πολλὰ μὲν καὶ ἄλλα μαρτύρια ἔστι. Τέρπανδρον δ' ἄν τις παραλάβοι . . . καὶ Θαλήταν τὸν Κρῆτα, ὅν φασι κατά τι πυθόχρηστον Λακεδαιμονίους παραγενόμενον διὰ μουσικῆς ἰάσασθαι ἀπαλλάξαι τε τοῦ κατασχόντος λοιμοῦ τὴν Σπάρτην, καθάπερ φησὶ Πρατίνας.

Ibid. 10 καὶ περὶ Θαλήτα δὲ τοῦ Κρητός, εἰ παιάνων γεγένηται ποιητής, ἀμφισβητεῖται. Γλαῦκος γὰρ μετ' Ἀρχίλοχον φάσκων γεγενῆσθαι Θαλήταν μεμιμῆσθαι μὲν αὐτόν φησι τὰ Ἀρχιλόχου μέλη, ἐπὶ δὲ τὸ μακρότερον ἐκτεῖναι, καὶ Παίωνα[1] καὶ Κρητικὸν ῥυθμὸν εἰς τὴν μελοποιΐαν ἐνθεῖναι· οἷς Ἀρχίλοχον μὴ κεχρῆσθαι, ἀλλ' οὐδ' Ὀρφέα οὐδὲ Τέρπανδρον· ἐκ γὰρ τῆς Ὀλύμπου αὐλήσεως Θαλήταν φασὶν ἐξειργάσθαι ταῦτα καὶ δόξαι ποιήτην ἀγαθὸν γεγονέναι.

Porph. *Vit. Pyth.* 32 τὰς γοῦν διατριβὰς καὶ αὐτὸς ἕωθεν μὲν ἐπὶ τῆς οἰκίας ἐποιεῖτο, ἁρμοζόμενος πρὸς λύραν τὴν ἑαυτοῦ φωνὴν καὶ ᾄδων παιᾶνας ἀρχαίους τινας τῶν Θάλητος.

is best ascribed to Thaletas of Gortyn, Xenodamus . . ., Xenocritus . . ., Polymnastus . . ., and Sacadas. For we are told that the Feast of Naked Youths at Sparta[1] . . . was due to these musicians . . . Thaletas, Xenodamus, and Xenocritus were composers of Paeans.

Plutarch *on Music*: Many circumstances could be cited to show that good music has been a matter of concern to the best-regulated states, and not least among these the quelling of a rising at Sparta by Terpander . . . And according to Pratinas, Thaletas the Cretan who is said to have been invited thither at the instance of the Delphic oracle to heal the Spartans by his music, rid their city of the plague which ravaged it.

The Same: As for Thaletas of Crete, it is doubted whether he composed Paeans. Glaucus, who puts him later than Archilochus, declares that he imitated that poet with the difference that his songs were longer and he employed the Paeonic and Cretic rhythms. These had not been used by Archilochus, nor indeed by Orpheus or Terpander, but are said to have been derived by Thaletas, who thus showed himself a great poet, from the flute-music of Olympus.

Porphyrius *Life of Pythagoras*: He used to amuse himself alone in his own house of a morning by singing certain ancient paeans of Thales to his own accompaniment on the lyre.

See also Plut. *Ag.* 10, *Princ. phil.* 4, Strab. 10. 482, Philod. *Mus.* xix.

[1] cf. Ath. 15. 678 b (on Alcm. p. 47)

---

[1] Ritschl: mss μαρῶνα

ΠΟΛΥΜΝΑΣΤΟΥ

Βίος

Str. 14. 643 [π. Κολοφῶνος]· λέγει δὲ Πίνδαρος καὶ Πολύμναστόν τινα τῶν περὶ τὴν μουσικὴν ἐλλογίμων· 'Φθέγμα μὲν πάγκοινον ἔγνωκας Πολυμνάστου Κολοφωνίου ἀνδρός.'

Plut. *Mus.* 3 ὁμοίως δὲ Τερπάνδρῳ Κλονᾶν, τὸν πρῶτον συστησάμενον τοὺς αὐλῳδικοὺς νόμους καὶ τὰ προσόδια, ἐλεγειῶν τε καὶ ἐπῶν ποιητὴν γεγονέναι. καὶ Πολύμναστον τὸν Κολοφώνιον τὸν μετὰ τοῦτον γενόμενον τοῖς αὐτοῖς χρήσασθαι ποιήμασιν. οἱ δὲ νόμοι οἱ κατὰ τούτους, ἀγαθὲ Ὀνησίκρατες, αὐλῳδικοὶ ἦσαν, Ἀπόθετος, Ἔλεγος,[1] Κωμάρχιος, Σχοινίων, Κηπίων, Ἐπικήδειος,[2] καὶ Τριμελής· ὑστέρῳ δὲ χρόνῳ καὶ τὰ Πολυμνάστεια καλούμενα ἐξευρέθη.

Ibid. 5 μετὰ δὲ Τέρπανδρον καὶ Κλονᾶν Ἀρχίλοχος παραδίδοται γενέσθαι. ἄλλοι δέ τινες τῶν συγγραφέων Ἄρδαλόν φασι Τροιζήνιον πρότερον Κλονᾶ τὴν αὐλῳδικὴν συστήσασθαι μοῦσαν, γεγονέναι δὲ καὶ Πολύμναστον ποιητὴν Μέλητος τοῦ Κολοφωνίου υἱόν· ὃν τὸν Πολυμνήστειον νόμον[3] ποιῆσαι. περὶ δὲ Κλονᾶ, ὅτι τὸν Ἀπόθετον νόμον καὶ Σχοινίωνα πεποιηκὼς εἴη, μνημονεύουσιν οἱ ἀναγεγραφότες· τοῦ δὲ Πολυμνάστου

[1] mss ἔλεγοι [2] Westphal: mss τε καὶ δεῖος [3] mss ὃν Πολύμνηστόν (gloss on ὃν) τε καὶ Πολυμνήστην νόμους

POLYMNASTUS

Life

Strabo *Geography* [on Colophon]: According to Pindar, Polymnastus was one of the famous musicians; for he says: 'Thou knowest the world-wide saying of Polymnastus the man of Colophon.'[1]

Plutarch *On Music*: What was done in the lyric sphere by Terpander was done in that of the flute by Clonas, the first composer of flute-sung nomes and of processional songs: he used elegiac and epic verse. His successor Polymnastus of Colophon followed his example. The nomes of these flute-poets, my excellent Onesicrates, were sung to the flute, and are called the Apothetus or Special, the Elegy or Lament, the Comarchius or Rout-Leader's, the Schoenion or Rope-Song, the Cepion or Garden-Song, the Dirge, and the Three-part. To these were added afterwards the Polymnastian Songs, as they are called.

The Same: The successor of Terpander and Clonas is given as Archilochus. But some historians make out that Ardalus of Troezen composed music for flute and voice before the time of Clonas, and that the poet Polymnastus son of Meles of Colophon flourished before his day and composed the Polymnastian nome. The claim of Clonas to be the author of the Special nome and the Rope-Song is borne out by the compilers of the registers, and Polymnastus

[1] Pind. *fr.* 188

καὶ Πίνδαρος καὶ Ἀλκμὰν οἱ τῶν μελῶν ποιηταὶ ἐμνημόνευσαν.

Paus. 1. 14. 4 Θαλῆς δὲ ὁ Λακεδαιμονίοις τὴν νόσον παύσας . . . Θαλῆτα δὲ εἶναί φησι Γορτύνιον Πολύμναστος Κολοφώνιος ἔπη Λακεδαιμονίοις ἐς αὐτὸν ποιήσας.

Plut. *Mus*. 8 [π. Σακάδα]· τόνων γοῦν τριῶν ὄντων κατὰ Πολύμναστον καὶ Σακάδαν, τοῦ τε Δωρίου καὶ Φρυγίου καὶ Λυδίου . . .

Ibid. 9 ἡ μὲν οὖν πρώτη κατάστασις τῶν περὶ τὴν μουσικὴν ἐν τῇ Σπάρτῃ Τερπάνδρου καταστήσαντος γεγένηται· τῆς δευτέρας δὲ Θαλήτας τε ὁ Γορτύνιος καὶ Ξενόδαμος ὁ Κυθήριος καὶ Ξενόκριτος ὁ Λοκρὸς καὶ Πολύμναστος ὁ Κολοφώνιος καὶ Σακάδας ὁ Ἀργεῖος μάλιστα αἰτίαν ἔχουσιν ἡγεμόνες γενέσθαι· τούτων γὰρ εἰσηγησαμένων τὰ περὶ τὰς Γυμνοπαιδίας τὰς ἐν Λακεδαίμονι λέγεται κατασταθῆναι, τὰ περὶ τὰς Ἀποδείξεις τὰς ἐν Ἀρκαδίᾳ, τῶν τε ἐν Ἄργει τὰ Ἐνδυμάτια καλούμενα. ἦσαν δ' οἱ περὶ Θαλήταν τε καὶ Ξενόδαμον καὶ Ξενόκριτον ποιηταὶ παιάνων, οἱ δὲ περὶ Πολύμναστον τῶν ὀρθίων καλουμένων, οἱ δὲ περὶ Σακάδαν ἐλεγείων . . . καὶ Πολύμναστος δ' αὐλῳδικοὺς νόμους ἐποίησεν· εἰ δ' ἐν[1] τῷ ὀρθίῳ νόμῳ τῇ μελοποιίᾳ κέχρηται, καθάπερ οἱ ἁρμονικοί φασιν, οὐκ ἔχομεν ἀκριβῶς εἰπεῖν· οὐ γὰρ εἰρήκασιν οἱ ἀρχαῖοί τι περὶ τούτου.

Ibid. 29 Πολυμνάστῳ δὲ τόν θ' Ὑπολύδιον νῦν ὀνομαζόμενον τόνον ἀνατιθέασι, καὶ τὴν

[1] mss ἐν δὲ and ἔχομεν δ' below

is mentioned by two of the lyric poets, Pindar and Alcman.

Pausanias *Description of Greece*: The Thales who stayed the plague at Sparta . . . according to Polymnastus of Colophon, who composed some epic lines upon him for the Spartans, was a native of Gortyn.

Plutarch *On Music*: There were three modes employed by Polymnastus and Sacadas, the Dorian, the Phrygian, and the Lydian . . .

The Same: The first establishment of music at Sparta was due to Terpander. The second is best ascribed to Thaletas of Gortyn, Xenodamus of Cythera, Xenocritus of Locri, Polymnastus of Colophon, and Sacadas of Argos. For we are told that the institution of the Feast of Naked Youths at Sparta, of the Provings in Arcadia, and of the Feast of Garments as it is called at Argos, was due to these musicians. Thaletas, Xenodamus, and Xenocritus were composers of Paeans, Polymnastus of the so-called Orthian or High-pitched Songs, and Sacadas of Elegies . . . Polymnastus, too, composed nomes to be sung to the flute. But whether, as the writers on the theory of music aver, he employed his musical powers upon the Orthian, in the absence of ancient testimony we cannot tell for certain.

The Same: Polymnastus is credited with the invention of what is now called the Hypolydian mode,

ἔκλυσιν καὶ τὴν ἐκβολὴν πολὺ μείζω πεποιηκέναι φασὶν αὐτόν.

Ar. *Eq.* 1281 . . . Ἀριφράδης πονηρός . . .
καὶ Πολυμνήστεια ποιῶν καὶ ξυνὼν Οἰωνίχῳ·
ὅστις οὖν τοιοῦτον ἄνδρα μὴ σφόδρα βδελύττεται
οὔποτ' ἐκ ταὐτοῦ μεθ' ἡμῶν πίεται ποτηρίου.

Hesych. Πολυμνήστειον ᾄδειν· εἶδός τι μελοποιΐας τὸ Πολυμνήστειον. ἦν δὲ Κολοφώνιος μελοποιὸς ὁ Πολύμνηστος εὐήμερος[1] πάνυ.

Suid. Πολύμνηστος . . . Πολυμνήστεια δὲ <ᾄσματα Πολυμνήστου ὃς> καὶ αὐτὸς[2] κωμῳδεῖται ἐπὶ αἰσχρότητι. Κρατῖνος· 'Καὶ Πολυμνήστει' ἀείδει μουσικήν τε μανθάνει.'

[1] ms εὐημερὴς: al. εὐμερὴς, εὐμελὴς [2] mss αὕτη

and is said to have greatly increased the three-quarter-tone lowering, and five-quarter-tone raising, of notes in the scale.[1]

Aristophanes *Knights*: . . . That scoundrel Ariphrades . . . and doing, not singing, the 'Polymnestian' and consorting with Oeonichus. Now whoever is not utterly disgusted by such a man as this, shall never drink out of the same cup as I.[2]

Hesychius *Glossary*: To sing the Polymnestian: This was a kind of musical piece. Polymnestus was a lyric poet of Colophon, of a very merry type.

Suidas *Lexicon*: Polymnestus: . . . the Polymnestian are songs of Polymnestus who, like the above, is satirised for his obscenity. Compare Cratinus: 'And learns music and sings the Polymnestian songs.'

[1] the reading is doubtful, but cf. *Mus. Script. Gr.* Janus pp. 301, 302 (= Baccheius 41, 42), and p. 300 (Bacch. 37) where these are said to be features peculiar to the Enharmonic scale [2] cf. Sch. Luc. p. 235 Jacobitz

ΑΛΚΜΑΝΟΣ

Βίος

Suid. Ἀλκμάν. Λάκων ἀπὸ Μεσσόας, κατὰ δὲ τὸν Κράτητα πταίοντα Λυδὸς ἐκ Σάρδεων. λυρικός, υἱὸς Δάμαντος, ἢ Τιτάρου. ἦν δὲ ἐπὶ τῆς λζʹ[1] Ὀλυμπιάδος, βασιλεύοντος Λυδῶν Ἄρδυος τοῦ Ἀλυάττου πατρός. καὶ ὢν ἐρωτικὸς πάνυ εὑρετὴς γέγονε τῶν ἐρωτικῶν μελῶν. ἀπὸ οἰκετῶν δέ. ἔγραψε βιβλία ϛʹ μέλη,[2] πρῶτος δὲ εἰσήγαγε τὸ μὴ ἑξαμέτροις μελῳδεῖν. κέχρηται δὲ Δωρίδι διαλέκτῳ, καθάπερ Λακεδαιμόνιος.[3]

Ael. *V.H.* 12. 50

Vell. Pat. 1. 18. 2 Alcmana Lacones falso sibi vindicant.

Anth. Pal. 7. 709 Ἀλεξάνδρου·

Σάρδιες ἀρχαῖαι, πατέρων νομός, εἰ μὲν ἐν ὑμῖν
 ἐτρεφόμαν, κερνᾶς ἦν τις ἂν ἢ βακέλας
χρυσοφόρος, ῥήσσων καλὰ τύμπανα· νῦν δέ μοι
 Ἀλκμάν
 οὔνομα καὶ Σπάρτας εἰμὶ πολυτρίποδος,
καὶ Μούσας ἐδάην Ἑλικωνίδας αἵ με τύραννον
 θῆκαν καὶ Γύγεω μείζονα Δασκυλίου.[4]

Ibid. 7. 18 Ἀντιπάτρου Θεσσαλονικέως εἰς Ἀλκμᾶνα·

[1] mss κζʹ [2] mss add καὶ Κολυμβώσας [3] mss add ἔστι δὲ καὶ ἕτερος Ἀλκμάν, εἷς τῶν λυρικῶν, ὃν ἤνεγκεν ἡ Μεσσήνη
[4] ms τυράννων θ. δυσκύλεω μ. κ. γ.

ALCMAN

Life

Suidas *Lexicon*: Alcman:—A Laconian of Messoa, wrongly called by Crates a Lydian of Sardis. A lyric poet, the son of Damas or, according to some authorities, of Titarus. He flourished in the 37th Olympiad (B.C. 631–625), when Ardys father of Alyattes was king of Lydia. He was of an extremely amorous disposition and the inventor of love-poems, but by birth a slave. He wrote six Books of lyric poems, and was the first to adopt the practice of not accompanying the hexameter with music.[1] Being a Spartan, he uses the Doric dialect.

Aelian *Historical Miscellanies* [see above on Terpander, p. 27].

Velleius Paterculus *Roman History*: The Spartan claim to Alcman is false.

Palatine Anthology: Alexander of Aetolia:

Ancient Sardis, abode of my fathers, had I been reared in you I should have been a maund-bearer unto Cybelè or beaten pretty tambours as one of her gilded eunuchs; but instead my name is Alcman and my home Sparta, town of prize-tripods, and the lore I know is of the Muses of Helicon, who have made me a greater king even than Gyges son of Dascylus.

The Same: Antipater of Thessalonica on Alcman:

[1] or: 'of singing to the lyre or flute songs whose (chief) metre was not hexameter'?

Ἀνέρα μὴ πέτρῃ τεκμαίρεο. λιτὸς ὁ τύμβος
ὀφθῆναι, μεγάλου δ' ὀστέα φωτὸς ἔχει.
εἰδήσεις Ἀλκμᾶνα, λύρης ἐλατῆρα Λακαίνης
ἔξοχον, ὃν Μουσέων ἐννέ' ἀριθμὸς ἔχει.[1]
κεῖται δ' ἠπείροις διδύμοις ἔρις εἴθ' ὅ γε Λυδός,
εἴτε Λάκων· πολλαὶ μητέρες ὑμνοπόλων.

Heracl. Pont. *Pol.* 2 ὁ Ἀλκμὰν οἰκέτης ἦν Ἀγησίδα, εὐφυὴς δὲ ὢν ἐλευθερώθη.

Euseb. *Sync.* 403. 14: Ol. 42. 2 Ἀλκμὰν κατά τινας ἐγνωρίζετο.

Ath. 15. 678 b [π. στεφάνων]: θυρεατικοί· οὕτω καλοῦνταί τινες στέφανοι παρὰ Λακεδαιμονίοις, ὥς φησι Σωσίβιος ἐν τοῖς περὶ Θυσιῶν, ψιλίνους αὐτοὺς φάσκων νῦν ὀνομάζεσθαι, ὄντας ἐκ φοινίκων. φέρειν δὲ αὐτοὺς ὑπόμνημα τῆς ἐν Θυρέᾳ γενομένης νίκης τοὺς προστάτας τῶν ἀγομένων χορῶν ἐν τῇ ἑορτῇ ταύτῃ, ὅτε καὶ τὰς Γυμνοπαιδίας ἐπιτελοῦσιν. χοροὶ δ' εἰσὶ <γ'>, ὁ μὲν πρόσω παίδων, <ὁ δ' ἐκ δεξιοῦ γερόντων>, ὁ δ' ἐξ ἀριστεροῦ ἀνδρῶν,[2] γυμνῶν ὀρχουμένων καὶ ᾀδόντων Θαλητᾶ καὶ Ἀλκμᾶνος ᾄσματα καὶ τοὺς Διονυσοδότου τοῦ Λάκωνος παιᾶνας.

Arist. *H.A.* 557 *a* 1 [π. φθειριάσεως]: ἐνίοις δὲ τοῦτο συμβαίνει τῶν ἀνθρώπων νόσημα ὅταν ὑγρασία πολλὴ ἐν τῷ σώματι ᾖ. καὶ διεφθάρησάν τινες ἤδη τοῦτον τὸν τρόπον ὥσπερ Ἀλκμᾶνά τέ φασι τὸν ποιητὴν καὶ Φερεκύδην τὸν Σύριον.

Paus. 3. 15. 1 [π. Σπάρτης]· ἔστι δὲ τῆς στοᾶς, ᾗ παρὰ τὸν Πλατανιστᾶν πεποίηται, ταύτης

[1] perh. ὃς Μουσέων ἐννέα ῥυθμὸν ἔχει
[2] suppl. Kaib: mss τὸ μὲν and ἀρίστου

Judge not the man by the gravestone. The tomb you see is small, but it holds the bones of a great man. You shall know this for Alcman, striker pre-eminent of the Laconian lyre, one possessed of the nine Muses.[1] And twin continents dispute whether he is of Lydia or Laconia; for the mothers of a minstrel are many.

Heracleides of Pontus *Constitutions*: Alcman was the slave of Agesidas, but received his freedom because he was a man of parts.[2]

Eusebius *Chronicle*: Olympiad 42. 2 (B.C. 611): Flourished Alcman, according to some authorities.

Athenaeus *Doctors at Dinner* [on garlands]: 'Thyreatic':—This, according to Sosibius in his tract *On Sacrifices*, is the name of a kind of garland at Sparta, made of palm-leaves, and known nowadays as *psilinos*. These garlands, he says, are worn in memory of the victory at Thyrea by the leaders of the choruses which dance on the festival of that victory, which coincides with the *Gymnopaidiae* or Feast of Naked Youths. These choruses are three in number, the youths in front, the old men on the right, and the men on the left; and they dance naked, singing songs by Thaletas and Alcman and the paeans of the Spartan Dionysodotus.

Aristotle *History of Animals* [on the *morbus pedicularis*]: Mankind is liable to this disease when the body contains too much moisture, and several victims of it are recorded, notably the poet Alcman and Pherecydes the Syrian.

Pausanias *Description of Greece* [on Sparta]: Behind the colonnade which runs beside the Grove of Planes

[1] or 'who hath in him the disposition of the nine Muses'?
[2] the names of both his 'fathers,' however, are Greek

ὄπισθεν ἡρῷα, τὸ μὲν Ἀλκίμου, τὸ δὲ Ἐναρσφόρου καὶ ἀφεστηκὸς οὐ πολὺ Δορκέως, τὸ δὲ ἐπὶ τούτῳ Σεβροῦ· παῖδας δὲ Ἱπποκόωντος εἶναι λέγουσιν. ἀπὸ δὲ τοῦ Δορκέως κρήνην τὴν πλησίον τοῦ ἡρῴου Δορκείαν, τὸ δὲ χωρίον τὸ Σέβριον καλοῦσιν ἀπὸ τοῦ Σεβροῦ. τοῦ Σεβρίου δέ ἐστιν ἐν δεξιᾷ μνῆμα Ἀλκμᾶνος, ᾧ ποιήσαντι ᾄσματα οὐδὲν ἐς ἡδονὴν αὐτῶν ἐλυμήνατο τῶν Λακώνων ἡ γλῶσσα,[1] ἥκιστα παρεχομένη τὸ εὔφωνον. Ἑλένης δὲ ἱερὰ καὶ Ἡρακλέους, τῆς μὲν πλησίον τοῦ τάφου τοῦ Ἀλκμᾶνος, τοῦ δὲ ἐγγυτάτω τοῦ τείχους, ἐν αὐτῷ δὲ ἄγαλμα Ἡρακλέους ἐστὶν ὡπλισμένον· τὸ δὲ σχῆμα τοῦ ἀγάλματος διὰ τὴν πρὸς Ἱπποκόωντα καὶ τοὺς παῖδας μαχὴν γενέσθαι λέγουσι.

Ath. 14. 638 e καὶ ὁ τοὺς Εἵλωτας δὲ πεποιηκώς φησιν·

τὰ Στησιχόρου τε καὶ Ἀλκμᾶνος Σιμωνίδου τε
ἀρχαῖον ἀείδειν. ὁ δὲ Γνήσιππος ἔστ'
ἀκούειν . . .

Suid. Φιλόχορος· . . . ἔγραψεν . . . περὶ Ἀλκμᾶνος.

Ath. 14. 646 a ὁμοίως καὶ Σωσίβιος ἐν τρίτῳ Περὶ Ἀλκμᾶνος.

Steph. Byz. Ἀράξαι· . . . ὡς Ἀλέξανδρος Κορνήλιος ἐν τῷ περὶ Τῶν παρ' Ἀλκμᾶνι Τοπικῶς Εἰρημένων.

Heph. 138 π. Σημείων· ἡ δὲ διπλῆ ἡ ἔξω βλέπουσα παρὰ μὲν τοῖς κωμικοῖς καὶ τοῖς τραγικοῖς ἐστὶ πολλή, παρὰ δὲ τοῖς λυρικοῖς σπανία· παρὰ Αλκμᾶνι γοῦν εὑρίσκεται· γράψας

there are shrines of Alcimus and Enarsphorus and, close by, one of Dorceus, and adjoining this again one of Sebrus, all of whom are said to have been sons of Hippocoön. The spring near one of them is called Dorceian after Dorceus, and the plot near another, Sebrian after Sebrus. On the right of this plot is a monument to Alcman 'whose poems were not made the less sweet because he used the tongue of Sparta,' a dialect not too euphonious. The temples of Helen and Heracles lie the one near the tomb of Alcman, the other close to the wall. In the latter there is a statue of Heracles armed, this form being due, it is said, to the fight he had with Hippocoön and his sons.

Athenaeus *Doctors at Dinner*: The author of the comedy called *The Helots* says: 'It is old-fashioned to sing Stesichorus, or Alcman, or Simonides. We can listen to Gnesippus . . .'

Suidas *Lexicon*: Philochorus . . . wrote . . . a treatise on Alcman.

Athenaeus *Doctors at Dinner*: Similarly Sosibius in the 3rd Book of his *Treatise on Alcman*.

Stephanus of Byzantium *Lexicon*: . . . as Alexander Cornelius says in his tract *On the Topical Allusions of Alcman*.

Hephaestion *On Graphical Signs*: The outward-looking diplè (>) is frequent in the works of the comic and tragic writers, but unusual in those of the lyrists. It occurs in Alcman, who in writing a poem

[1] apparently the inscr. ran Ἀλκμᾶνος τόδε σᾶμα τῷ (or μνᾶμα τόδ' Ἀλκμαίωνος ᾧ) ᾄσματα ποιήσαντι | οὐδὲν ἐς ἁδοσύναν λυμάνατο γλῶσσα Λακώνων, but it would hardly be contemporary with A. (cf. *e.g.* *A.P.* 7. 3)

γὰρ ἐκεῖνος δεκατεσσάρων στροφῶν ᾆσμα[1] τὸ μὲν ἥμισυ τοῦ αὐτοῦ μέτρου ἐποίησεν ἑπτάστροφον, τὸ δὲ ἥμισυ ἑτέρου· καὶ διὰ τοῦτο ἐπὶ ταῖς ἑπτὰ στροφαῖς ταῖς ἑτέραις τίθεται ἡ διπλῆ σημαίνουσα τὸ μεταβολικῶς τὸ ᾆσμα γεγράφθαι.

ΑΛΚΜΑΝΟΣ

ΜΕΛΩΝ Α′ καὶ Β′

ΠΑΡΘΕΝΕΙΩΝ

1

Sch. Clem. Al. 4. 107 Klotz Ἱπποκόων τις ἐγένετο Λακεδαιμόνιος, οὗ υἱοὶ ἀπὸ τοῦ πατρὸς λεγόμενοι Ἱπποκοωντίδαι ἐφόνευσαν τὸν Λικυμνίου υἱὸν Οἰωνὸν ὀνόματι, συνόντα τῷ Ἡρακλεῖ, ἀγανακτήσαντες ἐπὶ τῷ πεφονεῦσθαι ὑπ' αὐτοῦ κύνα αὐτῶν· καὶ δὴ ἀγανακτήσας ἐπὶ τούτοις ὁ Ἡρακλῆς πόλεμον συγκροτεῖ κατ' αὐτῶν καὶ πολλοὺς ἀναιρεῖ, ὅτε καὶ αὐτὸς τὴν χεῖρα ἐπλήγη· μέμνηται καὶ Ἀλκμὰν ἐν α′.

Mariette Papyrus[2]:

. . . . . .[3]
[. . . . .][4] Πωλυδεύκης.
[οὐκ ἐγὼ]ν Λύκαιϝον[5] ἐν καμοῖσιν ἀλέγω,
[ἀλλ' Ἐνα]ρσφόρον τε καὶ Σέβρον ποδώκη

[1] mss ᾄσματα ὧν [2] the new readings come of a detailed study of an excellent photograph and of a revision in the light of a still better one, kindly sent me by the Bibliothèque Nationale in 1913 and 1914. I regret that I have not yet been able to confirm them by the actual papyrus [3] half of the first strophe, and prob. one or more whole strophes before it, missing [4] I have tested

of fourteen stanzas made the first seven alike of one metre, and the rest alike of another; in these the diplè is placed where the second part begins, to indicate that the poem is written in two different metres.

See also A.P. 7. 19, Plin. *N.H.* 11. 112, Plut. *Sulla* 36, Christod. *Ecphr.* 395.

THE POEMS OF ALCMAN

Books I and II

MAIDEN-SONGS

1

Scholiast on Clement of Alexandria: There was a Spartan called Hippocoön whose sons, called after him the Hippocoöntids, killed in anger Oeonus son of Licymnius, a companion of Heracles, because he had killed a dog of theirs. Heracles' revenge was to levy war upon them, and he killed many of them and was wounded in the hand himself. The story is told by Alcman in his first Book.

From a First-Century Papyrus:

. . . .

. . . . . Polydeuces.[1] Among the slain 'tis true I cannot reckon Lycaeus, but both Enarsphorus I can and the swift Sebrus, Alcimus the mighty and

[1] Heracles was aided by Tyndareüs and the Dioscuri

the suggestions of Egger and others for filling these gaps ll. 1–34 by tracing letter-groups on photographs of the extant parts, l. 6, which is quoted in Cram. *A. O.*, giving the length; cf. Paus. 3. 15. 1 (above), Apollod. *Bibl.* 3. 10. 5: l. 1 no suggestion fits: l. 7 Jur. but without authority (must begin with a vowel) [5] so pap. cf. *πρώϜονες fr.* 36

["Αλκιμό]ν τε τὸν βιατὰν
5 [Ἱππόσ]ων τε τὸν κορυστὰν
Εὐτείχη τε Ϝάνακτά[1] τ' Ἀρήϊον
["Ακμον]ά τ' ἔξοχον ἡμισίων.

[ἦ ΣκαῖϜο]ν τὸν ἀγρόταν
[στρατῶ] μέγαν Εὔρυτόν τε
10 ["Αρεος ἀ]ν πώρω κλόνον
["Αλκων]ά τε τὼς ἀρίστως
[ἡρόων][2] παρήσομες;
[κράτησ]ε γὰρ Αἶσα παντῶν
[καὶ Πόρο]ς γεραίτατοι
15 [σιῶν· ἀπ]έδιλος ἀλκά.
[μήτις ἀν]θρώπων ἐς ὠρανὸν ποτήσθω,
[μηδὲ π]ηρήτω γάμεν τὰν Ἀφροδίταν
[τὰν Πάφω Ϝ]άνασσαν ἤ τιν'
[ἀργυρείδ]η παίδα Πόρκω
20 [εἰναλίω· Χά]ριτες δὲ Διὸς δόμον
[ἰαρὸν ἔχοι]σιν ἐρογλεφάροι.

. . .]τάτοι
. . .]γα[3] δαίμων
. . .]. φίλοις
25 . . . δ]ῶκε δῶρα
. . . ἀ]λγαρέον
. . .]ώλεσ' ἥβα
. . .]χρόνον
. . . μ]αταίᾱς
30 . . .]έβα· τῶν δ' ἄλλος ἰῷ
[ἔφθιτ ἄλλος αὖτε][4] μαρμάρῳ μυλάκρῳ
[ἔστ' ἅπαντας εἶ]λεν Ἅιδας.
[τοὶ σφεαῖσι Κᾶρα]ς αὐτοὶ

Hippothoüs the helmeted, Euteiches and chieftain Areïus, and [Acmon] noblest of demigods. And shall we pass Scaeus by, that was so great a captain of the host, and Eurytus and Alcon that were supremest of heroes in the tumult of the battle-mellay? Not so; vanquished were they all by the eldest of Gods, to wit by Destiny and Device, and their strength had not so much as a shoe to her foot. Nay, mortal man may not go soaring to the heavens, nor seek to wed the Queen of Paphos or to wive any silver-shining daughter of Porcus[1] of the sea; inviolate also is that chamber of Zeus where dwell the Graces whose eyes look love[2] . . . .

. . . .

. . . .

. . . .

. . . .

. . . . . went; and they perished one of them by an arrow and another by a millstone of hard rock, till one and all were had to Hell. These by their own folly did seek them their dooms, and their evil

[1] Nereus [2] the mutilated strophe prob. described the war of the Giants against Heaven

---

[1] pap. Ϝανακτά [2] pap. prob. ἡρώων [3] less prob. τα
[4] gap too wide 31–34 for quite certain restoration

[ἀφραδίαισιν ἐπε]΄σπον, ἄλαστα δὲ
35 ἔργα πάσον κακὰ μησάμενοι.

ἔστι τις σιῶν τίσις·
ὁ δ' ὄλβιος ὅστις εὔφρων
ἁμέραν διαπλέκει
ἄκλαυστος. ἐγὼν δ' ἀείδω
40 Ἀγιδῶς τὸ φῶς· ὁρῶ
ϝ' ὥτ'[1] ἅλιον ὅνπερ ἇμιν
Ἀγιδὼ μαρτύρεται
φαίνην· ἐμὲ δ' οὔτ' ἐπαίνεν[2]
οὔτε μώμεσθαί νιν[3] ἁ κλεννὰ χοραγὸς
45 οὐδ' ἁμῶς ἐῇ· δοκεῖ τ' ἄρ' ἦμεν αὐτὰ
ἐκπρέπης τὼς ὥπερ αἴ τις
ἐν βοτοῖς στάσειεν ἵππον
παγὸν ἀϝεθλοφόρον[4] καναχάποδα
τοῖσιν ὑποπτεριδίων[5] ὀνείρων.

50 ἦ οὐχ ὅρης; ὁ μὲν κέλης
Ἐνετικός· ἁ δὲ χαίτα
τᾶς ἐμᾶς ἀνεψιᾶς
Ἁγησιχόρας ἐπανθεῖ
χρυσὸς ὥτ'[6] ἀκήρατος·
55 τό τ' ἀργύριον πρόσωπον
διαφάδαν τί τοι λέγω;
Ἁγησιχόρα μὲν αὔτα.[7]
ἁ δὲ δευτέρα πεδ' Ἀγιδὼν τὸ ϝεῖδος
ἵππος Εἰβηνῷ Κολαξαῖος δραμείται·
60 ταὶ πελειάδες γὰρ ἇμιν
Ὀρθίᾳ φάρος[8] φεροίσαις

[1] pap. ϝ ὥιτ [2] pap. επηνὲν [3] pap. νιν· [4] pap. αεθλ.
[5] *E*: pap., Sch., and *E.M.* τῶν ὑποπετριδίων, but in Gk.

imaginations brought them into suffering never to be forgot.

Verily there is a vengeance from on high, and happy he that weaveth merrily one day's weft without a tear. And so, as for me, I[1] sing now of the light that is Agido's. Bright I see it as the very sun's which the same Agido now invoketh to shine upon us.[2] And yet neither praise nor blame can I give at all to such as she without offence to our splendid leader, who herself appeareth as pre-eminent as would a well-knit steed of ringing hoof that overcometh in the race, if he were set to graze among the unsubstantial cattle[3] of our dreams that fly.

See you not first that the courser is of Enetic blood, and secondly that the tresses that bloom upon my cousin Hagesichora[4] are like the purest gold? and as for her silvern face, how shall I put it you in express words? Such is Hagesichora; and yet she whose beauty shall run second not unto hers but unto Agido's, shall run as courser Colaxaean to pure Ibenian-bred; for as we bear along her robe to Orthia, these our Doves[5] rise to fight for us[6]

[1] each of the performers [2] the invocation was prob. part of the ritual and took place in dumb-show as these words were sung [3] *i. e.* horses [4] she takes her nickname from her position as Choir-leader, Agido being second in command; it was prob. part of the ritual that the dancers should be cousins (cf. Pind. *Parth.*, Procl. *ap.* Phot. *Bibl.* 239 [5] the leader and her second were apparently called, and perhaps dressed as, doves; this was also the name of the constellation of the Pleiades; Orthia (later Artemis Orthia) was a bird-goddess [6] against the competing choruses

---

dreams give us unsubstantial, not wonderfully fine, types (Sheppard) [6] pap. [.]ς [7] pap. ἄυτα [8] ορθιαι Sch.: text ορθρίαι: pap. φᾶρος: Hdn. π. μον. λέξ. 36. 31 φάρος

νυκτα δι᾽ ἀμβροσίαν ἅτε Σήριον
ἄστρον ἀϝειρομέναι [1] μάχονται.
οὔτε [2] γάρ τι πορφύρας
65 τόσσος κόρος ὥτ᾽ ἀμύναι [3]
οὔτε ποικίλος δράκων
παγχρύσιος, οὐδὲ μίτρα
Λυδία νεανίδων
ἰανογλεφάρων ἄγαλμα·
70 οὐδὲ ταὶ Ναννῶς κόμαι,
ἀλλ᾽ οὐδ᾽ Ἀρέτα σιειδής,
οὐδὲ Συλακίς τε καὶ Κλεησισήρα·
οὐδ᾽ ἐς Αἰνησιμβρότας ἐνθοίσα φασεῖς·
'Ἀσταφίς τέ μοι γένοιτο
75 καὶ ποτιγλέποι [4] Φίλυλλα
Δαμαρέτα τ᾽ ἐρατά τε Ϝιανθεμίς,'
ἀλλ᾽ Ἁγησιχόρα με τηρεῖ.
οὐ γὰρ ἁ καλλίσφυρος
Ἁγησιχόρα πάρ᾽ αὐτεῖ, [5]
80 Ἀγιδοῖ τ᾽ ἴκταρ μένει
Θωστήριά τ᾽ ἅμ᾽ ἐπαινεῖ;
ἀλλὰ τᾶν ἀράς, σιοί,
δέξασθε· σιῶν γὰρ ἄνα.
καὶ τέλος μάλ᾽ ἐς τάφος
85 εἴποιμί κ᾽· ἐγὼν μὲν αὐτὰ
παρσένος μάταν ἀπὸ θράνω λέλακα
γλαύξ· ἐγὼν δὲ τᾷ μὲν Ἀῶτι μαλίστα
ἁνδάνην ἐρῶ· πόνων γὰρ
ἆμιν ἰάτωρ ἔγεντο·
90 ἐξ Ἁγησιχόρας δὲ νεάνιδες
[ἰρ]ήνας ἐράτας ἐπέβαν·
[ὥ]τε [6] γὰρ σηρ[αφόρ]ῳ [7]

[1] pap. σιριον (first ι erased) ασ. αυειρ. [2] pap. ουτι [3] pap.

amid the ambrosial night not as those heavenly Doves but brighter, aye even as Sirius himself.

For neither is abundance of purple defence enough,[1] nor speckled snake of pure gold, nor the Lydian wimple that adorns the sweet and soft-eyed maid, nor yet the tresses of our Nanno, nay nor Areta the goddess-like, nor Thylacis and Cleësithera, nor again shalt thou go to Aenesimbrota's and say 'Give me Astaphis and let me see Philylla, and Damareta and the lovely Ianthemis;' there is no need of that, for I am safe[2] with Hagesichora.

For is not the fair-ankled Hagesichora here present and abideth hard by Agido to commend our Thosteria[3]? Then O receive their prayers, ye Gods; for to the Gods belongeth the accomplishment. And for the end of my song I will tell you a passing strange thing. My own singing hath been nought; I that am a girl have yet shrieked like a very owl from the housetop—albeit 'tis the same girl's desire to please Aotis[4] so far as in her lies, seeing the Goddess is the healer of our woe[5]—; 'tis Hagesichora's doing, hers alone, that the maidens have attained the longed-for peace.[6]

For 'tis true the others have run well beside her

[1] this strophe names the chorus and their teacher, and describes their dress [2] from defeat in the competition [3] the festival of Orthia, of which this song and dance was part of the ritual [4] (the a is long) epithet of Orthia prob. meaning 'dawn-goddess,' cf. the invocation of the sun mentioned l. 41; the procession seems to have taken place at daybreak [5] the ritual was apparently apotropaic [6] either a modest way of describing their expected victory, or ref. to the object of the ritual

---

ὥσταμύναι [4] pap. ποτιβλεποι [5] pap. πάρ'αὐτεῖ [6] pap.]στε [7] the brackets 92–101 mark very faint and uncertain traces

α[ὐ]τῶς ἕδ[ραν ἵκταρ ἄλλαι],
τῷ[1] κυβερνά[τ]ᾳ δ' ἔχεν
95 κὴν ναὶ[2] μα[κρὰν ὄπ]α χ[ρή·]
ἁ δὲ τᾶν Σηρη[νί]δων
ἀοιδοτέρα μὲν [οὐχί·]
σιαὶ γάρ· ἀν[θρώπων δέ νιν]
παίδων ἀέρ[αιμ' ὕπερθ]ι·[3]
100 φθέγγεται δ'[ἄρ' ὥτ' ἐπὶ] Ξάνθω ῥοαῖσι
κύκνος· ἁ δ' ἐ[πὶ σχερ]ῷ ξανθᾷ κομίσκᾳ[4]

. . . .

2 A–C εἰς Διοσκούρους

Steph. Byz. *s.* Ἐρυσίχη· πόλις Ἀκαρνανίας . . . τὸ ἐθνικὸν Ἐρυσιχαῖος, περὶ οὗ πολὺς λόγος τοῖς ἀρχαίοις. ὁ τεχνικὸς γάρ φησιν ὅτι σεσημείωται τὸ Ἐρυσίχαιος προπαροξυνόμενον ἐν τοῖς ἐθνικοῖς· μήποτε οὖν τὸ χαῖον ἐγκεῖσθαι, ὅ ἐστιν ἡ βουκολικὴ ῥάβδος, καὶ τὸν ἐρύσω μέλλοντα. διχῶς οὖν ἔσται, ὡς ἐστὶ δῆλον, παρ' Ἀλκμᾶνι ἐν ἀρχῇ τοῦ δευτέρου τῶν Παρθενείων ᾀσμάτων· φησὶ γάρ·

οὐκ εἶς ἀνὴρ ἄγροικος[5] οὐδὲ
σκαιὸς οὐδὲ παράσυφός τις[6]
οὐδὲ Θέσσαλος γένος
οὐδ' Ἐρυσιχαῖος οὐδὲ ποιμήν,
ἀλλὰ Σαρδίων ἀπ' ἀκρᾶν.

εἰ γὰρ τῷ Θεσσαλὸς γένος συναπτέον, ἐθνικόν ἐστι καὶ προπερισπάσθω· Ἡρωδιανὸς ἐν ταῖς Καθόλου Προσῳδίαις καὶ Πτολεμαῖος ἔφη· Εἰ δὲ τῷ οὐδὲ ποιμὴν συνάψειέ τις λέγων 'οὐδ' ἐρυσίχαιος οὐδὲ ποιμήν,' πρόδηλον ὡς προπαροξυνθήσεται καὶ δηλοῖ τὸν βουκόλον ἢ τὸν αἰπόλον, πρὸς ὃ τὸ ποιμὴν ἁρμόδιον ἐπαχθήσεται.

[1] pap. corrects to ται bec. Hages. is fem. [2] pap. ν`ᾱ ϊ
[3] aor. of αἴρω cf. Hesych. ἀέρῃς· ἄρῃς, βαστάσῃς, Sa. 148. 3: for -θι cf. Alc. 122. 10 ἄγι [4] a coronis or dividing-mark on the edge of the lost fourth column shows that there were 4 lines more to the poem [5] so Chrys. ἀποφ. 21 quoting l. 1: mss here ἄγριος [6] *E*, *cf.* παράκοιτος, παράσιτος: mss παρὰ σοφοῖσιν: *B* sugg. παρὰ σύφοισι

even as horses beside the trace-horse; but here as on shipboard the steersman must needs have a good loud voice, and Hagesichora—she may not outsing the Sirens, for they are Gods, but I would set her higher than any child of human breed. Aye, she sings like a very swan beside the yellow streams of Xanthus, and she that cometh next to that knot of yellow hair . . . [1]

---

2 A–C To the Dioscuri

Stephanus of Byzantium *Lexicon*: Erysichè: A city of Acarnania . . . its adjective is Ἐρυσιχαῖος 'Erysichaean,' about which there is much discussion in the old writers. For Herodian says that Ἐρυσίχαιος is marked in our texts because it is accented proparoxytone though an ethnic adjective; and perhaps therefore it really contains χαῖος 'a cowherd's staff' and the future of ἐρύω 'to draw.' It will be ambiguous then, as is clear, in Alcman near the beginning of the second of his *Maiden-Songs*, where he says:

No boor art thou nor a lubber, nor yet a tender of sties, nay nor Thessalian-born, nor Erysichaean (*or* drag-staff), nor a keeper of sheep, but a man of highest Sardis.

"For if it is to be joined with 'Thessalian-born' it is an ethnic adjective and should be accented circumflex on the penultimate"—thus Herodian, in his *Universal Prosody*, and Ptolemaeus: "but if it is connected with 'a keeper of sheep,' it is obvious that the accent should be acute on the last but two, and that it means 'cowherd' or 'goatherd,' an appellation which is properly followed by 'keeper of sheep.'" [2]

[1] the yellow streams of X. are her own hair which is called golden above (l. 53); the pap. breaks off as we begin a final ref. to Agido with an explanation of the jest; A. follows H. in the processional dance [2] cf. Sch. Ap. Rh. 4. 972, Str. 10. 460 (Ἐρυσ. glossed Καλυδάνιος)

2 B

Hdn. π. σχήμ. 61 Ἀλκμανικὸν σχῆμα τὸ μεσάζον τὴν ἐπαλλήλων ὀνομάτων[1] θέσιν πληθυντικοῖς ἢ δυϊκοῖς ὀνόμασιν ἢ ῥήμασι. τέσσαρα δὲ παρὰ τῷ ποιητῇ τοιαῦτα . . . πλεονάζει δὲ τοῦτο τὸ σχῆμα παρ' Ἀλκμᾶνι τῷ λυρικῷ, ὅθεν καὶ Ἀλκμανικὸν ὠνόμασται. εὐθὺς γοῦν ἐν τῇ δευτέρᾳ ᾠδῇ παρείληπται·

Κάστορ τε πώλων ὠκέων δαμάντορ' ἱππότα
σοφὼ
καὶ Πολλυδεύκες κυδρὲ[2]

2 C

Heph. 3 [π. μακρῶν θέσει]· ἤτοι γὰρ λήγει εἰς δύο σύμφωνα, οἷον . . . καί·

καὶ κῆνος ἐν σάλεσσι πολλοῖς κήμενος μακαρς
ἀνήρ[3]

3–7 εἰς Διοσκούρους (ἢ εἰς Δία Λυκαῖον)

Sch. Bern. Verg. *G.* 3. 89 [Talis Amyclaei domitus Pollucis habenis | Cyllarus]: . . . equos a Neptuno Iunoni datos Alcman lyricus dicit Cyllarum et Xanthum, quorum Polluci Cyllarum, Xanthum fratri eius concessum esse.

4

Ael. *H.A.* 12. 3 Ὁμήρῳ μὲν οὖν φωνὴν Ξάνθῳ τῷ ἵππῳ δόντι συγγνώμην νέμειν ἄξιον· ποιητὴς γάρ· καὶ Ἀλκμὰν δὲ μιμούμενος ἐν τοῖς τοιούτοις Ὅμηρον οὐκ ἂν φέροιτο αἰτίαν.

[1] mss ὀνομ. ἢ ῥημάτων [2] Κάστορ τε *E*: mss Κάστορε: *B* Κάστωρ τε ὠκέων: Sch. Pind. ταχέων δαμάντορε *E*: mss -τορες or -τῆρες: Sch. *Od.* ἐλατῆρες, Eust. ἐλατῆρε, Sch. Pind. δματῆρες Πολλυδεύκες *E*: mss Πολυδεύκεις, -ης: *B*

2 B

Herodian *on Grammatical Figures*: The Alcmanic 'figure' is that whereby plural or dual nouns[1] or verbs are placed between singular nouns which go together. It occurs four times in Homer . . . ; but it is more frequent in the lyric poet Alcman; whence its name. One has only to go as far as his second ode to find:

O Castor—ye tamers of swift steeds, ye skilful horsemen—and noble Polydeuces[2]

2 C

Hephaestion *Handbook of Metre* [on syllables long by position]: For either the word will end in two consonants, for instance . . . and *μάκαρς* 'blessed,' in this:

And reclining yonder in manifold content among the Blest . . .[3]

3–7 To the Dioscuri (*or* To Lycaean Zeus)

Scholiast on Vergil [Such was Cyllarus when he bent to the rein of Pollux]: . . . According to the lyric poet Alcman, the horses given by Neptune to Juno were named Cyllarus (or Bowlegs) and Xanthus (or Bayard), Cyllarus being given to Pollux and Xanthus to his brother.

4

Aelian *On Animals*: Homer, being a poet, deserves our pardon for giving the horse Xanthus speech; and Alcman should not be blamed for imitating Homer in such matters.

[1] includes adjectives [2] cf. Sch. Pind. *P.* 4. 318, Sch. *Od.* 10. 513, Eust. *Od.* 1667. 34 [3] ref. to Heracles? cf. Apoll. *Pron.* 335b (Ἀλκμὰν)

Πωλυδεύκης κυδρὲ *E*: mss nom. [3] σάλεσσι: mss σάλεσιν κήμενος *E*: mss κείμενος, ἥμενος πολλοῖς: Heph. om.

5

Paus. 1. 41. 5 [π. Ἀλκάθου]· Ἀλκμὰν ποιήσας ᾆσμα ἐς τοὺς Διοσκούρους ὡς Ἀφίδνας[1] ἕλοιεν καὶ τὴν Θησέως ἀγάγοιεν μητέρα αἰχμάλωτον, ὅμως Θησέα φησὶν αὐτὸν ἀπεῖναι.

6

Hesych.

Ἀσανέων πόλιν . . .

τὰς Ἀφίδνας.

7

Paus. 3. 26. 2 [π. Πέφνου]· Θαλαμῶν δὲ ἀπέχει σταδίους εἴκοσιν ὀνομαζομένη Πέφνος ἐπὶ θαλάσσῃ, προκεῖται δὲ νησὶς πέτρας τῶν μεγάλων οὐ μείζων, Πέφνος καὶ ταύτῃ τὸ ὄνομα· τεχθῆναι δὲ ἐνταῦθα τοὺς Διοσκούρους φασὶν οἱ Θαλαμᾶται· τοῦτο μὲν δὴ καὶ Ἀλκμᾶνα ἐν ᾄσματι οἶδα εἰπόντα, τραφῆναι δὲ οὐκέτι ἐν τῇ Πέφνῳ φασὶν αὐτούς, ἀλλ' Ἑρμῆν τὸν ἐς Πελλάναν κομίσαντα εἶναι.

8–15 εἰς Δία Λυκαῖον

Max. Plan. ad Herm. *Rh. Gr.* Walz 5. 510 στροφὴ καὶ ἀντίστροφος καὶ ἐπῳδὸς συστήματα μέτρων ἐστὶν ἐν λυρικοῖς ποιήμασιν· ἡ μὲν οὖν στροφή ἐστιν ἡ πρώτη τιθεμένη περίοδος ἐκ δύο ἢ πλειόνων κώλων ὁμοίων ἢ ἀνομοίων συγκειμένη, ὡς παρὰ Ἀλκμᾶνι· (43) αὕτη γὰρ ἡ στροφὴ ἐκ τριῶν ἐστὶ κώλων δακτυλικῶν ἰσομέτρων συγκειμένη· ἐξ ἀνομοίων δὲ ὡς τόδε·

Μῶσ' ἄγε, Μῶσα λίγεια πολυμμελὲς
αἰενάοιδε,[2] μέλος
νεοχμὸν ἄρχε παρσένοις ἀείδεν.

[1] mss Ἀθήνας [2] *B*: mss ἀεὶ δὲ, ἀεὶν ἄειδε, αἰὲν ἄειδε

5

Pausanias *Description of Greece* [on Alcathous]: Alcman in a song to the Dioscuri tells us how they seized Aphidnae and took prisoner the mother of Theseus, but says that Theseus himself was not there.[1]

6

Hesychius *Glossary*:

City of the Athenians:

that is, Aphidnae.

7

Pausanias *Description of Greece* [on Pephnus]: Twenty furlongs from Thalamae there is a place on the sea called Pephnus, off which there stands a pile of rock of some considerable size, known by the same name. This according to the people of Thalamae was the birthplace of the Dioscuri, and their testimony, I know, agrees with that of a song of Alcman's; but they say that though born they were not bred there, and that it was Hermes who carried them to Pellana.

8–15 To Lycaean Zeus

Maximus Planudes *On Hermogenes*: The metrical systems of lyric poetry consist of strophe, antistrophe and epode. Of these the strophe comes first, and consists of two or more similar or dissimilar lines, as in this of Alcman (43), where it is composed of three dactylic lines of the same metre, and in this, where it is made up of unlike lines:

Hither, Muse, sweet clear Muse of the many tunes and everlasting song, and begin a new lay for maids to sing.[2]

[1] cf. Sch. *Il.* 3. 242 [2] cf. *E.M.* 589. 47, Apoll. *Synt.* 1. 4, Erotian 99. 2 (Ἀλκμὰν ἐν α' μελῶν), Prisc. *Metr. Ter.* 2. 428 Keil (*Alcman in primo*), Him. *Or.* 5. 3

9

Vita Arati Buhle 2. 437 ἀγνοοῦσι δὲ ὅτι καὶ Πίνδαρος κατεχρήσατο τῷ ἔπει τούτῳ λέγων· "Ὅθενπερ καὶ Ὁμηρίδαι ἄρχονται, Διὸς ἐκ προοιμίου·" καὶ Ἀλκμάν·

. . . . . ἐγώνγα δ' ἀείσομαι
ἐκ Διὸς ἀρχομένα.[1]

10

Apoll. *Pron.* 109. 23 πλεῖστα γοῦν ἔστι παρ' ἑτέροις εὑρεῖν σφέτερον πατέρα ἀντὶ τοῦ ὑμέτερον . . . καὶ πάλιν παρ' αὐτῷ ἀντὶ τοῦ σφωΐτερον· Ἀλκμάν·

ὑμέ τε καὶ σφετέρως
ἵππως . . .

11

Sch. Eur. *Tro.* 210 οἰκητήριόν φασι τὰς Θεράπνας τῶν Διοσκούρων παρ' ὅσον ὑπὸ τὴν γῆν τῆς Θεράπνης εἶναι λέγονται ἀποθανόντες,[2] ὡς Ἀλκμάν φησιν.

[1] Valck.-*B*: mss ἐγὼ δὲ ἀεί σοι με ἐκ Δ. ἀρχόμενα [2] mss ζῶντες

---

[1] *Nem.* 2. 1 [2] the feminine shows the song was sung by girls (cf. fr. 8) [3] prob. the Dioscuri, mention of whom seems to have been added to this hymn at the request of

9

Life of Aratus: They are unaware that Pindar, too, made use of this line, saying 'Where the children of Homer also do begin, to wit the proem unto Zeus,'[1] and Alcman:

But of this song of mine the beginning shall be Zeus.[2]

10

Apollonius *The Pronouns*: This is often found among other writers; for instance, σφέτερον πατέρα instead of ὑμέτερον πατέρα, 'your father' . . . and again in the same author [Hesiod] σφέτερον is used for σφωΐτερον; Alcman says:

Ye[3] and your horses

11

Scholiast on Euripides *Trojan Women*: They call Therapnae the dwelling of the Dioscuri because they are said to be beneath the land of Therapnè when they are dead, as Alcman says.

the Spartans when A. passed through Sparta on his way with the poem to the temple of Lycaean Zeus in Arcadia; cf. Him. l.c.

12, 13

Prisc. *Metr. Ter.* 3. 428 Keil: Alcman autem in primo catalecticum trimetrum fecit habentem in quarto loco modo iambum modo spondeum, sic [—*fr.* 8 *l.* 3; *then*—]

καὶ ναὸς ἁγνὸς[1] εὐπύργω Σεράπνας,

hic quarto loco spondeum habet. Similiter

χερσόνδε κωφὸν ἐν φύκεσσι πιτνεῖ

quarto loco spondeum posuit, nam φυ producitur . . .

14

Aristid. 2. 508 π. τοῦ Παραφθέγματος· ἀκούεις δὲ καὶ τοῦ Λάκωνος λέγοντος εἰς αὑτόν τε καὶ τὸν χορόν Ἁ Μῶσα κ.τ.λ. . . . προστίθει δὲ κἀκεῖνο, ὅτι αὐτῆς τῆς Μούσης δεηθεὶς κατ' ἀρχὰς ὁ ποιητής, ἵν' ἐνεργὸς ὑπ' αὐτῆς γένοιτο, εἶτα ὥσπερ ἐξέστη καί φησιν ὅτι τοῦτο ἐκεῖνο <ὁ> χόρος αὐτὸς ἀντὶ τῆς Μούσης πεποίηκε.[2]

ἁ Μῶσα κέκλαγ', ἁ λίγεια Σειρήν·[3]
e.g.[4] ἀλλά νιν οὐκ ἄρ' ἔδευε[5] καλῆν ἐμέ,
| τῷ Ϝόπα, παρθενικαί,
| ὔμμες τοσαύταν ἐμπεπνεύκατ' αὐταί.[6]

15

Sch. Ap. Rh. 1. 146 [Αἰτωλίς . . . Λήδη]· Φερεκύδης δὲ ἐν τῇ β' ἐκ Λαοφόντης τῆς Πλευρῶνος Λήδαν καὶ Ἀλθαίαν Θεστίῳ γενέσθαι φησίν· ὅτι δὲ Γλαύκου ἐστὶ καὶ Ἀλκμὰν[7] αἰνίττεται λέγων·

. . . τὼς τέκε <Ϝοι> θυγάτηρ
Γλαύκω μάκαιρα[8]

---

[1] Herm. -*B*: mss ἁγνᾶς [2] *E*: mss γεγένηται [3] κέκλᾰγ' ἁ Welck. -*B*: mss κεκλήγη or -ει [4] *E*: cf. Hes. *Th.* 31 [5] cf. Sa. 2. 15 ἐπιδεύϜην [6] cf. 1. 95 [7] *B*: mss Ἀλθαίας from above [8] suppl. *B*

12, 13

Priscian *Metres of Terence:* Moreover Alcman in his first book has a catalectic trimeter sometimes with and sometimes without an iambus in the fourth foot thus [—*frag.* 8. *l.* 3; *then* —]

. . . And the temple pure of towered Therapnae;[1]

here he has a spondee in the fourth foot. Similarly:

. . . Falleth dumb upon the shore among the tangle;[2]

here, too, he has given the fourth foot a spondee, for the first syllable of φύκεσσι is long.

14

Aristides *On the Extemporised Addition*[3]: You hear the Laconian, too, saying to himself and the chorus: 'The Muse' etc.; note also that having at the outset asked the Muse herself to inspire him, he then seems to change about and says that the chorus who is singing the song has itself done this instead of the Muse.

The Muse crieth aloud, that Siren clear and sweet. But I had no need, it seems, to invoke her aid, seeing that you yourselves, ye maidens, have inspired me with so loud a voice.

e.g.

15

Scholiast on Apollonius of Rhodes *Argonautica* [Aetolian Leda]: It is true that Pherecydes says in his second Book that Leda and Althaea were daughters of Thestius by Laophontè daughter of Pleuron; but that Leda was daughter of Glaucus is implied by Alcman thus:

. . . his sons by the blessed daughter of Glaucus

---

[1] cf. Harp. 151. 14 ('Αλκμὰν ἐν ά), Phot. and Suid. Θεράπναι, Paus. 3. 20. 1, Sch. Pind. *I.* 4. 3, Steph. Byz. Θεράπναι
[2] the calm sea [3] to a written speech of his own

16 εἰς Ἥραν[1]

Ath. 15. 680f [π. ἑλιχρύσου]· μνημονεύει αὐτοῦ Ἀλκμὰν ἐν τούτοις·

καὶ τὶν εὔχομαι φέροισα[2]
τόνδ' ἑλιχρύσω πυλεῶνα
κἠράτω κυπαίρω.[3]

17–23 εἰς Ἄρτεμιν

E.M. Vet. Miller *Misc.* 263 ῥύτειρα·

Ἄρταμι, ῥύτειρα τόξων[4]

18

Apoll. *Pron.* 75. 12 ἡ σέο καταβάλλει τὸ σ εἰς τὸ τ παρὰ Δωριεῦσιν. Ἀλκμάν·

Ἐμὲ Λατοΐδα τέο θ' ἁγεόχορον[5]

19

Sch. *Il.* 21. 485 περιάπτεται γὰρ νεβρίδας, Ἀλκμάν·

ἐπαμμένᾳ πέρι[6] δέρματα θηρῶν

20

E.M. 486. 39 καλά· τὸ καλά παρ' Ἀλκμᾶνι καλλά ἐστιν, οἷον

καλλὰ μελισδομένᾳ

[1] Ath. 15. 678a [2] τὶν *B*: mss τιν' [3] πυλεῶνα κἠρ. Boiss: mss πύλεω ἀκηράτων κυπαίρω Welck., cf. Eust. *Od.* 1648. 7: mss κυπέρω [4] *B Adesp.* 46B [5] i.e. ἁγιόχορον *E*: mss δ' αχοσχορον [6] *B-E*: mss ἐπάμειαι (or ἐσσαμένᾳ) παρὰ

16 To Hera

Athenaeus *Doctors at Dinner* [on the helichryse or cassidony]: Alcman speaks of it thus:

To thee also I pray with this garland of cassidony and lovely bedstraw[1] for an offering.

17–23 To Artemis[2]

Old Etymologicum Magnum: Drawer:

O Artemis, drawer of bowstrings

18

Apollonius *The Pronouns*: The pronoun σέο changes σ to τ in Doric; compare Alcman:

Me who am choirmaster as well to thee as to the Son of Leto

19

Scholiast on the *Iliad*: For Artemis is clad in fawnskins; compare Alcman:

clad in the skins of the beasts of the field

20

Etymologicum Magnum καλά, 'pretty': the word appears as καλλά in Alcman:

sung of so prettily[3]

[1] I thus translate because it was used for lying on (at meals), though it is not *our* bedstraw; sometimes translated 'galingale' [2] all these fragments are not necessarily from the same hymn [3] cf. Cram. *A.P.* 4. 63. 13, Apoll. *Adv.* 155. 9

21

Apoll. *Pron.* 50. 28 οἱ αὐτοὶ Δωριεῖς ἐγώνγα καὶ ἐγώνη·

οὐ γὰρ ἐγώνγα, Ϝάνασσα Διὸς θύγατερ[1]

Ἀλκμάν.

22

Choer. ad Heph. 13 [π. παιωνικοῦ]· Ἡλιόδωρος δέ φησι κοσμίαν εἶναι τῶν παιωνικῶν τὴν κατὰ πόδα τομήν . . . οἷον·

οὐδὲ τῷ Κνακάλῳ οὐδὲ τῷ Νυρσύλα

23

Ath. 14. 646a [π. κριβανῶν]· κριβάνας πλακοῦντάς τινας ὀνομαστικῶς Ἀπολλόδωρος παρ' Ἀλκμᾶνι· ὁμοίως καὶ Σωσίβιος ἐν τρίτῳ Περὶ Ἀλκμᾶνος, τῷ σχήματι μαστοειδεῖς εἶναι φάσκων αὐτούς· χρῆσθαι δ' αὐτοῖς Λάκωνας πρὸς τὰς τῶν γυναικῶν ἑστιάσεις, περιφέρειν τε αὐτοὺς ὅταν μέλλωσιν ᾄδειν τὸ παρεσκευασμένον ἐγκώμιον τῆς Παρθένου αἱ ἐν τῷ χορῷ ἀκόλουθοι.

Ibid. 3. 114f [π. μαζῶν]· αἱ δὲ παρ' Ἀλκμᾶνι θριδακίσκαι λεγόμεναι αἱ αὐταί εἰσι ταῖς Ἀττικαῖς θριδακίναις, λέγει δὲ οὕτως ὁ Ἀλκμάν·

θριδακίσκας τε καὶ κριβάνας νῶντος[2]

---

24 εἰς Ἀφροδίτην

Str. 8. 340 [π. Ἤλιδος]· ποιητικῷ δέ τινι σχήματι συγκαταλέγειν τὸ μέρος τῷ ὅλῳ φασὶ τὸν Ὅμηρον, ὡς τὸ 'ἂν' Ἑλλάδα καὶ μέσον Ἄργος' . . . καὶ Ἀλκμὰν δέ·

Κύπρον ἱμερτὰν λιποῖσα καὶ Πάφον περιρρύταν

[1] mss ἔγωνγα [2] *B*, cf. Phot. νῶντος· σωρεύοντος: mss κριβανωτὸς or -τως

21

Apollonius *Pronouns*: The same Dorians say ἐγώνγα and ἐγώνη 'I': compare:

Never [did] I, O queen born of Zeus

from Alcman.

22

Choeroboscus on Hephaestion *Handbook of Metre* [on the paeonic]: Heliodorus says that the foot-by-foot caesura is regular in paeonics, as for instance:

nor yet from Cnacalus nor yet from Nyrsylas [1]

23

Athenaeus *Doctors at Dinner* [on 'pan-baked' loaves]: According to Apollodorus this is the name of a kind of cake in Alcman; and similarly Sosibius in the third Book of his treatise *On Alcman*, declaring that they are shaped like a woman's breast and are used at Sparta for women's feasts, being carried round just before the attendants in the chorus sing the eulogy they have prepared in honour of the Maid.

The Same [on loaves]: The θριδακίσκαι of Alcman are the same as the Attic θριδακῖναι or lettuces; the passage of Alcman runs thus:

making a pile of lettuces and pan-baked loaves

---

24 To Aphrodite

Strabo [on Elis]: They say that Homer, by a poetic figure, puts the part side by side with the whole, as 'throughout Greece and midmost Argos' . . . and Alcman, too, says:

From the lovely Cyprus and the sea-girt Paphos [2]

[1] haunts of Artemis, cf. Paus. 8. 23. 4 [2] cf. Men. *Rh. Gr.* Walz 9. 135 (on hymns of invocation; 'calls Aphrodite from Cyprus, Cnidus,' etc.)

25

Ath. 9. 390a καλοῦνται δὲ οἱ πέρδικες ὑπ' ἐνίων κακκάβαι, ὡς καὶ ὑπ' Ἀλκμᾶνος, λέγοντος οὕτως·

ἔπη δέ γε[1] καὶ μέλος Ἀλκμὰν
εἶρε[2] γεγλωσσάμενον
κακκαβίδων στόμα συνθέμενος,

σαφῶς ἐμφανίζων ὅτι παρὰ τῶν περδίκων ᾄδειν ἐμάνθανε.

26

Ant. Car. *Hist. Mir.* 27 (23) τῶν δὲ ἀλκυόνων οἱ ἄρσενες κηρύλοι καλοῦνται· ὅταν οὖν ὑπὸ τοῦ γήρως ἀσθενήσωσι καὶ μηκέτι δύνωνται πέτεσθαι, φέρουσιν αὐτοὺς αἱ θήλειαι ἐπὶ τῶν πτερῶν λαβοῦσαι· καί ἐστι τὸ ὑπὸ τοῦ Ἀλκμᾶνος λεγόμενον τούτῳ συνῳκειωμένον· φησὶν γὰρ ἀσθενὴς ὢν διὰ τὸ γῆρας καὶ τοῖς χοροῖς οὐ δυνάμενος συμπεριφέρεσθαι οὐδὲ τῇ τῶν παρθένων ὀρχήσει·

οὔ μ' ἔτι, παρθενικαὶ μελιγάρυες ἱερόφωνοι,[3]
γυῖα φέρειν δύναται· βάλε δὴ βάλε κηρύλος εἴην,
ὅς τ' ἐπὶ κύματος ἄνθος ἅμ' ἀλκυόνεσσι ποτῆται
νηδεὲς[4] ἦτορ ἔχων, ἁλιπόρφυρος εἴαρος[5] ὄρνις.

27

Aristid. 2. 40 π. Ῥητορικῆς· τί δὲ ὁ τῶν παρθένων ἐπαινέτης τε καὶ σύμβουλος λέγει ὁ Λακεδαιμόνιος ποιητής;[6]

Πολλυλέγων[7] ὄνυμ' ἀνδρί, γυναικὶ δὲ Πασιχάρηα.[8]

πολλά, φησίν, ὁ ἀνὴρ λεγέτω, γυνὴ δὲ οἷς ἂν ἀκούσῃ χαιρέτω.

[1] *E*: mss ἐπῆγε δὲ: *B* ἔπη τάδε [2] Emperius: mss εὗρε [3] loud-voiced, cf. 1. 95 [4] Boiss: mss νηλεὲς but Phot. ἀδεὲς [5] if right, this use of the gen. of the noun instead of an adj. personifies spring; Heck. ἰαρὸς = ἱερὸς perh. rightly; the halcyon was popularly connected with winter [6] Sch. ὁ Ἀλκμάν [7] *E*, cf. Πολυμέδων: mss πολλὰ λέγων: Herm. Πολλαλέγων [8] Herm: mss πᾶσι (πάσῃ) χαρηά

25

Athenaeus *Doctors at Dinner*: Partridges are called by some writers κακκάβαι, notably by Alcman, who says:

Aye, and Alcman did put together the tongued utterance of the *caccabis*, to make his twine of words and music,

clearly indicating that he learnt to sing from the partridges.[1]

26

Antigonus of Carystus *Marvels*: The cock halcyons are called ceryls, and when they grow old and weak and unable to fly, their mates carry them upon their wings; and with this is connected the passage in Alcman where he says that age has made him weak and unable to whirl round with the choirs and with the dancing of the maidens:

O maidens of honey voice so loud and clear, my limbs can carry me no more. Would O would God I were but a ceryl, such as flies fearless of heart with the halcyons over the bloom of the wave, the Spring's own bird that is purple as the sea![2]

27

Aristides *On Rhetoric*: And what saith the praiser and counsellor of the maidens, the poet of Sparta?

Be the man's name Say-much, the woman's Glad-of-all,

by which he means 'let the man speak and the woman be content with whatsoever she shall hear.'

[1] the poet is jestingly praising his choir at his own expense [2] cf. Bek. *An.* 2. 522, 568, 946, Cram. *A.O.* 1. 265, 1, *E.M.* 186. 43, Sch. Ar. *Av.* 250, 299, Suid. κηρύλος, Phot. s. ὄρνις, Ath. 9. 347 d, Zon. 121 (Goettl.)

28–35

Ath. 9. 373e [π. ὀρνίθων]· ὅτι δὲ καὶ ἐπὶ τοῦ πληθυντικοῦ ὄρνεις λέγουσιν, πρόκειται τὸ Μενάνδρειον μαρτύριον· ἀλλὰ καὶ Ἀλκμάν που φησί·

δῦσαν δ' ἄπρακτα νεάνιδες ὧτ'
ὄρνῑς ἱέρακος ὑπερπταμένω.[1]

29

Apoll. *Pron.* 58. 13 ἀλλὰ καὶ Ἀλκμὰν πρωτῷ

Μάκαρς ἐκεῖνος

φησί.

30

Ibid. 366c ἡ σέ . . . Δωριεῖς διὰ τοῦ τ . . . Ἀλκμὰν καὶ ἔτι μετὰ τοῦ ι . . . καὶ ἔτι κοινῶς·

σὲ γὰρ ἄζομαι.

31

Sch. *Od.* 6. 244 [αἲ γὰρ ἐμοὶ τοιόσδε πόσις κεκλημένος εἴη | ἐνθάδε ναιετάων, καί οἱ ἅδοι αὐτόθι μίμνειν]· ἄμφω μὲν ἀθετεῖ Ἀρίσταρχος· διστάζει δὲ περὶ τοῦ πρώτου ἐπεὶ καὶ Ἀλκμὰν αὐτὸν μετέλαβε,[2] παρθένους λεγούσας εἰσάγων·

Ζεῦ πάτερ, αἰ γὰρ ἐμὸς πόσις εἴη

32

Apoll. *Pron.* 109. 23 πλεῖστα γοῦν ἔστι παρ' ἑτέροις εὑρεῖν σφέτερον πατέρα ἀντὶ τοῦ ὑμέτερον . . . Ἀλκμάν (—*fr.* 10; *then*—)

σφεὰ δὲ προτὶ γούνατα πίπτω.[3]

[1] δῦσαν *B*, cf. *Il.* 18. 145: mss λῦσαν [2] Lehrs: mss -έβαλε [3] προτὶ Bek: mss ποτὶ

---

[1] prob. from a poem dealing with Nausicaa and Odysseus' entertainment by Alcinous, *Od.* 6 and 7: with 28 cf. *Od.* 6. 138

28–35 [1]

Athenaeus *Doctors at Dinner* [on poultry]: That they say ὄρνεις for ὄρνιθες 'birds' in the plural is obvious from the above testimony of Menander; but Alcman also says somewhere:

Down sank the damsels helpless, like birds beneath a hovering hawk.

29 [2]

Apollonius *The Pronouns*: But Alcman, too, says in his first Book:

Blest is he

30 [3]

The same: The pronoun σέ, 'thee' . . . The Dorians use the form in τ; compare Alcman (132), and that in ι (52), and also the ordinary form in σ:

For of thee stand I in awe.[4]

31 [5]

Scholiast on the *Odyssey* [Would that such a man might be my husband here dwelling, and would be pleased to abide with me!]: Aristarchus athetises both these lines, but is doubtful about the first because Alcman has adopted it, making some maidens say:

O Father Zeus! that he were but my husband!

32 [6]

Apollonius *The Pronouns*: This is often found among other writers; for instance, σφέτερον πατέρα instead of ὑμέτερον πατέρα 'your father' . . . Alcman (*—fragment* 10; *then*—)

Before your knees I fall.

(N.'s companions on seeing O.) [2] cf. *Od.* 6. 158 O. to N. [3] cf. *Od.* 6. 168 O. to N. [4] cf. Apoll. *Synt.* 139 [5] cf. *Od.* 6. 244 N. on seeing O. dressed [6] cf. *Od.* 7. 146 O. supplicates Arete

33

Cram. *A.P.* 4. 181. 27 εἴκω· τὸ ὑποχωρῶ . . . ὡς Ἀλκμάν·

τῷ δὲ γυνὰ ταμία[1] σφεὰν ἔειξε χώραν.[2]

34

Id. *A.O.* 1. 343. 11 καὶ πλῆτρον τὸ πηδάλιον, καὶ ὑποκοριστικῶς εἶπεν Ἀλκμὰν

πληṫρίον[3]

35

Eust. *Il.* 110. 25 μονῆρες δὲ ἐν θηλυκοῖς ἡ χείρ, ἣ κλίνεται διχῶς, ποτὲ μὲν διὰ τοῦ ε . . ., ποτὲ δὲ διὰ τῆς ει διφθόγγου, ποτὲ δὲ κατὰ Ἡρωδιανὸν καὶ μετατεθείσης αὐτῆς εἰς η, ᾧ μαρτυρεῖ φησὶν Ἀλκμὰν ἐν τῷ·

ἐπ' ἀριστερὰ χηρὸς ἔχων

36

Apoll. *Lex. Hom.* κνώδαλον· . . . ἔνιοι δὲ θῆρας μὲν καὶ θηρία λέγουσι[4] λέοντας καὶ παρδάλεις καὶ λύκους καὶ πάντα τὰ παραπλήσια τούτοις, ἑρπετὰ δὲ πάλιν κοινῶς τὰ γένη τῶν ὄφεων, κνώδαλα δὲ τὰ θαλάσσια κήτη, φαλαίνας καὶ ὅσα τοιαῦτα, καθάπερ καὶ Ἀλκμὰν διαστέλλει λέγων οὕτως·

εὕδοισιν δ' ὀρέων κορυφαί τε καὶ φάραγγες
πρώϝονές τε καὶ χαράδραι,[5]
φῦλά θ' ἑρπετὰ τόσσα[6] τρέφει μέλαινα γαῖα,
θῆρες τ' ὀρεσκῷοι καὶ γένος μελισσᾶν,
καὶ κνώδαλ' ἐν βένθεσι πορφυρέας[7] ἁλός·
εὕδοισιν δ' οἰωνῶν
φῦλα τανυπτερύγων.

[1] *B*, cf. Od. 7. 175: mss τὸ δὲ γύναι ταμίας [2] *E*: mss σφεὰς εἶξε χώρας (σφεὰς from ταμίας): ἔειξε Apoll. (τῷ ε πλεονάζει) [3] *E*: mss πλήθριον: πλῆτρον prob. Aeol. for πλῆκτρον; for simplification of consonant-compounds cf. ὄθματα, ἔσλος [4] mss λέγοντες [5] Vill.-Baunack: mss

33[1]

Cyrillus in Cramer's *Inedita (Paris)*: εἴκω 'to withdraw' . . . as Alcman:

And the housewife gave up her place to him.[2]

34

Cramer *Inedita (Oxford)*: And πλῆτρον 'rudder,' and in the diminutive-form Alcman said πλητρίον

'tiller'[3]

35

Eustathius on Homer: χείρ 'hand' is peculiar among feminines in being declined in two ways, both with ε and with ει, and, according to Herodian, with the change to η, for which he quotes Alcman:

having upon his[4] left hand

36

Apollonius *Homeric Lexicon*: Some writers give the name of beast to lions, leopards, wolves, and all similar animals, that of creeping-thing generically to the various kinds of snakes, that of monster to cetaceans such as whales; which is the distinction made by Alcman in the lines:

Asleep lie mountain-top and mountain-gully, shoulder also and ravine; the creeping-things that come from the dark earth, the beasts whose lying is upon the hillside, the generation of the bees, the monsters in the depths of the purple brine, all lie asleep, and with them the tribes of the winging birds.

[1] cf. *Od.* 7. 175 Alcinous entertains O. [2] cf. Apoll. *Pron.* 112. 2 [3] cf. Ammon. 109 [4] or 'my': cf. *Od.* 5. 276: perh. O. is telling A. how he came to Scheria 'keeping the Bear upon his left hand'

εὕδουσιν and φάλαγγες πρωτονέστε [6] Schoemann: mss φ. τε ἑρπ. θ' ὅσσα [7] mss μελισσῶν and πορφυρῆς

37

Apoll. *Pron.* 95. 9 ἡ ἁμῶν παρὰ Δωριεῦσι, καὶ σύναρθρον γενικὴν σημαίνει ἀκόλουθον τῇ ἁμός· τῇ μέντοι διαιρέσει ἡ πρωτότυπος διαλλάσσει τῆς κτητικῆς . . . Ἀλκμάν·

ὅσαι δὲ παῖδες ἁμέων ἐντί, τὸν κιθαρίσταν αἰνέοντι . . .[1]

38

Eust. *Il.* 1147. 1 λῆδος . . . ὃ Δωριεῖς λᾶδός φασιν ὡς Ἀλκμάν·

λᾶδος εἱμένα καλόν

ὅ ἐστιν λήδιον ἐνδεδυμένη εὐειδές.

39

Eust. *Od.* 1618. 23 κατὰ δὲ τὴν παρὰ Ἡρωδιανῷ Ἀλκμανικὴν χρῆσιν καὶ Ἀρτέμιδος Ἀρτάμιτος,[2] οἷον·

Ἀρτάμιτος θεράποντα

οὕτω θέμις θέμιτος.

40

Ach. Tat. *Isag.* 2. 166 (Petavius *Uranologium*) εἰσὶν οὖν τέσσαρες σφαῖραι· ἃ στοιχεῖα καλοῦσιν οἱ παλαιοὶ διὰ τὸ στοίχῳ καὶ τάξει ἕκαστον αὐτῶν ὑποκεῖσθαι· ὥς που καὶ Ἀλκμὰν

ὁμοστοίχους

ἐκάλεσε τὰς ἐν τάξει χορευούσας παρθένους.

41

Suid. ψιλεύς· ἐπ' ἀκροῦ χοροῦ ἱστάμενος· ὅθεν καὶ

φιλόψιλος

παρ' Ἀλκμᾶνι ἡ φιλοῦσα ἐπ' ἀκροῦ χοροῦ ἵστασθαι.[3]

[1] mss παῖδες [2] sugg. *B* (bis): mss Ἀρτέμ. [3] cf. ψίλον = πτίλον and Hesych. ψιλεῖς· οἱ ὕστατοι χορεύοντες

37

Apollonius *Pronouns*: The pronoun ἁμῶν is Doric, and shows an articular genitive corresponding to ἁμός. But the primitive, ἁμέων 'us,' is distinguished from the possessive, ἁμῶν 'our,' by diaeresis . . . Alcman:

All of us that are girls do praise our lyre-player.[1]

38

Eustathius on the *Iliad*: λῆδος 'muslin gown' . . . which the Dorians call λᾶδος, as Alcman:

and she is clad in a fair muslin gown,

that is, clothed in a handsome summer dress.

39

Eustathius on the *Odyssey*: And also, according to the instance quoted by Herodian from Alcman, Ἀρτάμιτος for Ἀρτέμιδος 'of Artemis,' as:

minister of Artemis;

So θέμις, θέμιτος.

40

Achilles Tatius *Introduction to Aratus' Phaenomena*: There are four spheres, and these are called by the ancients στοιχεῖα because each of them lies in a row or rank, just as Alcman somewhere called girls dancing in a line

maidens all a-row

41

Suidas *Glossary*: ψιλεύς, 'winger': one who stands on the edge of a band of singers; whence Alcman's

lover of the wings,

'she who loves to stand on the edge of the choir.'[2]

[1] the poet's choir to the poet [2] cf. Phot. s. ψιλεύς

42

Bek. *An.* 2. 855 ὁ ὑποκορισμὸς ὄνομά ἐστι μικρότητος ἐμφαντικὸν καὶ κόραις ἐοικός· λαμβάνεται δὲ ἕνεκεν τοῦ πρέποντος ὡς παρ' Ἀλκμᾶνι· . . . κόραι γὰρ αἱ λέγουσαι.

Γ'

43

Heph. 43 [π. δακτυλικοῦ]· Ἀλκμὰν δὲ καὶ ὅλας στροφὰς τούτῳ τῷ μέτρῳ κατεμέτρησε·

Μῶσ' ἄγε, Καλλιόπα, θύγατερ Διός,
ἄρχ' ἐρατῶν ἐπέων, ἐπὶ δ' ἵμερον [1]
ὕμνον καὶ χαρίεντα τίθει χορόν.[2]

44

Sch. *Od.* 3. 171 Ψυρίης· νησίδιον μικρὸν ἔχον λίμενα νηῶν εἴκοσιν· Ἀλκμάν·

πάρ θ' ἱερὸν σκόπελον παρά τε Ψύρα [3]

45

Aristid. 2. 509 π. τοῦ Παραφθέγματος· ἀλλαχῇ δὲ οὕτω σφόδρα ἔνθεος γίγνεται (ὁ Ἀλκμὰν) ὥστε φαίης ἂν οὐδ' οὑτωσὶ κατὰ τὸ ῥῆμα ἔνθεός ἐστιν, ἀλλ' αὐτὸ δὴ τοῦτο ὥσπερ θεὸς τῶν ἀπὸ μηχανῆς λέγει·

εἴπατέ μοι τάδε, φῦλα βροτήσια.

[1] ἐφ' ἵμερον the phrase whence came ἐφίμερος [2] Max. ὕμνῳ [3] πάρ θ' Buttmann : mss παρά τε

42

Bekker *Inedita*: The diminutive or pet-name is a name expressive of smallness and suitable to girls. It is used for this reason, for instance, by Alcman: . . . ; for the speakers are girls.[1]

Books III[2]

43

Hephaestion *Handbook of Metre* [on the dactylic]: Alcman has whole stanzas of this metre:

Come, Muse Calliopè, daughter of Zeus, begin thy lovely lines, and make a hymn to our liking and a dance that shall please.[3]

44

Scholiast on the *Odyssey*: Psyria, a little islet with anchorage for twenty ships . . . compare Alcman:

to the sacred rock, to Psyra

45

Aristides *On the Extemporised Addition*: In another place Alcman becomes so God-inspired that you may say he is not only ἔνθεος in the ordinary sense of the word but speaks the God's actual words like a God from the machine, *deus ex machina*:

Tell me this, ye mortal breeds.

[1] the quotation is lost: cf. Cram. *A.O.* 4. 273. 12 [2] in this book I have placed all other fragments of choral or otherwise general type [3] cf. Max. Plan. 5. 510 Walz, Ars. 360, *Paroem.* 2. 540, Heph. 44 and Sch.

46

Ath. 10. 416c [π. πολυφαγίας]· καὶ Ἀλκμὰν δὲ ὁ ποιητὴς ἑαυτὸν ἀδηφάγον εἶναι παραδίδωσιν ἐν τῷ τρίτῳ διὰ τούτων·

καὶ τόκα τοι δώσω τρίποδος κύτος,[1]
ᾧ κ' ἔνι <δεῖπνον ἀολλέ'> ἀγείρῃς·[2]
ἀλλ' ἔτι νῦν γ' ἄπυρος, τάχα δὲ πλέος
ἔτνεος, οἷον ὁ παμφάγος Ἀλκμὰν
ἠράσθη χλιερὸν πεδὰ[3] τὰς τροπάς·
οὔτι γὰρ ἠῢ τετυγμένον ἔσθει,[4]
ἀλλὰ τὰ κοινὰ γάρ, ὥσπερ ὁ δᾶμος,
ζατεύει . . .[5]

47

Ibid. 11. 498 f [π. σκύφου]· Ἀσκληπιάδης δὲ ὁ Μυρλεανὸς ἐν τῷ Περὶ τῆς Νεστορίδος φησὶν ὅτι τῷ σκύφει καὶ τῷ κισσυβίῳ τῶν μὲν ἐν ἄστει καὶ μετρίων οὐδεὶς ἐχρῆτο, συβῶται δὲ καὶ νομεῖς καὶ οἱ ἐν ἀγρῷ . . . καὶ Ἀλκμὰν δέ φησι·

πολλάκι δ' ἐν κορυφαῖς ὀρέων, ὅκα
θεοῖσι Ϝάδῃ πολύφανος ἑορτά,[6]
χρύσιον ἄγγος ἔχοισα μέγαν σκύφον
οἷά τε ποιμένες ἄνδρες ἔχοισιν,
χερσὶ λεόντεον ἐν γάλα θεῖσα[7]
τυρὸν ἐτυρήσας μέγαν ἄτρυφον
ἀργιφόεντα . . .[8]

[1] τόκα sugg. *B*: mss πόκα [2] δεῖπνον *E*, ἀολλέ' Jur: mss by haplogr. ὦκένιλεα γ̄ειρης (ΛΕ for ΔΕ, cf. ΧΑ for ΧΛ below): *B* ἀγείραις perh. rightly [3] Cas: mss χαιερον παῖδα [4] mss also τετυμμ. [5] κοινὰ Cas: mss καινὰ [6] mss θεοῖς ᾄδῃ [7] Fiorillo-Herm, cf. Aristid. 1. 49: mss ἐπαλαθεῖσα [8] *E*, cf. late poet Cram. *A.P.* 4. 350 (epithet of νῶτα θαλάσσης, mss ἀργυφ.): mss ἀργύφεόν τε, ἀργειόφεονται, -φόνται: Gram. (see opp.) ἀργίφοντα

46

Athenaeus *Doctors at Dinner* [on voracity]: And in his third Book the poet Alcman records that he was a glutton, thus:

And then I'll give you a fine great caldron wherein you may gather a plentiful dinner. But unfired is it yet, though soon to be full of that good pottage the all-devouring Alcman loves piping hot when the days are past their shortest. He'll none of your fine confections, not he; for, like the people, he seeketh unto the common fare.[1]

47

The same [on the *scyphus*]: Asclepiades of Myrlea, in his treatise on *the Cup of Nestor*, says that the *scyphus* or 'can,' and the *cissybium* or 'mazer' were never used by town-dwellers and people of means, but only by swineherds and shepherds and country-folk. . . . And Alcman says:

Time and again 'mid the mountain-tops, when the Gods take their pleasure in the torch-lit festival, you have carried a great can of the sort that shepherds carry, but all of gold and filled by your fair hand with the milk of a lioness, and thereof have made a great cheese, whole and unbroken and shining white.[2]

[1] *i. e.* when you, the chorus-leader, have won the singing-contest for Alcman, I, the judge (A. makes him say) will give you—and him—the prize [2] ref. to a Maenad at a midnight festival of Dionysus: cf. a Grammarian quoted *Philologus* 10. 350

48

Plut. *Qu. Conv.* 3. 10. 3 δροσοβολεῖ γὰρ ταῖς πανσελήνοις μάλιστα διατηκόμενος (ὁ ἀήρ), ὥς που καὶ Ἀλκμὰν ὁ μελοποιὸς αἰνιττόμενος τὴν δρόσον ἀέρος θυγατέρα καὶ σελήνης·

οἷα Διὸς θυγάτηρ
ἔρσα τρέφει καὶ δίας Σελάνας [1]

49

Nat. Com. *Myth.* 3. 255 Quidam tradiderunt Lunam fuisse uxorem Aeris, e quo Rorem filium conceperit et genuerit, ut ait Alcman melicus in eo carmine:

ἄγρωστιν δρόσος αὔξει
μήνας τε καὶ ἀέρος υἱός.[2]

50

Sch. *Il.* 13. 588: . . . τῇ φι παραγωγῇ ὁ ποιητὴς κατὰ τριῶν κέχρηται πτώσεων, ἐπὶ γενικῆς, δοτικῆς, αἰτιατικῆς . . . ἐπὶ δὲ κλητικῆς Ἀλκμὰν ὁ μελοποιὸς οὕτως·

Μῶσα Διὸς θύγατερ,
ὠρανίαφι λίγ' ἀείσομαι·

ἔστι γὰρ οὐρανία.

51

Sch. *Il.* 22. 305 [ἀλλὰ μέγα ῥέξας τι καὶ ἐσσομένοισι πυθέσθαι]· λείπει τὸ ἀγαθόν, ὡς Ἀλκμάν·

μέγα γείτονι γείτων.

[1] Bernardakis: mss κ. ἀσελ: *Qu. Nat.* κ. Σ. δίας [2] mss δρόσον αὔξ. μὲν μήνης

---

[1] cf. Plut. *Fac. Orb.* 25, *Qu. Nat.* 24, Macr. *Sat.* 7. 16
[2] the bona fides of this author is open to doubt [3] cf.

48

Plutarch *Dinner-Table Problems*: For the melting air drops the most dew at full moon, as the lyric poet Alcman implies when he says that the dew is daughter of the Air and the Moon:

such as are nursed by the dew that is the daughter of Zeus and the divine Moon [1]

49

Natalis Comes *Mythology*: [2] Some authorities have held that the Moon was the wife of the Air, and by him the mother of the Dew; compare the lyric poet Alcman in the well-known poem:

The dew that is son of moon and air makes the deergrass to grow.

50

Scholiast on the *Iliad*: The termination -φι is used by Homer in three cases, genitive, dative, and accusative. . . . And Alcman the lyric poet uses it in the vocative, thus:

Muse, daughter of Zeus, heavenly Muse, sweet and clear will I sing;

for ὠρανίαφι stands for οὐρανία 'heavenly.' [3]

51

Scholiast on the *Iliad* ['but having done some great thing that shall be known even to them that are yet to be']: there is an omission of the word 'good,' as in Alcman:

Neighbour is a great thing unto neighbour.

Sch. *Il.* 2. 233, Apoll. *Adv.* 165. 7, Cram. *A.O.* 1. 293. 23 (οὐρανίαφί γ' ἀείσομαι), *E.M.* 800. 10, *E.G.* 411. 16, but metre and grammar alike point to some early corruption, perh. of οὐρανία λίγ' ἀείσομαι

52

Apoll. *Pron.* 83. 3 ἡ σέ ὁμοίως πρὸς πάντων κοινή· Δωριεῖς διὰ τοῦ τ· . . . (132) Ἀλκμάν καὶ ἔτι μετὰ τοῦ ι·

τεὶ γὰρ Ἀλεξάνδρῳ δαμάσαι.[1]

53

Sch. *Il.* 3. 39 Δύσπαρι· ἐπὶ κακῷ ὠνομασμένε Πάρι, κακὲ Πάρι· καὶ Ἀλκμάν φησι·

Δύσπαρις, αἰνόπαρις, κακὸν Ἑλλάδι βωτιανείρᾳ

54

Ibid. 16. 236 [ἠμὲν δήποτ' ἐμὸν ἔπος ἔκλυες εὐχομένοιο]· τὴν ἀπὸ τῆς μητρὸς δέησιν ἑαυτοῦ εὐχὴν νενόμικεν· ὁ γὰρ τὴν Θέτιν αὐτῷ ἀνεὶς Ἀχιλλεὺς ἦν καὶ εἰς αὐτὸν ἄγεται <ἡ εὐχή>· καὶ Ἀλκμὰν γάρ φησι·

καί ποτ' Ὀδυσσῆος ταλασίφρονος ὤαθ' ἑταίρων
Κίρκα ἐπαλείψασα . . .[2]

οὐ γὰρ αὐτὴ ἤλειψεν, ἀλλ' ὑπέθετο Ὀδυσσεῖ.

55

Bek. *An.* 2. 566. 11 ἑξῆς ῥητέον ἐστὶ καὶ περὶ τοῦ ῥᾴ· Ἀλκμάν·

Τίς κα, τίς ποκα ῥᾷ ἄλλω νόον ἀνδρὸς ἐνίσποι;[3]

56

Ammon. ἶπες· . . . ἶκες δὲ τὰ διεσθίοντα τοὺς ὀφθαλμοὺς τῶν ἀμπέλων· Ἀλκμάν·

καὶ ποικίλον ἶκα τὸν ὀφθαλμῶν ὀλετῆρα[4]

[1] mss δάμασαι [2] ὤαθ' Schn: mss ὦτά θ': for ἐπᾱλ. cf. ἠλαίνω ἀλαίνω [3] κα: mss ἂν: ἄλλω Bek: mss ἀλλὰ [4] Schn.: mss ὀφθ. ἀμπέλων ὀλ. from above: for metre cf. Heph. 54

52

Apollonius *Pronouns*: The pronoun σέ, 'thee,' occurs in all dialects—in the Dorian in the form τέ . . . (132), as Alcman says, and in the form τεί:

Thy overcoming shall fall to the lot of Paris.[1]

53

Scholiast on the *Iliad*: Δύσπαρι: that is, 'called Paris for ill, evil Paris'; compare Alcman:

Paris-of-ill, Paris-of-dread, an evil unto Greece, the nurse of heroes.[2]

54

The Same [even as once thou heardst my voice in prayer]: He reckons his mother's prayer (*Il.* 1. 503) as his own. For it was Achilles who sent Thetis up to Zeus and the prayer is transferred to him. Similarly Alcman says:

And Circè once, having anointed the ears of the comrades of strong-heart Odysseus . . .,

though she did not anoint them herself but charged Odysseus to anoint them.

55

Apollonius *Adverbs*: Next we must treat of the adverb ῥᾴ; compare Alcman:

And prithee who may read with ease the mind of another?[3]

56

Ammonius *Words Alike but Different*: ἶπες . . . But ἶκες are the creatures that eat through the buds of vines; compare Alcman:

and the wily worm that destroyeth the buds

[1] prob. addressed to Achilles, cf. Arist. *Rh.* 1359a. 3
[2] cf. Eust. *Il.* 379. 38 [3] cf. Theocr. 25. 67

57

Hdn. *μον. λέξ.* 44. 10 [πιέζω]· παρὰ δὲ Ἀλκμᾶνα διὰ τοῦ α·

τῶ δὲ σκόλλυν θεὰ[1]
κατταν καρὰν λαβῶσ' ἐπίαζε.[2]

58

Apoll. *Pron.* 365 A [π. τῆς σοι]· ὀρθοτονεῖται δὲ καὶ παρ' Ἀλκμᾶνι συνηθῶς Δωριεῦσιν·

ἅδοι Διὸς νόϝῳ χόρος ἁμὸς
καὶ τοί, ϝάναξ.[3]

59

Ibid. 112. 20 πάλιν δὴ ὁ Ἀλκμὰν τὸ σφέας ἀντὶ ἑνικοῦ ἔταξε καὶ τὸ <σφοῖς>·[4]

σφοῖς ἀδελφιδεοῖς
κᾶρα καὶ φόνον[5]

60

E.M. Vet. (cf. Zon. 1338) μέγας παρὰ τὸ μήγας, ὁ μὴ ὢν ἐν τῇ γῇ ἀλλ' ὑπερέχων αὐτῆς· τὸ δὲ μέ[6] Ἀλκμάν·

εἶπε μὲ δαῦτε φαίδιμος Αἴας.

61

Ath. 15. 682 a [π. κάλχης ἄνθους]· τῶν δὲ καλχῶν μέμνηται καὶ Ἀλκμὰν ἐν τούτοις·

χρύσιον ὅρμον ἔχων ῥαδινᾶν πετάλοισι
καλχᾶν[7]

[1] τῶ *E*: mss τῷ: σκ. θεὰ *B*: mss σκομύνθεα (*B*), σηομύνθια Egenolff *Rh. Mus.* 35, 105 [2] Nauck: mss κάτ' ἂν καρρὰν μάβως ἐπ. [3] νόϝῳ Sitz. -*E*: mss δόμῳ (through νότῳ): mss ὁ χορὸς: ϝάναξ Maittaire: mss γ' ἄναξ [4] *E* [5] κᾶρα Bek: mss κάραν [6] sugg. *E*, originally μέγ 'greatly, loudly,' cf. ὑπόδρα for ὑπόδρακ (ἔδρακον): mss μὴ context, με quotation:

57

Herodian *On Peculiarities*: In Alcman the word πιέζω, 'to press,' takes the form πιάζω; compare:

And the Goddess took and pressed in her hand the crown-lock of his head.

58

Apollonius *Pronouns* [on the pronoun σοι]: τοί 'to thee' is accented by Alcman, in accordance with Doric idiom:

I pray my dance may both please the heart of Zeus and be acceptable, O Lord, to thee.

59

The Same: Again, Alcman has used σφέας 'them' in place of the singular (possessive), and also the adjective σφοῖς 'their,' for 'his':

the death and death-spirit of his brother's children [1]

60

Old Etymologicum Magnum: μέγας, 'great,' is for μήγας, 'that which is not in the earth (μὴ γῇ) but extends above it'; Alcman uses the form μέ:

Lo! the illustrious Ajax bragged (talked great).[2]

61

Athenaeus *Doctors at Dinner* [on the flower *calcha*]: This flower is mentioned by Alcman, thus:

wearing a golden chain of dainty-petalled calcha-flowers

[1] cf. 33 [2] cf. the death of Ajax son of Oïleus (called 'illustrious' *Il.* 23. 779) *Od.* 4. 499 ff., *E.M.* 574. 38, Eust. *Od.* 1447. 10

B's suggestions leave no point in the illustration: mss δ' αὖτε
[7] Dalecamp: mss ῥαδινὰν π. καλχὰν

62

Plut. *Lycurg.* 21 μουσικωτάτους γὰρ ἅμα καὶ πολεμικωτάτους ἀποφαίνουσιν αὐτούς·

ῥέπει γὰρ ἄντα τῷ σιδάρῳ
τὸ καλῶς κιθαρίσδην·[1]

ὥς ὁ Λακωνικὸς ποιητὴς εἴρηκε.

63

Et. Va. ap. Gais. *E.M.* p. 327 τὸ γὰρ Λακωνικόν ἐστιν ἀείδην[2] ἢ ἀείδεν·

μηδέ μ' ἀείδην ἀπέρυκε.

64

Sch. Soph. *O.C.* 1248 [ἐννυχιᾶν ἀπὸ Ῥιπᾶν]· . . . λέγει δὲ αὐτὰ ἐννύχια διὰ τὸ πρὸς τῇ δύσει κεῖσθαι· μέμνηται δὲ καὶ Ἀλκμὰν λέγων οὕτω·

Ῥίπας ὄρος ἀνθέον ὕλᾳ
νυκτὸς μελαίνας στέρνον[3]

65

Bek. *An.* 2. 490 παρ' Ἀλκμᾶνι·

ἦρα τὸν Φοῖβον ὄνειρον εἶδον;

66

Plut. *Fort. Rom.* 4 οὐ μὲν γὰρ ἀπείθης κατὰ τὸν Πίνδαρον . . . ἀλλὰ μᾶλλον·

Εὐνομίας <τε> καὶ Πειθοῦς ἀδελφὰ
καὶ Προμαθείας θυγάτηρ,[4]

ὡς γενεαλογεῖ Ἀλκμάν.

[1] ῥέπει Scal: mss ἕρπει [2] *B* (bis): mss ἀείδειν
[3] Lobeck: mss ἔνθεον ὕλαι and στέρνων [4] τε *B*

62

Plutarch *Life of Lycurgus*: These quotations show that the Spartans were at once most musical and very warlike:

For to play well upon the lyre weigheth even-poise with the steel,

as the Spartan poet has said.[1]

63

MS. in Gaisford's *Etymologicum Magnum*: For the Laconian form is ἀείδην or ἀείδεν, 'to sing':

Nor yet stay me from singing.[2]

64

Scholiast on Sophocles [from the night-wrapt Rhipae]: . . . and he calls them night-wrapt because they lie towards the west; and Alcman also mentions them thus:

The wood-beflowered mount of Rhipè that is the breast of murky night

65

Bekker *Inedita*: In Alcman:

Then have I dreamt of Phoebus?

66

Plutarch *Fortune of Rome*: For Fortune is not intractable as Pindar says . . ., but rather

Sister of Orderliness and Persuasion, and daughter of Foresight,

which is her pedigree in Alcman.

[1] cf. Plut. *Fort. Alex.* 2. 2, Terp. 6 [2] cf. Fav. 115

67

Sch. Pind. *I.* 1. 56 [ὁ πονήσαις δὲ νόῳ καὶ προμαθείαν φέρει]· ὁ παθὼν καὶ τῷ νῷ προμαθὴς γίνεται· Ἀλκμάν·

πεῖρά τοι μαθήσιος ἀρχά.

68

Eust. *Od.* 1787. 43 λέγουσιν οἱ Αἰολεῖς ἐκ τοῦ φιλῶ μετοχὴν φίλεις . . . μήποτε οὖν καὶ τὸ εἴη ῥῆμα Αἰολικόν ἐστιν ἀπὸ τῆς εἴς μετοχῆς, ἧς κλίσιν παρὰ τοῖς ποιηταῖς εἰπὼν φυλάττεσθαι (Ἡρακλείδης) παράγει χρῆσιν ἐξ Ἀλκμᾶνος τό·

ἔστι παρέντων μνᾶστιν ἐπιθέσθαι.

69

Apoll. *Pron.* 93. 5 ἅμες Δώριον· Ἀλκμάν·

ὡς ἁμὲς τὸ καλὸν μελίσκον . . .

οὐκ ἐπίληπτος δὲ ἡ τάσις.

70

Ath. 9. 374 d [π. ὀρνίθων]· οἱ δὲ Δωριεῖς λέγοντες ὄρνιξ τὴν γενικὴν διὰ τοῦ χ λέγουσιν ὄρνιχος· Ἀλκμὰν δὲ διὰ τοῦ σ τὴν εὐθεῖαν ἐκφέρει . . . (26. 4), καὶ τὴν γενικὴν <διὰ τοῦ χ>.[1]

οἶδα δ' ὀρνίχων νόμως
πάντων.[2]

[1] *E* [2] δ' Herm : mss δι'

67

Scholiast on Pindar [For he who has suffered, beareth for it forethought in his mind]: A man's mind wins forethought or prudence by his experience; compare Alcman:

Trial surely is the beginning of wisdom.

68

Eustathius on the *Odyssey*: The Aeolians use as participle of φιλῶ, 'I love,' φίλεις . . . It may be therefore that the optative εἴη, 'would be,' is an Aeolic word derived from the participle εἴς, 'being, the declension of which, Heracleides says, is observed by the poets, and he gives the following instance of it from Alcman:

Remembrance belongs to them that were there.

69

Apollonius *Pronouns*: ἄμες 'we' is Doric; compare Alcman:

as we the pretty roundelay . . .

and the accentuation ἁμές is not to be censured.

70

Athenaeus *Doctors at Dinner* [on poultry]: The Dorians, who say ὄρνιξ for ὄρνις, 'bird,' use the genitive ὄρνιχος with a χ, though Alcman uses the σ-form in the nominative . . . (26. 4) and the χ-form in the genitive; compare:

I know the tunes of all the birds.

71

Bek. *An.* 3. 1182 ἀλλὰ καὶ τὸ Αἴας τὸ παρ' Ἀλκμᾶνι ἔχομεν σεσημειωμένον ὡς συστέλλον τὸ α . . .

δουρὶ δὲ ξυστῷ μέμηνεν Αἶας αἱματᾷ[1] τε Μέμνων.

. . . ἐν τῇ πέμπτῃ γὰρ χώρᾳ κεῖται, ἐν ᾗ οὐ τίθεται σπονδεῖος ἐν τροχαϊκῷ μέτρῳ.

72

Sch. *Il.* 1. 222 οὕτως δαίμονας καλεῖ θεοὺς ἤτοι ὅτι . . . ἢ ὅτι διαιτηταί εἰσι καὶ διοικηταὶ τῶν ἀνθρώπων, ὡς Ἀλκμὰν ὁ λυρικός φησιν·

ὃς Ϝέθεν πάλοις ἔπαλε διανομάς τ' ἐδάσσατο·[2]

τοὺς μερισμούς, τὰς διαιρέσεις αὐτῶν.

73, 74

Ath. 4. 140 c ἔτι φησὶν ὁ Πολέμων (ἐν Τῷ παρὰ Ξενοφῶντι Κανάθρῳ) καὶ τὸ δεῖπνον ὑπὸ τῶν Λακεδαιμονίων ἄϊκλον προσαγορεύεσθαι . . . Ἀλκμὰν μὲν γὰρ οὕτω φησί·

κἠπὶ τᾷ μύλᾳ δρυφᾶται[3] κἠπὶ ταῖς συναικλίαις·

οὕτω τὰ συνδείπνια καλῶν· καὶ πάλιν

ἄϊκλον Ἀλκμάων ἁρμόξατο.[4]

75

Cram. *A.O.* 1. 159. 30 ἔσκε· . . . καὶ ὁ μὲν ποιητὴς τὴν ἄρχουσαν συστέλλει ἐν τῷ ἔσκεν, ὁ δὲ Ἀλκμὰν φυλάττει·

ἦσκέ τις σκαφεὺς ἀνάσσων.

[1] Herm: mss αἷμα τά [2] ὃς: mss also οἱ: mss ἔπαλλεν: διανομάς *B*: mss δαίμονάς an ancient corruption, cf. Aesch. *Eum.* 727, Sch. Eur. *Alc.* 12: Nauck δαιμονάς [3] mss δρυφῆται, apparently δρυφάω 'tear the flesh, lament,' cf. δρύπτω [4] mss also ἀρμ.

71

Choeroboscus in Bekker's *Inedita*: Moreover Αἴας, 'Ajax,' we find marked in the texts of Alcman with the α short . . .

With polished spear raves Ajax, and Memnon is athirst for blood.

. . . For it occurs in the fifth place, in which spondees are not found in the trochaic metre.[1]

72

Scholiast on the *Iliad*: He calls the gods δαίμονες either because . . . or else because they are the arbitrators or dispensers of men, as the lyric poet Alcman says:

who hath allotted them with his own lots and divided unto them his own portions;

that is, divisions.[2]

73, 74

Athenaeus *Doctors at Dinner*: Moreover Polemo (in his tract *on the Word* Κάναθρον *in Xenophon*) says that for δεῖπνον 'supper' the Spartans use ἄϊκλον . . . Alcman at any rate says:

He is mourned at the mill, he is mourned at the mess;[3]

meaning by συναικλίαι the public suppers; and again:

Alcman hath prepared himself a supper,

ἄϊκλον.

75

Cramer *Inedita* (*Oxford*): And Homer shortens the vowel of the first syllable in the word ἔσκεν 'was,' but Alcman keeps it long:

There was once a ditcher was a king.

[1] cf. Zon. 564, Cram. *A.O.* 3. 283. 14, *E.M. Vet.* 92, Draco Strat. 12 and 64 [2] cf. Cram. *A.O.* 4. 409. 16, Matr. *An.* 409, Sch. Cod. Vind. 49, Cod. Vind. 61 [3] *i.e.* by slave and freeman, cf. *Carm. Pop.* 43 Bergk

76

Apoll. *Adv.* Bek. *An.* 2. 563 πρόσθε, πρόσθα, καὶ παρ' Ἀλκμᾶνι οὕτω δεκτέον τὴν συναλοιφήν·

πρόσθ' Ἀπόλλωνος Λυκήω[1]

77

E.M. Vet. ἀφθονέστατον· . . . καὶ τὸ αἰδοιέστατον, ὡς παρ' Ἀλκμᾶνι, οἷον·

σίοισι κἀνθρώποισιν αἰδοιέστατον

78, 79

Apoll. *Pron.* 96. 23 ἡ ἅμιν Δωρικὴ ἐγκλινομένη συστέλλει τὸ ι ἐν οἷς προπερισπᾶται·

. . . αἰ γὰρ ἆμιν
τούτων μέλοι·

ὀξύνομέν τε·

ἀμὶν δ' ὑπαυλήσει μέλος·

Ἀλκμάν.

80

Strab. 12. 580 λέγεται δέ τινα φῦλα Φρύγια οὐδαμοῦ δεικνύμενα ὥσπερ οἱ Βερέκυντες· καὶ Ἀλκμὰν λέγει·

Φρύγιον αὔλησεν μέλος Κερβήσιον.[2]

81

Heph. 71 καὶ ὅλα μὲν οὖν ᾄσματα γέγραπται ἰωνικά, ὡς παρ' Ἀλκμᾶνι·

ἕκατον μὲν Διὸς υἱὸν τάδε Μῶσαι κροκόπεπλοι[3]

[1] προσθ' Bast: mss πρὸς [2] mss ηὔλησε: Κερβ. *B*: mss τὸ Κερβ. (Κειρβ.): Mein. Κιρβ. cf. Hesych. Κιρβιαῖον [3] ἕκατον Urs: mss ἑκατὸν

76

Apollonius *Adverbs*: πρόσθε, 'before,' appears as πρόσθα, and the elision is to be so taken in Alcman:

before Lycean Apollo

77

Old Etymologicum Magnum: ἀφθονέστατον 'most plentiful': . . . and the superlative αἰδοιέστατον 'most reverend' as in Alcman, for instance:

most reverend unto Gods and men

78, 79

Apollonius *Pronouns*: The pronoun ἅμιν 'to us,' as declined in Doric, shortens the ι when it is circumflexed upon the last syllable but one:

Would this were business of ours!

and an acute accent also is put upon the last:

He will accompany our song with music of the flute,

as Alcman says.

80

Strabo *Geography*: There is mention of some Phrygian tribes which cannot be traced, as the Berecyntians; and Alcman says:

He piped a Phrygian tune Cerbesian.[1]

81[2]

Hephaestion *Handbook of Metre* [on the *Ionicum a minore*]: And indeed whole poems have been written in this metre, as in Alcman:

The saffron-robèd Muses this to the far-flinging Son of Zeus

[1] see Lewis and Short *Berecyntus* [2] cf. Gram. ap. Herm. *Elem. Doctr. Metr.* 472, Gram. Harl. 332 (as a tetrameter), Tricha 8 fin.

82

E.M. Vet.

λιγύκορτον πάλιν ἄχει [1]

παρ' Ἀλκμᾶνι ἀντὶ τοῦ λιγύκροτον μεταθέσει τοῦ ρ.

83

Plut. *Mus.* 14 οὐ μόνη δὲ κιθάρα Ἀπόλλωνος, ἀλλὰ καὶ αὐλητικῆς καὶ κιθαριστικῆς εὑρετὴς ὁ θεός . . . ἄλλοι δὲ καὶ αὐτὸν τὸν θεόν φασιν αὐλῆσαι, καθάπερ ἱστορεῖ ὁ ἄριστος μελῶν ποιητὴς Ἀλκμάν.

84

Sch. Theocr. 5. 83 [Κάρνεα]· Πράξιλλα μὲν ἀπὸ Κάρνου φησὶν ὠνομάσθαι τοῦ Διὸς καὶ Εὐρώπης υἱοῦ . . . Ἀλκμὰν δὲ ἀπὸ Καρνέου τινὸς Τρωϊκοῦ.

85, 86

Heph. 86 ἀπ' ἐλάσσονός τε ἐπιωνικὸν τρίμετρόν ἐστι παρ' Ἀλκμᾶνι· ὃ τὴν μὲν πρώτην ἔχει ἰαμβικὴν ἑξάσημον ἢ ἑπτάσημον, τὰς δὲ ἑξῆς δύο ἑξασήμους ἰωνικὰς καθαράς, οἷον·

περισσόν· αἰ γὰρ Ἀπόλλων ὁ Λύκηος·

Ἰνὼ σαλασσομέδοισ', ἃν ἀπὸ μάσδων [2]

[1] *B*, cf. Hesych. κορτεῖν: mss λιγυκρύτον (marg. λιγύκυρτον)· πάλιν παρ' Ἀ. ἔχει ἀντὶ τοῦ λιγύκυρτον κ.τ.λ.: cf. Suid. λιγυρώτατον· λιγύκροτον, where there has been omission and displacement: ἄχει intrans. as Theocr. 2. 36 [2] ἃν Pors: mss σαλασσομέδοισὰν, σάλας ὁμέδοισαν

82

Old Etymologicum Magnum:

Sound anew the clear-twanging [lyre].

in Alcman; λιγύκορτον 'clear-twanging,' instead of λιγύκροτον by metathesis of ρ.

83

Plutarch *On Music*: Not only the lyre belongs to Apollo, but he is the inventor of flute-playing as well as lyre-playing . . . Others say that he played the flute himself, for instance the great lyric poet Alcman.

84

Scholiast on Theocritus [the Carneian Festival]: Praxilla says that this festival is so called from Carnus son of Zeus and Europa . . . but Alcman from a Trojan named Carneüs.

85, 86

Hephaestion *Handbook of Metre*: The epionic trimeter *a minore* acatalectic occurs in Alcman; its first part comprises an iambic of six or seven beats, and the rest two six-beat ionics pure, as:

too much; for if Apollo Lycean

and

The sea-queen Ino, who from her breast [1]

[1] Pors. sugg. for next line ῥίπτεν φάτις γαλασηνὸν Μελικέρταν, 'cast, 'tis said, the suckling Melicertes'

87

Strab. 10. 482 [π. Κρήτης]· τὰ δὲ συσσίτια ἀνδρεῖα παρὰ μὲν τοῖς Κρησὶν καὶ νῦν ἔτι καλεῖσθαι, παρὰ δὲ τοῖς Σπαρτιάταις μὴ διαμεῖναι καλούμενα ὁμοίως <ὥς> πρότερον· παρ' Ἀλκμᾶνι γοῦν οὕτω κεῖσθαι·

φοίναις δὲ καὶ ἐν θιάσοισιν [1]
ἀνδρείων παρὰ δαιτυμόνεσσιν
πρέπει παιᾶνα κατάρχειν.[2]

88

Ath. 2. 39 a [π. νέκταρος]· οἶδα δ' ὅτι Ἀλεξανδρίδης τὸ νέκταρ οὐ ποτὸν ἀλλὰ τροφὴν εἶναι λέγει θεῶν· . . . καὶ Ἀλκμὰν δέ φησι·

τὸ νέκταρ ἔδμεναι αὔτως [3]

89

Sch. Pind. *O.* 1. 91 [ἄταν . . . ἄν οἱ πατὴρ ὕπερ | κρέμασε κάρτερον αὐτῷ (Ταντάλῳ) λίθον]· Ἀλκαῖος δὲ καὶ Ἀλκμὰν λίθον φασὶν ἐπαιωρεῖσθαι τῷ Ταντάλῳ· ὁ μὲν Ἀλκαῖος . . ., ὁ δὲ Ἄλκμαν οὕτως·[4]

ἀνὴρ δ' ἐν ἀρμένοισιν [5]
ἀλιτηρὸς ἧστ' ἐπὶ θάκας καταπέτρας [6]
ὁρέων μὲν οὐδὲν δοκέων δέ.

90

Cram. *A.O.* 1. 418. 8 [ὕπαιθα]· λέγεται δὲ καὶ ἄνευ τῆς θα παρὰ Ἀλκμᾶνι καὶ σημαίνει τὸ πρότερον·

. . . . ἔπετεν ὕπαι
Ἱππόλοχος, κλέος δ' ἔλαβεν
οὐ νῦν ἀπόσταν· [7]

ἀντὶ τοῦ πρότερον· βαρύνεται.

[1] mss also θοίναις perh. rightly [2] πρέπει Urs: mss πρέπε [3] *E*: mss αὐτούς [4] *B*: mss ὅπως or ὅπη part of quotation [5] Heck: mss ἀσμ. [6] *E*, θάκας = θάκου, cf. κατάγειος: mss θ. κατὰ π. [7] *E*: mss ὅποτε ὑπὸ τοῦ Ἱππολόχου κ. δ' ἔβαλλον ο. ν. ὑπεστάντων: cf. Hesych. ὑπαί· πρὸ τοῦ

87

Strabo *Geography* [on Crete]: Ephorus says that the public mess is still called ἀνδρεῖα or 'the men's mess' in Crete, but that at Sparta that name is obsolete, though it occurs in Alcman as follows:

At feasts and in the companies of the men's mess 'tis well beside them that sit at meat to strike up and sing the Paean.[1]

88

Athenaeus *Doctors at Dinner* [on nectar]: I know that Alexandrides says that nectar is not the Gods' drink but their food; . . . and Alcman says:

to do nothing but eat of the nectar.[2]

89

Scholiast on Pindar [woe . . . which his father hung over him, that mighty stone]: Alcaeus and Alcman say that a stone hung over Tantalus; Alcaeus thus (*fr.* 57), and Alcman thus:

He sat, a wicked man, among pleasant things, upon a seat rock-o'erhung, thinking he saw and seeing not.[3]

90

Cramer *Inedita* (Oxford) [on ὕπαιθα]: This word is also used without the syllable θα in Alcman, and it means πρότερον 'formerly':

'Twas long ago that Hippolochus did fall, but he hath received a fame that even now hath not deserted him;

instead of πρότερον; it is accented on the first syllable.

[1] cf. Eust. *Il.* 305. 34, Men. *Rh. Gr.* Walz 9. 135 [2] cf. Eust. 1633. 1 [3] the feast was a phantom: cf. Eust. *Od.* 1701. 23

91

Apoll. *Synt.* 212 ἡ εὐκτική, ὡς ἔχει τὸ παρ' Ἀλκμᾶνι·

νικῴ δ' ὁ κάρρων.

92

E.M. 506. 20 Κέρκυρ· . . . Ἀλκμάν φησι·

καὶ Κέρκυρος ἄγεῖται

ἀπὸ εὐθείας τῆς Κέρκυρ, ἀλλ' οὐκ εἴρηται.

93

Ibid. 620. 35

ὅκκα δὴ γυνὰ εἴην [1]

παρὰ Ἀλκμᾶνι· τὸ ὅτε ὅκα λέγει ἡ διάλεκτος, εἶτα διπλασιάσασα ὅκκα· περὶ Παθῶν.

94

Eust. *Od.* 1547. 60 λέγει δὲ καὶ Ἀλκμάν·

τὰν Μῶσαν καταΰσεις·[2]

ἀντὶ τοῦ ἀφανίσεις.

95

Sch. *Il.* 12. 66 στεῖνος· οὕτως καὶ τὸ κλειτός, οὐδέτερον γὰρ γενόμενον βαρύνεται παρ' Ἀλκμᾶνι·

τῶν ἐν Θεσσαλίᾳ κλείτει [3]

[1] mss τύνη, Apoll. Bek. *An.* γυνή [2] *B*: mss καταύσεις
[3] *B*: mss τῷ ἐν Θεσσαλίῳ κ.: cf. Suid. κλῆτος· δόξα, Hesych. κλειτή

91

Apollonius *Syntax*: The optative, as it is in Alcman:

And may the better win!

92

Etymologicum Magnum: Κέρκυρ, 'Corcyraean': . . . compare Alcman:

And leads a Corcyraean;

from the nominative Κέρκυρ, which however does not occur.

93

The Same: Compare Alcman:

[Would that,] when I am a woman grown

The dialect uses ὄκα for ὅτε 'when,' and then doubles the κ (*On Inflexions*).[1]

94

Eustathius on the *Iliad*: And Alcman says:

Thou'lt shout down the Muse;

instead of 'consume.'[2]

95

Scholiast on the *Iliad*: στεῖνος, 'a narrow place': so too the adjective κλειτός, 'famous,' when it becomes a neuter noun, is accented on the first syllable, as in Alcman:

by whose fame in Thessaly

[1] cf. Bek. *An.* 606. 31 [2] he wrongly connects it with αὔω, 'to burn'

96

E.M. Vet. ὑλακόμωροι· ὑλακτικοί, οἱ περὶ τὸ ὑλακτεῖν πονούμενοι, τινὲς δὲ τοὺς ὀξυφώνους ὡς καὶ ἐγχεσιμώρους διὰ τὴν ὀξύτητα τῶν δοράτων· μόρον γὰρ λέγουσι Κύπριοι τὸ ὀξύ· βέλτιον δὲ περὶ τὴν ὑλακὴν μεμορημένοι διὰ τὸ ἐγρηγορέναι· ἢ τὴν ὑλακὴν ὠροῦντες,[1] ὅ ἐστιν ὀξείᾳ χρώμενοι ὑλακῇ· Ἀλκμάν·

μελίσκον ἆτον ἔμ' ὠρῇ[2]

97

Sch. Ar. *Pac.* 457 [Ἄρει δὲ μή; Μή. Μηδ' Ἐνυαλίῳ γε; Μή]· πρὸς τοὺς οἰομένους τῶν νεωτέρων τὸν αὐτὸν εἶναι Ἄρεα καὶ Ἐνυάλιον . . . Ἀλκμᾶνα δὲ λέγουσιν ὅτε μὲν τὸν αὐτὸν λέγειν, ὅτε δὲ διαιρεῖν.

98

Paus. 3. 18. 6 [π. Ἀμυκλῶν]· ἐς Ἀμύκλας δὲ κατιοῦσιν ἐκ Σπάρτης ποταμός ἐστι Τίασα . . . καὶ πρὸς αὐτῇ Χαρίτων ἐστὶν ἱερὸν Φαέννας καὶ Κλητᾶς, καθὰ δὴ καὶ Ἀλκμὰν ἐποίησεν.

99

Athenag. *Leg. Christ.* 14 Ἀλκμὰν καὶ Ἡσίοδος Μήδειαν (θεὸν φέρουσι).

100

Ael. *V.H.* 12. 36 ἐοίκασιν οἱ ἀρχαῖοι ὑπὲρ τοῦ ἀριθμοῦ τῶν τῆς Νιόβης παίδων μὴ συνᾴδειν ἀλλήλοις . . . Ἀλκμὰν δέκα φησίν.

[1] *E*: *i. e.* ἑωροῦντες or αἰωροῦντες: mss τῇ ὑλακῇ ὠρ.
[2] *E*: ms μελισκόνα τὸν ἀμόρη

96

Old Etymologicum Magnum: ὑλακόμωροι (an epithet of dog *Od.* 14. 29): given to barking busy with barking; or, according to another view, sharp-voiced, like ἐγχεσίμωρος, because of the sharpness of the spears (ἔγχη), for μόρος in the Cyprian dialect means sharp. But it is better to take it as toiling (μορέω) over their barking, because of their keeping awake. Or perhaps raising their bark, that is giving a shrill bark; compare Alcman:

raises for me his insatiable little tune[1]

97

Scholiast on Aristophanes [Not to Ares? No. Nor yet to Enyalius? No]: This refers to those of the younger generation who identified Ares with Enyalius . . . Alcman is said sometimes to identify and sometimes to distinguish them.

98

Pausanias *Description of Greece* [on Amyclae]: On the way thither from Sparta is the river Tiasa . . . and near by there is a shrine of the Graces Phaënna and Cleta, as Alcman calls them in a poem.

99

Athenagoras *Mission on behalf of the Christians*: Alcman and Hesiod make a Goddess of Medea.

100

Aelian *Historical Miscellanies*: The ancients appear to disagree upon the number of Niobe's children . . . Alcman says it was ten.

[1] perh. of a bird's song, or of a rival poet's chorus (the God speaking)?

101

Plut. *Hdt. mal.* 14 καίτοι τῶν παλαιῶν καὶ λογίων ἀνδρῶν οὐχ Ὅμηρος, οὐχ Ἡσίοδος, οὐκ Ἀρχίλοχος, οὐ Πείσανδρος, οὐ Στησίχορος, οὐκ Ἀλκμάν, οὐ Πίνδαρος, Αἰγυπτίου ἔσχον λόγον Ἡρακλέους ἢ Φοίνικος, ἀλλ' ἕνα τοῦτον ἴσασι πάντες Ἡρακλέα τὸν Βοίωτον ὁμοῦ καὶ Ἀργεῖον.

102

Tz. *Il.* 65. Herm: Θαλῆς, Πυθαγόρας, Πλάτων τε καὶ οἱ Στωϊκοὶ διαφορὰν ἴσασι δαιμόνων τε καὶ ἡρώων . . . Ὀρφεὺς δὲ καὶ Ὅμηρος, Ἡσίοδός τε καὶ Ἀλκμὰν ὁ λυροποιὸς καὶ οἱ λοιποὶ ποιηταὶ ἀλλὴν ἄλλως ταῦτα ἐκδέχονται.

103

Eust. *Il.* 1154. 25 καὶ ὅτι Ἀκμονίδαι οἱ Οὐρανίδαι δηλοῦσιν οἱ παλαιοί, ὡς δὲ Ἄκμων[1] ὁ οὐρανὸς ὁ Ἀλκμάν, φασιν, ἱστορεῖ.

104

Ath. 14. 624 b [π. τῆς Φρυγιστὶ ἁρμονίας]· ταύτην δὲ τὴν ἁρμονίαν Φρύγες πρῶτοι εὗρον καὶ μετεχειρίσαντο. διὸ καὶ τοὺς παρὰ τοῖς Ἕλλησιν αὐλητὰς Φρυγίους καὶ δουλοπρεπεῖς τὰς προσηγορίας ἔχειν· οἷός ἐστιν ὁ παρὰ Ἀλκμᾶνι Σάμβας καὶ Ἄδων καὶ Τῆλος.[2]

105

Sch. *Il.* 3. 250 [Λαομεδοντιάδη]· μήτηρ Πριάμου, ὥς φησι Πορφύριος ἐν τῷ Περὶ τῶν Παραλελειμμένων τῷ Ποιητῇ Ὀνομάτων, κατὰ μὲν Ἀλκμᾶνα τὸν μελοποιὸν Ζευξίππη, κατὰ δὲ Ἑλλάνικον Στρυμώ.

106

Plut. *Mus.* 5 τοῦ δὲ Πολυμνάστου καὶ Πίνδαρος καὶ Ἀλκμὰν οἱ τῶν μελῶν ποιηταὶ ἐμνημόνευσαν.

[1] *B*, cf. Eust. *Il.* 1150. 59, Hesych. ἄκμων: mss Ἄκμονος
[2] *B* sugg. Τύλος

101

Plutarch *Malignity of Herodotus*: And yet among the ancient men of letters neither Homer, nor Hesiod, nor Archilochus, nor Peisander, nor Stesichorus, nor Alcman, nor Pindar, knew anything of an Egyptian or Phoenician Heracles, but all know this one Heracles who was both of Boeotia and of Argos.

102

Tzetzes on the *Iliad* : Thales, Pythagoras, Plato, and the Stoics, know of a distinction between *daemones* or 'spirits' and *heroes* or 'demigods' . . . but Orpheus, Homer, Hesiod, Alcman the lyrist, and the other poets sometimes distinguish them and sometimes not.

103

Eustathius on the *Iliad*: The ancients explain that the sons of Heaven were Acmonidae or 'sons of Acmon,' and Alcman is said to tell us that Acmon is Heaven.[1]

104

Athenaeus *Doctors at Dinner* [on the Phrygian 'mode']: This mode was first invented and practised by the Phrygians, and that is why flute-players in Greece have Phrygian names like those of slaves, for instance Sambas, and Adon, and Telus, in Alcman.

105

Scholiast on the *Iliad* [Son of Laomedon]: Priam's mother, as we are told by Porphyrius in his book *On the Names omitted by Homer*, was according to the lyric poet Alcman Zeuxippè, but according to Hellanicus Strymo.

106

Plutarch *Music*: Polymnastus is mentioned by the lyric poets Pindar and Alcman.

[1] Some make Acmon father of Heaven

107

Aristid. 2. 272 ὑπὲρ τῶν Τεττάρων· ἀλλ' ὅμως ἐῶ ταῦτα Πλάτωνος χάριν· ἔστω τὸ γειτόνημα ἁλμυρόν, ὥς φησιν.

Sch. *ad loc.* ἁλμυρὸν γειτόνημα· Ἀλκμὰν ὁ λυρικὸς τοῦτο εἶπεν· ἀντὶ τοῦ τί κακόν ἐστιν γείτονα ἔχειν τὴν θάλασσαν . . . λέγει οὖν ὁ ῥήτωρ· Συγχωρῶμεν, φησί, ταῖς Ἀθήναις τὴν θάλατταν προσοικεῖν.

Arsen. 43

ἁλμυρὸν γειτόνημ' ἔμβλεπε πρόσω.[1]

108

Aristid. 2. 508 π. τοῦ Παραφθέγματος· ἑτέρωθι τοίνυν, καλλωπιζόμενος παρ' ὅσοις εὐδοκιμεῖ τοσαῦτα καὶ τοιαῦτα ἔθνη καταλέγει (ὁ Ἀλκμὰν), ὥστ' ἔτι νῦν τοὺς ἀθλίους γραμματιστὰς ζητεῖν οὗ γῆς ταῦτ' ἐστί,[2] λυσιτελεῖν δ' αὐτοῖς καὶ μακράν, ὡς ἔοικεν, ἀπελθεῖν ὁδὸν μᾶλλον ἢ περὶ τῶν Σκιαπόδων ἀνήνυτα πραγματεύεσθαι.

109

Strab. 1. 43 Ἡσίοδου δ' οὐκ ἄν τις αἰτιάσαιτο ἄγνοιαν, Ἡμίκυνας λέγοντος . . . οὐδ' Ἀλκμᾶνος Στεγανόποδας ἱστοροῦντος.

110

Diod. Sic. 4. 7 ταύτας γὰρ οἱ πλεῖστοι τῶν μυθογράφων καὶ μάλιστα δεδοκιμασμένοι φασὶ θυγατέρας εἶναι Διὸς καὶ Μνημοσύνης, ὀλίγοι δὲ τῶν ποιητῶν, ἐν οἷς ἐστὶ καὶ Ἀλκμάν, θυγατέρας ἀποφαίνονται Οὐράνου καὶ Γῆς.

[1] *E*, for metre cf. 131 : mss πόρρω [2] mss εἶναι

107

Aristides *The Four Great Athenians*[1]: But I will admit this in Plato's favour; granted the 'brackish [*or* bitter] neighbour,' as he calls it (*Laws* 475 a).

Scholiast on the passage: Brackish neighbour: from Alcman the lyrist, meaning 'it is a bad thing to have the sea for a neighbour.' . . . So the orator means 'let us admit that Athens was situate near the sea.'

Arsenius *Violet-Bed*:

Look thou from afar upon a brackish neighbour.

108

Aristides *On the Extemporised Addition*: In another passage, by way of displaying the greatness of his own fame, Alcman makes so preposterous an enumeration of peoples, that the hapless scholar to this day is trying to find out where in the world they can be, and it would pay him better, I think, to retrace his steps for many miles than to spend his time over the Sciapods or Shadow-feet.

109

Strabo *Geography*: One can hardly charge Hesiod with ignorance for speaking of the Demi-dogs . . . nor yet Alcman for mentioning the Steganopods or Shelter-feet.[2]

110

Diodorus of Sicily *Historical Library*: For most of the mythologists, and these the most approved, say that the Muses are the daughters of Zeus and Memory, but a few of the poets, and among these Alcman, represent them as daughters of Heaven and Earth.[3]

[1] Miltiades, Themistocles, Pericles, Cimon [2] cf. Strab. 7. 299, Cram. *A.O.* 3. 370. 8 [3] see however 43 and 50; cf. Sch. Pind. *N.* 3. 16

111

Hesych.

ἄανθα·

εἶδος ἐνωτίου παρὰ Ἀλκμᾶνι, ὡς Ἀριστοφάνης.[1]

112

Cram. *A.O.* 1. 55. 7 ἀγάζω . . . τὸ θαυμάζω, ὅπερ παρὰ ἀγῶ, ἔστιν δὲ παρ' Ἀλκμᾶνι·

αὐτὸν ἀγᾷ,

ἀφ' οὗ καὶ ἄγημι καὶ ἄγαμαι.

113

Eust. *Il.* 314. 41 [ἀγέρωχοι]· . . . δηλοῖ δέ φασιν οὕτως ἡ λέξις τοὺς σέμνους, ὡς Ἀλκμὰν βούλεται.

114

Steph. Byz. Αἰγιαλός . . . τὸ ἐθνικὸν Αἰγιαλεύς, τὸ θηλυκὸν Αἰγιάλεια, καὶ

Αἰγιαλίς

παρ' Ἀλκμᾶνι.

115

Arg. Theocr. 12 καὶ Ἀλκμὰν τὰς ἐπεράστους κόρας[2]

ἀΐτιας

λέγει.

[1] *B*: mss ἢ Ἀριστοφάνει [2] there was an ancient corruption χορδάς appearing elsewhere in this Arg. and in *E.M.* 43. 40; cf. *E.G.* 23. 3. 12

111

Hesychius *Glossary*: ἄανθα, a kind of

earring

in Alcman, according to Aristophanes.[1]

112

Cramer *Inedita (Oxford)*: ἀγάζω . . . 'to wonder,' from ἀγῶ, which occurs in Alcman; compare:

marvels at him;

from this come ἄγημι and ἄγαμαι.

113

Eustathius on the *Iliad*: They say that the word ἀγέρωχοι thus used means 'the proud,' as Alcman intends it.

114

Stephanus of Byzantium: Αἰγιαλός . . . the ethnic adjective is Αἰγιαλεύς, with feminine Αἰγιάλεια and in Alcman Αἰγιαλίς,

woman of Aegialus

115

Argument to Theocritus: And Alcman calls beloved maidens ἀΐτίαι

darlings.[2]

[1] cf. Cram. *A.P.* 4. 84. 18 (ἀάνθα) [2] cf. *E.G.* 25. 3 and 12

116

Hesych. ἀλιβάπτοις· <πορφυροῖς. |

ἀλίβαπτον·>[1]

πορφυρᾶν ὄρνιν· Ἀλκαῖος καὶ Ἀλκμάν.[2]

117

Steph. Byz.

Ἀννίχωρον·

μέμνηται Ἀλκμάν· οἱ οἰκοῦντες Ἀννίχωροι καὶ Ἀννίχωρες, πλησίον Περσῶν κείμενοι.

118

Ibid.

Ἀράξαι

ἢ Ἄραξοι· ἔθνος Ἰλλυρίας, ὡς Ἀλέξανδρος Κορνήλιος ἐν τῷ περὶ τῶν Παρ' Ἀλκμᾶνι Τοπικῶς Εἰρημένων.

119

Ibid. Ἄρρυβα· τὸ ἐθνικὸν

Ἀρρύβας·

οὕτω καὶ Ἀλκμάν.[3]

120

Ibid.

Ἀσσός

. . . Ἀλέξανδρος δ' ὁ Κορνήλιος ἐν τῷ περὶ τῶν Παρ' Ἀλκμᾶνι Τοπικῶς Ἱστορημένων Μυτιληναίων ἄποικον ἐν τῇ Μυσίᾳ φησὶν Ἀσσόν, ὅπου ὁ σαρκοφάγος γίγνεται λίθος.

[1] two separate entries: so *B* [2] mss Ἀχαιὸς καὶ ἀλ.μάς
[3] mss also Ἄρρυββα and Ἀρρύββας

116

Hesychius *Glossary*:

Dipt-in-the-Sea:

a purple bird, Alcaeus and Alcman.

117

Stephanus of Byzantium *Lexicon*:

Annichorum:

mentioned by Alcman: the inhabitants are Annichori or Annichores and are situate near Persia.

118

The Same:

Araxae

or Araxi: a race of Illyria, according to Alexander Cornelius in his tract on the *Place-Allusions of Alcman*.

119

The Same: Arrhyba: the adjective is Ἀρρύβας,

Arrhyban,

for it is so in Alcman.

120

The Same:

Assus

. . . But Alexander Cornelius in his tract on the *Place-Allusions of Alcman* says that it is a Mytilenaean colony in Mysia, where they find the sarcophagus or flesh-consuming stone.

121

Steph. Byz. Γάργαρα· πόλις τῆς Τρῳάδος . . . Ἀλκμὰν δὲ θηλυκῶς τὴν

Γάργαρον

φησίν.

122

Ibid. Γραικός· ὁ Ἑλλῆν, ὀξυτόνως, ὁ Θεσσαλοῦ υἱός, ἀφ' οὗ Γραικοί οἱ Ἕλληνες.

Γραίκα

δὲ παρὰ Ἀλκμᾶνι ἡ τοῦ Ἑλλῆνος μήτηρ.[1]

123

Ibid. Ἰσσηδόνες· ἔθνος Σκυθικόν . . . Ἀλκμὰν δὲ μόνος

Ἐσσηδόνας [2]

αὐτούς φησιν· εὑρίσκεται δὲ ἡ δευτέρα παρ' ἄλλοις διὰ τοῦ ε.

124

E.G. 395. 52 μνήμη· . . . Ἀλκμὰν δὲ

φρασίδορκον [3]

αὐτὴν καλεῖ· βλέπομεν γὰρ τῇ διανοίᾳ τὰ ἀρχαῖα.

125

Cram. *A.O.* 1. 55. 21 σεσημείωται τὸ κάρχαρος . . . καὶ τὸ θηλυκὸν παρ' Ἀλκμᾶνι·

καρχάραισι φωναῖς [4]

[1] *E*: mss Γραῖκες (or Γραῖες) δ. π. Ἀ. αἱ τῶν Ἑλλήνων μητέρες
[2] mss also Ἀσσεδ., Ἀσεδ. [3] O. Müller: mss φασὶ δόρκον: Headl. φασὶ δορκῶν, cf. Ἀγιδῶν (1), κινῶ, φυσῶ κ.τ.λ. [4] mss καρχάρεσσι φ.

121

Stephanus of Byzantium *Lexicon*: Gargara: a city of the Troad . . . Alcman makes it

Gargarus

of the feminine gender.

122

The Same: Γραικός, 'Graecus': Hellen—accented oxytone—the son of Thessalus, whence the Hellenes came to be called Greeks. And

Graeca

in Alcman is the mother of Hellen.

123

The Same: Issedones: a tribe of Scythia . . . Alcman is peculiar in calling them

Essedones;

the second syllable is found with the e short in other writers.

124

Etymologicum Gudianum: μνήμη, 'Memory': Alcman calls her

she that looks with the mind;

for we view the past with the eye of the intellect.

125

Cramer *Inedita* (*Oxford*): The word κάρχαρος 'sharp' has been marked in our texts . . . and it is found in the feminine in Alcman; compare

with sharp voices

126

Zonar. 1190

κερκολύρα·

οὕτως ὁ Ἀλκμὰν ἐχρήσατο ἀντὶ τοῦ κρεκολύρα . . . τὸ δὲ κερκολύρα ἠχητικὴ λύρα· τὸ γὰρ κρέκε κρέκε ἦχός ἐστι τῆς κιθάρας.

127

Steph. Byz. Πιτυοῦσσαι· νῆσοι διάφοροι, ἃς

Πιτυώδεις

καλεῖ Ἀλκμάν.

128

E.M. 663. 54

Περίηρς·

ἐκ τοῦ Περιήρης, ἆρον τὸ η Περίηρς· ταύτῃ ἐάν σοι προτεθῇ παρ' Ἀλκμᾶνι ὅτι κλῖνον αὐτό, μὴ κλίνῃς· οὐ γὰρ ἀκολουθεῖ ἡ κατάληξις, εἰ γένοιτο Περιήρους, πρὸς τὴν Περίηρς[1] εὐθεῖαν. περὶ Παθῶν.

129

Suid. χθονία . . . καὶ παρ' Ἀλκμᾶνι δέ, ὅτε φησὶ

χθόνιον τέρας

ἐπὶ τῆς Ἔριδος, τινὲς ἀντὶ τοῦ στυγνὸν ἐδέξαντο, ἔνιοι δὲ ἀντὶ τοῦ μέγα, ἐπεὶ πρὸς αὐτὴν λέγει.

[1] mss Περιήρης

126

Zonaras *Lexicon*: κερκολύρα: Alcman used this form instead of κρεκολύρα . . . it means

sounding lyre,

krekè-krekè being the sound of the cithara.[1]

127

Stephanus of Byzantium: Pityussae: various islands, called

Pityōdes

by Alcman.[2]

128

Etymologicum Magnum: Περίηρς,

Periers,

from Περιήρης, 'Perieres,' with loss of η; if it is set you to decline in this form in Alcman, refuse to do so; for the termination, if it becomes Περιήρους in the genitive, does not correspond to the nominative Περίηρς.[3] (*On Inflexions.*)[4]

129

Suidas' *Lexicon*: χθονία 'earthy, infernal': . . . and in Alcman, when he says of Strife

infernal monster,

some commentators take it in the sense of 'abhorrent,' others in the sense of 'great' because he is addressing her.

[1] cf. *E.M.* 506. 17, Suid. κερκολύρα [2] cf. Eust. *Il.* 355. 45
[3] cf. μάκαρς (29): P. was father of Tyndareüs [4] cf. *fr.* 133

Δʹ

ʼΕΡΩΤΙΚΩΝ

130

Ath. 13. 600 f [π. ἔρωτος]· Ἀρχύτας δʼ ὁ ἁρμονικός, ὥς φησι Χαμαιλέων, Ἀλκμᾶνα γεγονέναι τῶν ἐρωτικῶν μελῶν ἡγεμόνα καὶ ἐκδοῦναι πρῶτον μέλος ἀκόλαστον ὂν τὰ[1] περὶ τὰς γυναῖκας καὶ τὴν τοιαύτην μοῦσαν εἰς τὰς διατριβάς· διὸ καὶ λέγειν ἔν τινι τῶν μελῶν·

> Ἔρως με δαὖτε Κύπριδος ϝέκατι[2]
> γλυκὺς κατείβων καρδίαν ἰαίνει.

λέγει δὲ καὶ ὡς τῆς Μεγαλοστράτης οὐ μετρίως ἐρασθείη,[3] ποιητρίας μὲν οὔσης δυναμένης δὲ καὶ διὰ τὴν ὁμιλίαν τοὺς ἐραστὰς προσελκύσασθαι· λέγει δὲ οὕτως περὶ αὐτῆς·

> τῷ ϝαδεᾶν Μωσᾶν[4] ἔδειξε
> δῶρον μάκαιρα παρθένων[5]
> ἁ ξανθὰ Μεγαλοστράτα.

131

Heph. 82 [π. κρητικοῦ]· καὶ εἴη ἂν ἑξάμετρον καταληκτικὸν τὸ καλούμενον τοῦ Ἀλκμᾶνος ἐκ μόνων ἀμφιμάκρων·

> Ἀφροδίτα μὲν οὐκ ἔστι, μάργος δʼ Ἔρως οἷα <παῖς>[6] παίσδει
> ἄκρʼ ἐπʼ ἄρθρʼ ἧκα βαίνων[7] τὸ ʻ μή μοι θίγῃς τῷ κυπαιρίσκῳ.ʼ

[1] mss ὄντα καὶ [2] *B*: mss δʼ αὖτε and ἕκατι [3] μετρίως Schw: ἐρασθείη Cob: mss συμμέτρως ἐρασθεὶς [4] τῷ ϝαδεᾶν *E*, context requires ʻmeʼ: Μωσᾶν Steph: mss τοῦ θʼ ἀδεῖαν μοῦσαν [5] mss also μακαίρᾳ παρθένῳ [6] Bent: [7] *E*: mss ἄνθης καββαίνων, ἄνθηκα βαίνων: Pauw ἄνθη καβαίνων, *E* once ἄνθρυσκα βαίνων, but a *child* cannot walk on, or down on to, the tips of flowers

Book IV

LOVE-SONGS

130

Athenaeus *Doctors at Dinner* [on love]: Archytas the writer on musical theory maintains according to Chamaeleon that the originator of love-songs was Alcman, and that he was the first to give out to the schools[1] song that was licentious in matters concerning women, and other poetry of that kind, and that hence he says in one of his songs:

Lo, at the Cyprian's hest, sweet Love distils upon me and melts my heart.

And he says too that he fell wildly in love with Megalostrata, who was both a poetess and had the power of attracting lovers by her conversation. He speaks of her thus:

. . . to whom hath been shown the gift of the sweet Muses at the hands of one that is right happy among maidens, to wit the flaxen-haired Megalostrata.

131

Hephaestion *Handbook of Metre* [the cretic]: And it will be a catalectic hexameter—namely that called Alcman's—composed entirely of cretics, as:

It is not Aphroditè; but wild Love, like a child, plays me touch-me-not-with-your-little-reed, treading softly on tiptoe.[2]

[1] *i.e.* set choruses to learn in the song-schools: cf. Theophr. *Char.* 30. 18 ἱμάτιον ἐκδοῦναι πλῦναι, 'send his cloak to be cleaned' [2] ref. to some game like our 'touch' or 'tig'; he means he is not really in love, it is 'only a flutter'

132

Apoll. *Pron.* 83. 3 ἡ σέ ὁμοίως πρὸς πάντων κοινή· Δωριεῖς διὰ τοῦ τ . . .·

πρὸς δὲ τὲ τῶν φίλων

Ἀλκμάν.

133

E.M. 622. 44 ὀλοοίτροχος· . . . ἐκ δὲ τοῦ ὀλοός γίνεται ἡ κλητικὴ ὀλοέ, καὶ κατὰ συγκοπὴν ὀλέ, ἐὰν δὲ ὀλός ᾖ ἡ εὐθεῖα, γένοιτ᾽ ἂν ἡ κλητικὴ ὀλέ καὶ οὐκ ἔστι συγκοπή· οἷον·

ἔχει μ᾽ ἄχος, ὦ ᾽λὲ δαῖμον·[1]

τοῦτο περὶ Παθῶν Ἡρωδιανός.

134

Prisc. 2. 17. 11 Keil: Hiatus quoque causa solebant illi interponere *F*, quod ostendunt et poetae Aeolide usi, Alcman:

καὶ χεῖμα πῦρ τε δάϜιον

135

Cram. *A.O.* 1. 287. 4 καὶ εἶκα, ὃ σημαίνει τὸ ὁμοιῶ·

εἶκας μὲν ὡραίῳ λίνῳ·[2]

παρὰ Ἀλκμᾶνι.

136

Ath. 3. 81 f [π. μήλων]· Ἀλκμὰν δὲ τὸ στρουθίον μῆλον, ὅταν λέγῃ·

μῆον ἢ κοδύμαλον·

Ἀπολλόδωρος δὲ καὶ Σωσίβιος τὸ Κυδώνιον μῆλον ἀκούουσιν.

[1] ὦ ᾽λὲ: mss ὦ ὀλὲ here, elsewh. ὦλε [2] mss here, Bek, 1404, Hdn., οἶκας, elsewhere εἶκας

132

Apollonius *Pronouns*: The pronoun σέ, 'thee,' occurs in all dialects—in the Dorian in the form τέ; compare Alcman:

By our friends I adjure thee

133

Etymologicum Magnum: The vocative of ὀλοός, 'destructive,' is ὀλοέ or by syncope ὀλέ, or if ὀλός be taken for the nominative then there is no syncope, as:

I am in pain, thou destroying spirit.[1]

This comes from Herodian *On Inflexions.*

134

Priscian *Principles of Grammar*: To avoid hiatus, too, they inserted digamma, as the poets who use Aeolic show, for instance Alcman:

And storm and destroying fire [2]

135

Cramer *Inedita* (*Oxford*): And εἶκα, which means 'to be like,' as

Thou 'rt like to ripe flax;

in Alcman.[3]

136

Athenaeus *Doctors at Dinner* [on apples]: Alcman means the *struthian* apple when he says:

As small as a codymalon,[4]

though Apollodorus and Sosibius take it as a quince.

[1] cf. Cram. *A.O.* 2. 461. 32 (Ἀλκμανικόν), 1. 442, Sch. *Il.* 10. 134 [2] cf. Ibid. 21 [3] cf. Ibid. 4. 368. 19, 415. 22, Bek. *An.* 3. 1294. 5, 1404, Choer. *Epim.* Gais. 2. 587, 871, Hdn. μον. λέξ. 24. 9 [4] perh. = medlar

Ε′

ΣΥΜΠΟΤΙΚΩΝ

137

Ath. 10. 416 d [π. πολυφαγίας τῆς Ἀλκμᾶνος]· κἀν τῷ ε′ δὲ ἐμφανίζει αὑτοῦ τὸ ἀδηφάγον λέγων οὕτως·

ὥρας δ' ἔσηκε τρεῖς, θέρος
καὶ χεῖμα χὠπάραν[1] τρίταν,
καὶ τέτρατον τὸ Ϝῆρ, ὅκα[2]
σάλλει μὲν ἐσθίεν δ' ἅδαν[3]
οὐκ ἔστι . . .

138

Ibid. 3. 110 f μακωνίδων δ' ἄρτων μνημονεύει Ἀλκμὰν ἐν τῷ πέμπτῳ[4] οὕτως·

κλῖναι μὲν ἕπτα καὶ τόσαι τράπεσδαι
μακωνίδων ἄρτων ἐπιστεφεῖσαι
λίνω[5] τε σασάμω τε, κὴν πελίχναις
πέδεστι χρυσόκολλα·[6]

ἔστι βρωμάτιον διὰ μέλιτος καὶ λίνου.

[1] cf. Boisacq *s.v.* ὀπώρα: mss χεῖμαχω παραν, χειμὰν ὀπώραν [2] Schw.-*B*: mss τὸ ηρυκας, τὸ κρόκας [3] Pors: mss ἀλλ' εἰ μὲν ἔσθει ἐν δάδαν [4] Schw: mss ε′, ιεω, ἶεω, πεντεκαιδεκάτῳ [5] Kaib: mss ἐπιστεφοῖσαι λ., -φοι σε λ., -φεῖς σελίνῳ: gen.

Book V

DRINKING-SONGS

137

Athenaeus *Doctors at Dinner* [on the voracity of Alcman]: And in his fifth Book he shows his gluttony thus:

And seasons made he three, summer and winter and the third the autumn, and a fourth also, to wit the spring, when things do flourish and grow but one cannot eat his fill.

138

The Same: Poppy-cakes are mentioned by Alcman in his fifth Book thus:

Seven couches and as many tables crowned with poppy-cakes and linseed and sesame,[1] and set among the flagons cups of damaskt gold;

it is a sweetmeat made with honey and linseed.[2]

[1] *i.e.* cakes flavoured with them, or 'poppy-cakes both of linseed and of sesame'; this is a drinking-bout not a feast
[2] *i.e.* these and poppy

Schn: mss dat: πελίχναις: cf. Ath. 11. 495 c   [6] πέδεστι *B*; mss πέδεσσι, πέδαισι: χρυσ.: sc. ἐκπώματα

139

Ath. 1. 31 c [π. οἰνῶν]· Ἀλκμὰν δέ που ἄπυρον οἶνον καὶ ἄνθεος ὄσδοντά φησι τὸν ἐκ Πέντε λόφων, ὅς ἐστι τόπος Σπάρτης ἀπέχων στάδια ἑπτά, καὶ τὸν ἐκ Δενθιάδων, ἐρύματός τινος, καὶ τὸν ἐκ Καρύστου, ὅς ἐστι πλησίον Ἀρκαδίας,[1] καὶ τὸν ἐξ Οἰνοῦντος καὶ τὸν ἐξ Ὀνόγλων καὶ Σταθμῶν· χωρία δὲ ταῦτα πάντα πλησίον Πιτάνης· φησὶν οὖν οἶνον δ' Οἰνουντιάδαν ἢ Δένθιν ἢ Καρύστιον ἢ Ὄνογλιν[2] ἢ Σταθμίταν· ἄπυρον δὲ εἶπε τὸν οὐχ ἡψημένον.

e.g. ἄπυρον τε Ϝοῖνον κἄνθεος
ὄσδοντα, τὸν μὲν Πέντε λόφων,
τὸν δὲ τὸν Ϝοινουντιάδαν
ἢ Δένθιν ἢ Καρύστιον ἢ
Ὄνογλιν ἢ Σταθμίταν.

140

Hesych. κλεψίαμβοι· Ἀριστόξενος· μέλη τινὰ παρ' Ἀλκμᾶνι.

141

Ath. 14. 648 b πόλτου δὲ μνημονεύει Ἀλκμὰν οὕτως·

ἤδη παρέξει πυάνιόν τε πόλτον
χίδρον τε λευκὸν κηρίναν θ' ὀπάραν·[3]

ἔστι δὲ τὸ πυάνιον, ὥς φησι Σωσίβιος, πανσπερμία ἐν γλυκεῖ ἡψημένη, χίδρον δὲ οἱ ἑφθοὶ πυροί, κηρίναν δὲ ὀπώραν λέγει τὸ μέλι.

[1] καὶ τὸν ἐκ Καρ. — Ἀρκαδίας transp. Pors. from after Σταθμίταν [2] cf. Hesych. ὄνιγλιν· εἶδος οἴνου and Δένθις· οἶνος· Λακῶνες [3] cf. 137: mss τ' ὀπώραν

---

[1] cf. Strab. 10. 446, Eust. *Il.* 281. 10, 1449. 12, 1633. 51, Steph. Byz. Κάρυστος [2] these iambic fragments may be of

139

Athenaeus *Doctors at Dinner* [on wines]: Alcman says, I think: 'That wine unfired and of finest scent which comes from the Five Hills,' which is about a mile from Sparta, and that of Denthiades, a frontier-post, and that of Carystus, which is nearly in Arcadia, and that of Oenus, Onogli, and Stathmus, which are all in the neighbourhood of Pitanè—in his own words:

That wine unfired and of the finest scent, either that which comes from the Five Hills, or that which is the wine of Oenus, or else the Denthian or the Carystian, or the wine of Onogli or of Stathmi . . .

where by 'unfired' he means 'not boiled.'[1]

140

Hesychius *Glossary*: κλεψίαμβοι, 'hidden iambics': according to Aristoxenus these are certain lyric poems in the works of Alcman.[2]

141

Athenaeus *Doctors at Dinner*: Porridge is mentioned by Alcman, thus:

Forthwith shall you have raisin-wine porridge, white frumenty, and the waxen fruits of the bee;

and this kind of porridge, according to Sosibius, is all-seeds boiled in wine of raisins, frumenty is boiled wheat-corns, and the waxen fruits are honey.[3]

this sort; they were recited to music, cf. Ath. 14, 636 b, where for κλεψιάμβους we should read κλεψιαμβύκας, the instrument used [3] cf. Eust. *Od.* 1563. 1, 1735. 50

142

Cram. *A.O.* 1. 60. 24 ἐὰν δ' ὦσιν ἐκ τοῦ ε οὐκέτι (γίνεται τροπὴ τοῦ η εἰς α μακρόν)· ἔλατος ἱππήλατος· Ἀλκμάν·

λεπτὰ δ' ἄταρπος νηλεὴς δ' ἀνάγκα·[1]

ἐκ γὰρ τοῦ ἐλεεινή.

143

Ath. 14. 636 f [π. μαγάδιδος]· καὶ Ἀλκμὰν δέ φησι·

μάγαδιν δ' ἀποθέσθαι

144

E.M. 171. 7 αὔσιον· καὶ ὁ μὲν Ἴβυκος αὔσιον λέγει . . . ὁ δὲ Ἀλκμάν·

ταυσία πάλλα κέω.[2]

ϛ'

145

Apoll. *Pron.* 107. 11 Αἰολεῖς μετὰ τοῦ F κατὰ πᾶσαν πτῶσιν καὶ γένος . . . καὶ Ἀλκμὰν δὲ συνεχῶς Αἰολίζων φησί·

τὰ Fὰ κάδεα[3]

[1] νηλεὴς *B*: mss ἀνηλὴς [2] *E* (perh. ταὔσία): mss παλλακίω, πολλακίω [3] Fὰ *B*: mss εα

142

Cramer *Inedita* (*Oxford*): But if they begin with ε the change from η to long α does not take place, for instance *ἔλατος ἱππήλατος*; compare Alcman:

Thin is the thread and pitiless the necessity;[1]

for *νηλεής*, 'pitiless,' is derived from *ἐλεεινή*, 'pitiable.'

143

Athenaeus *Doctors at Dinner* [on the musical instrument called *magadis*]: And Alcman, too, says:

to lay aside the lute

144

Etymologicum Magnum: *αὔσιον*, 'idle, useless': Ibycus uses this form . . . but Alcman *ταύσιος*; compare:

I will lie an idle ball.[2]

Book VI[3]

145

Apollonius *Pronouns*: The Aeolians use the digamma-forms in every case and gender . . . and Alcman is regularly Aeolic in:

his own troubles

[1] thread *B*; 'one of the Fates was Ἀταρπώ Sch. *Od.* 7, 197'
[2] *i. e.* thrown down and not played with
[3] the contents of this Book being unknown, I have put into it all the remaining fragments of a personal type

146

Sch. Aristid. ὑπὲρ τῶν Τεττάρων 3. 490 ὁ Κρὴς δὴ τὸν πόντον· παροιμία ἐπὶ τῶν εἰδότων μὲν προσποιουμένων δ' ἀγνοεῖν· ἀντὶ τοῦ νησιώτης ἀγνοεῖ τὴν θάλατταν . . . λέγεται δὲ ἡ παροιμία καὶ οὕτως· ὁ Σικελὸς τὴν θαλάτταν . . . Ἀλκμὰν δ' ὁ λυρικὸς μέμνηται τῆς παροιμίας.

147

E.M. 22. 23 ἅζω . . . ὁ δὲ Ἡρωδιανὸς ἐν τῷ περὶ Παθῶν λέγει ὅτι παράγωγόν ἐστιν ἀπὸ τοῦ ἅγος ἁγίζω καὶ κατὰ συγκοπὴν ἅζω . . . πόθεν δὲ δῆλον; ἐκ τοῦ τὸν Ἀλκμᾶνα εἰπεῖν

ἁγίσδεο

ἀντὶ τοῦ ἅζεο.

148

Hesych.

βλήρ·

δέλεαρ· τὸ δὲ αὐτὸ καὶ αἶθμα·[1] παρὰ Ἀλκμᾶνι[2] ἡ λέξις.

149

E.M. 228. 25 γεργύρα· ὁ ὑπόνομος, κυρίως δι' οὗ τὰ ὕδατα φέρεται τὰ ὄμβρια . . . ζήτει εἰς τὰ γόργυρα· ὁ δὲ Ἀλκμὰν διὰ τοῦ ε

γεργύρα[3]

φησί.

150

Bek. *An.* 2. 949 τὸ

δοάν

παρ' Ἀλκμᾶνι Δωρικῶς ὀξύνεται, γεγονὸς οὕτω· δήν, δάν, δοάν.

[1] Schmidt, cf. Hesych. αἶθμα· δέλεαρ: mss ἆσθμα [2] Mein: mss Ἀλκμαίωνι [3] mss γέργυρα

146

Scholiast on Aristides *On behalf of the Four Great Athenians*: The Cretan and the sea: Proverbial of those who know but pretend they do not; it means 'the islander does not know the sea' . . The proverb also has this form: 'The Sicilian and the sea' . . It is mentioned by the lyric poet Alcman.[1]

147

Etymologicum Magnum: ἅζω . . . Herodian in his treatise *On Inflexions* declares that it is derived from ἅγος, 'guilt or expiation,'—ἀγίζω by syncope ἅζω . . . and why he says so, is clear from Alcman's use of ἀγίσδεο for ἅζεο

stand thou in awe

148

Hesychius *Glossary*: βλῆρ·

bait;

and another word for it is αἶθμα; the word occurs in Alcman.

149

Etymologicum Magnum: γεργύρα:

underground;

properly that which carries off rainwater; see the note on γόργυρα; but Alcman uses the ε-form, γεργύρα.[2]

150

Bekker *Inedita*: The word δοάν,

for a long while,

in Alcman has an acute accent on the last syllable, arriving at this form thus: δήν, δάν, δοάν.[3]

[1] cf. Strab. 10. 481, *Paroem*. 1. 131 (where, however, *Alcaeus* is quoted as mentioning the proverb) [2] cf. Bek. *An*. 1. 233. 27 [3] cf. Jo. Alex. 42, Bek. *An*. 2. 570

151

E.M. Vet. 136 τὸ δὲ

ζάτραφα

παρὰ Ἀλκμᾶνι κανονιστέον κατὰ μεταπλασμὸν ἀπὸ τοῦ ζάτροφον.

152

E.M. 420. 28 ἥδυμος . . . τὸ δὲ ὑπερθετικὸν

ἁδυμέστατον[1]

Ἀλκμὰν ἔφη.

153

Eust. *Od.* 1892. 44 ἔτι ἰστέον καὶ ὅτι τὸ εἰρημένον ἦν ἐπὶ τρίτου ἑνικοῦ προσώπου ὁ Ἀλκμὰν

ἦς

λέγει μετειλημμένου τοῦ ν εἰς σ Δωρικῶς.

154

Cram. *A.O.* 1. 190. 20

ἠτί

δὲ λέγει Ἀλκμὰν ἀντὶ τοῦ ἠσίν.

155

Eust. Il. 756. 30 . . . ἀντιθέσει τοῦ ν εἰς λ, ᾧ ἀντιστοιχοῦσι Δωριεῖς ἐν τῷ φίλτατος φίντατος . . . κέλετο

κέντο

παρὰ Ἀλκμᾶνι.

[1] mss ἡδυμέστατον

151

Old Etymologicum Magnum: The form ζάτραφα[1]

well-fed

in Alcman is to be classed as a metaplasm of ζάτροφον.

152

Etymologicum Magnum: ἥδυμος, 'pleasant'; . . . Alcman uses the superlative ἁδυμέστατον,

pleasantest

153

Eustathius on the *Odyssey*: It should be understood, too, that the third person singular ἦν takes the form ἦς,

he was,

in Alcman, by the Doric change of ν to σ.[2]

154

Cramer *Inedita* (*Oxford*): Alcman uses the form ἠτί,

saith,

instead of ἠσί.

155

Eustathius on the *Iliad*: . . . by the change of ν to λ, a substitution which the Dorians make in saying φίντατος for φίλτατος 'dearest'; . . . κέντο for κέλετο,

he prayed,

in Alcman.

[1] apparently acc. sing. [2] cf. Fav. 234

156

Ath. 3. 81 d

Κυδωνίων μήλων

μνημονεύει Στησίχορος . . . καὶ Ἀλκμάν.

157

Sch. *Od.* 23. 76 [μάστακα]· ὁ δὲ Ἀλκμὰν καὶ τὰς γνάθους

μάστακας

φησὶ παρὰ τὸ μασᾶσθαι.

158

Sch. *Il.* 17. 40 τὰ γὰρ εἴς τις λήγοντα θηλυκὰ δισύλλαβα, μὴ ὄντα ἐπιθετικά, παραληγόμενα δὲ τῷ ο ἤτοι μόνῳ ἢ σὺν ἑτέρῳ φωνήεντι, ὀξύνεσθαι θέλει, κοιτίς, . . .

οὐτίς

τὸ ζῷον παρ' Ἀλκμᾶνι.

159

E.M. Vet. πείρατα· πέρατα, καὶ παρ' Ἀλκμᾶνι

πέρασα·

<περὶ> Παθῶν.[1]

160

Sch. *Il.* 12. 137 [αὔας]· ἴσως δὲ βεβαρυτόνηται, ἐπεὶ καὶ τὸ ναῦος ἐβαρύνετο . . . καὶ τὸ

φαῦος[2]

παρ' Ἀλκμᾶνι.

[1] Reitz. cf. 128, 133: perh. A. said πέρρατα [2] *E*: mss ψαῦος

156

Athenaeus *Doctors at Dinner*:

Cydonian apples

or quinces are mentioned by Stesichorus . . . and Alcman.

157

Scholiast on the *Odyssey*: Alcman calls the

jaws

μάστακες, from μασάομαι 'to chew.'

158

Scholiast on the *Iliad*: Feminine dissyllables ending in -τις, which are not epithets and of which the penultimate syllable contains ο either simple or in a diphthong, have the acute accent on the last syllable, for instance κοιτίς, . . . and

outis,

the animal, in Alcman.[1]

159

Old Etymologicum Magnum: πείρατα:

ends,

and in Alcman in the form πέρασα. (*On Inflexions*).

160

Scholiast on the *Iliad*: αὖας: perhaps it has been circumflexed on the first like ναῦος for ναός 'temple,' . . . and φαῦος for φάος,

light,

in Alcman.

[1] cf. Arc. 35. 3

161

Sch. Luc. *Anach.* 32

γέρρον

. . . Ἀλκμὰν δὲ ἐπὶ τῶν οἰστῶν τέθεικε τὴν λέξιν.

162

E.M. Vet. βάλε· . . . ὁ δὲ Ἀλκμὰν τὸ ἀβάλε, οἷον·

ἀβάλε καὶ νοέοντα[1]

γίνεται.

163

Hdn. μον. λέξ. 9. 31 (2. 915 Lentz) εὐρυπῶν· Ἀλκμάν·

οἷσι δ' εὐρυπῶν[2]

164

Sch. Theocr. 5. 92 [ἀνεμώνα]· . . . Σωσίβιος δὲ τὰς ἀνεμώνας παρὰ Λάκωσι

φαινίδας

καλεῖσθαί φησιν.

165

Reitz. *Ind. Lect.* Rostock cod. Coislin. 394

ὁλκάς·

πλοῖον, <ναῦς φορτηγός,>[3] καὶ παρὰ Ἀλκμᾶνι ἀηδών[4] καὶ Σειρήν.[5]

[1] ms νέοντα [2] *B*: mss εὐρυοπῶν ἀλκμοῖς ἥδε ῥυπῶν [3] Hesych. [4] so Hesych: mss here ἀειδῶν [5] Voss: mss εἰρήνη

161

Scholiast on Lucian: γέρρον . . . Alcman uses the word of

arrows

162

Old Etymologicum Magnum: βάλε 'would that': . . . Alcman uses the form ἀβάλε, 'O would that,' for instance

O would that both discreet . . .

163

Herodian *Words without Parallel* εὐρυπῶν 'splay-footed': compare Alcman

But they to whom splay-footed . . .

164

Scholiast on Theocritus [windflower]: . . . according to Sosibius the anemone or windflower is called by the Spartans

shine-bright.

165

From a manuscript quoted by Reitzenstein: ὁλκάς: A ship; a merchant-ship; and in Alcman

alluring

of the nightingale and the Siren.[1]

[1] the word means 'that which draws' cf. Hesych. s.v.

ΑΡΙΟΝΟΣ

Βίος

Hdt. 1. 23 ἐτυράννευε δὲ ὁ Περίανδρος Κορίνθου. τῷ δὴ λέγουσι Κορίνθιοι—ὁμολογέουσι δέ σφι Λέσβιοι—ἐν τῷ βίῳ θῶμα μέγιστον παραστῆναι, Ἀρίονα τὸν Μηθυμναῖον ἐπὶ δελφῖνος ἐξενειχθέντα ἐπὶ Ταίναρον, ἐόντα κιθαρῳδὸν τῶν τότε ἐόντων οὐδενὸς δεύτερον καὶ διθύραμβον πρῶτον ἀνθρώπων τῶν ἡμεῖς ἴδμεν ποιήσαντά τε καὶ ὀνομάσαντα καὶ διδάξαντα ἐν Κορίνθῳ. τοῦτον τὸν Ἀρίονα λέγουσι τὸν πολλὸν τοῦ χρόνου διατρίβοντα παρὰ Περιάνδρῳ, ἐπιθυμῆσαι πλῶσαι ἐς Ἰταλίην τε καὶ Σικελίην· ἐργασάμενον δὲ χρήματα μεγάλα θελῆσαι ὀπίσω ἐς Κόρινθον ἀπικέσθαι· ὁρμᾶσθαι μέν νυν ἐκ Τάραντος, πιστεύοντα δὲ οὐδαμοῖσι μᾶλλον ἢ Κορινθίοισι μισθώσασθαι πλοῖον ἀνδρῶν Κορινθίων· τοὺς δὲ ἐν τῷ πελάγει ἐπιβουλεύειν τὸν Ἀρίονα ἐκβαλόντας ἔχειν τὰ χρήματα . . . τὸν δὲ ἐνδύντα τε πᾶσαν τὴν σκευὴν καὶ λαβόντα τὴν κιθάρην, στάντα ἐν τοῖσι ἑδωλίοισι διεξελθεῖν νόμον τὸν ὄρθιον· τελευτῶντος δὲ τοῦ νόμου ῥῖψαί μιν ἐς τὴν θάλασσαν ἑωυτὸν ὡς εἶχε σὺν τῇ σκευῇ πάσῃ· καὶ τοὺς μὲν ἀποπλέειν ἐς Κόρινθον· τὸν δὲ δελφῖνα λέγουσι ὑπολαβόντα ἐξενεῖκαι ἐπὶ Ταίναρον . . . καὶ Ἀρίονός ἐστι ἀνάθημα χάλκεον οὐ μέγα ἐπὶ Ταινάρῳ, ἐπὶ δελφῖνος ἐπεὼν ἄνθρωπος.

ARION

Life

Herodotus *Histories*: Periander was despot of Corinth. During his lifetime, according to the Corinthians—and indeed the Lesbians—a very marvellous thing took place, namely the rescue of Arion of Methymna from the sea at Taenarum by a dolphin. This Arion was the finest singer to the lyre then known, and is the first recorded composer of dithyrambs, which he named and trained Corinthian choirs to perform. It seems that he spent most of his life at the court of Periander; but one day conceiving a desire to visit Italy and Sicily, he did so, and some time afterwards, having made large sums of money there, determined to return to Corinth. Accordingly he set sail from Tarentum, chartering a vessel manned by Corinthians, a people whom he thought, of all men, he could trust. But when they reached the open sea the crew conspired to secure his money by throwing him overboard. . . . Putting on all his harper's dress and grasping his lyre, he took his stand in the stern-sheets, and went through the Orthian or High-pitched Nome from beginning to end. Then he threw himself just as he was, dress and all, into the sea. The crew continued their voyage to Corinth; but meanwhile a dolphin, it seems, took Arion upon his back and carried him ashore at Taenarum. . . . There is a small bronze votive-offering of Arion on the promontory of Taenarum, consisting of a man upon a dolphin's back.

Procl. *Chrest.* ap. Phot. *Bibl.* p. 320 Bek. εὑρεθῆναι δὲ τὸν διθύραμβον Πίνδαρος ἐν Κορίνθῳ λέγει· τὸν δὲ ἀρξάμενον τῆς ᾠδῆς Ἀριστοκλῆς[1] Ἀρίονά φησιν εἶναι, ὃς πρῶτος τὸν κύκλιον ἤγαγε χορόν.

Euseb. *Ol.* 40. 4 Ἀρίων ἐγνωρίζετο Μηθυμναῖος· οὗτος ἐπὶ δελφῖνος εἰς Ταίναρον διεσώθη.

Sch. Ar. *Av.* 1403 [κυκλιοδιδάσκαλον]· Ἀντίπατρος καὶ Εὐφρόνιος . . . φασὶ τοὺς κυκλίους χοροὺς στῆσαι πρῶτον Λασόν . . . οἱ δὲ ἀρχαιότεροι, Ἑλλάνικος καὶ Δικαίαρχος, Ἀρίονα τὸν Μηθυμναῖον, Δικαίαρχος μὲν ἐν τῷ Περὶ Μουσικῶν Ἀγώνων, Ἑλλάνικος δὲ ἐν τοῖς Καρνεονίκαις.[2]

Suid. Ἀρίων· Μηθυμναῖος, λυρικός, Κυκλέως υἱός, γέγονε κατὰ τὴν λη' Ὀλυμπιάδα. τινὲς δὲ καὶ μαθητὴν Ἀλκμᾶνος ἱστόρησαν αὐτόν. ἔγραψε δὲ ᾄσματα, προοίμια εἰς ἔπη β'. λέγεται καὶ τραγικοῦ τρόπου εὑρετὴς γενέσθαι, καὶ πρῶτος χορὸν στῆσαι, καὶ διθύραμβον ᾆσαι καὶ ὀνομάσαι τὸ ᾀδόμενον ὑπὸ τοῦ χοροῦ, καὶ Σατύρους εἰσενεγκεῖν ἔμμετρα λέγοντας.

Vide Luc. *D.M.* 8, Strab. 13. 618, Paus. 3. 25. 7; Ael. *N.A.* 12. 45 quotes the hymn of thanks to

[1] mss Ἀριστοτέλης [2] mss Κραναΐκοῖς

Proclus *Chrestomathy*: According to Pindar the dithyramb was invented at Corinth, and we are told by Aristocles that the originator of this song was Arion, the first trainer of the cyclic or circular chorus.

Eusebius *Chronicle*: Fourth year of the 40th Olympiad (B.C. 617): Flourished Arion of Methymna, who was rescued by a dolphin off Taenarum.

Scholiast on Aristophanes [cyclic-chorus-trainer]: Antipater and Euphronius . . . declare that the cyclic or circular choruses were first assembled by Lasus. . . . The earlier authorities, however, namely Hellanicus and Dicaearchus, ascribe their origin to Arion of Methymna, the former in his *List of Carnean Victors* and the latter in his *Treatise on the Musical Contests.*

Suidas *Lexicon*: Arion: Of Methymna, lyric poet, son of Cycleus, flourished in the 38th Olympiad (B.C. 628–625). According to some authorities he was a pupil of Alcman. He composed songs, namely two Books of Preludes to Epic poems. He is also said to have been the inventor of the tragic style, and to have been the first to assemble a chorus, to sing a dithyramb, to give that name to the song of the chorus, and to introduce Satyrs speaking in metre.

Poseidon ascribed to Arion; this hymn being of much later date will be found in vol. iii; for other refs. see Pauly-Wiss. *Real-Encycl.*

ΣΑΠΦΟΥΣ

Βίος

Stob. *Fl.* 29. 58 Αἰλιανοῦ· Σόλων ὁ Ἀθηναῖος Ἐξηκεστίδου παρὰ πότον τοῦ ἀδελφιδοῦ αὐτοῦ μέλος τι Σαπφοῦς ᾄσαντος, ἥσθη τῷ μέλει καὶ προσέταξε τῷ μειρακίῳ διδάξαι αὐτόν. ἐρωτήσαντος δέ τινος διὰ ποίαν αἰτίαν τοῦτο ἐσπούδακεν, ὅδε ἔφη· ‘Ἵνα μαθὼν αὐτὸ ἀποθάνω.’

Hdt. 2. 135 Ῥοδῶπις δὲ ἐς Αἴγυπτον ἀπίκετο Ξάνθεω τοῦ Σαμίου κομίσαντος· ἀπικομένη δὲ κατ' ἐργασίην ἐλύθη χρημάτων μεγάλων ὑπὸ ἀνδρὸς Μυτιληναίου Χαράξου τοῦ Σκαμανδρωνύμου παιδὸς ἀδελφεοῦ δὲ Σαπφοῦς τῆς μουσοποιοῦ. . . . φιλέουσι δέ κως ἐν τῇ Ναυκράτι ἐπαφρόδιτοι γίγνεσθαι αἱ ἑταῖραι· τοῦτο μὲν γὰρ αὕτη τῆς πέρι λέγεται ὅδε ὁ λόγος οὕτω δή τι κλεινὴ ἐγένετο ὡς καὶ πάντες οἱ Ἕλληνες Ῥοδώπιος τὸ οὔνομα ἐξέμαθον . . . Χάραξος δὲ ὡς λυσάμενος Ῥοδῶπιν ἀπενόστησε ἐς Μυτιλήνην, ἐν μέλεϊ Σαπφὼ κατεκερτόμησέ μιν.

Ibid. 134 κατὰ Ἄμασιν βασιλεύοντα ἦν ἀκμάζουσα Ῥοδῶπις.

Str. 17. 808 [π. πυραμίδων]· λέγεται δὲ τῆς ἑταίρας τάφος γεγονὼς ὑπὸ τῶν ἐραστῶν, ἣν Σαπφὼ μὲν ἡ τῶν μελῶν ποιήτρια καλεῖ Δωρίχαν, ἐρωμένην τοῦ ἀδελφοῦ αὐτῆς Χαράξου γεγονυῖαν,

SAPPHO

Life

Stobaeus *Anthology*: Aelian:—One evening over the wine, Execestides the nephew of Solon the Athenian sang a song of Sappho's which his uncle liked so much that he bade the boy teach it him, and when one of the company asked in surprise 'What for?' he replied 'I want to learn it and die.'

Herodotus, *Histories*: Rhodopis was brought to ply her trade in Egypt by Xanthes of Samos, from whom she was bought at a great price and given her freedom by a Mytilenaean named Charaxus, the son of Scamandronymus and brother of the poetess Sappho. . . . It seems that the courtesans of Naucratis are particularly attractive. At any rate the one of whom we are speaking became so famous as to be a household word throughout the Greek world. . . . When Charaxus returned to Mytilene after setting Rhodopis free, Sappho soundly rated him in a poem.

The Same: Rhodopis flourished in the reign of King Amasis.

Strabo *Geography* [the Pyramids]: There is a story that this one was built by her lovers as the tomb of the courtesan who is sometimes called Rhodopis but is known as Doricha to the lyric poetess Sappho, whose brother Charaxus made her

οἶνον κατάγοντος εἰς Ναύκρατιν Λέσβιον κατ' ἐμπορίαν, ἄλλοι δ' ὀνομάζουσι Ῥοδῶπιν.

Ath. 10. 424 e ᾠνοχόουν τε παρὰ τοῖς ἀρχαίοις οἱ εὐγενέστατοι παῖδες . . . Σαπφώ τε ἡ καλὴ πολλαχοῦ Λάριχον τὸν ἀδελφὸν ἐπαινεῖ ὡς οἰνοχοοῦντα ἐν τῷ πρυτανείῳ τοῖς Μυτιληναίοις.

Str. 13. 617 [π. Μυτιλήνης]· συνήκμασε δὲ τούτοις (Πιττακῷ καὶ Ἀλκαίῳ) καὶ ἡ Σαπφώ, θαυμαστόν τι χρῆμα· οὐ γὰρ ἴσμεν ἐν τῷ τοσούτῳ χρόνῳ τῷ μνημονευομένῳ φανεῖσάν τινα γυναῖκα ἐνάμιλλον οὐδὲ κατὰ μικρὸν ἐκείνῃ ποιήσεως χάριν.

Ibid. 618 [π. Ἐρέσου]· ἐξ Ἐρέσου δ' ἦσαν Θεόφραστός τε καὶ Φανίας οἱ ἐκ τῶν περιπάτων φιλόσοφοι.

Sch. Plat. *Phaedr.* 235 c Σαπφὼ λυρικὴ ποιήτρια, Σκαμανδρωνύμου, Μυτιληναία.

Marm. Par. 36 ἀφ' οὗ Σαπφὼ ἐκ Μυτιλήνης εἰς Σικελίαν ἔπλευσε φυγοῦσα [τὸ δεύτερ]ον [1] [ἔτη ΗΗΗΔΔΔΙΙΙΙ, ἄρχο]ντος Ἀθήνησιν μὲν Κριτίου τοῦ προτέρου, ἐν Συρακούσσαις δὲ τῶν γαμόρων κατεχόντων τὴν ἀρχήν.

Euseb. Ol. 45. 2 [2] Sappho et Alcaeus poetae clari habentur.

[1] *E*, cf. Sch. Berl.-Aberd. Alcaeus *C.R.* 1917. 33 [2] some mss 45. 1

---

[1] cf. Suid. Αἴσωπος, Phot. *Lex.* Ῥοδώπιδος ἀνάθημα, Ov.

his mistress on one of his visits to Naucratis with a cargo of Lesbian wine.[1]

Athenaeus *Doctors at Dinner*: It was the custom among the ancients for the boys of noblest birth to pour out the wine. . . . The beautiful Sappho often sings the praises of her brother Larichus as serving the wine in the town-hall of Mytilene.[2]

Strabo *Geography* [on Mytilene]: Contemporary with Pittacus and Alcaeus was Sappho—a marvel. In all the centuries since history began we know of no woman who could be said with any approach to truth to have rivalled her as a poet.

The Same [on Eresus]: This was the birthplace of Theophrastus and Phanias, the Peripatetic philosophers.[3]

Scholiast on Plato *Phaedrus*: Sappho: A lyric poetess, daughter of Scamandronymus; a native of Mytilene.[4]

Parian Chronicle: From the time when Sappho went from Mytilene to Sicily when banished [the second time, 334 years,] in the archonship of the earlier Critias at Athens and the rule of the Gamori or Landowners at Syracuse (B.C. 598).[5]

Eusebius *Chronicle*: Olympiad 45. 2 (B.C. 598): Flourished the poets Sappho and Alcaeus.

Ep. 15. 63, *Paroem.* App. 4. 51 [2] cf. Sch. *Il.* 20. 234 [3] he would have mentioned S. had he believed her to have been born there [4] cf. Mosch. 3. 92 [5] the date occurs in a gap, but is prob. right; in any case it must lie betw. 605 and 591

Hermes. ap. Ath. 598 b . . .

Λέσβιος Ἀλκαῖος δὲ πόσους ἀνεδέξατο κώμους
  Σαπφοῦς φορμίζων ἱμερόεντα πόθον
γινώσκεις. ὁ δ' ἀοιδὸς ἀηδόνος ἠράσαθ' ὕμνων
  Τήϊον ἀλγύνων ἄνδρα πολυφραδίῃ . . .

Ath. 599 c ἐν τούτοις ὁ Ἑρμησιάναξ σφάλλεται συγχρονεῖν οἰόμενος Σαπφὼ καὶ Ἀνακρέοντα, τὸν μὲν κατὰ Κῦρον καὶ Πολυκράτην γενόμενον, τὴν δὲ κατ' Ἀλυάττην τὸν Κροίσου πατέρα.

Ov. *Ep.* 15. 61 [Sappho Phaoni]
Sex mihi natales ierant, cum lecta parentis
  ante diem lacrimas ossa bibere meas.

Sch. Pind: εἰς τοὺς Ἐννέα Λυρικούς·
Ἐννέα τῶν πρώτων λυρικῶν πάτρην γενεήν τε
  μάνθανε, καὶ πατέρας καὶ διάλεκτον ἄθρει.
ὧν Μυτιληναῖος μὲν ἔην γεραρώτερος ἄλλων
  Ἀλκαῖος πρότερος ἠχικὸς Αἰολίδης.
ἡ δ' ἐπὶ τῷ ξυνὴν πάτρην φωνήν τε δαεῖσα
  Σαπφὼ Κλῆιδος καὶ πατρὸς Εὐρυγύου . . .

Suid. Σαπφὼ (α')· Σίμωνος· οἱ δὲ Εὐνομίνου·[1] οἱ δὲ Εὐρυγύου·[2] οἱ δὲ Ἐκρύτου· οἱ δὲ Σήμου· οἱ δὲ Σκάμωνος·[3] οἱ δὲ Εὐάρχου·[4] οἱ δὲ Σκαμανδρωνύμου· μητρὸς δὲ Κλειδός· Λεσβία ἐξ Ἐρέσου,[5] λυρική· γεγονυῖα κατὰ τὴν μβ' Ὀλυμπίαδα, ὅτε καὶ Ἀλκαῖος ἦν καὶ Στησίχορος καὶ Πιττακός. ἦσαν δὲ αὐτῇ ἀδελφοὶ τρεῖς Λάριχος,

[1] mss also Εὐμήνου [2] mss Ἠεριγύου but Eud. Εὐριγύου [3] mss Κάμωνος [4] mss Ἐτάρχου [5] mss and Str. 13. 618 Ἐρέσσου but coins have σ

LIFE OF SAPPHO

Hermesianax quoted by Athenaeus *Doctors at Dinner*: . . . And Lesbian Alcaeus, thou knowest in how many a serenade he thrummed out his delightful love of Sappho; the poet loved that nightingale of hymns and vexed the man of Teos with his eloquence.[1]

Athenaeus [on the Same]: In these lines Hermesianax is wrong in making Sappho contemporary with Anacreon. She belongs to the time of Alyattes father of Croesus, whereas he is coeval with Cyrus and Polycrates.

Ovid *Letters of the Heroines* [Sappho to Phaon]: I was but six years old when the bones of a parent received the too-early drink-offering of my tears.

Preserved by the Scholiast on Pindar: On the Nine Lyric Poets: Now shall you learn the birthplace and lineage of the great lyric poets, and behold both their fathers and their language. First was Alcaeus of Mytilene, the most honoured [*or* eldest] of them all, a resonant son of Aeolus; and next to him one of the same city and speech, Sappho daughter of Eurygyus and Cleïs . . .

Suidas *Lexicon*: Sappho (1*st notice*): Daughter of Simon or of Eunominus, or of Eurygyus,[2] or of Ecrytus, or of Semus, or of Scamon,[3] or of Euarchus, or of Scamandronymus; mother's name Cleïs. A Lesbian of Eresus,[4] a lyric poetess; flourished in the 42nd Olympiad (B.C. 612–609) along with Alcaeus, Stesichorus, and Pittacus. She had three brothers,

[1] cf. Ov. *Ep.* 15. 29 [2] the exact form of the name is doubtful; cf. Ἐρίγυιος son of Larichus of Mytilene, *temp.* Alexander, Diod. 17. 27 [3] abbrev. of Scamandronymus [4] perh. wrong, see above

Χάραξος, Εὐρύγυος.[1] ἐγαμήθη δὲ Κερκώλᾳ[2] ἀνδρὶ πλουσιωτάτῳ, ὁρμωμένῳ ἀπὸ Ἄνδρου· καὶ θυγατέρα ἐποίησατο ἐξ αὐτοῦ ἣ Κλεὶς ὠνομάσθη. ἑταῖραι δὲ αὐτῆς καὶ φίλαι γεγόνασι τρεῖς, Ἀτθίς, Τελεσίππα, Μεγάρα· πρὸς ἃς καὶ διαβολὴν ἔσχεν αἰσχρᾶς φιλίας. μαθήτριαι δὲ αὐτῆς Ἀναγόρα[3] Μιλησία, Γογγύλα Κολοφωνία, Εὐνείκα Σαλαμινία. ἔγραψε δὲ μελῶν λυρικῶν βιβλία θ'. καὶ πρώτη πλῆκτρον εὗρεν. ἔγραψε δὲ καὶ ἐπιγράμματα καὶ ἰάμβους καὶ μονῳδίας.

Suid. Σαπφὼ (β')· Λεσβία ἐκ Μυτιλήνης, ψ'λτρια. αὕτη δι' ἔρωτα Φάωνος τοῦ Μυτιληναίου ἐκ τοῦ Λευκάτου κατεπόντισεν ἑαυτήν. τινὲς δὲ καὶ ταύτης εἶναι λυρικὴν ἀνέγραψαν ποίησιν.

Ael. *V.H.* 12. 19 τὴν ποιήτριαν Σαπφὼ τὴν Σκαμανδρωνύμου θυγατέρα· ταύτην καὶ Πλάτων ὁ Ἀρίστωνος σοφὴν ἀναγράφει· πυνθάνομαι δὲ ὅτι καὶ ἑτέρα ἐν τῇ Λέσβῳ ἐγένετο Σαπφώ, ἑταῖρα οὐ ποιήτρια.

Ath. 13. 571 d καλοῦσι γοῦν καὶ αἱ ἐλεύθεραι γυναῖκες ἔτι καὶ νῦν καὶ αἱ παρθένοι τὰς συνήθεις καὶ φίλας ἑταίρας, ὡς ἡ Σαπφώ . . .

Ov. *Trist.* 2. 365
Lesbia quid docuit Sappho nisi amare puellas?
tuta tamen Sappho . . .

[1] mss Εὐρυγίου [2] mss also Κερκύλᾳ [3] Ἀνακτορία?

---

[1] *or* plied as a trader between A. (an Ionian city) and Lesbos? [2] cf. Ov. *Ep.* 15. 70, 120 [3] Anactoria? [4] 'quill' prob. a mistake for *pēctis*, a kind of lyre, cf. Ath. 14. 635 e (below) [5] this must come from another source.

Larichus, Charaxus, Eurygyus. She was married to a very rich man called Cercōlas [*or* Cercylas] who came from Andros,[1] and had by him a daughter named Cleïs.[2] She had three companions or friends, Atthis, Telesippa, and Megara, to whom she was slanderously declared to be bound by an impure affection. Her pupils or disciples were Anagora[3] of Miletus, Gongyla of Colophon, Euneica of Salamis. She wrote nine Books of Lyric Poems, and was the inventor of the quill for striking the lyre.[4] [She wrote also 'inscriptions,' iambic verse, and monodies.][5]

Suidas *Lexicon*: Sappho (*2nd notice*): A Lesbian of Mytilene, a lyre-player. She threw herself from the Leucadian Cliff for love of Phaon the Mytilenaean. Some authorities say that she too was a lyric poetess.

Aelian *Historical Miscellanies* [in the next article to that on Phaon[6]]: The poetess Sappho daughter of Scamandronymus: Even Plato son of Ariston calls her wise.[7] I understand that there was another Sappho in Lesbos, a courtesan, not a poetess.

Athenaeus *Doctors at Dinner*: Freeborn women to this day, and girls, call their intimates and friends *hetaerae* or companions [the usual word for courtesan], as Sappho does in this passage (*fr.* 12).

Ovid *Songs of Sadness*: What lore did Sappho teach but how to love maidens?[8] Yet Sappho was safe . . .

as the term 'monodies' would cover most of the contents of her nine Books [6] n.b. he gives no other hint of a connexion between the two [7] the Greek means 'good at one's art or trade' [8] *or* teach her maidens but how to love

Sen. *Ep.* 88 quattuor milia librorum Didymus grammaticus scripsit. misererer si tam multa supervacua legisset. in his libris de patria Homeri quaeritur, in his de Aeneae matre vera, in his libidinosior Anacreon an ebriosior vixerit, in his an Sappho publica fuerit, et alia quae erant dediscenda si scires; i nunc et longam esse vitam nega.

Ath. 13. 596 b ἐνδόξους δὲ ἑταίρας καὶ ἐπὶ κάλλει διαφερούσας ἤνεγκεν καὶ ἡ Ναύκρατις· Δωρίχαν τε, ἣν ἡ καλὴ Σαπφὼ ἐρωμένην γενομένην Χαράξου τοῦ ἀδελφοῦ αὐτῆς κατ' ἐμπορίαν εἰς τὴν Ναύκρατιν ἀπαίροντος διὰ τῆς ποιήσεως διαβάλλει ὡς πολλὰ τοῦ Χαράξου νοσφισαμένην. Ἡρόδοτος δ' αὐτὴν Ῥοδῶπιν καλεῖ,[1] ἀγνοῶν ὅτι ἑτέρα τῆς Δωρίχης ἐστὶν αὕτη, ἡ καὶ τοὺς περιβοήτους ὀβελίσκους ἀναθεῖσα ἐν Δελφοῖς, ὧν μέμνηται Κρατῖνος διὰ τούτων . . . εἰς δὲ τὴν Δωρίχαν τόδ' ἐποίησε τοὐπίγραμμα Ποσείδιππος, καίτοι καὶ ἐν τῇ Αἰσωπείᾳ[2] πολλάκις αὐτῆς μνημονεύσας. ἐστὶ δὲ τόδε·

Δωρίχα, ὀστέα μὲν σ' ἁπαλῆς κόσμησ' ἀπόδεσμα[3]
 χαίτης ἥ τε μύρων ἔκπνοος ἀμπεχόνη
ᾗ ποτε τὸν χαρίεντα περιστείλασα[4] Χάραξον
 σύγχρους ὀρθρίνων ἥψαο κισσυβίων.
Σαπφῷας[5] δὲ μένουσι φίλης ἔτι καὶ μενέουσιν
 ᾠδῆς αἱ λευκαὶ φθεγγόμεναι σελίδες·
οὔνομα σὸν μακάριστον, ὃ Ναύκρατις ὧδε φυλάξει
 ἔστ' ἀνίῃ Νείλου ναῦς ἔφαλος τενάγη.[6]

[1] cf. Str. 17. 808 [2] Wil: mss Αἰθιοπίᾳ [3] *E*, cf. ἀπόδεσμος, δέσμα and for rhythm *A.P.* 12. 98. 1: mss ἁπαλὰ (taking δέσμα for plur.) κοιμήσατο δεσμῶν (gen. due to ἀπὸ) [4] *E*: mss pres. [5] mss Σαπφῷαι [6] mss εσταν εἴη and γεγανη

Seneca *Letters to Lucilius*: The grammarian Didymus wrote four thousand books. I should pity him if he had merely read so many useless works. The list includes treatises in which he discusses the birthplace of Homer, the true mother of Aeneas, whether Anacreon was more of a rake than a sot, whether Sappho was a prostitute, and other questions the answers to which you ought to forget if you knew them. And then people complain that life is short.[1]

Athenaeus *Doctors at Dinner*: Naucratis too was the home of some famous and extremely beautiful courtesans. Doricha, who became the mistress of Sappho's brother Charaxus when his business took him to Naucratis, is trounced by his sister in a poem for having fleeced him.[2] But Herodotus calls her Rhodopis,[3] not understanding that Doricha is not the same as the woman who dedicated at Delphi the famous spits mentioned by Cratinus . . .[4] The following epigram was written on Doricha by Poseidippus, who speaks of her many times in the *Aesopeia*: ''Tis but your bones they adorn now, Doricha, that band for your dainty hair, that spice-breathing mantle you wrapped the fair Charaxus in, to lie breast to breast with you till 'twas time for the morning cup; yet the white speaking pages of Sappho's dear song abides and ever will. Happy your name, which Naucratis thus will keep for her own so long as sea-going ship sails up the shallows of the Nile.'[5] Moreover there was a certain

[1] cf. Mart. 7. 69, 10. 35, Apul. *Apol.* 413, Ov. *A.A.* 3. 331, *Rem.* 761 [2] cf. Ov. *Ep.* 15. 63, 117 [3] cf. Str. 17. 808 [4] quotation lost [5] *i. e.* steers its way among the lagoons; N. was 30 miles from the sea

καὶ Ἀρχεδίκη δ' ἦν τις ἐκ τῆς Ναυκράτεως καὶ αὐτὴ ἑταίρα καλή . . . καὶ ἡ ἐξ Ἐρέσου δὲ τῆς <ἑτέρας Σαπφοῦς ὁμώνυμος> ἑταίρα [1] τοῦ καλοῦ Φάωνος ἐρασθεῖσα περιβόητος ἦν, ὥς φησι Νύμφις [2] ἐν Περίπλῳ Ἀσίας.

Str. 10. 452 [π. Λευκάδος]· ἔχει δὲ τὸ τοῦ Λευκάτα Ἀπόλλωνος ἱερὸν καὶ τὸ ἅλμα τὸ τοὺς ἔρωτας παύειν πεπιστευμένον, 'Οὗ δὴ λέγεται πρώτη Σαπφώ,' ὥς φησιν ὁ Μένανδρος,

> τὸν ὑπέρκομπον θηρῶσα Φάων'
> οἰστρῶντι πόθῳ ῥῖψαι πέτρας
> ἀπὸ τηλεφανοῦς· ἀλλὰ κατ' εὐχὴν
> σόν, δέσποτ' ἄναξ, εὐφημείσθω
> τέμενος περὶ Λευκάδος ἀκτῆς.[3]

ὁ μὲν οὖν Μένανδρος πρώτην ἁλέσθαι λέγει τὴν Σαπφώ, οἱ δ' ἔτι ἀρχαιολογικώτεροι Κέφαλόν φασιν ἐρασθέντα Πτερέλα τὸν Δηϊονέως. ἦν δὲ καὶ πάτριον τοῖς Λευκαδίοις κατ' ἐνιαυτὸν ἐν τῇ θυσίᾳ τοῦ Ἀπόλλωνος ἀπὸ τῆς σκοπῆς ῥιπτεῖσθαί τινα τῶν ἐν αἰτίαις ὄντων ἀποτροπῆς χάριν, ἐξαπτομένων ἐξ αὐτοῦ παντοδαπῶν πτερωτῶν [4] καὶ ὀρνέων ἀνακουφίζειν δυναμένων τῇ πτήσει τὸ ἅλμα, ὑποδέχεσθαι δὲ κάτω μικραῖς ἁλιάσι κύκλῳ περιεστῶτας πολλοὺς καὶ περισῴζειν εἰς δύναμιν τῶν ὅρων ἔξω τὸν ἀναληφθέντα.

Serv. Verg. *Aen.* 3. 279 Phaon cum esset navicularius solitus a Lesbo in continentem proximos quosque mercede transvehere Venerem mutatam in anus formam gratis transvexit. quapropter ab ea donatus unguenti alabastro, cum se indies inditum

[1] Kaib. -*E*: mss τῆς ἑταίρας Σαπφὼ [2] Wil. Νυμφόδωρος

Archedicè of Naucratis, who was a beautiful courtesan. . . . And according to Nymphis in his *Voyage around Asia*, the courtesan of Eresus, who was a namesake of the other Sappho and lover of the fair Phaon, won great notoriety.

Strabo *Geography* [the Leucadian Cliff]: This rock is surmounted by the temple of Apollo Leucātes, and from it is the leap which is supposed to cure love, 'Where Sappho first,' to quote Menander, 'in wild love-chase of the proud Phaon, leapt from the far-seen rock. But now in accordance with my vow shall thy precinct be praised, great Lord, by reason of the Cliff Leucadian.'[1] Though Menander thus gives priority to Sappho, greater antiquaries than he assign it to Cephalus son of Deïoneus. It was an old custom of the Leucadians, every year at the sacrifice to Apollo, as an apotropaic or averting rite, to throw from the cliff some guilty person to whom they had previously fastened all sorts of birds and other winged creatures which by their fluttering might break his fall, a large crowd waiting below in small boats to pick him up and if possible carry him off to safety beyond the frontier.

Servius on the *Aeneid*: Phaon, who was a ferryman plying for hire between Lesbos and the mainland, one day ferried over for nothing the Goddess Venus in the guise of an old woman, and received from her for the service an alabaster box of unguent

[1] cf. Hesych. Mil. Σαπφώ

[3] last line and a half added by Bentley from Hesych. Λευκάδος: σόν: mss σήν [4] *E*: mss πτερῶν

ungeret, feminas in suum amorem trahebat, in quis fuit una quae de monte Leucate, cum potiri eius nequiret, abiecisse se dicitur, unde nunc auctorare se quotannis solent qui de eo monte iaciantur in pelagus.[1]

Suid. Φάων· <Φάων ὑπάρχεις τῷ κάλλει καὶ τῷ τρόπῳ·> φασὶν ἐπὶ τῶν ἐρασμίων καὶ ὑπερηφάνων. τοῦ γὰρ Φάωνος ἐρασθῆναί φασι σὺν πολλοῖς καὶ Σαπφώ, οὐ τὴν ποιήτριαν, ἀλλὰ <ἄλλην> Λεσβίαν· καὶ ἀποτυγχάνουσαν ῥῖψαι ἑαυτὴν ἀπὸ τῆς Λευκάδος πέτρας.

Ath. 2. 69 d Κρατῖνος δέ φησι Φάωνος ἐρασθεῖσαν τὴν Ἀφροδίτην ἐν 'καλαῖς θριδακίναις' αὐτὸν ἀποκρύψαι, Μαρσύας δ' ὁ νεώτερος ἐν χλόῃ κριθῶν.

Ov. *Ep.* 15. 51

Nunc tibi Sicelides veniunt nova praeda puellae;
quid mihi cum Lesbo? Sicelis esse volo.

Ath. 10. 450 e ἐν δὲ Σαπφοῖ ὁ Ἀντιφάνης αὐτὴν τὴν ποιήτριαν προβάλλουσαν ποιεῖ γρίφους . . . :—13. 572 c Ἔφιππος ἐν Σαπφοῖ φησιν . . . :—8. 339 c καὶ Τιμοκλῆς δ' ἐν Σαπφοῖ φησιν . . . :—13. 599 d καὶ γὰρ Δίφιλος ὁ κωμῳδιοποιὸς πεποίηκεν ἐν Σαπφοῖ

[1] Ael. *V.H.* 12. 18 adds τά γε μὴν τελευταῖα ἀπεσφάγη μοιχεύων ἁλούς

---

[1] prob. basis of the plot of the *Phaon* of the comedy-writer Plato [2] Aelian adds 'Finally he was taken in adultery and murdered' [3] from Apostolius *Par.* 2. 707 who appends a slightly different version derived from *Epit.* Palaeph. *Incred.*

the daily use of which made women fall in love with him.[1] Among those who did so was one who in her disappointment is said to have thrown herself from Mount Leucates, and from this came the custom now in vogue of hiring people once a year to throw themselves from that place into the sea.[2]

Suidas *Lexicon*: Phaon: <You are a Phaon both in looks and deeds>[3]; this proverb is used of those who are lovely and disdainful. They say that this Phaon was beloved by many women, among them Sappho, not the poetess but another Lesbian, who failing to win him threw herself from the Leucadian Cliff.

Athenaeus *Doctors at Dinner*: According to Cratinus, Aphrodite when beloved by Phaon concealed him among the 'fair wild-lettuces'; but according to the younger Marsyas the hiding-place was among the growing barley.

Ovid *Letters of the Heroines* [Sappho to Phaon]: The maidens of Sicily are now thy prey; what have I to do with Lesbos? I am fain to be a Sicilian.

Athenaeus *Doctors at Dinner*: Antiphanes in his *Sappho* makes the poetess propound riddles . . . ;—To quote the *Sappho* of Ephippus . . . ;—Compare Timocles' *Sappho* . . . ;—Diphilus, the

49 with the inconsistent addition, 'this is the P. in whose honour as her lover many a song has been written by Sappho'; cf. Phot. *Lex.* Λευκάτης, Φάων, Phot. *Bibl.* 153 (list of Leucadian Cliff leapers without mention of S.), Luc. *D. Mort.* 9. 2 (substitutes Chios for Lesbos), Ov. *Ep.* 15. 175f (confuses the 'two Sapphos'), *Am.* 2. 18. 34, Stat. *Silv.* 5. 3. 155 (substitutes Calchis (sic) for Leucas), Apost. *Paroem.* 17. 80, Alciphr. 3. 1, Aus. *Id.* 6. 21, *Ep.* 92, Plin. *N.H.* 22. 9, Plaut. *Mil.* 1246

δράματι Σαπφοῦς ἐραστὰς Ἀρχίλοχον καὶ Ἱππώνακτα.[1]

Max. Tyr. 24 (18) ὁ τῆς Λεσβίας (ἔρως), εἴ τοι χρὴ πρεσβύτερα τοῖς νεοῖς εἰκάσαι, τί ἂν εἴη ἄλλο ἢ ἡ Σωκράτους τέχνη ἐρωτική; δοκοῦσι γάρ μοι τὴν κατὰ ταὐτὸ ἑκάτερος φιλίαν, ἡ μὲν γυναικῶν, ὁ δὲ ἀρρένων ἐπιτηδεῦσαι. καὶ γὰρ πολλῶν ἐρᾶν ἔλεγον καὶ ὑπὸ πάντων ἁλίσκεσθαι τῶν καλῶν. ὅτι γὰρ ἐκείνῳ Ἀλκιβιάδης καὶ Χαρμίδης καὶ Φαῖδρος, τοῦτο τῇ Λεσβίᾳ Γύριννα καὶ Ἄτθις καὶ Ἀνακτορία· καὶ ὅτιπερ Σωκράτει οἱ ἀντίτεχνοι Πρόδικος καὶ Γοργίας καὶ Θρασύμαχος καὶ Πρωταγόρας, τοῦτο τῇ Σαπφοῖ Γοργὼ καὶ Ἀνδρομέδα· νῦν μὲν ἐπιτιμᾷ ταύταις, νῦν δὲ ἐλέγχει καὶ εἰρωνεύεται αὐτὰ ἐκεῖνα τὰ Σωκράτους.

Ov. *Ep.* 15. 15

Nec me Pyrrhiades Methymniadesve puellae
nec me Lesbiadum cetera turba iuvant;
vilis Anactorie, vilis mihi candida Cydro,[2]
non oculis grata est Atthis ut ante meis,
atque aliae centum, quas hic[3] sine crimine amavi;
improbe, multarum quod fuit, unus habes.

[1] cf. Ibid. 11. 487 a [2] mss also *Cydno*, but see L. & S. κυδνός [3] some mss *non*

---

[1] cf. Bek. *An.* p. 89, Poll. 7; it will be seen that the ancient testimony for connecting the poetess with the Leucadian Cliff and with Phaon is conflicting; there were many White Rocks, and her leap, which if it was more than a threat or a

writer of comedies, in his play *Sappho* has made the poetess beloved by Archilochus and Hipponax.[1]

Maximus of Tyre *Dissertations*: The love of the fair Lesbian, if it is right to argue from one age to another, was surely the same as the art of love pursued by Socrates. They both appear to me to have practised the same sort of friendship, he of males, she of females, both declaring that their beloved were many in number and that they were captivated by all beautiful persons. What Alcibiades, Charmides, and Phaedrus were to him, Gyrinna,[2] Atthis, and Anactoria were to her, and what his rival craftsmen, Prodicus, Gorgias, Thrasymachus and Protagoras were to Socrates, that Gorgo and Andromeda were to Sappho, who sometimes takes them to task and at others refutes them and dissembles with them exactly like Socrates.

Ovid *Letters of the Heroines* [Sappho to Phaon]: I take no pleasure in the maids of Pyrrha or Methymna nor in any of the daughters of Lesbos; Anactoria is a paltry jade, and so is the fair Cydro; my eyes see no beauty now in Atthis, or in a hundred others whom I have loved here so innocently.[3] Bold man! what once belonged to many is now thine alone.

metaphor, can hardly have been fatal (cf. Max. Tyr. 18. 9 below), was apparently transferred to Leucates from one of these; the second Sappho is prob. a late invention intended to reconcile the testimony of S.'s own works with the dramatic adaptations of the popular tradition to the myth of Phaon and the Goddess (cf. Jason and Hera Ap. Rhod. 3. 68) [2] cf. Suid. Ἤριννα, Eust. *Il.* 2 p. 247 [3] *or* not without evil imputation

Philostr. *Vit. Ap.* 1. 30 εἰσῄει μὲν δὴ (ὁ Ἀπολλώνιος) παραπεμπόμενος ὑπὸ πλειόνων· τουτὶ γὰρ ᾤοντο καὶ τῷ βασιλεῖ χαρίζεσθαι μαθόντες ὡς χαίροι ἀφιγμένῳ· διϊὼν δὲ ἐς τὰ βασίλεια οὐ διέβλεψεν ἐς οὐδὲν τῶν θαυμαζομένων, ἀλλ ὥσπερ ὁδοιπορῶν διῄει αὐτά, καὶ καλέσας τὸν Δάμιν 'Ἥρου με' ἔφη 'πρώην, ὅτι ὄνομα ἦν τῇ Παμφύλῳ γυναικὶ ἣ δὴ Σαπφοῖ τε ὁμιλῆσαι λέγεται καὶ τοὺς ὕμνους οὓς ἐς τὴν Ἄρτεμιν τὴν Περγαίαν ᾄδουσι συνθεῖναι τὸν Αἰολέων τε καὶ Παμφύλων τρόπον.' 'Ἠρόμην' ἔφη, 'τὸ δὲ ὄνομα οὐκ εἶπας.' 'Οὐκ, ὦ χρηστέ, εἶπον ἀλλ' ἐξηγούμην σοι τοὺς νόμους τῶν ὕμνων καὶ τὰ ὀνόματα καὶ ὅπη τὰ Αἰολέων ἐς τὸ ἀκρότατόν τε καὶ τὸ ἴδιον Παμφύλων παρήλλαξε· πρὸς ἄλλῳ μετὰ ταῦτα ἐγενόμεθα, καὶ οὐκέτ' ἤρου με περὶ τοῦ ὀνόματος· καλεῖται τοίνυν ἡ σοφὴ αὕτη Δαμοφύλη, καὶ λέγεται τὸν Σαπφοῦς τρόπον παρθένους τε ὁμιλητρίας κτήσασθαι ποιήματά τε συνθεῖναι τὰ μὲν ἐρωτικά, τὰ δὲ ὕμνους. τά τοι ἐς τὴν Ἄρτεμιν καὶ παρῴδηται αὐτῇ καὶ ἀπὸ τῶν Σαπφῴων ᾖσται.'

Hor. *Od.* 2. 13. 21 [Ille et nefasto te posuit die . . ., arbos . . .]:

> Quam paene furvae regna Proserpinae
> et iudicantem vidimus Aeacum
> sedesque discriptas piorum et
> Aeoliis fidibus querentem
>
> Sappho puellis de popularibus
> et te sonantem plenius aureo,
> Alcaee, plectro . . .

LIFE OF SAPPHO

Philostratus *Life of Apollonius of Tyana*: So Apol lonius entered the king's palace, accompanied by a number of people who, knowing that he had been pleased to hear of his arrival in Babylon, thought that this would gratify the king. As he passed in however, the philosopher paid no attention whatever to the wonders of the house, but walking by them as though he were travelling on the high road, called Damis to him and said: 'You asked me the other day the name of the fair Pamphylian who is said to have been associated with Sappho and to have composed the hymns they sing to Artemis of Perga in the Aeolian and Pamphylian modes.' 'So I did,' he replied; 'but received no answer.' 'No, my friend, but you received an account of the tunes of the hymns and the names they are known by, and how she changed the Aeolian peculiarities into her own noble Pamphylian. We then turned to something else, and you did not repeat your original request. Well, this clever woman's name was Damophyla, and she is said to have had girl-companions like Sappho, and to have composed love-poems and hymns just as she did. The hymns to Artemis are her adaptations of her teacher's work, deriving ultimately from Sapphic originals.'

Horace *Odes* [Ill-omened was the day of your planting, good tree . . .]: How near was I to beholding the realm of gloomy Proserpine with Aeacus holding court, how near to seeing the abodes assigned the holy dead, with Sappho singing elegies to the Aeolian string upon the girls of her city, and thee, Alcaeus, chanting with fuller note and quill of gold . . .

Ov. *Ep.* 15. 201

Lesbides, infamem quae me fecistis amore,
desinite ad citharas turba venire meas.

Arist. *Rh.* 1398 b πάντες τοὺς σοφοὺς τιμῶσιν· Πάριοι γοῦν Ἀρχίλοχον καίπερ βλάσφημον ὄντα τετιμήκασι, καὶ Χῖοι Ὅμηρον οὐκ ὄντα πολίτην, καὶ Μυτιληναῖοι Σαπφὼ καίπερ γυναῖκα οὖσαν, καὶ Λακεδαιμόνιοι Χίλωνα τῶν γερόντων ἐποίησαν ἥκιστα φιλόλογοι ὄντες . . .

Poll. 9. 84 Μυτιληναῖοι Σαπφὼ τῷ νομίσματι ἐνεχαράξαντο.

Anth. Pal. 7. 14 Ἀντιπάτρου Σιδωνίου εἰς Σαπφὼ τὴν Μυτιληναίαν τὴν λυρικήν·

Σαπφώ τοι κεύθεις, χθὼν Αἰολί, τὰν μετὰ Μούσαις
ἀθανάταις θνατὰν Μοῦσαν ἀειδομέναν,
ἃν Κύπρις καὶ Ἔρως συνάμ' ἔτραφον, ἇς μέτα Πειθὼ
ἔπλεκ' ἀείζωον Πιερίδων στέφανον,
Ἑλλάδι μὲν τέρψιν, σοὶ δὲ κλέος. ὦ τριέλικτον
Μοῖραι δινεῦσαι νῆμα κατ' ἠλακάτας,
πῶς οὐκ ἐκλώσασθε πανάφθιτον ἦμαρ ἀοιδῷ
ἄφθιτα μησαμένᾳ δῶρ' Ἑλικωνιάδων;

Plat. *Phaedr.* 235 b ΣΩ. Τοῦτο ἐγώ σοι οὐκέτι οἷος τ' ἔσομαι πίθεσθαι· παλαιοὶ γὰρ καὶ σοφοὶ ἄνδρες τε καὶ γυναῖκες περὶ αὐτῶν εἰρηκότες καὶ γεγραφότες ἐξελέγξουσί με, ἐάν σοι χαριζόμενος συγχωρῶ.—ΦΑΙ. Τίνες οὗτοι; καὶ ποῦ σὺ βελτίω

LIFE OF SAPPHO

Ovid *Letters of the Heroines* [Sappho to Phaon]: Daughters of Lesbos, whose love has made me of ill-report, throng ye no more to hear my lyre.

Aristotle *Rhetoric*: . . . The wise are honoured universally. The Parians have honoured Archilochus despite his slanderous tongue, the Chians Homer though he was not of their city, and the Mytilenaeans Sappho for all she was a woman;[1] while the Spartans, who have no love for learning, elected Chilon of their senate . . .[2]

Pollux *Vocabulary*: The Mytilenaeans engraved Sappho on their coinage.[3]

Palatine Anthology: Antipater of Sidon on Sappho the lyric poetess of Mytilene: That which thou coverest, Aeolian soil, is Sappho,[4] one that is sung for a mortal Muse among Muses immortal, one that was reared by Cypris and by Eros too, one that helped Persuasion weave the everlasting garland of the Pierian Maids, a delight unto Greece, a glory unto thee. O ye Fates that twirl the three-ply thread from the distaff, why span ye not a never-dying day for the songstress who devised the deathless gifts of the Daughters of Helicon?

Plato *Phaedrus*: SOCRATES: I cannot go so far with you as that. There are wise ancients, both men and women, whose sayings or writings will refute me if I allow you to persuade me of it.—PHAEDRUS: Who may these be? and where have they given you

[1] n.b. he does not say 'an *evil* woman' [2] cf. Aristid. 12. 85. [3] where she may still be seen, as also on that of Eresus; in both cases the coins are of Imperial times [4] Antipater (c. 120 B.C.) evidently believed that S. died in Lesbos; cf. Max. Tyr. 18. 9 below

τούτων ἀκήκοας ;—ΣΩ. Νῦν μὲν οὕτως οὐκ ἔχω εἰπεῖν· δῆλον δὲ ὅτι τινῶν ἀκήκοα, ἤ που Σαπφοῦς τῆς καλῆς ἢ Ἀνακρέοντος τοῦ σοφοῦ ἢ καὶ συγγραφέων τινῶν.

Max. Tyr. 24 (18). 7 . . . Σαπφοῦς τῆς καλῆς—οὕτω γὰρ αὐτὴν ὀνομάζων χαίρει (ὁ Σωκράτης) διὰ τὴν ὥραν τῶν μελῶν, καίτοι μικρὰν οὖσαν καὶ μέλαιναν.

Ov. *Ep.* 15. 31

Si mihi difficilis formam natura negavit,
 ingenio formae damna rependo meae:
nec me despicias, si sim tibi corpore parva
 mensuramque brevis nominis ipsa feram [1];
sum brevis, at nomen quod terras impleat omnes
 est mihi; mensuram nominis ipsa fero.
candida si non sum, placuit Cepheïa Perseo
 Andromede, patriae fusca colore suae;
et variis albae iunguntur saepe columbae,
 et niger a viridi turtur amatur ave.

Luc. *Imag.* 18 [π. τὴν σοφίας καὶ συνέσεως εἰκόνα]· δεύτερον δὲ καὶ τρίτον παράδειγμα Θεανώ τε ἐκείνη καὶ ἡ Λεσβία μελοποιὸς καὶ Διοτίμα ἐπὶ ταύταις, ἡ μὲν τὸ μεγαλόνουν ἡ Θεανὼ συμβαλλομένη εἰς τὴν γραφήν, ἡ Σαπφὼ δὲ τὸ γλαφυρὸν τῆς προαιρέσεως . . .

Sch. *ad loc.* ὅσον εἰς σῶμα εἰδεχθεστάτη <ἡ> Σαπφώ, μικρά τε καὶ μέλαινα ὁρωμένη, καὶ τί γὰρ ἄλλο ἢ ἀηδὼν ἀμόρφοις τοῖς πτίλοις ἐπὶ σμικρῷ τῷ σώματι περιειλημένη.

Porph. Hor. *Sat.* 2. 1. 30 [ille velut fidis arcana sodalibus olim | credebat libris]: Aristoxeni sententia

better information in this matter?—SOCRATES: I cannot say off-hand; but I have certainly got it from one of them, from the beautiful Sappho perhaps, or from the wise Anacreon, or some writer of history.

Maximus of Tyre: . . . the beautiful Sappho, for so Socrates rejoices to call her because of the beauty of her lyric verse, although she was small and dark.

Ovid *Letters of the Heroines* [Sappho to Phaon]: If crabbed Nature has denied me beauty, I make up for the lack of it with wit; nor should you despise me for one that hath both small stature and little fame. Little I am indeed, but I have a name which fills the world, and 'tis by the measure of that I go. If I am not fair, remember that Cepheian Andromeda found favour with Perseus, dark though she was with the hue of her birthplace, remember that white doves mate with pied, dark turtle-doves with green.

Lucian *Portraits* [on an ideal picture of Wit and Wisdom]: For a second and third model (after Aspasia) we might take Theano and the Lesbian lyrist, and for a fourth Diotima, Theano contributing to our picture greatness of mind and Sappho refinement of character . . .

Scholiast on the passage: Physically Sappho was very ill-favoured, being small and dark, like a nightingale with ill-shapen wings enfolding a tiny body.

Porphyrio on Horace [Lucilius used to confide his secrets to his books as though to a faithful comrade]: This idea comes from Aristoxenus, who

[1] mss *fero*

est; ille enim in suis scriptis ostendit Sapphonem et Alcaeum volumina sua loco sodalium habuisse.

Max. Tyr. 24 (18). 9 ἀναίθεται (ὁ Σωκράτης) τῇ Ξανθίππῃ ὀδυρομένῃ ὅτε[1] ἀπέθνησκεν, ἡ δὲ Σαπφὼ τῇ θυγατρί·

οὐ γὰρ θέμις ἐν μοισοπόλῳ οἰκίᾳ
θρῆνον θέμεν· οὐκ ἄμμι πρέπει τάδε.

Anth. Pal. 9. 506 Πλάτωνος εἰς Σαπφώ·

Ἐννέα τὰς Μούσας φασίν τινες· ὡς ὀλιγώρως·
ἠνίδε καὶ Σαπφὼ Λεσβόθεν ἡ δεκάτη.

Ibid. 7. 718: Νοσσίδος εἰς Νοσσίδα·

Ὦ ξεῖν', εἰ τύ γε πλεῖς ποτὶ καλλίχορον Μυτιλάναν
τὰν Σαπφοῦς χαρίτων αἶθος[2] ἐναυσαμέναν,
εἰπὼν[3] ὡς Μούσαισι φίλα τ' ἦν ἅ τε Λοκρὶς γᾶ
τίκτε μ'[4] ἴσαις δ' ὅτι μοι τοὔνομα Νόσσις, ἴθι.[5]

Ibid. 7. 407 Διοσκορίδου εἰς Σαπφὼ τὴν Μυτιληναίαν, τὴν μελοποιόν, τὴν ἐν τῇ λυρικῇ ποιήσει θαυμαζομένην·

Ἥδιστον φιλέουσι νέοις προσανάκλιμ' ἐρώτων,[6]
Σαπφώ, σὺν Μούσαις ἦ ῥά σε Πιερίη
ἢ Ἑλικὼν εὔκισσος ἴσα πνείουσαν ἐκείναις
κοσμεῖ, τὴν Ἐρέσῳ Μοῦσαν ἐν Αἰολίδι,
ἢ καὶ Ὑμὴν Ὑμέναιος ἔχων εὐφεγγέα πεύκην
σύν σοι νυμφιδίων ἵσταθ' ὑπὲρ θαλάμων,

[1] mss ὅτι [2] *E*: mss ἄνθος [3] *E*: mss εἰπεῖν [4] Mein: mss φίλα (φίλαν) τῆναιτε λόκρισσα τίκτειν (τίκτεν, τίκτ' ἔμ') [5] ἴσαις 2nd person sing. as Theocr. 14. 34 *E*, al. partcp. [6] Salm: mss πρὸς ἀνάκλιν' ἐρ.

points out in his writings that Sappho[1] and Alcaeus made comrades of their books.

Maximus of Tyre *Dissertations*: Socrates chides Xanthippè for weeping when he is about to die, and so does Sappho chide her daughter: 'No house that serveth the Muses hath room for grief, and so it ill-beseemeth this.'[2]

Palatine Anthology: Plato on Sappho: Some say there are nine Muses; but they should stop to think. Look at Sappho of Lesbos; she makes a tenth.

The Same: Nossis on herself: If you are bound for Mytilene, stranger, the city of fair dances which kindled the fierce flame of Sappho's lovelinesses,[3] go not away till you have told them that I was dear to the Muses, and a daughter of Locris, and that you know my name is Nossis.[4]

The Same: Dioscorides on Sappho of Mytilene, the lyric poetess, the wonder of lyric poetry: Sweetest of all love-pillows unto the burning young, sure am I that Pieria or ivied Helicon must honour thee, Sappho, along with the Muses, seeing that thy spirit is their spirit, thou Muse of Aeolian Erĕsus; or that Hymen God of Weddings hath thee with him when he standeth bright torch in hand over bridal beds,

[1] Acro says 'Anacreon' [2] this little poem is printed here because it proves with its context that S. died quietly at home: for her age at death cf. *fr.* 42 [3] or 'Graces,' the name of her book? cf. *A.P.* 9. 184 [4] see also *A.P.* 5. 132

ἢ Κινύρεω νέον ἔρνος ὀδυρομένῃ Ἀφροδίτῃ
σύνθρηνος μακάρων ἱερὸν ἄλσος ὁρῇς·
πάντῃ, πότνια, χαῖρε θεοῖς ἴσα· σὰς γὰρ ἀοιδὰς[1]
ἀθανάτων ἄγομεν[2] νῦν ἔτι θυγατέρας.

Anth. Pal. 4. 1 Μελεάγρου στέφανος·
Μοῦσα φίλα, τίνι τάνδε φέρεις πάγκαρπον ἀοιδάν;
ἢ τίς ὁ καὶ τεύξας ὑμνοθετᾶν στέφανον;
ἄνυσε μὲν Μελέαγρος, ἀριζάλῳ δὲ Διοκλεῖ
μναμόσυνον ταύταν ἐξεπόνησε χάριν,
πολλὰ μὲν ἐμπλέξας Ἀνύτης κρίνα, πολλὰ δὲ Μοιροῦς
λείρια, καὶ Σαπφοῦς βαιὰ μὲν ἀλλὰ ῥόδα . . .

Ibid. 7. 15 Ἀντιπάτρου εἰς τὴν αὐτήν·
Οὔνομά μευ Σαπφώ· τόσσον δ' ὑπερέσχον ἀοιδᾶν
θηλειᾶν, ἄνδρων ὅσσον ὁ Μαιονίδας.[3]

Ibid. 9. 66 Ἀντιπάτρου Σιδωνίου εἰς Σαπφὼ τὴν Μυτιληναίαν ἐγκωμιαστικόν·
Μναμοσύναν ἕλε θάμβος, ὅτ' ἔκλυε τᾶς μελιφώνου
Σαπφοῦς, μὴ δεκάταν Μοῦσαν ἔχουσι βροτοί.

Ibid. 9. 571 Ἀδέσποτον· εἰς τοὺς Ἐννέα Λυρικούς·
Ἔκλαγεν ἐκ Θηβῶν μέγα Πίνδαρος· ἔπνεε τερπνὰ
ἡδυμελεῖ φθόγγῳ μοῦσα Σιμωνίδεω·
λάμπε[4] Στησίχορός τε καὶ Ἴβυκος· ἦν γλυκὺς Ἀλκμάν·
λαρὰ δ' ἀπὸ στομάτων φθέγξατο Βακχυλίδης·

[1] Reiske-Tyrwhitt: mss θεοῖς γὰρ ἴσας ἀοιδὰς [2] Heck:

or Aphrodite with her when she bewails the fair young offspring of Cinÿras in the sacred grove of the Blest. Howsoe'er it be, I bid thee all hail, Great Lady, even as any God; for we still hold thy songs to be daughters of an Immortal.

Palatine Anthology: The Garland of Meleager:[1] To whom, dear Muse, bring you this song so rich in fruit? and who is the fashioner of this your garland of minstrels? It is the work of Meleager, and he hath made it to be a keepsake for the admired Diocles. Inwoven here is many a lily of Anytè's, many a white lily of Moero's, and of the flowers of Sappho few, but roses . . .

The Same: Antipater on Sappho: My name is Sappho, and my song surpasses the songs of women even as Homer's the songs of men.

The Same: Antipater of Sidon, encomium on Sappho of Mytilene: Memory was astonished when she heard the honey-voiced Sappho, wondering whether mankind possessed a tenth Muse.

The Same: Anonymous on the Nine Lyric Poets: Pindar of Thebes clanged amain; the Muse of Simonides breathed a joy of delicious-noted sound; Stesichorus and Ibycus rang clear; Alcman was sweet; and the lips of Bacchylides uttered pleasant

[1] poem introductory to M.'s collection of Greek 'Epigrams,' in which each poet's works are likened to a flower

---

mss ἀθανάτας ἔχομεν -ων -ων [3] mss ἀοιδὰν (-ῶν) θηλειᾶν (-ων), stone [4] mss λάμπει

Πειθὼ Ἀνακρείοντι συνέσπετο· ποικίλα δ' ηὔδα[1]
Ἀλκαῖος πυκνῇ Λέσβιος Αἰολίδι.[2]
ἀνδρῶν δ' οὐκ ἐνάτη Σαπφὼ πέλεν, ἀλλ' ἐρατειναῖς
ἐν Μούσαις δεκάτη Μοῦσα καταγράφεται.

Cat. 35. 16 . . . . . . Sapphica puella
Musa doctior.

Hor. *Od.* 4. 9. 11 . . . . . spirat adhuc amor
vivuntque commissi calores
Aeoliae fidibus puellae.

Id. *Ep.* 1. 19. 28
Temperat Archilochi Musam pede mascula Sappho.

Anth. Pal. 7. 16 Πινύτου εἰς Σαπφώ·
Ὀστέα μὲν καὶ κωφὸν ἔχει τάφος οὔνομα Σαπφοῦς·
αἱ δὲ σοφαὶ κείνης ῥήσιες ἀθάνατοι.

Ibid. 17 Τυλλίου Λαυρέα εἰς τὴν αὐτήν·
Αἰολικὸν παρὰ τύμβον ἰών, ξένε, μή με θανοῦσαν
τὰν Μυτιληναίαν ἔννεπ' ἀοιδοπόλον·
τόνδε γὰρ ἀνθρώπων ἔκαμον χέρες, ἔργα δὲ φωτῶν
ἐς ταχινὴν ἔρρει τοιάδε ληθεδόνα·
ἢν δέ με Μουσάων ἐτάσῃς χάριν, ὧν ἀφ' ἑκάστης
δαίμονος ἄνθος ἐμῇ θῆκα παρ' ἐννεάδι,
γνώσεαι ὡς Ἀΐδεω σκότον ἔκφυγον, οὐδέ τις ἔσται
τῆς λυρικῆς Σαπφοῦς νώνυμος ἠέλιος.

Plut. *Pyth. Or.* 6 'οὐχ ὁρᾷς,' εἶπεν, 'ὅσην χάριν ἔχει τὰ Σαπφικὰ μέλη κηλοῦντα καὶ καταθέλγοντα τοὺς ἀκροωμένους;'

[1] mss *αὐδᾷ* [2] *E e. g.* or *πτυκτῷ* 'book' cf. *πτυκτεῖον*?: mss *κυκνω* (*κύκνῳ*) Λ. *αἰολίδι*, *κύκνος* Λ. *Αἰολίσιν*

things; Anacreon was attended by Persuasion; and Lesbian Alcaeus spake varied notes unto the wise Aeolian dame.[1] But Sappho was not ninth among the men; rather is she written tenth in the list of the lovely Muses.

Catullus: . . . thou maiden more cultured than the Sapphic Muse.

Horace: . . . Still breathes the love, still lives the flame, which the Aeolian maid confided to her strings.

The Same: The virile Sappho shapes her Muse with the metre of Archilochus.

Palatine Anthology: Pinytus on Sappho: This tomb hath the bones and the dumb name of Sappho, but her wise utterances are immortal.

The Same: Tullius Laureas on the same: When you pass my Aeolian grave, stranger, call not the songstress of Mytilene dead. For 'tis true this was built by the hands of men, and such works of humankind sink swiftly into oblivion; yet if you ask after me for the sake of the holy Muses from each of whom I have taken a flower for my posy of nine,[2] you shall know that I have escaped the darkness of Death, and no sun shall ever be that keepeth not the name of the lyrist Sappho.

Plutarch *Pythian Oracles*: 'Do you not see,' he asked, 'what a charm the songs of Sappho have to enchant and bewitch the listener?'

[1] *or* in his Aeolian book? [2] her nine 'Books'

Plut. *Symp.* 7. 8. 2. [τίσι μάλιστα χρηστέον ἀκροάμασι παρὰ δεῖπνον]· ἡμεῖς γάρ ἐσμεν οἱ πρῶτοι τοῦ πράγματος εἰσαγομένου δυσχεράναντες ἐν Ῥώμῃ καὶ καθαψάμενοι τῶν ἀξιούντων Πλάτωνα διαγωγὴν ἐν οἴνῳ ποιεῖσθαι καὶ τῶν Πλάτωνος διαλόγων ἐπὶ τραγήμασι καὶ μύροις ἀκούειν διαπίνοντας· ὅτε καὶ Σαπφοῦς ἀναλεγομένης[1] καὶ τῶν Ἀνακρέοντος ἐγώ μοι δοκῶ καταθέσθαι τὸ ποτήριον αἰδούμενος.

Id. *Amat.* 18 ἄξιον δὲ Σαπφοῦς παρὰ ταῖς Μούσαις μνημονεῦσαι· τὸν μὲν γὰρ Ἡφαίστου παῖδα Ῥωμαῖοι Κᾶκον ἱστοροῦσι πῦρ καὶ φλόγας ἀφιέναι διὰ τοῦ στόματος ἔξω ῥεούσας· αὕτη δ' ἀληθῶς μεμειγμένα πυρὶ φθέγγεται καὶ διὰ τῶν μελῶν ἀναφέρει τὴν ἀπὸ τῆς καρδίας θερμότητα 'Μούσαις εὐφώνοις ἰωμένη τὸν ἔρωτα' κατὰ Φιλόξενον.

Id. *Symp.* 1. 5. 1 Πῶς εἴρηται τὸ 'ποιητὴν δ' ἄρα Ἔρως διδάσκει κἂν ἄμουσος ᾖ τὸ πρίν' ἐζητεῖτο παρὰ Σοσσίῳ, Σαπφικῶν τινῶν ᾀσθέντων . . .

Gell. 19. 3 Is (Antonius Julianus), ubi eduliis finis et poculis mox sermonibusque tempus fuit, desideravit exhiberi quos habere eum adulescentem sciebat, scitissimos utriusque sexus qui canerent voce et qui psallerent. Ac posteaquam introducti pueri puellaeque sunt, iucundum in modum Ἀνακρεόντεια pleraque et Sapphica et poetarum quoque recentium ἐλεγεῖα quaedam erotica dulcia et venusta cecinerunt.

[1] Wyttenbach: mss ἀναδεχ.

Plutarch *Dinner-Table Problems* [on what is the best sort of entertainment during dinner]: We were the first to fall foul of the new fashion when it came to Rome, and to deprecate the use of Plato as an after-dinner diversion and his dialogues as things to be listened to over the wine and the dessert. Why, even when they recite us Sappho or Anacreon I feel I must put down my cup for very shame.

The Same *Amatorius*: Sappho fully deserves to be counted among the Muses. The Romans tell how Cacus son of Vulcan sent forth fire and flames from his mouth; and Sappho utters words really mingled with fire, and gives vent through her song to the heat that consumes her heart, thus 'healing' in the words of Philoxenus 'the pain of love with the melodies of the Muse.'[1]

The Same *Dinner-Table Problems*: One day at Sossius's, after the singing of some songs of Sappho's, a discussion arose of the line 'Love makes a poet of the veriest boor.'

Aulus Gellius *Attic Nights*: When the chief courses were disposed of and the time was come for wine and conversation, Antonius expressed a wish that we might be favoured with a performance by the first-rate singers and players of both sexes whom he knew our young friend to have at command. In due time the young musicians were summoned, and proceeded to give delightful renderings not only of a number of the songs of Anacreon and Sappho but also of some charming erotic elegies, as they are called, of modern composers.

[1] see *fr.* 2

Luc. *Am.* 30 εἰ γυναιξὶν ἐκκλησία καὶ δικαστήρια καὶ πολιτικῶν πραγμάτων ἦν μετουσία, στρατηγὸς ἂν ἢ προστάτης ἐκεχειροτόνησο καί σε χαλκῶν ἀνδριάντων ἐν ταῖς ἀγοραῖς, ὦ Χαρίκλεις, ἐτίμων. σχεδὸν γὰρ οὐδὲ αὐταὶ περὶ αὐτῶν, ὁπόσαι προὔχειν κατὰ σοφίαν ἐδόκουν, εἴ τις αὐταῖς τὴν τοῦ λέγειν ἐξουσίαν ἐφῆκεν, οὕτω μετὰ σπουδῆς ἂν εἶπον, οὐχ ἡ Σπαρτιάταις ἀνθωπλισμένη Τελέσιλλα, δι' ἣν ἐν Ἄργει θεὸς ἀριθμεῖται γυναικῶν Ἄρης· οὐχὶ τὸ μελιχρὸν αὔχημα Λεσβίων Σαπφὼ καὶ ἡ τῆς Πυθαγορείου σοφίας θυγάτηρ Θεανώ· τάχα δ' οὐδὲ Περικλῆς οὕτως ἂν Ἀσπασίᾳ συνηγόρησεν.

Id. *Merc. Cond.* 36 καὶ γὰρ αὖ καὶ τόδε ὑπὸ τῶν γυναικῶν σπουδάζεται, τὸ εἶναί τινας αὐταῖς πεπαιδευμένους μισθοῦ ὑποτελεῖς ξυνόντας καὶ τῷ φορείῳ ἑπομένους· ἓν γάρ τι καὶ τοῦτο τῶν ἄλλων καλλωπισμάτων αὐταῖς δοκεῖ, ἢν λέγηται ὡς πεπαιδευμέναι τέ εἰσι καὶ φιλόσοφοι καὶ ποιοῦσιν ᾄσματα οὐ πολὺ τῆς Σαπφοῦς ἀποδέοντα.

Cic. Verr. 2. 4. 57 Nam Sappho, quae sublata de prytaneo est, dat tibi iustam excusationem, prope ut concedendum atque ignoscendum esse videatur. Silanionis opus tam perfectum, tam elegans, tam elaboratum, quisquam non modo privatus sed populus potius haberet, quam homo elegantissimus atque eruditissimus Verres? . . . atque haec Sappho sublata quantum desiderium sui reliquerit, dici vix potest. nam cum ipsa fuit egregie facta, tum

---

[1] this, with the ref. to Syracuse in the Parian Chronicle

Lucian *Loves*: If women had a parliament and law-courts and a share in politics, you would have been elected general or president, Charicles, and they would have put up bronze statues in your honour in the market-place. Indeed, had all the wisest and cleverest of their own sex been given the opportunity, they could hardly have proved better champions of its cause, not even Telesilla, who took arms against the Spartan nobles and thus caused Ares to be reckoned at Argos a woman's God, nor yet Sappho, the delicious glory of the Lesbians, or Theano the daughter of the wisdom of Pythagoras. Nay, Pericles could hardly have made out so good a case for Aspasia.

The Same *On Paid Companions*: For ladies make a great point of having persons of education in their pay, to attend upon them and accompany them when they go abroad in their chairs, since there is nothing on which they pride themselves more than that it should be said that they are ladies of culture and learning and write poems almost as good as Sappho's.

Cicero *Orations against Verres*: The Sappho which was stolen from the town-hall of Syracuse,[1] that, I admit, almost grants you extenuation. Could this work of Silanion, so perfect, so refined, so finished, be in fitter hands public or private than those of a man so refined and cultured as Verres? . . . And how sorely this stolen Sappho was missed is almost more than words can tell. Not only was the poetess exquisitely portrayed, but there was a world-famous

(above), is thought to be an indication that Sappho's Sicilian exile was spent at Syracuse

epigramma Graecum pernobile incisum habuit in basi, quod iste eruditus homo et Graeculus, qui haec subtiliter iudicat, qui solus intelligit, si unam litteram Graecam scisset, certe non reliquisset.[1] nunc enim, quod inscriptum est inani in basi, declarat quid fuerit et id ablatum indicat.

Dion. Hal. *Dem.* 40 ἡ δὲ μετὰ ταύτην (ἁρμονία) ἡ γλαφυρὰ καὶ θεατρικὴ καὶ τὸ κομψὸν αἱρουμένη πρὸ τοῦ σεμνοῦ τοιαύτη· ὀνομάτων αἰεὶ βούλεται λαμβάνειν τὰ λειότατα καὶ μαλακώτατα, τὴν εὐφωνίαν θηρωμένη καὶ τὴν εὐμέλειαν, ἐξ αὐτῶν δὲ τὸ ἡδύ. ἔπειτα οὐχ ὡς ἔτυχεν ἀξιοῖ ταῦτα τιθέναι οὐδὲ ἀπερισκέπτως συναρμόττειν θἄτερα τοῖς ἑτέροις, ἀλλὰ διακρίνουσα τὰ ποῖα τοῖς ποίοις παρατιθέμενα μουσικωτέρους ποιεῖν δυνήσεται τοὺς ἤχους, καὶ σκοποῦσα κατὰ ποῖον σχῆμα ληφθέντα χαριεστέρας ἀποτελέσει τὰς συζυγίας, οὕτως συναρμόττειν ἕκαστα πειρᾶται, πολλὴν σφόδρα ποιουμένη φροντίδα τοῦ συνέχεσθαι[2] καὶ συνηλεῖφθαι καὶ προπετεῖς ἁπάντων αὐτῶν εἶναι τὰς ἁρμονίας . . . τοιαῦτά τινά μοι καὶ ταύτης εἶναι φαίνεται χαρακτηριστικὰ τῆς ἁρμονίας. παραδείγματα δ' αὐτῆς ποιοῦμαι ποιητῶν μὲν Ἡσίοδόν τε καὶ Σαπφὼ καὶ Ἀνακρέοντα, τῶν δὲ πεζῇ λέξει χρησαμένων Ἰσοκράτην τε τὸν Ἀθηναῖον καὶ τοὺς ἐκείνῳ πλησιάσαντας.

Demetr. *Eloc.* 132 τὰ μὲν οὖν εἴδη τῶν χαρίτων τοσάδε καὶ τοιάδε. εἰσιν δὲ αἱ μὲν ἐν τοῖς πράγμασι χάριτες οἷον νυμφαῖοι κῆποι, ὑμέναιοι, ἔρωτες, ὅλη ἡ Σαπφοῦς ποίησις. τὰ γὰρ τοιαῦτα

[1] mss *sustulisset* which some edd. keep, reading *una* for *non*
[2] mss συνέξ.

Greek couplet inscribed upon the base, which this cultured Grecian who can really criticise such things, who is the only man who understands such things, would never have dreamt of leaving behind if he had known a single letter of the Greek alphabet. For the inscription on the empty base declares to-day what the statue was, thus proclaiming the theft.[1]

Dionysius of Halicarnassus[2] *Demosthenes*: Next comes the finished or decorative style, the style which makes for elegance rather than grandeur. In the first place it invariably prefers the smoothest and gentlest words, seeking euphony and melodiousness and their resultant charm. Secondly, it does not put its words just as they come or combine them without consideration, but first decides what elements will combine to give the most musical effect, and what arrangement will produce the most taking combinations, paying very great attention to the coherence of the parts and the perfection of the joinery. . . . Such appear to me to be the characteristics of this style. For examples of it I may mention, in poetry, Hesiod, Sappho, and Anacreon, and in prose, Isocrates the Athenian and his school.

Demetrius *on Style*: The forms, then, of literary charm are many and various. But charm may also reside in the subject. For instance, it may be the Gardens of the Nymphs, a wedding, a love-affair, in short the entire subject-matter of the poetry of Sappho. Such themes are charming even if treated

[1] Plin. *N.H.* 35, 34 mentions a picture of S. by Leon, on which (?) cf. *Anth. Plan.* 310; see also Tat. *adv. Gr.* 130
[2] see also *Comp.* 19. 23

κἂν ὑπὸ Ἱππώνακτος λέγηται, χαρίεντά ἐστι καὶ αὐτὸ ἱλαρὸν τὸ πρᾶγμα ἐξ ἑαυτοῦ· οὐδεὶς γὰρ ἂν ὑμέναιον ᾄδοι ὀργιζόμενος, οὐδὲ τὸν Ἔρωτα Ἐρινὺν ποιήσειεν τῇ ἑρμηνείᾳ ἢ Γίγαντα, οὐδὲ τὸ γελᾶν κλαίειν.

Him. *Or.* 1. 4 *Οὐκοῦν ὥρα καὶ ἡμῖν, ὦ παῖδες, ἐπεὶ καὶ τὰς ἡμετέρας καλοῦμεν Μούσας πρὸς γαμήλιον χόρον καὶ ἔρωτα, ἀνεῖναι τὴν ἁρμονίαν τὴν σύντονον, ἵν' ἅμα μετὰ παρθένων ἐπ' Ἀφροδίτῃ χορεύσωμεν. ὅτι δὲ μέγας ὁ κίνδυνος οὕτως ἁπαλὸν μέλος εὑρεῖν ὡς τὴν θεὸν ἀρέσαι τῷ μέλει, παρ' αὐτῶν ποιητῶν μανθάνειν ἔξεστιν, <ὧν> οἱ πλείους οἶμαι δεινοὶ τὰ ἐρωτικὰ γενόμενοι, κατὰ μὲν ἠϊθέους καὶ παρθένους ἐπιτολμώσαντες*[1] *τὴν Ἥραν ἔδειξαν, τὰ δὲ Ἀφροδίτης ὄργια μόνῃ παρῆκαν τῇ Λεσβίᾳ Σαπφοῖ καὶ ᾄδειν πρὸς λύραν καὶ ποιεῖν τὸν ἐπιθαλάμιον.*[2] *ἣ καὶ εἰσῆλθε μετὰ τοὺς ἀγῶνας εἰς θάλαμον, πλέκει παστάδα, τὸ λέχος στρώννυσι, ἀγείρει παρθένους <εἰς> νυμφεῖον, ἄγει καὶ Ἀφροδίτην ἐφ' ἅρματι χαρίτων καὶ χόρον Ἐρώτων συμπαίστορα· καὶ τῆς μὲν ὑακίνθῳ τὰς κόμας σφίγξασα, πλὴν ὅσαι μετώπῳ μερίζονται, τὰς λοιπὰς ταῖς αὔραις ἀφῆκεν ὑποκυμαίνειν ἢ πνεύσαιεν·*[3] *τῶν δὲ τὰ πτέρα καὶ τοὺς βοστρύχους χρυσῷ κοσμήσασα πρὸ τοῦ δίφρου σπεύδει πομπεύοντας καὶ δᾷδα κινοῦντας μετάρσιον.*

Anth. Pal. 9. 189 *ἄδηλον εἰς Σαπφὼ τὴν Μυτιληναίαν μελοποιόν·*

[1] mss *ἠιθέων κ. παρθένων ἐπιτολμῶσαν* [2] mss *θάλαμον*
[3] mss *εἰ πλήττοιεν*

by an Hipponax, the subject being pleasing in its nature. It is as impossible to sing a wedding-song in a rage, or make Love a Fury or a Giant by mere choice of expression, as it is to turn laughter into tears.

Himerius *Orations*: So it is time for us, my children, since we are summoning our Muses to marriage-dance and marriage-love, to relax the graveness of our music, so that we may the better trip it with the maidens in honour of Aphrodite. How hard it is to find a tune gentle enough to please the Goddess, we may judge from the poets themselves, most of whom, though past masters in love-poetry, went as bravely to the description of Hera as any boy or girl, but when it came to the rites of Aphrodite, left the song for the lyre and the making of the epithalamy entirely to Sappho, who when the contests[1] are over enters the chamber, weaves the bower, makes the bride-bed, gathers the maidens into the bride-chamber, and brings Aphrodite in her Grace-drawn car with a bevy of Loves to be her playfellows; and her she adorns with hyacinths about the hair, leaving all but what is parted by the brow to float free upon the wayward breeze, and them she decks with gold on wing and tress and makes to go on before the car and wave their torches on high.[2]

Palatine Anthology: Anonymous on Sappho the lyric poetess of Mytilene: Come, ye daughters of

[1] part of the ceremony apparently consisted of a mock contest of suitors [2] cf. Him. ap. Schenkl *Hermes* 1911. 421, Dion. Hal. *Rhet.* 247

Ἔλθετε πρὸς τέμενος ταυρώπιδος[1] ἀγλαὸν Ἥρης,
Λεσβίδες, ἁβρὰ ποδῶν βήμαθ' ἑλισσόμεναι,
ἔνθα καλὸν στήσεσθε[2] θεῇ χόρον· ὔμμι δ' ἀπάρξει
Σαπφὼ χρυσείην χερσὶν ἔχουσα λύρην.
ὄλβιαι ὀρχηθμοῦ πολυγηθέος· ἦ γλυκὺν ὕμνον
εἰσαΐειν αὐτῆς δόξετε Καλλιόπης.

Jul. *Ep.* 30 Ἀλυπίῳ· ἤδη μὲν ἐτύγχανον ἀνειμένος τῆς νόσου, τὴν γεωγραφίαν ὅτε ἀπέστειλας· οὐ μὴν ἔλαττον διὰ τοῦτο ἡδέως ἐδεξάμην τὸ παρὰ σου πινάκιον ἀποσταλέν. ἔχει γὰρ καὶ τὰ διαγράμματα τῶν πρόσθεν βελτίω, καὶ κατεμουσώσας αὐτὸ προσθεὶς τοὺς ἰάμβους, οὐ μάχην ἀείδοντας τὴν Βουπάλειον κατὰ τὸν Κυρηναῖον ποιητὴν, ἀλλ' οἵους ἡ καλὴ Σαπφῶ βούλεται τοῖς νόμοις ἁρμόττειν.

Paus. 1. 25. 1 . . . Ἀνακρέων ὁ Τήϊος, πρῶτος μετὰ Σαπφὼ τὴν Λεσβίαν τὰ πολλὰ ὧν ἔγραψεν ἐρωτικὰ ποιήσας.

Ath. 13. 605 e κἀγὼ δὲ κατὰ τὴν Ἐπικράτους Ἀντιλαΐδα
τἀρωτίκ' ἐκμεμάθηκα πάντα[3] παντελῶς
Σαπφοῦς, Μελήτου, Κλεομένους, Λαμυνθίου.

Ibid. 14. 639 a Κλέαρχος δὲ ἐν δευτέρῳ Ἐρωτικῶν τὰ ἐρωτικά φησιν ᾄσματα καὶ τὰ Λοκρικὰ καλούμενα οὐδὲν τῶν Σαπφοῦς καὶ Ἀνακρέοντος διαφέρειν.

[1] Heck. cf. Nonn. 9. 68 : mss γλαυκώπ. [2] mss στήσασθε
[3] mss ταῦτα

Lesbos, trip it delicately in the whirling measure on your way to the shining precinct of the bull-faced Hera, and there take up the fair dance unto the Goddess with Sappho for your leader golden lyre in hand. Happy ye in that delightsome round! ye shall think, for sure, that ye are hearing some sweet hymn of Calliopè herself.[1]

Julian *Letters*: To Alypius:—I was already recovered when I received the Geography, though your missive was none the less welcome for that. Not only are the maps in it better done, but you have given it a touch of literary distinction by prefixing the iambic motto—not such iambics as sing the fight with Bupalus, to adapt Callimachus,[2] but of the sort which the beautiful Sappho chooses to fit to her melodies.

Pausanias *Description of Greece*: . . . Anacreon of Teos, who was the first poet after Sappho to make love his principal theme.

Athenaeus *Doctors at Dinner*: I, too, to quote Epicrates' *Anti-Laïs* 'am letter-perfect in all the love-songs of Sappho, Meletus, Cleomenes, and Lamythius.'

The Same: Clearchus, in the second Book of his *Treatise on Love Poetry*, declares that the love-songs of Gnesippus and his *Locrian Ditties*, as they are called, are quite as good as Sappho's or Anacreon's.

[1] cf. *A.P.* 7. 407 (above) [2] *i.e.* the choliambics prefixed by Callim. to his *Iambics* referring to Hipponax' lampoons (in that metre) on Bupalus and containing the words φέρων ἴαμβον οὐ μάχην ἀείδοντα | τὴν Βουπάλειον, cf. *Ox. Pap.* 1011

Them. *Or.* 13. p. 170d . . . καὶ τὸ καλὸν δὲ αὐτὸ σὺν τῇ ἀληθείᾳ καλόν ἐστι, ψεῦδος δὲ οὐδὲν καλόν, οὔτε θωπεία οὔτε κολακεία. Σαπφοῖ μὲν γὰρ καὶ Ἀνακρέοντι συγχωροῦμεν ἀμέτρους εἶναι καὶ ὑπερμέτρους ἐν τοῖς ἐπαίνοις τῶν παιδικῶν· σωμάτων γὰρ ἤρων ἰδιωτικῶν ἰδιῶται καὶ οὐδεὶς κίνδυνος ἐπῆν εἰ χαυνωθεῖεν ὑπὸ τοῦ ἐπαίνου αὐτοῖς οἱ ἐρώμενοι. ἐνταῦθα δὲ βασιλικὸς μὲν ὁ ἔρως, βασιλικὸς δὲ ὁ ἐρώμενος . . .

Plut. *Mus.* 16 καὶ ἡ Μιξολύδιος (ἁρμονία) παθητική τίς ἐστι τραγῳδίαις ἁρμόζουσα. Ἀριστόξενος δέ φησι Σαπφὼ πρώτην εὕρασθαι τὴν Μιξολυδιστί, παρ' ἧς τοὺς τραγῳδοποιοὺς μαθεῖν.

Ath. 14. 635e καὶ τὴν Σαπφὼ δέ φησιν οὗτος (ὁ Μέναιχμος ὁ Σικυώνιος ἐν τοῖς Περὶ Τεχνιτῶν) . . . πρώτην χρήσασθαι τῇ πηκτίδι.

Ibid. 13. 599c Χαμαιλεὼν δὲ ἐν τῷ Περὶ Σαπφοῦς . . .

Suid. Δράκων Στρατονικεύς· γραμματικός . . . Περὶ τῶν Σαπφοῦς Μέτρων.

Phot. *Bibl.* ἀνεγνώθησαν ἐκλογαὶ διάφοροι ἐν βιβλίοις ιβ' Σωπάτρου σοφιστοῦ. συνείλεκται δὲ αὐτῷ τὸ βιβλίον ἐκ πολλῶν καὶ διαφόρων ἱστοριῶν καὶ γραμμάτων . . . ὁ δὲ δεύτερος (λόγος) ἔκ τε τῶν Σωτηρίδα Παμφίλης Ἐπιτομῶν πρώτου λόγου . . . καὶ ἐκ τῶν Ἀρτέμωνος τοῦ Μάγνητος τῶν Κατ' Ἀρετὴν Γυναιξὶ Πεπραγματευμένων Διηγημάτων, ἔτι δὲ καὶ ἐκ τῶν

---

[1] see also Ibid. 20. 36 [2] Gratian [3] ascribed however Ibid. 28 to Terpander [4] a kind of lyre played with the

Themistius *Orations*:[1] . . . And beauty itself is beautiful only when accompanied by truth, whereas no falsehood is beautiful, be it called cajolery or adulation. We may acquiesce in the unbounded—or shall I say excessive—praises given their beloved by Sappho and Anacreon, because both loved and lover were private individuals and there was no danger to be apprehended if their praises should turn the beloved head. But the love of which I speak now is Imperial, and so is the beloved.[2] . . .

Plutarch *On Music*: The Mixolydian 'mode' is particularly sensuous or emotional, suited to tragedy. According to Aristoxenus this mode was invented by Sappho, from whom it was taken by the writers of tragedy.[3]

Athenaeus *Doctors at Dinner*: Menaechmus of Sicyon in his *Treatise on Artists* declares that Sappho was the first to use the *pēctis*.[4]

The Same: Chamaeleon in his treatise *On Sappho*. . . .

Suidas *Lexicon*: Dracon of Stratoniceia:—A grammarian, the writer of books . . . *On the Metres of Sappho*.

Photius *Library*: Excellent selections were read from the twelve Books of Sopater the Sophist. The work is a compilation from many excellent histories and tracts. . . . The second Book includes passages from the first Book of the *Epitomes* of Pamphila daughter of Soteridas . . ., from Artemon the Magnesian's *Tales of Feminine Virtue*, and from the

fingers (Ibid. 635 b, d), confused by Suidas (above) with the πλῆκτρον or quill

Διογένους τοῦ Κυνικοῦ Ἀποφθεγμάτων . . . ἀλλά γε καὶ ἀπὸ ὀγδόου λόγου τῆς Σαπφοῦς.

Heph. 43 ἐπιχοριαμβικὸν μὲν οὖν τὸ Σαπφικὸν καλούμενον ἑνδεκασύλλαβον οἷον (*fr.* 1) . . . ἔστι δὲ καὶ παρ' Ἀλκαίῳ—καὶ ἄδηλον ὁποτέρου ἐστὶν εὕρημα, εἰ καὶ Σαπφικὸν καλεῖται.

Sch. Heph. 293. Cons. [π. διαφορῶν τοῦ ἡρωϊκοῦ]· Σαπφικὸν δέ ἐστι τὸ ἀρχόμενον ἀπὸ σπονδείου καὶ λῆγον εἰς σπονδεῖον οἷον (*Il.* 2. 1) . . .

Heph. 60 [π. ποιήματος]· κοινὰ δὲ (τὰ ποιήματα) ὅσα ὑπὸ συστήματος μὲν καταμετρεῖται, <τοῖς> αὐτο<ῖς>[1] δὲ τὸ σύστημα ἔχει πληρούμενον, οἷά ἐστι τὰ ἐν τῷ δευτέρῳ καὶ τρίτῳ Σαπφοῦς· ἐν οἷς καταμετρεῖται μὲν ὑπὸ διστιχίας αὐτὴ δὲ ἡ διστιχία ὁμοία ἐστί.[2]

ΣΑΠΦΟΥΣ ΜΕΛΩΝ

1a

Mus. Ital. Ant. Class. vi:

Ἀερίων ἐπέων ἄρχομαι ἀλλ' ὀνάτων.[3]

[1] *E* [2] see also Dion. Hal. *Comp.* 19, Dion Chr. *Or.* 2. 24
[3] *E*: vase ηεριων κ.τ.λ. see *C.Q.* 1922

---

[1] this seems to indicate the existence of an edition of S.'s works arranged not according to metre but according to

Obiter Dicta of Diogenes the Cynic . . ., and lastly from the eighth Book of Sappho.[1]

Hephaestion *Handbook of Metre*: First the epichoriambic, called the Sapphic eleven-syllable, as (fr. 1) . . . It occurs also in Alcaeus—and it is uncertain which of the two poets invented it, though it is called after Sappho.

Scholiast on the Same [on varieties of the heroic hexameter]: The Sapphic variety is the line which both begins and ends with a spondee, thus (*Iliad* 2. 1) . . .

Hephaestion *Handbook* [on poems]: Poems are called 'common' when they are formed of 'systems' or stanzas and have those systems all composed of lines in the same metre, as for instance the poems in the Second and Third Books of Sappho, in which the stanzas are of two lines and those lines similar.[2]

THE POEMS OF SAPPHO

1 a

Column i. of a book entitled Ἔπεα πτερόεντα or *Winged Words* held by Sappho in an Attic vase-picture c. 430 B.C.:[3]

The words I begin are words of air, but, for all that,
good to hear.

subject [2] see also for S.'s metres Heph. etc. Consbruch *passim*, Atil. Fort., Terent., Mar. Vict., Plot. [3] this introductory poem apparently stood first in S.'s own collection of her poems; cf. Jul. *Ep.* 30 quoted p. 176

Α′

1 εἰς Ἀφροδίτην

Dion. H. *Comp.* 23 ἡ δὲ γλαφυρὰ καὶ ἀνθηρὰ σύνθεσις . . . χαρακτῆρα τοιόνδε ἔχει· . . . ἀκόλουθον δ' ἂν εἴη καὶ τοὺς ἐν αὐτῇ πρωτεύσαντας καταριθμήσασθαι. ἐποποιῶν μὲν οὖν ἔμοιγε κάλλιστα τουτονὶ δοκεῖ τὸν χαρακτῆρα ἐξεργάσασθαι Ἡσίοδος, μελοποιῶν δὲ Σαπφώ, καὶ μετ' αὐτὴν Ἀνακρέων τε καὶ Σιμωνίδης· τραγῳδοποιῶν δὲ μόνος Εὐριπίδης· συγγραφέων δὲ ἀκριβῶς μὲν οὐδείς, μᾶλλον δὲ τῶν πολλῶν Ἔφορός τε καὶ Θεόπομπος, ῥητόρων τε Ἰσοκράτης. θήσω δὲ καὶ ταύτης παραδείγματα τῆς ἁρμονίας, ποιητῶν μὲν προχειρισάμενος Σαπφώ, ῥητόρων δὲ Ἰσοκράτην. ἄρξομαι δὲ ἀπὸ τῆς μελοποιοῦ·

Ποικιλόθρον' ἀθάνατ' Ἀφρόδιτα,
παῖ Δίος δολόπλοκα, λίσσομαί σε·[1]
μή μ' ἄσαισι μηδ' ὀνίαισι δάμνα,
πότνια, θῦμον,

5 ἀλλὰ τυίδ' ἔλθ', αἴ ποτα κἀτέροττα
τᾶς ἔμας αὔδως ἀΐοισα πήλυι
ἔκλυες, πάτρος δὲ δόμον λίποισα
χρύσιον ἦλθες

ἄρμ' ὐπασδεύξαισα, κάλω[2] δέ σ' ἆγον
10 ὤκεε στρούθω προτὶ γᾶν μέλαιναν[3]
πύκνα δίννεντε πτέρ' ἀπ' ὠράνω αἴθε-
ρος διὰ μέσσω,

[1] mss also ποικίλοφρον (less likely in view of δολόπλοκα): δολοπλόκα Choer. on Heph. 85 (251 Consb.) cf. 134: mss here δολοπλόκε [2] (9–11) dual Piccolomini -*E Proc. Camb. Philol. Soc.* 1920 [3] προτὶ γᾶν μέλαιναν *E* l.c.: mss περὶ γᾶς (Ald. πτέριγας) (τὰς) μελαίνας: apogr. Vict. π. γᾶν μέλαιναν

SAPPHO

Book I

1 To Aphrodite

Dionysius of Halicarnassus *Literary Composition*:[1] The finished and brilliant style of composition . . . . has the following characteristics: . . . . It would not be out of place for me to enumerate here the finest exponents of it. Among epic writers I should give the first place in this style to Hesiod, among lyrists to Sappho, with Anacreon and Simonides next to her; among tragic poets there is only one example, Euripides. Among historians, to be exact, there is none, but Ephorus and Theopompus show it more than most; among the orators I should choose Isocrates. I will now give illustrations of this style, taking Sappho to represent the poets and Isocrates the orators; and I will begin with the lyrist:

Aphrodite splendour-throned[2] immortal, wile-weaving child of Zeus, to thee is my prayer. Whelm not my heart, O Queen, with suffering and sorrow, but come hither I pray thee, if ever ere this thou hast heard and marked my voice afar, and stepping from thy Father's house harnessed a golden chariot, and the strong pinions of thy two swans[3] fair and swift, whirring from heaven through mid-sky, have

[1] cf. Heph. 83 with sch., Prisc. 1. 37, Hdn. 2. 948 Lentz, *E.M.* 485. 41, Ath. 9. 391 e, Hesych. ὠκέες στροῦθοι: used by Heph. to illustrate the metre, and hence to be regarded as the 1st ode of S.'s 1st Book in the (?) Alexandrian edition, which was entirely composed of poems in this metre
[2] prob. = 'sitting on a throne of inlaid wood or metal'
[3] cf. 172, Alc. 2.: not sparrows, see *Proc.* (opp.), Stat. *S.* 1. 2.

αἶψα δ' ἐξίκοντο· σὺ δ', ὦ μάκαιρα,
μειδιάσαισ' ἀθανάτῳ προσώπῳ
15 ἤρε' ὄττι δηὖτε πέπονθα, κὤττι
δηὖτε κάλημι,
κὤττ' ἔμῳ μάλιστα θέλω γένεσθαι
μαινόλᾳ θύμῳ· 'τίνα δηὖτε πείθω
καὶ σ' ἄγην ἐς Fὰν φιλότατα; τίς τ', ὦ
20 Ψάπφ', ἀδικήει;[1]
καὶ γὰρ αἰ φεύγει, ταχέως διώξει,
αἰ δὲ δῶρα μὴ δέκετ', ἀλλὰ δώσει,
αἰ δὲ μὴ φίλει, ταχέως φιλήσει
κωὐκ ἐθέλοισα·
25 ἔλθε μοι καὶ νῦν, χαλέπαν δὲ λῦσον
ἐκ μερίμναν, ὄσσα δέ μοι τέλεσσαι
θῦμος ἰμμέρρει, τέλεσον, σὺ δ' αὔτα
σύμμαχος ἔσσο.

ταύτης τῆς λέξεως ἡ εὐέπεια καὶ ἡ χάρις ἐν τῇ συνεχείᾳ καὶ λειότητι γέγονε τῶν ἁρμονιῶν. παράκειται γὰρ ἀλλήλοις τὰ ὀνόματα καὶ συνύφανται κατά τινας οἰκειότητας καὶ συζυγίας φυσικὰς τῶν γραμμάτων . . .

2

[Longin.] *Subl.* 10 οὐκοῦν ἐπειδὴ πᾶσι τοῖς πράγμασι φύσει συνεδρεύει τινὰ μόρια ταῖς ὕλαις συνυπάρχοντα, ἐξ ἀνάγκης γένοιτ' ἂν ἡμῖν ὕψους αἴτιον τὸ τῶν ἐμφερομένων ἐκλέγειν ἀεὶ τὰ καιριώτατα, καὶ ταῦτα τῇ πρὸς ἄλληλα ἐπισυνθέσει καθάπερ ἕν τι σῶμα ποιεῖν δύνασθαι· τὸ μὲν γὰρ τῇ ἐκλογῇ τὸν ἀκροατὴν τῶν λημμάτων, τὸ δὲ τῇ πυκνώσει τῶν ἐκλελεγμένων προσάγεται. οἷον ἡ Σαπφὼ τὰ συμβαίνοντα ταῖς ἐρωτικαῖς μανίαις παθήματα ἐκ τῶν παρεπομένων καὶ ἐκ τῆς ἀληθείας αὐτῆς ἑκάστοτε λαμβάνει. ποῦ δὲ τὴν ἀρετὴν ἀποδείκνυται; ὅτε τὰ ἄκρα αὐτῶν καὶ ὑπερτεταμένα δεινὴ <γίγνεται> καὶ ἐκλέξαι καὶ εἰς ἄλληλα συνδῆσαι·

[1] *E* (Ibid.): mss καὶ, και (not καί), or μαι (from above) corrected to και, then σαγήνεσαν, σαγηνεύσαν, σαγήν εσσαν, or σαγήνεσσαν κ.τ.λ.: σ' emph. τ' *E*: mss (cf. above) σ or omit

drawn thee towards the dark earth, and lo! were there; and thou, blest Lady, with a smile on that immortal face, didst gently ask what ailed me, and why I called, and what this wild heart would have done, and 'Whom shall I make to give thee room in her heart's love, who is it, Sappho, that does thee wrong? for even if she flees thee, she shall soon pursue; if she will not take thy gifts, she yet shall give; and if she loves not, soon love she shall, whether or no;'—

O come to me now as thou camest then, to assuage my sore trouble and do what my heart would fain have done, thyself my stay in battle.

The verbal beauty and the charm of this passage lie in the cohesion and smoothness of the joinery. Word follows word inwoven according to certain natural affinities and groupings of the letters . . .

2

[Longinus] *The Sublime*: Since everything is naturally accompanied by certain affixes or accidents coexistent with its substance, it follows that we should find the source of sublimity in the invariable choice of the most suitable ideas, and the power to make these a single whole by combining them together. The first attracts the listener by the choice of subject-matter, the second by the cohesion of the ideas we choose. Sappho, for instance, always expresses the emotions proper to love-madness by means of its actual and visible concomitants. If you ask where she displays her excellence, I reply that it is where she shows her skill, first in choosing, and then in combining, the best and the most marked of those concomitants. Compare this:

Φαίνεταί μοι κῆνος ἴσος θέοισιν
ἔμμεν ὤνηρ ὄττις ἐνάντιός τοι
ἰζάνει καὶ πλάσιον ἆδυ φωνεί-
σας ὐπακούει

5 καὶ γελαίσας ἰμμέροεν, τὸ δὴ 'μαν[1]
κάρζαν ἐν στήθεσσιν ἐπεπτόασεν·[2]
ὠς γὰρ ἔς τ' ἴδω, Βρόχε', ὤς με φώνας
οὖδεν ἔτ' ἴκει,[3]

ἀλλὰ κὰμ μὲν γλῶσσα ϝέαγε, λέπτον[4]
10 δ' αὔτικα χρῷ πῦρ ὐπαδεδρόμακεν,[5]
ὀππάτεσσι δ' οὖδεν ὄρημμ', ἐπιρρόμ-
βεισι δ' ἄκουαι,

ἀ δέ μ' ἴδρως κακχέεται,[6] τρόμος δὲ
παῖσαν ἄγρη, χλωροτέρα δὲ ποίας
15 ἔμμι, τεθνάκην δ' ὀλίγω 'πιδεύϝην[7]
φαίνομαι·—ἀλλὰ
πάντ<α νῦν τ>ολμάτε', ἐπεὶ πένησα.[8]

. . . .

οὐ θαυμάζεις, ὡς ὑπὸ τὸ αὐτὸ τὴν ψυχήν, τὸ σῶμα, τὰς ἀκοάς, τὴν γλῶσσαν, τὰς ὄψεις, τὴν χρόαν, πάνθ' ὡς ἀλλότρια διοιχόμενα ἐπιζητεῖ, καὶ καθ' ὑπεναντιώσεις ἅμα ψύχεται καίεται, ἀλογιστεῖ φρονεῖ, ἢ γὰρ φοβεῖται μὴ[9] παρ' ὀλίγον τεθνήκεν, ἵνα μὴ ἕν τι περὶ αὐτὴν πάθος φαίνηται, παθῶν δὲ σύνοδος; πάντα μὲν τοιαῦτα γίνεται περὶ τοὺς ἐρῶντας. ἡ λῆψις δ', ὡς ἔφην, τῶν ἄκρων καὶ ἡ εἰς ταὐτὸ συναίρεσις ἀπειργάσατο τὴν ἐξοχήν.

[1] Ahr: mss μὴ μὰν [2] Robortelli -*E* (*Camb. Philol. Soc. Proc.* 1920), cf. *E.M.* 407. 22: mss καρδίαν ἐν στήθεσσιν (-εσιν) ἐπτόασεν (corr. in one to ἐποπτόασεν) [3] *E* (Ibid.): mss ὡς γ. σἴδω βρόχεως (βροχέως) κ.τ.λ. [4] or γλῶσσ' ἐάγη ὃν δὲ λέπτον Ald. with Plut. [5] ᾱ perh. for αι = η cf. αἰμίονος

SAPPHO

It is to be a God, methinks, to sit before you and listen close by to the sweet accents and winning laughter which have made the heart in my breast beat so fast and high. When I look on you, Brocheo,[1] my speech comes short or fails me quite, I am tongue-tied[2]; in a moment a delicate fire has overrun my flesh, my eyes grow dim and my ears sing, the sweat runs down me and a trembling takes me altogether, till I am as green and pale as the grass,[3] and death itself seems not very far away;[4]—but now that I am poor, I must fain be content[5] . . . .

Is it not marvellous how she has recourse at once to spirit, body, hearing, tongue, sight, flesh, all as quite separate things, and by contraries both freezes and burns, raves and is sane, and indeed is afraid she is nearly dead, so that she expresses not one emotion but a concourse of emotions? Now all such things are characteristic of the lover, but it is the choice, as I said, of the best and the combination of them into a single whole, that has produced the excellence of the piece.[6]

[1] (*or* Brochea) dimin. of a compd. of βραχύς, cf. Catull. and see *Camb. Philol. Soc. Proc.* 1920 [2] the Greek is 'my tongue is broken up' [3] cf. *Macbeth* 1. 7 [4] the Greek words for swooning are mostly metaphors from dying [5] metaphorical ('beggars can't be choosers') and explained by the lost sequel; = 'if I cannot see you face to face I must fain be content with distant reverence' [6] cf. Plut. *Pr. in Virt.* 10, Cram. *A.P.* 1. 39, Plut. *Erot.* 18, *Demetr.* 38, Cram. *A.O.* 1. 208. 15, Sch. *Il.* 22. 2, Catull. 51

Wil. [6] Long. (cf. ψύχεται below) apparently read κὰδ δ' ἴδρως ψῦχρος χέεται: his mss ἐκ δὲ (ἐκαδε) μ' ἰδ. ψ. κακχέεται: but μοι is necessary and the above is quoted Cram. *A.O.* 1. 208 to show ἰδ. is fem. [7] *E* (Ibid.): mss πιδευσην, πιδευην, or πιδευκην [8] *E* (Ibid.): mss ἀ. παντόλματον ἐ. (ἐ. καὶ) πένητα [9] Heller-*E*: mss ἢ γὰρ φοβεῖται ἢ

3

Eust. 729. 20 (*Il.* 8. 555) ἰστέον δὲ ὅτι ἐν τῷ 'φαεινὴν ἀμφὶ σελήνην' οὐ τὴν πλησιφαῆ νοητέον καὶ πληροσελήνην· ἐν αὐτῇ γὰρ ἀμαυρά εἰσι τὰ ἄστρα ὡς ὑπεραυγαζόμενα, καθὰ καὶ ἡ Σαπφώ που φησίν·

Ἄστερες μὲν ἀμφὶ κάλαν σελάνναν
ἂψ ἀπυκρύπτοισι φάεννον εἶδος,
ὄπποτα πλήθοισα μάλιστα λάμπησ'
ἀργυρία γᾶν.[1]

4

Hermog. π. ἰδεῶν (*Rhet. Gr.* Walz 3. 315) [π. γλυκύτητος]· καὶ τὰς μὲν οὐκ αἰσχρὰς (τῶν ἡδονῶν) ἔστιν ἁπλῶς ἐκφράζειν, οἷον κάλλος χωρίου καὶ φυτείας διαφόραν καὶ ῥευμάτων ποικιλίαν καὶ ὅσα τοιαῦτα. ταῦτα γὰρ καὶ τῇ ὄψει προσβάλλει ἡδονὴν ὁρώμενα καὶ τῇ ἀκοῇ ὅτε ἐξαγγέλλει τις. ὥσπερ ἡ Σαπφώ·

. . . . . ἀμφὶ δ' ὔδωρ
ψῦχρον <ὤνεμος>[2] κελάδει δι' ὔσδων
μαλίνων, αἰθυσσομένων δὲ φύλλων
κῶμα κατάρρει·[3]

καὶ ὅσα πρὸ τούτων γε καὶ μετὰ ταῦτα εἴρηται.

5[4] εἰς Ἀφροδίτην

Str. 1. 40 εἰ δὲ Φοίνικας εἰπὼν ὀνομάζει (Ὅμηρος) καὶ Σιδωνίους τὴν μητρόπολιν αὐτῶν, σχήματι συνήθει χρῆται ὡς . . . "Ἴδην δ' ἴκανεν καὶ Γάργαρον" καὶ Σαπφώ·

Αἴ σε Κύπρος καὶ Πάφος ἢ Πάνορμος . . .[5]

[1] λάμπησ' ἀ. γ. (or ἄργυρα γαῖαν?) Blf. -*E*, cf. Jul. *Ep.* 19 Σ. ἡ καλὴ τὴν σελήνην ἀργυρέαν φησὶ καὶ διὰ τοῦτο τῶν ἄλλων ἀστέρων ἀποκρύπτειν τὴν ὄψιν: mss λάμπη γᾶν [2] *E* (wrongly read as ὢν ἐμὸς and then cut out) [3] mss καὶ αἰθ. κ.τ.λ. [4] cf. Men. *Rh. Gr.* Walz 9. 135 (π. τῶν κλητικῶν) ἅμα μὲν γὰρ ἐκ πολλῶν τόπων τοὺς θεοὺς ἐπικαλεῖν ἔξεστιν, ὡς παρὰ τῇ Σ. . . . πολλαχοῦ εὑρίσκομεν [5] αἴ *E*: mss ἥ καὶ *B*: mss ἤ.

3 [1]

Eustathius on the *Iliad*: Note that in the words 'around the bright moon' we are not to understand the moon at her full; for then the stars are dim because they are outshone, as Sappho somewhere says:

Around the fair moon the bright beauty of the stars is lost them when her silver light illumes the world at its fullest.

4 [2]

Hermogenes *Kinds of Style* [on sweetness or charm]: All clean and honest pleasures may be described simply, as for instance the beauty of a place, the variety of trees and plants, the sweet diversity of rivers and brooks. Such things give pleasure to the eye when they are seen, and to the ear when they are told of. Compare Sappho:

. . . And by the cool waterside the breeze rustles amid the apple-branches, and the quivering leaves shed lethargy;

and all that precedes and follows this.

5 To Aphrodite

Strabo *Geography*: Now if in speaking of the Phoenicians Homer [*Od.* 4. 83] adds mention of the inhabitants of their mother city Sidon, he is using a common form of speech, as for instance, ... and 'he came to Ida and Gargarus' (*Il.* 8. 48) and Sappho's line:

Whether thou [art at] Cyprus and Paphos or at Panormus . . .[3]

[1] cf. Cram. *A.P.* 3. 233, 31 [2] cf. *Sch.* Hermog. *Rh. Gr.* 7. 883 Walz (see *fr.* 150) [3] doubtless from an invocation to Cypris, perh. 1st line of 6

6 εἰς Ἀφροδίτην

Ath. 11. 463c διόπερ σινιοῦσι καὶ ἡμῖν ἐπὶ τὰς Διονυσικὰς ταύτας λαλιὰς 'οὐδὲ εἷς ἂν εὐλόγως φθονήσαι νοῦν ἔχων' κατὰ τοὺς Ἀλέξιδος Ταραντίνους· 'οἱ τῶν πέλας | οὐδέν' ἀδικοῦμεν οὐδέν . . . ὃς δ' ἂν πλεῖστα γελάσῃ καὶ πίῃ | καὶ τῆς Ἀφροδίτης ἀντιλάβηται τὸν χρόνον | τοῦτον ὃν ἀφεῖται, κἂν τύχῃ γ', ἐράνου τινος, | πανηγυρίσας ἥδιστ' ἀπῆλθεν οἴκαδε.' καὶ κατὰ τὴν καλὴν οὖν Σαπφώ·

. . . . . ἔλθε, Κύπρι,
χρυσίαισιν ἐν κυλίκεσσιν ἄβραις[1]
συμμεμείγμενον θαλίαισι νέκταρ
οἰνοχόεισα
5 τοῖς ἑταίροις τοίσδεσ' ἔμοις τε καὶ σοῖς.[2] . . .

7 [εἰς Ἀφροδίτην] and 8

Apoll. *Pron.* 81. 23 σοί· Ἀττικῶς. Ἴωνες, Αἰολεῖς ὁμοίως·

σοὶ δ' ἔγω λεύκας ἐπὶ δᾶμον αἶγος
<πίονα καύσω>,[3]

Σαπφώ· καὶ τὸ κατὰ πολὺ τὸ[4] διὰ τοῦ τ·

κἀπιλείψω τοι . . .

9 εἰς Ἀφροδίτην

Id. *Synt.* 350 (247) εἰσὶ τῆς εὐχῆς ἐπιρρήματα παραστατικά·

Αἴθ' ἔγω, χρυσοστέφαν' Ἀφρόδιτα,
τόνδε τὸν πάλον λαχόην[5] . . .

[1] Blf.: mss ἄβροις from l. 5 [2] τοίσδεσ(ι) *E*, cf. Alc. 126, *Od.* 10. 268, 21. 93, *Ad.* 51: mss τούτοισι τοῖς ἑταίροις ἔμοις τε καὶ σοῖς (masc. an adaptation? or see opp.) [3] Ahr: mss ἐπιδωμον αἶγ. [4] *E*: mss κατὰ ἀπόλυτον [5] *B*: mss -οίην

[1] either the gender of the 'comrades' is changed to suit the

6 To Aphrodite

Athenaeus *Doctors at Dinner*: This being so, our own gathering together like this for talk over the wine-cup, 'no man of sense could reasonably grudge us,' as Alexis says in *The Tarentines*; 'for we never do our neighbours injury . . .; and whoever laughs, drinks, loves, and, if he is lucky, dines out, the most during his time of liberty [from death and darkness], he goes home [to death] the best satisfied with his days at the festival.' And so let me say in the words of the beautiful Sappho:

. . . Come, Queen of Love, to bear round golden cups of nectar mingled with gentle cheer unto these comrades of thine and mine.[1]

7 [To Aphrodite] and 8

Apollonius *Pronouns*: Σοί 'to thee' Attic. Ionic and Aeolic have alike this form—compare Sappho:

and to thee I [will burn the rich] fat of a white goat,—[2]

and the form usual to them with τ, as

and I will leave behind for thee . . .

9[3] To Aphrodite

Id. *Syntax*: There are hortatory adverbs of supplication; compare:

O golden-wreathed Aphrodite, would that such a lot as this were mine . . . !

quoter's company (he proceeds 'for whose [masculine] benefit I must now remark'), or this was once the introductory poem to Sappho's *Epithalamia*, the masculine including the feminine: the nectar is of course metaphorical [2] white goats were sacrificed to Aphrodite Pandemos, cf. Luc. *D. Mer.* 7 [3] cf. Hdn. π. παθ. 2. 280. 31 Lentz, *E.M.* 558. 28

10

Apoll. *Pron.* 113. 8 Αἰολεῖς ἀμμέτερον καὶ ἄμμον καὶ ὔμμον καὶ σφόν. Σαπφώ·

αἴ με τιμίαν ἐπόησαν ἔργα
τὰ σφὰ δοῖσαι . . .

11

Aristid. 2. 508 π. Παραφθέγματος· οἶμαι δέ σε καὶ Σαπφοῦς ἀκηκοέναι πρός τινας τῶν εὐδαιμόνων δοκουσῶν εἶναι γυναικῶν μεγαλαυχουμένης καὶ λεγούσης ὡς αὐτὴν αἱ Μοῦσαι τῷ ὄντι ὀλβίαν τε καὶ ζηλωτὴν ἐποίησαν, καὶ ὡς οὐδ' ἀποθανούσης ἔσται λήθη.

e. g. ἀλλ' ἔμ' ὀλβίαν ἀδόλως ἔθηκαν
| χρύσιαι Μοῖσαι οὐδ' ἔμεθεν θανοίσας
| ἔσσεται λάθα. . . . . .

12

Ath. 13. 571 d καλοῦσι γοῦν καὶ αἱ ἐλεύθεραι γυναῖκες ἔτι καὶ νῦν καὶ αἱ παρθένοι τὰς συνήθεις καὶ φίλας ἑταίρας, ὡς ἡ Σαπφώ·

. . . τάδε νῦν ἐταίραις
ταῖς ἔμαισι τέρπνα κάλως ἀείσω.[1]

13

Et. Mag. 449. 36 ὥσπερ δαμῶ δαμείω, οὕτω θῶ θέω· καὶ παρὰ Σαπφοῖ·

. . . ὄττινας γὰρ
εὖ θέω, κῆνοι με μάλιστα σίννον-
ται . . .

[1] ἔμοισι Seid : mss ἔμαις

10

Apollonius *Pronouns*: Aeolic has the forms ἀμμέτερος and ἄμμος 'our,' ὔμμος 'your,' and σφός 'their'; compare Sappho:

. . . [the Muses?] who have made me honoured by the gift of their work

11

Aristides *On the Extemporised Addition*: I think you must have heard how Sappho, too, once boasted to certain women reputed prosperous, that the Muses had given herself the true happiness and good fortune, and even when she was dead she would not be forgotten.

e. g. But I have received true prosperity from the golden Muses, and when I die I shall not be forgot.

12[1]

Ath. *Doctors at Dinner*: For free women to this day and girls will call a friend or acquaintance 'hetaira' or 'comrade,' as Sappho does:

These songs I will sing right well to-day for the delight of my comrades.

13[2]

Etymologicum Magnum: As instead of δαμῶ 'subdue' we find δαμείω, so for θῶ 'do' we find θέω; compare Sappho:

For those I have done good to, do me the greatest wrong.

[1] prob. from a poem introductory to a 'Book' of poems to her friends [2] cf. Choer. 259; wrongly identified by Wil. with *Ox. Pap.* 1231. 16 (see 15 below)

14

Apoll. *Pron.* 98. 2 ὔμμιν Αἰολεῖς·

ταῖς κάλαισ' ὔμμιν <τὸ> νόημα τὦμον
οὐ διάμειπτον.[1]

15[2]

Oxyrh. Pap. 1231. 16. 11–12

. . . . . .
. . . .]λαν· ἔγων δ' ἔμ' αὔτᾳ
τοῦτο σύνοιδα·
. . . .

16

Sch. Pind. *P.* 1. 10 [Διὸς αἰετός]· πάνυ γὰρ διετύπωσεν, ὅτι δὴ ὁ ἀετὸς ἐπικαθήμενος τῷ τοῦ Διὸς σκήπτρῳ καὶ κατακηλούμενος ταῖς μουσικαῖς ᾠδαῖς εἰς ὕπνον κατάγεται, ἀμφοτέρας χαλάσας τὰς πτέρυγας . . . ἡ δὲ Σαπφὼ ἐπὶ τοῦ ἐναντίου ἐπὶ τῶν περιστερῶν·

ταῖσι <δὲ> ψαῦκρος μὲν ἔγεντο θῦμος,
πὰρ δ' ἴεισι τὰ πτέρα . . .[3]

17

Vet. Et. Mag. Miller p. 213 μελεδῶναι· αἱ τὰ μέλη ἔδουσαι φροντίδες . . . καὶ αἱ Αἰολεῖς σταλαγμὸν τὴν ὀδύνην λέγουσιν· Σαπφώ·

. . . . κατ' ἔμον στέλεγμον·[4]

ἀποστάζουσι γὰρ καὶ ῥέουσιν.

[1] τὸ Bek. [2] so Apoll. *Pron.* 51. 1, but 80. 10 ἔμ' αὔτᾳ τοῦτ' ἔγων συνόϊδα: Pap. εγωδεμ' [. . . | . . . .]νοιδα [3] ψαῦκρος Fick from Hesych: mss ψυχρὸς [4] σταλαγμόν and στελεγμόν mss; the first, the form the word would take in Attic, is necessary to the etymology; in the quotation perh.

14

Apollonius *Pronouns*: The form ὔμμιν 'to you' is used in Aeolic; compare:

Towards you pretty ones this mind of mine can never change.

15 [1]

From a Second-Century Papyrus:

. . . and as for me, I am conscious of this: . . .

16

Scholiast on Pindar: He has given a complete picture of the eagle sitting on Zeus's sceptre and lulled to sleep by the music, letting both his wings lie slack. . . . Sappho on the contrary says of the doves:

And as for them their heart grows light and they slacken the labour of their pinions.[2]

17 [3]

Old Etymologicum Magnum: μελεδῶναι 'cares': the thoughts which devour the limbs . . . and the Aeolic writers call pain σταλαγμός 'a dripping'; compare Sappho:

. . . because of my pain;

for they [pains or wounds ?] drip and flow.

[1] cf. Apoll. *Pron.* 51. 1, 80. 10 [2] when they reach the nest? [3] cf. *E.M.* 576. 22

στέλυγμον *E*, cf. ἀνασταλύζω and Hesych. ἀστυλάζει (sic) and ἀσταλυχεῖν

18

Et. Mag. 335. 38 τὰ γὰρ δύο σσ εἰς ζ τρέπουσιν οἱ Αἰολεῖς· τὸ γὰρ ἐπιπλήσσω ἐπιπλάζω· Σαπφώ·

τὸν δ' ἐπιπλάζοντ' ἄνοαι φέροιεν
καὶ μελέδωναι.[1]

19

Amm. π. διαφ. λέξ. 23 ἄρτι καὶ ἀρτίως διαφέρει. ἄρτι μὲν γάρ ἐστι χρονικὸν ἐπίρρημα, τὸ δ' ἀρτίως ἐπὶ τοῦ ἀπηρτισμένου ἔργου τελείως. ὥστε ἁμαρτάνει Σαπφὼ λέγουσα·

Ἀρτίως μ' ἀ χρυσοπέδιλλος αὔως
<ἦλθε καὶ>[2] . . .

ἀντὶ <τοῦ> χρονικοῦ ἐπιρρήματος.

20

Sch. Ar. *Pac.* 1174 διαφέρουσι γὰρ αἱ Λυδικαὶ βαφαί· . . . καὶ Σαπφώ·

. . . . . . πόδας δὲ
ποίκιλος μάσλης ἐπέτεννε, Λύδι-
ον κάλον ἔργον.[3]

21

Sch. Ap. Rh. 1. 727 ἐρευθήεσσα δὲ ἀντὶ τοῦ πυρρά, ὑπέρυθρος, καὶ ἔστι παρὰ τὸ Σαπφικόν·

. . . . παντοδάπαις μεμειγμένα χροΐαισιν

[1] Hdn. ἐπιπλάζοντες: ἄνοαι = ἄνοιαι (for pl. cf. μανίαι) *E*: mss ἄνεμοι, Hdn. ἂν ἐμοὶ: καὶ μελ. only in Hdn. [2] μ' ἀ Seid: mss μὲν ἁ: ἦλθε κ. *E*, cf. [Theocr.] *Meg.* 121 [3] mss μάσθλης but cf. Heph. 12: ἐπέτεννε *E*, cf. Eur. *Bacch.* 936: mss Sch. ἐκάλυπτε, Poll. εἶπε (both from corruption ἐπε)

18[1]

Etymologicum Magnum: For the Aeolic writers change double *s* to *z*; they write ἐπιπλήσσω ἐπιπλάζω; compare Sappho:

And as for him who blames [me?] may frenzies and cares seize upon him.

19

Ammonius *Words which Differ*: Ἄρτι differs from ἀρτίως; for ἄρτι is an adverb of time, whereas ἀρτίως is used of that which is fully completed; so Sappho is wrong in saying:

The golden-slippered Dawn had just [come] upon me [when] . . .;

instead of the adverb of time.

20[2]

Scholiast on Aristophanes *Peace*: For the Lydian dyes differ . . . and Sappho says:

. . . and a motley gown (?), a fair Lydian work, reached down to [her] feet.

21

Scholiast on Apollonius of Rhodes *Argonautica*: ἐρευθήεσσα [epithet of Jason's mantle] is used instead of πυρρά, ὑπέρυθρος, 'ruddy,' and is contrary to Sappho's description:

. . . mingled with all manner of colours

[1] cf. Hdn. 2. 929. 19 Lentz [2] cf. Poll. 7. 93, who says it was a sort of sandal, but the sing. and 'dyes' are against this

22

Apoll. *Pron.* 66. 3 ἐμέθεν· πυκνῶς αἱ χρήσεις παρὰ Αἰολεῦσιν· (124)·

. . . . ἤ τίν' ἄλλον
<μᾶλλον> ἀνθρώπων ἔμεθεν φίλησθα ;[1]

23

Et. Mag. 485. 45 οἱ Αἰολεῖς . . . ποθέω ποθήω, οἷον·

καὶ ποθήω καὶ μάομαι . . .

24 εἰς Ἑκάτην

Philod. π. εὐσεβ. 42 Gomperz [Σαπ]φὼ δὲ τ[ὴν θεὸν] χρυσοφαῆ θερ[άπαιν]αν Ἀφροδίτ[ης] (εἶναι λέγει).

e. g. Χρυσόφαες ὦ Ϝεκάτα θέραπνα
| Ἀφροδίτας . . .[2]

25

Mar. Plot. *Art. Gram.* 6. 516 Keil [de dactylico metro]: Adonium dimetrum dactylicum catalecticum a Sappho inventum est, unde etiam Sapphicum nuncupatur monoschematistum, semper enim dactylo et spondeo percutitur ;

ὦ τὸν Ἄδωνιν.

26

Apoll. *Pron.* 82. 16 [π. τῆς οἷ]: Αἰολεῖς σὺν τῷ Ϝ·

φαίνεταί Ϝοι κῆνος[3] . . . .

[1] μᾶλλον *B* [2] for ᾰ in voc. cf. Hfm. *Gr. Dial.* 2. 538: cf. Hesych. θεράπνη [3] probably not a variant of 2. 1

22

Apollonius *Pronouns*: ἔμεθεν 'of me'; it occurs frequently in the Aeolic writers; compare (124) and:

. . . O whom in all the world do you love better than me?

23[1]

Etymologicum Magnum: The Aeolic writers use . . . and ποθήω for ποθέω 'I long,' as:

. . . and I long and I yearn . . .

24 To Hecate

Philodemus *Piety*: And Sappho calls the Goddess (Hecate):

Aphrodite's golden-shining handmaid . . .

25

Marius Plotius *Art of Grammar* [on the Dactylic Metre]: The dactylic Adonian dimeter catalectic was invented by Sappho, and that is why it is also called the monoschematist Sapphic, for it is always composed of a dactyl and a spondee; compare:

Woe for Adonis!

26

Apollonius *Pronouns* [on οἷ 'to him']: Aeolic writers use the form with digamma (*w*):

That man seems to himself . . .

[1] also in *Et. Gud.* 294. 40

27

Apoll. *Pron.* 100. 5 ἄμμε Αἰολεῖς·

. . . ὄπταις ἄμμε . . . .

Σαπφὼ πρώτῳ.

28

Max. Tyr. 24 (18). 9 Διοτίμα λεγει, ὅτι θάλλει μὲν Ἔρως εὐπορῶν, ἀποθνήσκει δὲ ἀπορῶν· τοῦτο Σαπφὼ συλλαβοῦσα εἶπε γλυκύπικρον (81) καὶ

ἀλγεσίδωρον·

τὸν Ἔρωτα Σωκράτης σοφίστην λέγει, Σαπφὼ

μυθόπλοκον.

29

Jul. *Ep.* 18 ἀλλ' εἰς αὐτοὺς ἂν τῶν ὑμετέρων ὁρῶν τοὺς πρόποδας ἔπτην, ἵνα σε, τὸ μέλημα τοὐμόν, ὥς φησιν ἡ Σαπφώ, περιπτύξωμαι.

e.g. . . . . ὤς τε, μέλημα τὦμον,
| περπτύγω[1] . . .

30

Philostr. *Im.* 2. 1 τοσοῦτον ἁμιλλῶνται (αἱ παρθένοι) ῥοδοπήχεις καὶ ἑλικώπιδες καὶ καλλιπάρῃοι καὶ μελίφωνοι, Σαπφοῦς τοῦτο δὴ τὸ ἡδὺ πρόσφθεγμα.

Aristaen. 1. 10 πρὸ τῆς παστάδος τὸν ὑμέναιον ᾖδον αἱ μουσικώτεραι τῶν παρθένων καὶ μειλιχοφωνότεραι,[2] τοῦτο δὴ Σαπφοῦς τὸ ἥδιστον φθέγμα.

e.g. . . . . παρθένοισι
| μελλιχοφώναις[3]

[1] perh. imitated by Bion 1. 44 [2] *E*: mss -φωνοι [3] so *E*: Ar. prob. found the more easily corruptible μελλιχοφ. in his copy of Phil.

27

Apollonius *Pronouns*: Ἄμμε, 'us' or 'me,' is used in Aeolic; compare:

. . . you burn me . . .;

Sappho in her first Book.

28

Maximus of Tyre *Dissertations*: Diotima says (in Plato's *Symposium*) that Love flourishes when he has plenty and dies when he is in want; Sappho, putting these characteristics together, called him bitter-sweet (81) and

giver of pain.[1]

Socrates calls love sophistical, Sappho a

weaver of tales.

29

Julian *Letter to Eugenius*: . . . but I should fly to the very foot of your mountains

to embrace you, my beloved,

as Sappho says.

30

Philostratus *Pictures*: The maidens so vied with one another, rose-armed, saucy-eyed, fair-cheeked, honey-voiced (?) —this is Sappho's delightful epithet.

Aristaenetus *Letters*: Before the bride-chamber rang out the wedding-song from such of the maidens as were the more musical and gentle-voiced[2]—this is Sappho's most delightful word.

e. g. . . . to gentle-voiced maidens

[1] cf. *fr.* 42 [2] Ar. is prob. imitating Phil., in whose mss 'honey-voiced' is prob. a mistake

31 εἰς Ἔρωτα

Sch. Ap. Rh. 3. 26 [παιδὶ ἐῷ, *i. e.* Κύπριδος]· Ἀπολλώνιος μὲν Ἀφροδίτης τὸν Ἔρωτα γενεαλογεῖ, Σαπφὼ δὲ Γῆς καὶ Οὐράνου. Sch. Theocr. 13. 2 [ᾧτινι τοῦτο θεῶν ποκα τέκνον ἔγεντο]· ἀμφιβάλλει τίνος υἱὸν εἴπῃ τὸν Ἔρωτα· Ἡσίοδος μὲν γὰρ . . . Σαπφὼ Ἀφροδίτης <ἢ Γῆς> [1] καὶ Οὐράνου. Paus. 9. 27. 2 Ἡσίοδον δὲ . . . οἶδα γράψαντα ὡς Χάος πρῶτον, ἐπὶ δὲ αὐτῷ Γῆ τε καὶ Τάρταρος καὶ Ἔρως γένοιτο. Σαπφὼ δὲ ἡ Λεσβία πολλά τε καὶ οὐχ ὁμολογοῦντα ἀλλήλοις ἐς Ἔρωτα ᾖσε.

e. g. Φίλτατον Γαίας γένος Ὀρράνω τε

32 εἰς Ἕσπερον

Him. *Or.* 13. 9 ἀστὴρ οἶμαι σύ τις ἑσπέριος,

Ἀστέρων πάντων ὁ κάλιστος [2] . . .·

Σαπφοῦς τοῦτο δὴ τὸ εἰς Ἕσπερον ᾆσμα.

33 [εἰς Πειθώ]

Sch. Hes. *Op.* 73 [πότνια Πειθώ]· Σαπφὼ δέ φησι τὴν Πειθὼ Ἀφροδίτης θυγατέρα.

e. g. Ὦ γένος θελξίμβροτον Ἀφροδίτας

34

Berl. Klassikertexte 5 P 5006

. . . .]θε θῦμον
. . . .]μι πάμπαν
. . . .] δύνᾱμαι
. . . .]
. . . .]ας κεν ἦ μοι
. . . .]ς ἀντιλάμπην

31 To Love

Scholiast on Apollonius of Rhodes *Argonautica* 3. 26 ['her son']: Apollonius makes Love the son of Aphrodite, but Sappho of Earth and Heaven.

Scholiast on Theocritus 13. 2 ['from what God soever sprung']: He is doubtful of whom to call Love the son; for Hesiod . . . and Sappho, of Aphrodite or of Earth and Heaven.

Pausanias *Description of Greece*: Hesiod I know has made Chaos the first creation, and then Earth and Tartarus and Love. And in the poems of Sappho the Lesbian there are many mutually inconsistent sayings about Love.

e.g. Dearest Offspring of Earth and Heaven

32[1] To Hesperus

Himerius *Declamations*: You must be as it were an evening star,

Fairest of all the stars that shine,

as Sappho says in her Ode to Hesperus.

33 [To Persuasion]

Scholiast on Hesiod *Works and Days*: ['queenly Persuasion']: Sappho calls Persuasion the daughter of Aphrodite.

e.g. Man-beguiling daughter of Aphrodite

34

From a Seventh-Century Manuscript:

. . . . heart . . . . . altogether . . . . . [if]
I can . . . . shall be to me . . . . shine back

[1] cf. Him. 3. 17

---

[1] Wil. [2] *B*: mss κάλλιστος

. . . . . . κά]λον πρόσωπον
. . . .]
. . . . ἐ]γχροΐσθεις
. . . .]΄[. .]ρος

35 [πρὸς Χάραξον]

Berl. Klassikertexte 5 P 5006 verso + *Oxyrh. Pap.* 424 [1]

. . .]δώσην.
[αἰ κλ]ύτων μέν τ' ἐπ[πότεαι πεδ' ἄνδρων]
[κωὐ κ]άλων κἄσλων, ἐ[νέπ.εις δὲ χαίρην]
[τοὶς φι]΄λοις, λύπης τέ μ[ε σοὶ γένεσθαι]
5 [φαὶς ἔ]μ' ὄνειδος,
[ἦτορ] οἰδήσαις, ἐπὶ τα̣[ῦτ' ἀρέσκεο]
[καρδι]΄αν· ἄσαιο· τὸ γὰρ ν̣[όημα]
[τὤ]μον οὐκ οὕτω μ[αλάκως χόλα̣ παί-]
[δων] διάκηται·
10 [ἀλλὰ] μὴ δο̣αζε· [γέροντας ὄρνῑς]
[οὐκ ἄγρη βρό]χις· συνίημ[' ἔγω σε]
[οἶ πρὶν ἐσπό]λ̣ης [2] κακότατο[ς, οἴῳ]
[δ' ἀντετέθη]μεν
[δαΐῳ. σὺ δ' ὦ]ν ἀτέραις με[μήλων]
15 [λῳόνων τίθ]η φρένας· εὔ[κολον γὰρ]
[νῶν τράφοισ]α τοὶς μάκα[ρας σάφ' οἶδ' ἔ-]
[μοι παρέοντας.] [3]

36 εἰς Νηρηΐδας

Ox. Pap. 7

[Χρύσιαι] [4] Νηρήϊδες, ἀβλάβη[ν μοι]
[τὸν κασί]γνητον δότε τυίδ' ἴκεσθα[ι,]

[1] identification due to E. Lobel [2] i.e. ἐστάλης [3] restored by Blass, Buecheler, *B*, and *E*; cf. *C.R.* 1909, 1921 [4] epithet uncertain ; Κύπρι καὶ is too long

. . . . . . fair face . . . . en-grained . . .

35[1] [To Charaxus]

From the reverse of the same Manuscript and a Third-Century Papyrus

. . . will give. If you hover about the notable rather than the good and noble, and bid your friends go their ways, and grieve me by saying in your swelling pride that I, forsooth, am become a reproach to you, at such things as these you may rejoice your heart. Feed your fill. For as for me, my mind is not so softly disposed to the anger of a child. But make no mistake in this; the snare never catches the old bird; I know what was the depth of your knavery before, and of what sort is the foe I am opposed to. Be you better advised then, and change your heart; for well I know that being of a gentle disposition I have the Gods on my side.

36[2] To the Nereïds

From a Third-Century Papyrus:

Golden Nereïds, grant me I pray my brother's safe return, and that the true desires of his heart

[1] prob. a letter to her erring brother Charaxus [2] prob. a complete letter to the same (handed to him on his return from Egypt?) asking reconciliation

[κἂ μὲν] ᾧ θύμῳ κε θέλη γένεσθαι,
[ταῦτα τε]λέσθην·[1]

5 [ὄσσα δὲ πρ]όσθ' ἄμβροτε, πάντα λῦσα[ι,]
[καὶ φίλοι]σι Ϝοῖσι χάραν γένεσθαι
[καὶ δύαν ἔ]χθροισι· γένοιτο δ' ἄμμι
[δύσκλεα μ]ήδεις.

[τὰν κασιγ]νήταν δὲ θέλοι πόησθα[ι]
10 [ἔμμορον] τίμας·[2] ὀνίαν δὲ λύγραν
[καὶ λόγοις] ὄτοισι πάροιθ' ἀχεύων
[ἄμμον ἐδά]μνα

[κῆρ ὄνειδο]ς εἰσαΐων τό κ' ἐν χρῷ
[κέρρεν,[3] ἀλ]λ' ἐπ' ἀγ[λαΐ]ᾳ πολίταν
15 [ἀββάλην ἄ]λλως, [ὄτα] νῆ κε δαῦτ' οὖ-
[δεν διὰ μά]κρω·

[καὶ συνάορ]ον, αἴ κ[ε θέλη, ἀξίοι]σι
[ἐν λέχεσσ' ἔ]χην·[4] σὺ [δέ], κύνν[' ἔ]ρε[μ]να,[5]
[ρῖνα πρὸς γάᾳ] θεμ[έν]α κακάν[θην][6]
20 [ἄλλα πεδάγρ]η.[7]

37[8] [πρὸς Χάραξον]

Ox. Pap. 1231. 1. i. (α)

. . . Κύπρι, καί σε πι[κροτέρ]αν ἔπευρε·
10 οἰ δὲ καυχάσαντο τόδ' ἐννέ[ποντες·]
'Δωρίχα τὸ δεύτερον ὠς πόθε[ννον]
[εἰς] ἔρον ἦλθε.'

[1] or κῶσα μὲ]ν [2] replacement of fibre now makes θέλοι certain [3] Bell now admits]ς as poss., and rejects]λ [4] or ἀξίαισι ἐν κόραις εὔρην [5] *E*, for κύν-ια cf. Κύννα Hesych., Ar. *Eq.* 765 and for single ν in P. ὤρανος for ὄρρανος κ.τ.λ.: Bell agrees κυν[is poss. [6] for flattened accent cf. χάραν above [7] restored by Blass, Diels, Jurenka, Smyth, Wil, *E*; cf. *C.Q.* '09. 249, *C.R.* '20. 4, Bell ibid. 63, *Journ. Eg. Arch.*

shall be accomplished, and putting away his former errors he shall become a delight to his friends and a grief to his enemies; and may our house be disgraced of no man. And may he be willing to bring honour to his sister; and the sore pain and the words wherewith, in bitter resentment of a taunt that must have cut to the quick, he sought ere he departed to overwhelm my heart,—O, when return he does on some near day, may he choose amid his fellow-townsmen's mirth[1] to cast them clean away, and to have a mate, if he desire one, in wedlock due and worthy;[2] and as for thee, thou black and baleful she-dog,[3] thou mayst set that evil snout to the ground and go a-hunting other prey.

37 [To Charaxus]

From a Second-Century Papyrus:

. . . O Cypris, and he found thee more bitter. And the others, they boasted loud and said: 'What a delightful love-match hath Doricha made this second time!'[3]

[1] at a feast of welcome? [2] *or* find a mate . . . among worthy maids [3] Doricha or Rhodopis a famous courtesan beloved by S.'s brother Charaxus in Egypt; see p. 149

'21. 88 Lobel *C.Q.* '21. 164 [8] 1–8 fragmentary, containing μάκαιρα (1), [ἄμ]βροτε (5): 9–10 Wil, 11–12 Hunt

38 [1] πρὸς Ἀνακτορίαν

Ox. Pap. 1231. 1. i. (β)

Οἰ μὲν ἰππήων στρότον οἰ δὲ πέσδων
οἰ δὲ νάων φαῖσ' ἐπὶ γᾶν μέλαιναν
ἔμμεναι κάλιστον· ἔγω δὲ κῆν' ὄτ-
τω τις ἔραται.

5 πάγχυ δ' εὔμαρες σύνετον πόησαι
πάντι τοῦτ'· ἀ γὰρ πόλυ περσκόπεισα
κάλλος ἀνθρώπων Ἐλένα τὸν ἄνδρα
[κρίννε κάλ]ιστον

[ὃς τὸ πὰν] σέβας Τροΐας ὄλεσσε,
10 [κωὐδὲ πα]ῖδος οὐδὲ φίλων τοκήων
[μᾶλλον] ἐμνάσθη, ἀλλὰ παράγαγ' αὔταν
[πῆλε φίλει]σαν

[Ὦρος· εὔκ]αμπτον γὰρ [ἀεὶ τὸ θῆλυ]
[αἴ κέ] τις κούφως τ[ὸ πάρον ν]οήσῃ·
15 [ἄμ]με νυν, Ϝανακτορί[α, τὺ] μέμναι-
[σ' οὐ] παρεοίσαις,[2]

[τᾶ]ς κε βολλοίμαν ἔρατόν τε βᾶμα
κἀμάρυγμα λάμπρον ἴδην προσώπω
ἢ τὰ Λύδων ἄρματα κἀν ὄπλοισι
20 [πεσδομ]άχεντας·

[εὖ μὲν ἴδ]μεν οὐ δύνατον γένεσθαι
e. g. [λῷστ'] ὂν ἀνθρώποις· πεδέχην δ' ἄρασθαι
[τῶν πέδηχόν ἐστι βρότοισι λῷον]
[ἢ λελάθεσθαι.]

[1] restored by Hunt, Rackham, Wil, and *E* cf. *C.R.* 1914. 73, 1919. 125 [2] P παρεοισας

38 To Anactoria[1]

From a Second-Century Papyrus:

The fairest thing in all the world some say is a host of foot, and some again a navy of ships, but to me 'tis the heart's belovèd. And 'tis easy to make this understood by any. Though Helen surveyed much mortal beauty, she chose for most beautiful the destroyer of all the honour of Troy, and thought not so much either of child or parent dear, but was led astray by Love to bestow her heart afar; for woman is ever easy to be bent when she thinks lightly of what is near and dear. See to it then that you remember us Anactoria, now that we[2] are parted from one of whom I would rather the sweet sound of her footfall and the sight of the brightness of her beaming face than all the chariots and armoured footmen of Lydia. I know that in this world man cannot have the best; yet to wish that one had a share [in what was once shared is better than to forget it.][3]

[1] a complete letter to Anactoria who has apparently gone with a soldier husband to Lydia, cf. 86 [2] S. and Atthis? [3] ref. to the old friendship between her and S.

39

Ox. Pap. 1231. 1. ii (α)

. . . τ' ἐξ ἀδοκήτω.

40[1] [εἰς Ἥραν]

(β)

Πλάσιον δή μ[οι κατ' ὄναρ παρείη,]
πότνι' Ἥρα, σὰ χ[αρίεσσα μόρφα,]
τὰν ἀράταν Ἀτρ[έϊδαι Ϝίδον κλῆ-]
τοι βασίληες
5 ἐκτελέσσαντες [Τροΐας ὄλεθρον]·
πρῶτα μὲν πα[ρ' ὠκυρόω Σκαμάνδρω]
τυίδ' ἀπορμάθε[ντες ἐπ' οἶκον ἴκην]
οὐκ ἐδύναντο,
πρὶν σὲ καὶ Δί' ἀντ[ιάσαι μέγιστον]
10 καὶ Θυώνας ἰμμ[ερόεντα παῖδα.]
e. g. νῦν δὲ κ[ἄγω, πότνια, λίσσομαί σε]
κὰτ τὸ πά[ροιθεν]
ἄγνα καὶ κά[λ' ἐν Μυτιλανάαισι]
[π]αρθ[ένοις με δρᾶν πάλιν, αἰς χορεύην]
15 [ἀ]μφὶ σ[αῖσι πόλλ' ἐδίδαξ' ἐόρταις]
[πόλλα τ' ἀείδην.]
[ὤς τε νᾶας Ἀτρέϊδαι σὺν ὔμμι]
ἆραν Ἰλ[ίω, κέλομαί σε κἄμοι]
ἔμμεν[αι πρὸς οἶκον ἀπυπλεόισᾳ, Ἥ]ρ'
20 ἤπι', [ἄρωγον.]

[1] cf. *Pap. della Soc. ital.* 2. 123: 1–10 restored by Wil. and *E*: 11–20 by *E e. g.* cf. *A.P.* 9. 189 above (p. 174)

39

From a Second-Century Papyrus:

. . . unexpectedly.

40 [To Hera]

From the Same and another of the Third Century:

Make stand beside me in a dream, great Hera, the beauteous shape that appeared in answer to the prayer of the famous kings of Atreus' seed when they had made an end of the overthrow of Troy. At first when they put forth hither from Scamander's swift flood, they could not win home, but ere that could be, were fain to make prayer to thee and to mighty Zeus and to Thyone's lovely child.[1] So now *e.g.* pray I, O Lady, that of thy grace I may do again, as of old, things pure and beautiful among the maids of Mytilene, whom I have so often taught to dance and to sing upon thy feast-days; and even as Atreus' seed by grace of thee and thy fellow-Gods did put out then from Ilium, so I beseech thee, gentle Hera, aid thou now this homeward voyage of mine.

[1] the latter half is very tentatively restored on the supposition that S. writes this before embarking to return to Mytilene from Syracuse on hearing of the amnesty

41[1]

Ox. Pap. 1231. 9

e.g. [ἐν θυέλλαισι ζαφ]έλοισι ναῦται
[ἐκφοβήθεντες] μεγάλαις ἀήται[ς]
[ἄββαλον τὰ φόρτι]α κἀπὶ χέρσω
[πλοῖον ὄκελλαν·]

5 [μὴ μάλιστ' ἔγωγ' ἀ]'μοθεν πλέοιμ[ι]
[χειμάσαντος, μη]δὲ τὰ φόρτι' εἴκ[ᾱ]
[ἐς βάθηα πόντο]ν ἄτιμ' ἐπείκη
[πάντα βάλοιμι·]

[αἰ δε Νήρηϊ προ]ρέοντι πόμπᾳ
10 [ἐννάλῳ τἄμ' ἐξέσετ]αι δέκε[σθαι]
[φόρτι' . . . .]

42[2]

Ibid. 10

. . . [αἰ δέ μοι γάλακτο]ς ἐπάβολ' ἦσ[κε]
[τωὔθατ' ἢ παίδω]ν δόλοφυν[3] [ποήσ]ει
[ἀρμένα, τότ' οὐ] τρομέροις πρ[ὸς]ἄλλα
[λέκτρα κε πόσσι]

5 [ἠρχόμαν· νῦν δὲ] χρόα γῆρας ἤδη
[μυρίαν ἄμμον ρύτι]ν ἀμφιβάσκει,
[κωὐ πρὸς ἄμμ' Ἔρο]ς πέταται διώκων
[ἀλγεσίδωρος.[4]]

. . . .]τᾶς ἀγαύας
10 . . . .]μα· λάβοισα
. . . .]ἄεισον ἄμμι
τὰν ἰόκολπον[5]

. . . .

41

From a Second-Century Papyrus:

e.g. When tempests rage, the mariner, for fear of the great blasts of the wind, doth cast his cargo overboard and drive his vessel ashore; as for me, I pray I may be bound nowhither in time of storm,[1] nor be fain to cast all my cargo, precious or not, into the deep; but if so be it should fall to Nereus in his flowing pageant of the sea to receive the gift of my goods. . . .

42

From the Same:

. . . If my paps could still give suck and my womb were able to bear children, then would I come to another marriage-bed with unfaltering feet; but nay, age now maketh a thousand wrinkles to go upon my flesh, and Love is in no haste to fly to me with his gift of pain.— . . . . . . of the noble . . . taking . . . O sing us the praises of her of the violet-sweet breast. . . .[2]

[1] cf. Theocr. 9. 10. [2] this mutilated sentence does not necessarily belong to the same poem

---

[1] *E e.g.* cf. *C.R.* 1916. 99: preceded by 7 fragmentary lines not necessarily part of the same poem [2] restored by *E*, cf. *C.R.* 1919. 126 [3] = δελφύς, cf. κίνδυν, Φόρκυν [4] ἀλγεσίδωρος: from 28 [5] the last two words from Apoll. *Pron.* 384 B (see Alc. 138)

43[1]

Ox. Pap. 1231. 13

. . . [αἶσ' ἔγων ἔφ]αν· ' Ἄγα[ναι γύναικες,]
[οἶα μ]εμνάσεσθ' ἄ[ϊ μέχρι γήρᾱς]
[ὄττιν' ἄ]μμες ἐν νεό[τατι λάμπρᾳ]
[σῡνε]πόημμεν·

5 [ἄγνα μ]ὲν γὰρ καὶ κά[λα πόλλ' ἐν αὔτᾳ]
[δράσα]μεν· πόλι[ν δ' ἀπυλιππανοίσᾱν]
[σφῶϊν] ὀ[ξ]είαις δ[άκεν ἴμμερός μοι]
[θῦμον ἄσαισι.']

44[2]

Ibid. 14

. . . . . .]έρωτος ἦλγ[ει]
. . . .]

[ὄττα γάρ κ' ἐνάν]τιον εἰσίδω σ[ε]
[τόττ' ἔμοι οὐ φύνν' Ἑ]ρμιόνα τεαύ[τα][3]
5 [φαίνεται,] ξάνθᾳ δ' Ἐλένᾳ σ' ἐΐσ[κ]ην
[ἔστιν ἔπει]κες

[κωὐ κόρ]αις θνάταις· τόδε δ' ἴσ[θι], τᾷ σᾷ
[καλλόνᾳ] παίσᾱν κε με τᾶν μερίμνᾱν
[ταὶς θυήλ]αις ἀντιδ[ι]'δων, πό[θοις δὲ]
10 [παῖσί σε τίην.][4]

[1] so *E*, cf. *C.R.* 1916. 100 [2] *E*, *C.R.* 1916. 101
[3] = τοιαύτη [4] Sch. τ[ί]ην σε (a variant)

43

From a Second-Century Papyrus:

And them I answered: 'Gentle dames, how you will evermore remember till you be old, our life together in the heyday of youth! For many things did we then together both pure and beautiful. And now that you depart hence, love wrings my heart with very anguish.'

44

From the Same:

. . . For when I look upon you, then meseems Hermione[1] was never such as you are, and just it is to liken you rather to Helen than to a mortal maid; nay, I tell you, I render your beauty the sacrifice of all my thoughts and worship you with all my desires.

[1] as daughter of Helen, Hermione was one remove less divine

45[1] πρὸς Γογγύλην

Ox. Pap. 1231. 15

[Τ]ὰν τ[αχίσταν, ὤ κ]έλομαί σ' ὄ[νελθε,]
[Γό]γγυλα β̣[ρόδ]ανθι, λάβοισα μάν[δυν]
[γλα]κτίναν· σὲ δηὖτε πόθος τι[ς ἆμος]
ἀμφιπόταται

5 τὰν κάλαν· ἀ γὰρ κατάγωγις αὔτα
ἐπτόαισ' ἴδοισαν,[2] ἔγω δὲ χαίρω.
καὶ γὰρ αὔτα δή π[οτ'] ἐμεμ[φόμαν τὰν]
[Κ]υπρογέν[ηαν·]

[τ]ᾶς ἄρᾱμα[ι μὴ χάριν ἀβφέρην μοι]
10 τοῦτο τῶ[πος, ἀλλά σε, τὰν μάλιστα]
[β]όλλομα[ι θνάταν κατίδην γυναίκων]
[ἂψ πάλιν ἔλκην.]

46[3]

Ibid. 50

[. . .] καὶ γὰρ [οὖδεν ἄεικες ἦσκεν]
[αἴ τ]ινες μέμ[φοντό σ' ἄ μοι προσῆλθες]
[ἢ] ζαλέξᾱ, κα[ἴστισι μὴ πρόσηκεν]
[ἄ]δρα χαρίσσᾱ[·]

5 [σ]τείχομεν γὰρ [πάντοσ'· ἔγω δὲ φῶμεν]
[κα]ὶ σὺ τοῦτ'· Ἀλλ[' ἦ δύνατον βρότοισι]
[πα]ρ[θ]ένοις ἄπ[εμμεν ἔκας γυναίκων]
[αἴς κ]εν ἔχοιεν [;]

[1] *E* (Ibid.) [2] ἐπτόαισι = ἐπιπτοεῖ [3] *E* (Ibid.)

45 To Gongyla

From a Second-Century Papyrus:

Come back, and that speedily, my rosebud Gongyla, and in your milk-white gown; surely a desire of my heart hovers about your lovely self; for the sight of your very robe thrills me, and I rejoice that it is so. Once on a day, I too found fault with the Cyprus-born—whose favour I pray these words may lose me not, but rather bring me back again the maiden whom of all womankind I desire the most to see.[1]

46

From the Same:

. . . Indeed it were no matter for wonder if some blamed you for coming to me or talking with me as you have done, and for showing such favour to one to whom you should not; for we walk everywhere. But let us say this, you and me, 'Is it possible for any maid on earth to be far apart from the woman she loves?'

[1] a complete letter

47

Ox. Pap. 1231. 56

. . . νὺξ . [. . .] . [. . . .]

e. g. πάρθενοι δ[ὲ ταίσδεσι πρὸς θύραισι]
παννυχίσδομ[εν, πολύολβε γάμβρε,]
σὰν ἀείδοι[σαι φιλότατα καὶ νύμ-] [1]
5 φας ἰοκόλπω.
ἀλλ' ἐγέρθε[ις εὖτ' ἐπίησιν αὔως]
στεῖχε, σοὶς [δ' ἄγοι πόδας αὖτος Ἔρμας]
ἤπερ ὄσσον ἄ[μμορος ἔσσε' ὄσσον] [2]
ὔπνον ἴδωμε[ν.]

μελῶν α'

χηηηδδ'

B'

48 πρὸς Ἄτθιδα

Heph. 45 [π. Αἰολικοῦ ἔπους]· τῶν δὲ ἀκαταλήκτων τὸ μὲν πεντάμετρον καλεῖται Σαπφικὸν τεσσαρεσκαιδεκασύλλαβον, ὧ τὸ δεύτερον ὅλον Σαπφοῦς γέγραπται· Ἠράμαν . . . ποτά.

Plut. *Amat.* 5 χάρις γὰρ οὖν ἡ τοῦ θήλεος ὕπειξις τῷ ἄρρενι κέκληται πρὸς τῶν παλαιῶν, ὡς καὶ Πίνδαρος ἔφη (*P.* 2. 78) τὸν Κένταυρον ἄνευ χαρίτων ἐκ τῆς Ἥρας γενέσθαι, καὶ τὴν οὔπω γάμον ἔχουσαν ὥραν ἡ Σαπφὼ προσαγορεύουσά φησιν, ὅτι· Σμίκρα . . . κἄχαρις.

[1] so Wil: for the other restorations see *C.R.* Ibid.
[2] = τόσσον . . . ὄσσον cf. Theocr. 4. 39

---

[1] this being apparently an epithalamy, one would expect to find it in Book IX; there were perh. two editions current in Roman times, one arranged according to metre, the other

47 [1]

From a Second-Century Papyrus:

e.g. . . . And we maidens spend all the night at this door, singing of the love that is between thee, thrice happy bridegroom, and a bride whose breast is sweet as violets. But get thee up and go when the dawn shall come, and may great Hermes lead thy feet where thou shalt find just so much ill-luck as we shall see sleep to-night.

THE END OF BOOK I

1320 LINES

BOOK II

48 TO ATTHIS

Hephaestion *Handbook of Metre* [on the Aeolic line]: Of the acatalectic kinds of Aeolic verse the pentameter is called the Sapphic fourteen-syllable, in which is written the whole of Sappho's second Book; compare 'I loved . . . ago.'

Plutarch *Amatorius*: For the yielding of the female to the male is called by the ancients χάρις 'grace'; compare Pindar where he says that the Centaur was born of Hera 'without grace,' and Sappho's use of ἄχαρις 'graceless' of the girl who was not yet ripe for marriage, 'You seemed . . . child.'

preserving what was prob. S.'s own arrangement, that according to subject-matter; the former being presumably made from the latter, it is only to be expected that some at least of the metrically-arranged Books would end with epithalamies if they formed the last Book of the earlier edition; cf. the final poem of Book VII (135)

Ter. Maur. *de metr.* 6. 390 Keil: (Sappho) . . . cordi quando fuisse sibi canit Atthida | parvam, florea virginitas sua cum foret.

Ἠράμαν μὲν ἔγω σέθεν, Ἄτθι, πάλαι ποτά,
[ἆς ἔμ' ἀνθεμόεσσ' ἔτι παρθενία σὺ δὲ][1]
σμίκρα μοι πάϊς ἔμμεν ἐφαίνεο κἄχαρις.

49, 50

Apoll. *Pron.* 93. 23 ὑμεῖς . . . Αἰολεῖς ὔμμες.

οὔ τι μ' ὔμμες[2] . . .

ἆς θέλετ' ὔμμες . . .

ἐν δευτέρῳ Σαπφώ.

51

Hdn. π.μ.λ. 2. 932. 23 Lentz μᾶλλον· οὐδὲν ὅμοιον τῷ μᾶλλον κατὰ χρόνον. τὸ γὰρ α εἰ ἔχοι ἐν ἐπιφορᾷ διπλασιαζόμενον τὸ λλ ἐν μιᾷ λέξει, συστέλλεσθαι φιλεῖ, χωρὶς εἰ μὴ τροπή τις εἴη τοῦ η εἰς α παρὰ διαλέκτῳ . . . ἐφυλαξάμην δὲ διαλέκτους διὰ τόδ'·

ἀλλ' ὂν μὴ μεγαλύννεο δακτυλίω πέρι.[3]

52

Chrys. π. ἀποφατ. col. 14 fr. 23 (Letronne, *Notices et Extraits*): εἰ Σαπφὼ οὕτως ἀποφαινομένη·

Οὐκ οἶδ' ὄττι θέω· δύο μοι τὰ νοήματα . . .

[1] so Neue-*E* from Ter. Maur. see *Camb. Philol. Soc. Proc.* 1916 [2] = *Il.* 1. 335 and perh. does not belong to S: μ' = μοι (mss μοι) [3] Hartung: mss ἀλλ' ἄν (cf. *Ox. Pap.* 1231. 1. ii. 23) μοι μεγαλύνεο: Hdn. apparently mistakes this rare use (cf. *Il.* 18. 178) of ἀλλ' ἄνα for an instance (ἆλλα voc.

Terentianus Maurus *On Metres*: (Sappho) . . . when she sings that her Atthis was small in the days when her own girlhood was blossoming.

I loved you, Atthis, long ago, when my own girlhood was still all flowers, and you—you seemed to me a small ungainly child.[1]

49, 50

Apollonius *Pronouns*: ὑμεῖς 'you,' Aeolic ὔμμες; compare:

It is not you who are . . . . to me . . .

and

So long as you wish . . . ;

from Sappho's second Book.

51

Herodian *Words without Parallel*: μᾶλλον 'rather': There is no parallel to this word as regards quantity; for if *a* is followed by *ll* in the same word it is regularly short, except in the case of *a* for *ē* in a dialect. . . . I made the above exception of dialects because of the following examples:

But come, be not so proud of a ring.

52[2]

Chrysippus *Negatives*: If Sappho, declaring:

I know not what to do; I am in two minds . . .

[1] apparently the 1st poem of Bk. II (cf. Heph.): ll. 1, 3 certainly Sappho's, 2 possibly: cf. *Paroem.* 2. 449, Mar. Plot. 512, Sch. Pind. *P.* 2. 78, Max. Tyr. 24 (18). 9, Bek. *An.* 1. 473. 25, Hesych. κἄχαρις [2] cf. Aristaen. 1. 6

fem.) of ἆλλος = ἠλεός which does occur in his next quotation (*fr.* 93)

53

Hdn. π.μ.λ. 2. 912. 10 Lentz οὐρανός· τὰ εἰς νος λήγοντα ὀνόματα τρισύλλαβα ὀξυνόμενα καὶ ἔχοντα τὸ α συνεσταλμένον πρὸ τέλους μὴ καθαρεῦον οὐδέποτε τὴν ἄρχουσαν ἔχει φύσει μάκραν . . . σημειῶδες ἄρα τὸ οὐρανός, ὅτι ἤρξατο ἀπὸ φύσει μακρᾶς. Ἀλκαῖος δὲ εἰς ω <καὶ εἰς ο>[1] ἀποφαίνεται τὸ ὄνομα, καὶ ὠρανός λέγων κατὰ τροπὴν τῆς ου διφθόγγου εἰς τὸ ω, καὶ ἄνευ τοῦ υ ὀρανός, ὥστε τὸ ἐπιζητούμενον παρ' αὐτῷ λελύσθαι. καὶ Σαπφώ·

ψαύην δ' οὐ δοκίμοιμ' ὀράνω ἔσσα διπάχεα.[2]

54

Max. Tyr. 24. 9 ἐκβακχεύεται (ὁ Σωκράτης) ἐπὶ Φαίδρῳ ὑπὸ τοῦ ἔρωτος, τῇ δὲ (Σαπφοῖ) ὁ ἔρως ἐτίναξε τὰς φρένας ὡς ἄνεμος κατάρης δρυσὶν ἐμπεσών·

e.g. ἔμοι δ' ὡς ἄνεμος κατάρης δρύσιν ἐμπέτων
| ἐτίναξεν ἔρος φρένας . . . . .[3]

55

Thes. Corn. et Hort. Adon. Ald. 268 b . . . οἷον ἡ Σαπφώ τῆς Σαπφῶς καὶ ἡ Λητώ τῆς Λητῶς, καὶ δηλοῦσιν αἱ χρήσεις οὕτως ἔχουσαι· (*Ad.* 62)· καὶ παρ' αὐτῇ τῇ Σαπφοῖ·

. . . . . . μάλα δὴ κεκορημένοις
Γόργως . . . . . .[4]

56, 57

Hdn. π.μ.λ. 2. 945. 8 Lentz [τὰ εἰς λη λήγοντα]· ἀναδράμωμεν ἐπὶ τὸ προκείμενον, παραθέμενοι τὸ τύλη, ὅπερ οὐκ ἦν παρ' Ἀττικοῖς, ἀλλὰ μέμνηται Σαπφὼ ἐν δευτέρῳ·

[1] *E* [2] δοκίμοιμ' (opt.) Ahr. -*B*: mss δοκεῖ μοι: ὀρ. ἐ. δ. *E*: mss ὠρανῶ δυσπαχέα: *B* δύσι πάχεσιν cf. Ps.-Callisth. 2. 20 but δυσί is only late [3] *E*: κατάρης Nauck from Eust. *Il.* 603. 39: mss κατ' ὄρος (bis): (see Alc. 46) [4] *B* κεκορημένας

53[1]

Herodian *Words without Parallel*: οὐρανός 'heaven': Oxytone trisyllabic nouns ending in *-nos* preceded by ᾰ which has a consonant before it, never have the first syllable long by nature. . . . And so οὐρανός is remarkable in beginning with a syllable which is long by nature. But Alcaeus uses the form with either ō or ŏ, saying ὠρανός with the change of the diphthong *ou* to ō, and also, without the *u*, ὀρανός, so that the exception we are discussing does not hold in his case. And Sappho says, using the form with ŏ:

A little thing of two cubits' stature like me could not expect to touch the sky.

54

Maximus of Tyre *Dissertations*: Socrates is wild with love for Phaedrus; Sappho's heart is shaken by love as oaks by a down-rushing wind.

e. g. As for me, love has shaken my heart as a | down-rushing whirlwind that falls upon the oaks.

55

Aldus *Cornucopia*: . . . For example, Σαπφώ 'Sappho' genitive Σαπφῶς and Λητώ 'Leto' genitive Λητῶς, as is shown by such instances as (*Adespota* 62. Bgk.), and from Sappho herself:

. . . having had enough of Gorgo

56, 57

Herodian *Words without Parallel* (on nouns in *-lē*): Let us return to our subject, which was τύλη 'cushion,' a word not found in Attic writers but used by Sappho in her second Book:

[1] cf. Herodas 4. 75, Plut. *Demetr*. 22, Synes. *Ep*. 142. Herch.

. . . . . . ἔγω δ' ἐπὶ μαλθάκαν
τύλαν ὀσπολέω μέλε(α) . . . .[1]
<καὶ>.[2]

καίναν μέν τε τύλαν κατὰ σὰ σπολέω μέλεα·[3]

οὐ γὰρ ὁ τέ σύνδεσμος.

58

Galen *Protr.* 8 ἄμεινον οὖν ἐστιν, ἐγνωκότας τὴν μὲν τῶν μειρακίων ὥραν τοῖς ἠρινοῖς ἄνθεσιν ἐοικυῖαν ὀλιγοχρόνιόν τε τὴν τέρψιν ἔχουσαν, ἐπαινεῖν τε τὴν Λεσβίαν λέγουσαν·

ὀ μὲν γὰρ κάλος <εἶς κάλος>[4] ὄσσον ἴδην
  πέλει,
ὀ δὲ κἄγαθος αὔτικα καὶ κάλος ἔσσεται . . .[5]

59, 60, 61

Demetr. *Eloc.* 161 [π. ὑπερβολῆς]· ἐκ δὲ ὑπερβολῶν χάριτες μάλιστα αἱ ἐν ταῖς κωμῳδίαις, πᾶσα δὲ ὑπερβολὴ ἀδύνατος, ὡς Ἀριστοφάνης. . . . τοῦ δὲ αὐτοῦ εἴδους καὶ τὰ τοιαῦτά ἐστιν· ὑγιέστερος κολοκύντης, καὶ φαλακρότερος εὐδίας, καὶ τὰ Σαπφικά·

. . . . πόλυ πάκτιδος ἀδυμελεστέρα,

χρύσω χρυσοτέρα . . . . .[6]

Greg. ad Hermog. *Rhet. Gr.* 7. 1236 Walz αἰσχρῶς μὲν κολακεύει τὴν ἀκοὴν ἐκεῖνα ὅσα ἐστὶν ἐρωτικά, οἷον τὰ Ἀνακρέοντος, τὰ Σαπφοῦς, οἷον γάλακτος λευκοτέρα, ὕδατος ἁπαλωτέρα, πηκτίδων ἐμμελεστέρα, ἵππου γαυροτέρα, ῥόδων ἁβροτέρα, ἑανοῦ μαλακωτέρα,[7] χρυσοῦ τιμιωτέρα.

e.g. . . . . . ἰάνω μαλακωτέρα[8]

[1] *E*: ὀσπ. = ἀναστελῶ cf. ἀνακλίνω, ἀναπίπτω: mss σπολέω [2] *E* [3] *E*: mss κἂν μέν τε τύλαγκας ασπόλεα [4] *E*: εἷς = ὢν Eust. 1787. 45: mss κάλ. ὅσ. ἰ. πέλεται (-εται from below) [5] κἄγαθος: for καὶ cf. Plat. *Phaedr.* 23 a and Heindorf's note (Neue) [6] *i. e.* χρυσιοτέρα [7] *E*: mss ἱματίου ἑανοῦ μ. [8] *E*, cf. Hesych. ἴανον (sic)· ἱμάτιον

. . . And I will set [you] reclining on soft cushions;

and

You shall lie on new cushions;

where it should be noted that τε is not the copula.[1]

58

Galen *Exhortation to Learning*: It is better therefore, since we know that the prime of youth is like the spring flowers and its pleasures transitory, to approve the words of the Lesbian dame:

He that is fair is fair to outward show;
He that is good will soon be fair alsò.

59, 60, 61

Demetrius *On Style* [on hyperbole]: The charms of comedy, particularly, are those which arise from hyperbole, and every hyperbole is an impossibility; compare Aristophanes. . . . Of the same kind are phrases such as 'healthier than a cucumber,' 'balder than a calm sea,' and Sappho's:

far sweeter-tunèd than the lyre,

and:

more golden than gold.[2]

Gregorius on Hermogenes: The ear is improperly flattered by erotic turns of phrase such as those of Anacreon and Sappho; for instance, 'whiter than milk,' 'more delicate than water,' 'more tuneful than a lyre,' 'more wanton than a mare,' 'daintier than rosebuds,' 'softer than a fine robe,' 'more precious than gold.'

e.g. . . . softer than fine raiment

[1] for μέν τε cf. 35. 2 [2] cf. Demetr. *Eloc.* 127

62

Ath. 2. 57d [π. ᾠῶν]: Σαπφὼ δ' αὐτὸ τρισυλλάβως καλεῖ· (97) καὶ πάλιν·

ὠΐω πόλυ λευκότερον. . . .

63

Antiatt. Bek. *An.* 1. 108. 22:

μύρραν

τὴν σμύρναν Σαπφὼ δευτέρῳ.

64

Poll. 6. 107 Ἀνακρέων . . . στεφανοῦσθαί φησι καὶ . . . καὶ ἀνήτῳ, ὡς καὶ Σαπφὼ (117) καὶ Ἀλκαῖος· οὗτοι δὲ ἄρα καὶ σελίνοις

e.g. . . . . στεφάνοισι σελιννίνοις[1]

65

Ox. Pap. 1232. 1. i. 8–9

[. . . . . . .] ἀλλ' ἄγιτ', ὦ φίλαι,
e.g. [ἀοίδας ἀπυλήξομεν[2]], ἄγχι γὰρ ἀμέρα.
(Σα[φοῦς μ]ε[λῶν])[3]

66[4] <Ἕκτορος καὶ Ἀνδρομάχης γάμοι>

Ibid. 1232. 1. ii

. . . Κύπρο.[. . . . .]
κᾶρυξ ἦλθ[ε] θό[ων ὀυνάμι μ]ελέ[ων] ἔθεις

[1] *E*: cf. σέλιννα Cram. *A.O.* 2. 258. 6 [2] *E*, cf. *C.R.* 1919. 127: ἀπυλήξομεν subj. cf. Alc. 70. 9 [3] prob. but not certainly belongs here; if so, this was the end either of Bk. ii (reading μελῶν β') or of the whole collection (reading μελῶν) and the next poem was added as an afterthought perh. as only doubtfully S.'s; for the two different editions

62 [1]

Athenaeus *Doctors at Dinner* [on eggs]: Sappho makes three syllables of ᾤὸν 'egg' as (97), and again:

far whiter than an egg . . .

63

Antiatticist: Sappho uses μύρρα

myrrh

for σμύρνα in her second Book.

64

Pollux *Vocabulary*: Anacreon . . . . says that anise, too, was used for garlands, as indeed by Sappho (117) and Alcaeus; the two latter, moreover, speak also of celery.

e.g. . . . garlands of celery

65

From a Third Century Papyrus:

. . . But come, dear maidens, [let us end our song], for day is at hand.

([End of ?] the Poems of Sappho) [2]

66 [Marriage of Hector and Andromache]

From the Same:

. . . Cyprus . . . . . . came a herald sped by the might of his swift legs bringing speedily these

[1] cf. Eust. *Od.* 1686. 49 [2] see opp. n. 3

---

perh. current in antiquity see on 13 and 48; this *may* be the end of the last book (ix) in the edition arranged according to subject-matter (hence μέλη not μελῶν below as title of the whole collection?) [4] restored by Hunt, Lobel, Wil. and *E* (Ibid.)

Ἰδάοις τάδε κ[â]λα φ[όρ]εις τάχυς ἄγγελος
. . . . [1]
τᾶς τ' ἄλλας Ἀσίας τ[ά]δ' ἔσαν κλέος
ἄφθιτον.
5 '"Εκτωρ κοὶ [2] συνέταιροι ἄγοισ' ἐλικώπιδα
Θήβας ἐξ ἰάρας Πλακίας τ' ἀπ' ἀϊνάω
ἄβραν Ἀνδρομάχαν ἐνὶ ναῦσιν ἐπ' ἄλμυρον
πόντον· πόλλα δ' [ἐλί]γματα χρύσια κἄμ-
ματα
πορφύρ[ā] λία τ' αὖ τ[ρό]να, ποίκιλ'
ἀθρήματα, [3]
10 ἀργύρ[α τ'] ἀνάριθμα ποτήρια κἀλέφαις.' [4]
ὣς εἶπ'· ὀτραλέως δ' ὀνόρουσε [5] πάτ[ηρ] φίλος,
φάμα δ' ἦλθε κατὰ πτόλιν εὐρύχορον Fίλω. [6]
αὔτικ' Ἰλιάδαι σατίναις ὐπ' ἐϋτρόχοις
ἆγον αἰμιόνοις, ἐπέβαινε δὲ παῖς ὄχλος
15 γυναίκων τ' ἄμα παρθενίκαν τε τανυσφύρων·
χῶρις δ' αὖ Περάμοιο θύγατρες [ἐπήϊσαν.]
ἴππ[οις] δ' ἄνδρες ὔπαγον ὐπ' ἄρ[ματα, σὺν
δ' ἴσαν]
π[άντ]ες ἀΐθεοι· μεγάλωστι δ' [ἴεν μέγας]
δ[âμος] κἀνίοχοι φ[αλάροισ]ι [κεκαδμέναις]
20 π[ώλοις ἐ]'ξαγο[ν. . . . .]
. . . . [7]

Fr. 2 *e.g.* [ὄτα δεῦτ' ὀχέων ἐπέβαν ἴ]κελοι θέοι[ς]
["Εκτωρ Ἀνδρομάχα τε, σύν]αγνον ἀόλ[λεες] [8]
[Τρῶες Τρωΐαδες τ' ἐρ 'τεν]νον ἐς Ἴλιο[ν.]
[. . . . .]τον ἐμίγνυ[σαν]
5 [. . . . .] ὠς δ' ἄρα πάρ[θενοι]
[. . . . .]νεδε. . .[
[. . . . . [9]

fair tidings unto the people of Ida . . . . . . and [throughout] the rest of Asia these tidings were a fame that never died: 'Hector and his comrades bring from sacred Thebe[1] and ever-flowing Placia, by ship upon the briny sea, the dainty Andromache of the glancing eye; and many are the golden bracelets, and the purple robes, aye and the fine smooth broideries, indeed a richly-varied bride-gift; and without number also are the silver goblets and the ornaments of ivory.' So spake the herald; and Hector's dear father leapt up in haste, and the news went forth through Ilus' spacious city. Straightway the children of Ilus harnessed the mules to the wheelèd cars, and the whole throng of the women and of the slender-ankled maidens mounted therein, the daughters of Priam riding apart; and the men did harness horses to the chariots, and the young men went with them one and all; till a mighty people moved mightily along, and the drivers drove their boss-bedizened steeds out of [the city] . . . . [Then, when the] god-like [Hector and Andromache were mounted in the chariots, the men of Troy and the women of Troy] accompanied them in one great company into [lovely] Ilium . . . . . . they mingled . . . . . . And now, when the maidens . . . . . .

[1] in Mysia

---

[1] one or more lines omitted here in P [2] *E*: P *και* [3] *ἀθρήματα* *E*, cf. Hesych: P *ἀθύρματα* [4] Ath. 460 d [5] P *ανορουσε* [6] Fίλω *E* (Ibid.): P *φιλοις·* [7] number of lines lost unknown [8] for *συνάγνεον* (-νιον), cf. Hesych. *ἀγνεῖν* [9] number of lines lost unknown

Fr. 1 col. iii [........]φ[.]α.[.]ο[ν εὔ]ρυεδε[..]..εακ[.].[
[...... κα]ὶ κασία λίβανός τ' ὀνελίχνυτο.[1]
γύναικες δ' ἐλέλυσδον ὄσαι προγενέστεραι
πάντες δ' ἄνδρες ἐπήρατον ἴαχον ὄρθιον
5 πάων'[2] ὀγκαλέοντες ἐκάβολον εὐλύραν,
ὔμνην δ' Ἕκτορα κ' Ἀνδρομάχαν θεοεικέλο[ις.]

(Σαφ[ο]ὺς μέλη)

67

Sch. Ar. *Thesm.* 401 νεωτέρων καὶ ἐρωτικῶν τὸ στεφανηπλοκεῖν· πρὸς τὸ ἔθος, ὅτι ἐστεφανηπλόκουν αἱ παλαιαί. Σαπφώ·

αἴ τ' ὄρααι στεφαναπλόκην.[3]

Γ'

68 εἰς τὰς Χάριτας

Arg. Theocr. 28 γέγραπται δὲ Αἰολίδι διαλέκτῳ παρὰ τὸ Σαπφικὸν ἑκκαιδεκασύλλαβον τό·

Βροδοπάχεες ἄγναι Χάριτες δεῦτε Δίος κόραι.

[1] so P: cf. λίγνυς and μείχνυντες Alc. 73. 13 [2] P πάον' [3] *E*: *i. e.* ὡραῖαι, cf. *Comp.* 3. 18 Hoff. *Gr. Dial.* 2, p. 217

---

[1] see note 3 on p. 226 [2] this may belong to the above

. . . . . . and cassia and frankincense went up in smoke. Meanwhile the elder women raised a loud cry, and all the men shouted amain a delightful song of thanksgiving unto the Far-Darting God of the lyre, and hymned the praise of the god-like Hector and Andromache.

(END OF THE POEMS OF SAPPHO)[1]

67

Scholiast on Aristophanes: The weaving of garlands was done by young people and lovers;—this refers to the custom whereby the women wove the garlands among the ancients; cf. Sappho:

And the maids ripe for wedlock wove garlands.[2]

BOOK III

68[3] TO THE GRACES

Argument to Theocritus 28: And it is written in the Aeolic dialect and in the Sapphic sixteen-syllable metre of:

Hither, pure rose-armed Graces, daughters of Zeus.

poem [3] as it is taken as an example of the metre, this is probably the 1st line of the 1st poem of the Book: see also Philostr. *Im.* 2. 1, Eust. *Od.* 1429. 58 and cf. Heph. 35 (ᾧ τὸ τρίτον ὅλον Σαπφοῦς γέγραπται)

69

Poll. 10. 124 πρώτην δέ φασι χλαμύδα ὀνομάσαι Σαπφὼ ἐπὶ τοῦ Ἔρωτος εἰποῦσαν·

. . . ἔλθοντ' ἐξ ὀράνω πορφυρίαν προιέμενον χλάμυν.[1]

70

Prisc. *Inst. Gram.* 2. 277 Keil: Et contra tamen in quibusdam *es* productam terminantibus fecerunt Graeci poetae, *eus* pro *es* proferentes. . . . Ἄρευς pro Ἄρης ut Sappho;

ὀ δ' Ἄρευς φαῖσί κεν Ἄφαιστον ἄγην βίᾳ.

71

Stob. *Fl.* 4. 12 [π. ἀφροσύνης]· Σαπφοῦς· πρὸς ἀπαίδευτον γυναῖκα·

κατθάνοισα δὲ κείσεαι οὐδέ τινι μναμνοσύνα σέθεν
ἔσσετ' οὐδέποτ' <εἰς> ὔστερον·[2] οὐ γὰρ πεδέχεις βρόδων
τῶν ἐκ Πιερίας, ἀλλ' ἀφάνης κὴν Ἀΐδα δόμοις[3]
φοιτάσεις πεδ' ἀμαύρων νεκύων ἐκπεποταμένα.[4]

[1] πορφ. Bent.: mss π. ἔχοντα προιέμ. *E*: mss προϊέμ.: Seid. περθέμ. line 1 perh. νύκτι τᾷδ' ὔναρ, Ἄτθ', εἶδον Ἔρον τὸν δολομάχανον *E*, cf. Theocr. 30. 25 [2] οὐδέ τινι *E*: mss St. οὐδέποκα (from below), Pl. οὐδέ τις: εἰς Grotius (mss Pl. ἔσεται· οὐ γὰρ π.) [3] mss also δομο, whence Fick δόμῳ perh. rightly [4] *E*: mss ἐκπεπ.

69

Pollux *Vocabulary*: It is said that the first mention of the word χλαμύς 'mantle' is in Sappho, where she says of Love:

. . . come from heaven and throw off his purple mantle.[1]

70

Priscian *Grammar*: Conversely, in certain names ending in *ēs* the Greek poets give *-eus* for *-ēs*, as . . . Areus for Ares, for instance Sappho:

And Areus says that he could carry off Hephaestus by force.

71[2]

Stobaeus *Anthology* [on folly]: Sappho, to a woman of no education:

When you are dead you will lie unremembered for evermore; for you have no part in the roses that come from Pieria; nay, obscure here, you will move obscure in the house of Death, and flit to and fro among such of the dead as have no fame.

[1] perh. line 1 ran 'I dreamt last night, Atthis, that I saw the wily Love come' etc: cf. Didymus ap. Amm. 147
[2] cf. Plut. *Praec. Con.* 48 where S. is said to have written it 'to a wealthy woman,' and *Qu. Conv.* 3. 1. 2 where it is 'to a woman of no refinement or learning'

72

Chrys. π. ἀποφατ. col. 8 fr. 13 (cf. 52) εἰ Σαπφὼ οὕτως ἀπεφήνατο·

οὔδιαν δοκίμωμι προσίδοισαν φάος ἀλίω [1]
ἔσσεσθαι σοφίᾳ πάρθενον εἰς οὔδενά ποι χρόνον
τοιαύταν [2] . . . . . .

73

Thes. Corn. et Hort. Adon. Ald. 268 b τὴν δὲ αἰτιατικὴν οἱ Αἰολεῖς καὶ μόνοι προσθέσει τοῦ ν ἐποίουν τὴν Λητών, ὡς καὶ ἡ χρῆσις δηλοῖ·

Ἤρων ἐξεδίδαξ' ἐγ Γυάρων τὰν ἀνυόδρομον· [3]

αἰτιατικῶς γάρ ἐστιν ἀπὸ εὐθείας τῆς Ἡρώ.

Δ'

74

Et. Mag. 2. 43 ἀβακής . . . κέχρηται δὲ αὐτῷ Σαπφώ, οἷον·

. . . . ἀλλά τις οὐκ ἔμμι παλίγκοτος
ὄργαν, [4] ἀλλ' ἀβάκην τὰν φρέν' ἔχω . . . .

75

Max. Tyr. 24 (18). 9 τὸν Ἔρωτά φησιν ἡ Διοτίμα τῷ Σωκράτει οὐ παῖδα, ἀλλ' ἀκόλουθον τῆς Ἀφροδίτης καὶ θεράποντα εἶναι· λέγει που καὶ Σαπφοῖ ἡ Ἀφροδίτη ἐν ᾄσματι·

<Ὦ Ψάπφοι>, [5] σύ τε κἄμος θεράπων Ἔρος

[1] δοκίμωμι Ahr: P- οιμι [2] σοφίᾳ *E*: mss -ίαν awkward with τοιαύταν: ποι (= που) *E*: mss πω unlikely with fut. [3] Fick: mss ἐξεδίδαξε Γ. κ.τ.λ. [4] Urs: mss παλιγκότων

72

Chrysippus *Negatives*: If Sappho expressed herself thus:

I do not believe that any maiden that shall see the sunlight will ever rival [you] in [your] art. . . .

73

Aldus *Cornucopia*: The accusative of nouns like *Leto*, in Aeolic only, by the addition of *n* became *Leton*, as the example shows:

Well did [I] teach Hero of Gyara, the fleetly-running maid;

for *Heron* is used as an accusative from the nominative *Hero*.

Book IV

74

Etymologicum Magnum: ἀβακής 'infantile' . . . and Sappho has used it, for instance:

. . . Yet I am not resentful in spirit, but have the heart of a little child.

75

Maximus of Tyre *Dissertations*: Diotima [in Plato's *Symposium*] tells Socrates that Love is not the child but the attendant and servitor of Aphrodite; and Aphrodite somewhere says to Sappho in a poem:

My servitor Love and thou, O Sappho

ὀργάνων: Neue's *-κότων ὄργαν* (accus.) unlikely without *τῶν*
5 *E*

76, 77

Dio Chr. 37. 47:

Μνάσεσθαί τινά φαιμ' ὔστερον ἀμμέων·[1]

πάνυ γὰρ καλῶς εἶπεν ἡ Σαπφώ· καὶ πόλυ κάλλιον Ἡσίοδος (*Op.* 763–4)· 'Φήμη δ' οὔτις πάμπαν ἀπόλλυται, ἥντινα πολλοὶ | λαοὶ φημίξωσι· θέος νύ τίς ἐστι καὶ αὐτή.' ἐγώ σε ἀναστήσω παρὰ τῇ θεῷ, ὅθεν οὐδείς σε μὴ καθέλῃ, οὐ σεισμός, οὐκ ἄνεμος, οὐ νιφετός, οὐκ ὄμβρος, οὐ φθόνος, οὐκ ἐχθρός, ἀλλὰ καὶ νῦν σε καταλαμβάνω ἑστηκότα. λάθα[2] μὲν γὰρ ἤδη τινὰς καὶ ἑτέρους ἔσφηλε καὶ ἐψεύσατο, γνώμη δ' ἀνδρῶν ἀγαθῶν οὐδένα, ᾗ κατ' ἄνδρα μοι ὀρθὸς ἕστηκας.

e.g. λάθα μέν τινας ἐψεύσατο κἀτέροις
ἀ δ' ἄνδρων ἀγάθων οὔδενα πώποτα
γνώμα . . . .

78

Sch. Ap. Rh. 1. 1123 χέραδος ἡ τῶν βραχέων λίθων συλλογή . . . ἢ χεράδες λέγονται οἱ μικροὶ σωροὶ τῶν λίθων . . . μνημονεύει καὶ Σαπφώ·

μὴ κίνη χέραδας.[3]

79

Apoll. *Pron.* 107. 11 (π. τῆς ὅς): Αἰολεῖς μετὰ τοῦ F κατὰ πᾶσαν πτῶσιν καὶ γένος·

τὸν Fὸν παῖδα κάλει·[4]

Σαπφώ.

[1] μνάσεσθαι Cas: mss -σασθαι φαιμ(ι) *B*: mss φάμη ὔστερον Volg. -*E*: mss καὶ ἕτερον (correction of φήμηστερον from φαιμυστερον) [2] note the form [3] So Ahr: mss μὴ κενὴ χέραδος: mss *E.M.* μὴ κίνει χεράδας (τά παραθαλάσσια σκύβαλα) [4] Fὸν Heyne: mss εον

76, 77

Dio Chrysostom *Discourses*:

Somebody, I tell you, will remember us hereafter;

as Sappho has well said, and, as Hesiod has better said (*Works and Days*, 763): 'No fame told of by many peoples is altogether lost; for Fame is a God even as others are.' I will dedicate you [his present oration] in the temple of this Goddess, whence nothing shall ever remove you, neither earthquake, nor wind, nor snow, nor rain, nor envy, nor enemy—nay, I believe you are there already; for

[others have been disappointed by oblivion, but never one by the judgment of good men,[1]]

and in that, methinks, you for your part stand upright.

78

Scholiast on Apollonius of Rhodes *Argonautica*: χέραδος is a gathering of small stones . . . or small heaps of stones are known as χεράδες . . . compare also Sappho:

Stir not the jetsam.[2]

79

Apollonius *Pronouns* [on ὅς 'his' or 'her']: The Aeolic writers use the form with digamma (*w*) in every gender and case; compare:

. . . whom she calls her child;

Sappho.

[1] that is, disappointed of their hopes of undying fame by the (good) opinion of good judges; prob. a slightly adapted version of lines from the same poem of S. [2] *i. e.* or you will find something noisome; = 'let sleeping dogs lie': cf. *E.M.* 808. 37 (explained as 'seashore refuse')

E′

80

Hermog. π. ἰδεῶν *Rhet. Gr.* 3. 317 Walz [π. γλυκύτητος]· . . . καὶ ὅταν τὴν λύραν ἐρωτᾷ ἡ Σαπφὼ καὶ ὅταν αὔτη ἀποκρίνηται, οἷον·

. Ἄγε δῖα χέλυννά μοι
φωνάεσσά τε γίγνεο·[1]

καὶ τὰ ἑξῆς.

81 πρὸς Ἀτθίδα

Heph. 46 [π. Αἰολικοῦ ἔπους]· τὸ δὲ τετράμετρον ἀκατάληκτόν ἐστι τοιοῦτον·

Ἔρος δαὖτέ μ' ὁ λυσιμέλης δόνει
γλυκύπικρον ἀμάχανον ὄρπετον,
Ἄτθι, σοὶ δ' ἔμεθεν μὲν ἀπήχθετο
φροντίσδην, ἐπὶ δ' Ἀνδρομέδαν πότῃ.

82[2] [πρὸς Ἄτθιδα ?]

Berl. Klassikertexte P 9722. 1

. . . 'Ψάπφ', ἦ μὰν οὔτως ἔγω οὔ σε φιλήσω.
ὦ φαῖν' ἄμμι, κὴξ εὔναν λυῖε τέαν

πεφιλημμ[έν]αν ἴσχυν, ὔδατι δὲ
κρίνον [ὡς ἀ]κήρατον παρὰ κράναν
5 πέπλον Χῖον ἀπύσχοισα λούεο·

[1] so Neue -*E* cf. *fr.* 190 : mss Herm. ἀ. χέλυ δ. μ. (ἀ. δ. χ.) λέγε φ. δὲ γίνεο, Eust. ἀ. μ. δ. χέλυ φ. γένοιο : opt. with ἄγε unparalleled [2] very tentatively restored by *E* ; many words *even outside the brackets* are very doubtfully legible,

Book V

80 [1]

Hermogenes *On Kinds of Oratory* [on sweetness or charm] . . . And when Sappho addresses her lyre and when it answers her, as:

Up, my lute divine, and make thyself a thing of speech;

and the lines that follow.

81 To Atthis

Hephaestion *Handbook of Metre*: The acatalectic (Aeolic) tetrameter is like this:

Lo! Love the looser of limbs stirs me, that creature irresistible, bitter-sweet; but you, Atthis, have come to hate the thought of me, and run after Andromeda in my stead.[2]

82 [3] [To Atthis]

From a Seventh-Century Manuscript:

' . . . Sappho, I swear if you come not forth I will love you no more. O rise and shine upon us and set free your beloved strength from the bed, and then like a pure lily beside the spring hold aloof your Chian robe and wash you in the water. And

[1] cf. Eust. *Il.* 9. 41 [2] *B* divides the fragment saying l. 3 begins a poem, but δέ belies this [3] see opp. note 2

---

especially after l. 9, cf. *C.R.* 1916. 131: separation of the strophes uncertain

καὶ Κλεῖϊς[1] σάων καβφέροισα γρῦταν
κροκόεντα λώπεά σ' ἐββάλη καὶ
πέπλον πορφύριον· κἀββεβλημμένᾳ

χλαίνᾳ πέρ σ' ἐξ[ακ]ρισάντων ἄνθινοι
10 στέφανοι περ[ὶ κρᾶτά σοι] δέθεντες,
κἄλθ' ὄσᾳ μαίν[ης μ' ἄδεα καλλ]όνᾳ.

φρῦσσον, ὦ Πρα[ξίνω, κάρ]υ' ἄμμιν, ὡς
παρθένων πό[τον ἀδίω π]οήσω·
ἔκ τινος γὰρ θέων [ταῦτ' ἄ]μμι, τέκνον·

15 ἦ μὰν τᾷδ' ἀμέρ[ᾳ προτὶ] φιλτάταν
Μυτιλάνναν π[ολίων η]ὔξατ' ἤδη
γυναίκων ἀ κα[λίστα Ψ]άπφ' ἀπύβην

πεδ' ἀμμέω[ν, ἀ μάτ]ηρ πεδὰ τῶν τέκνων.'
φίλτα[τ' Ἄτθι, μῶν ἄρα] ταῦτα τὰ πρὶν
20 ἐπι[λάθεαι πάντ' ἢ] ὀμμναίσα' ἔτι ; . . .

83[2] [πρὸς Ἄτθιδα ?]

Berl. Klassikertexte P. 9722. 2.

[Ἄτθιδ' οὔποτ' ἄρ' ὄ]ψ[ομαι,][3]
τεθνάκην δ' ἀδόλως θέλω.
ἄ με ψισδομένα κατελίππανεν

πόλλα, καὶ τόδ' ἔειπέ μ[οι·]
5 Ὤιμ', ὡς δεῖνα πεπ[όνθ]αμεν·
Ψάπφ', ἦ μάν σ' ἀέκοισ' ἀπυλιππάνω.

[1] better Κλεῦις? [2] cf. *C.R.* 1916. 129, 1909. 100 [3] *E e.g.* : ll. 11–13 *E*, 14 Fraccaroli : ll. 16–17 Ath. 15. 674 d : ll. 18–21 *E*: cf. Ath. 15. 690 e : ll. 23–25 *E e.g.*

Cleïs shall bring down from your presses saffron smock and purple robe; and let a mantle be put over you and crowned with a wreath of flowers tied about your head; and so come, sweet with all the beauty with which you make me mad. And do you, Praxinoa, roast us nuts, so that I may make the maidens a sweeter breakfast;[1] for one of the Gods, child, has vouchsafed us a boon. This very day has Sappho the fairest of all women vowed that she will surely return unto Mytilene the dearest of all towns—return with us, the mother with her children.'

Dearest Atthis, can you then forget all this that happened in the old days? . . .[2]

83 [To Atthis?]

From the reverse of the same Manuscript:

So I shall never see Atthis more, and in sooth I might as well be dead. And yet she wept full sore to leave me behind and said 'Alas! how sad our lot; Sappho, I swear 'tis all against my will I leave

[1] the ordinary Greek breakfast was bread dipped in wine; this, the day of S.'s return (from the first exile at Pyrrha?), is a great day [2] doubtfully restored; see p. 238, n. 2: the speaker of the main portion is apparently Atthis

τὰν δ' ἔγω τάδ' ἀμειβόμαν·
Χαίροισ' ἔρχεο κἄμεθεν
μέμναισ'· οἶσθα γὰρ ὤς <τ'> ἐπεδήπομεν.
10 αἰ δὲ μή, ἀλλά σ' ἔγω θέλω
ὄμναισαι τ[ὰ σ]ὺ [λά]θεαι,
ὄσσ' ἄμμ[ες φίλα] καὶ κάλ' ἐπάσχομεν·
πό[λλοις ἃ στεφάν]οις ἴων
καὶ βρ[όδων γλυ]κίων γ' ὔμοι
15 κὰπ π[λόκων] πὰρ ἔμοι περεθήκαο,[1]
καὶ πόλλαις ὐπαθύμιδας
πλέκταις ἀμφ' ἀπαλᾳ δέρᾳ
ἀνθέων ἔκ[ατον] πεποημμέναις,

καὶ πόλλῳ ν[έαρο]ν σὺ χρῶ
20 βρενθείω πρ[οχόῳ μύρ]ω·
ἐξαλείψαο κα[ὶ βασιληΐω,]
e. g. καὶ στρώμν[ας ἔπι κημένα]
ἀπάλαν πὰν[2] [ὀνηάτων][3]
ἐξίης πόθο[ν ἤδε πότων γλυκίων] . . .

84[4]

Berl. Klassikertexte P 9722. 3

e. g. [. . . . . καὶ ταῦτά σ' ἀμειβόμαν ἔγ]ω·
['Νὴ θέαν ἔγω σοι τόδ' ὀμώ]μοκα,
[ὠς οὐδ' αὔτα πόλλαις, ἀ]λλ' ἴαν ἦχον
5 [μόναν ἂπ τῶ Δίος τὰν] παρθενίαν,
[ὔμως δ' οὐκ ὄδδον] ὠρρώδων[5] ὐπὲρ ὂν
[ἀπύ μοί Ϝ' ἐπέσκ]ηψ' Ἦρα βάλεσθαι.'
[ταῦτ' ἔγω σ' ἠ]ὔφραν' ἄρ' ὠξυβόων δ'·
['Ἄμμι μάν,] πάρθεν', ἀ νὺξ οὐκὶ βάρυ
10 [φαίνετ]' ἔμμεν· ὤστ' οὐ μὴ σύ γ' ἀτύξη'. . .

[1] περεθήκαο Jurenka : ms παρεθηκας [2] πὰν accus. masc.

thee'; and I answered her 'Go your way rejoicing and remember me, for you know how I doted upon you. And if you remember not, O then I will remind you of what you forget, how dear and beautiful was the life we led together. For with many[1] a garland of violets and sweet roses mingled you have decked your flowing locks by my side, and with many a woven necklet made of a hundred blossoms your dainty throat; and with many a jar of myrrh, both of the precious and the royal, have you anointed your fair young skin before me, and [lying upon] the couch have taken your fill of dainty [meats and of sweet drinks] . . .'

84

From the same Manuscript:

. . . [And I answered you], 'I swear [to you by the Goddess that although I, like you,] had [of Zeus] but one virginity, [nevertheless] I feared [not the threshold] beyond which Hera had bidden [me cast it away.' Aye, thus I] heartened you, and cried aloud, 'That night was sweet enough [to me,] neither have you, dear maid, anything to fear.' . . .

[1] *i.e.* on many separate occasions

[3] cf. Cram. *A.O.* 2. 245. 21 [4] *E, e.g.*, cf. *C.R.* 1916, p. 132: separation of strophes doubtful [5] we should perh. read ὠρρώδην here and ὠξυβόην below

84 A

Lib. *Or.* i. 402 εἰ οὖν Σαπφὼ τὴν Λεσβίαν οὐδὲν ἐκώλυσεν εὔξασθαι νύκτα αὐτῇ γενέσθαι διπλασίαν, ἐξέστω κἀμοί παραπλήσιον αἰτῆσαι.

e. g. . . . . τοῦτο δ' ἴσθι, διπλασίαν
| κήναν νύκτ' ἄρασθαί μ' ἄμμι γένεσθαι.

85 [1]

Berl. Klassikertexte P 9722. 4

. . . ἦρ' ἀ[. . .
δῆρα τό[. . .
e. g. Γογγύλα τ[' ἔφατ'· 'Οὔ τι πᾳ τόδ' ἔγνως;]
ἤ τι σᾶμ' ἐθέλ[ης δεικνύναι τέαις]
5 παῖσι;' 'Μάλιστ',' ἀμ[ειβόμαν ἔγω. ''Ερ-]
μας γ' εἰσῆλθ'· ἐπὶ [δὲ βλέποισ' ἔγω Ϝε]
εἶπον· ᾮ δέσποτ', ἔπ[παν ἀπωλόμαν·]
[ο]ὐ μὰ γὰρ μάκαιραν [ἔγω θέαν]
[ο]ὖδεν ἄδομ' ἔπαρθ' ἄγα[ν ἔτ' ὄλβῳ,]
10 κατθάνην δ' ἴμμερός τις ἄ[γρεσέ με·] [2]
λῶ στᾶσ' εἰς δροσόεντ' ἄγ[ρον σέ μ' οἶ]
'Ατρήδαν 'Αγαμ[έμνον' ἄγαγες πρὶν]
[πά]ν τε ταΐρη[τον ἄνθος 'Αχαιίων.] [3]
[χ]ρῆ δὲ τοῦτ[' ἀπυλιππάνην με φαῦ-]
15 [ο]ς, ἄτις ὀ.[. . . . .'

[1] *E* ibid. [2] ms η[[3] ms]νδεθαιρη[

84 A[1]

Libanius *Orations*: If therefore Sappho the Lesbian could wish the length of her night doubled, I may make a similar prayer.

e.g. . . . Nay, I tell you, I prayed that night of ours might be made twice as long.

85

From the reverse of the above Manuscript:

. . . ['It cannot be] long now,' [said I. 'Surely,' said] Gongўla, ['you cannot tell?] or will you show your children a sign?' 'That I will,' answered I; 'Hermes came in unto me, and looking upon him I said "O Master, I am altogether undone; for by the blessed Goddess I swear to thee I care not so much any longer that I am exalted unto prosperity, but a desire hath taken me to die. I would fain have thee set me in the dewy meadow whither aforetime thou leddest Atreus' son Agamemnon and all the chosen flower of the Achaeans. I must [leave] this [light of day,] seeing that I . . ."'

[1] perh, from the same poem

86 [1] [πρὸς Ἄτθιδα]

Berl. Klassikertexte P 9722. 5

[Ἄτθι, σοὶ κἄμ' Ἀνακτορία φίλα] [2]
[πηλόροισ' ἐνὶ] Σάρδε[σιν]
[ναίει, πό]λλακι τυίδε [ν]ῶν ἔχοισα, [3]

ὤς ποτ' ἐζώομεν βίον, ἆς ἔχε
5 σὲ θέᾳ Ϝικέλαν ἀρι-
-γνώτᾳ, σᾷ δὲ μάλιστ' ἔχαιρε μόλπᾳ.

νῦν δὲ Λύδαισιν ἐμπρέπεται γυναί-
κεσσιν ὤς ποτ' ἀελίω
δύντος ἀ βροδοδάκτυλος σελάννα

10 πὰρ τὰ περρέχοισ' ἄστρα, [4] φάος δ' ἐπί-
σχει θάλασσαν ἐπ' ἀλμύραν
ἴσως καὶ πολυανθέμοις ἀρούραις,

ἀ δ' ἐέρσα κάλα κέχυται τεθά-
λαισι δὲ βρόδα κἄπαλ' ἄν-
15 θρυσκα καὶ μελίλωτος ἀνθεμώδης.

πόλλα δὲ ζαφοίταισ' ἀγάνας ἐπι-
μνάσθεισ' Ἀτθίδος ἰμμέρω,
λέπταν ποι φρένα κῆρ' ἄσᾳ βόρηται. [5]

κῆθι τ' ἔλθην ἄμμ' ὀξυβόη· τὰ δ' οὐ
20 νῷν γ' ἄπυστα νὺξ πολύω[ς]
γαρυίει δι' ἄλος πα[ρε]ụρẹọ[ίσας.] [6]

[1] cf. *C.R.* 1916. 130 [2] *E*, *e.g.* [3] πηλόροις ἐνὶ and ναίει *E* [4] *i.e.* ἄστρα ἃ περιέχουσι [5] ms κηρ', *i.e.* κῆρι adv. cf. Hom. [6] κῆθι Wil: ms κηθυι: perh. κῆσι, = ἐκεῖσε *E*: παρενρ. *E*

86 [To Atthis]

From the same Manuscript:

[Atthis, our beloved Anactoria dwells in far-off] Sardis, but she often sends her thoughts hither, thinking how once we used to live in the days when you were like a glorious Goddess to her and she loved your song the best. And now she shines among the dames of Lydia as after sunset the rosy-fingered Moon[1] beside the stars that are about her, when she spreads her light o'er briny sea and eke o'er flowery field, while the dew lies so fair on the ground and the roses revive and the dainty anthrysc and the melilot with all its blooms. And oftentime while our beloved wanders abroad, when she calls to mind the love of gentle Atthis, her tender breast, for sure, is weighed down deep with longing; and she cries aloud for us to come thither; and what she says we know full well, you and I, for Night that hath the many ears calls it to us across the dividing sea.[2]

[1] was Atthis the Sun? [2] a letter to [Atthis]; cf. 38

87 [1] πρὸς Τιμάδα

Ath. 9. 410 e Σαπφὼ δ' ὅταν λέγῃ ἐν τῷ πέμπτῳ τῶν Μελῶν πρὸς τὴν Ἀφροδίτην·

. . . χερρόμακτρα δὲ κὰγ γενύων [2]
πορφύρα καταρτᾰμένα, τὰ Τῖμας
εἴς <τ'> ἔπεμψ' ἀπὺ Φωκάας,[3]
δῶρα τίμια· . . . .

κόσμον λέγει κεφαλῆς τὰ χειρόμακτρα, ὡς καὶ Ἑκαταῖος δηλοῖ ἢ ὁ γεγραφὼς τὰς Περιηγήσεις ἐν τῇ Ἀσίᾳ ἐπιγραφομένας·[4] 'γυναῖκες δ' ἐπὶ τῆς κεφαλῆς ἔχουσι χειρόμακτρα.'

88

Hesych.

. . . . Τιμαδία·

μικρὰ Τιμάς.[5]

89

Jul. *Ep.* 60:

Ἦλθες· κεῦ ἐποίησας· ἔγω δέ σε
μαόμαν, ὂν δ' ἔφλαξας ἔμαν φρένα
καυομέναν πόθῳ· χαῖρ' ἄμμι, <χαῖρε>
πόλλα καὶ Ϝισάρῑθμα τόσῳ χρόνῳ
5 ἀλλάλαν ἀπελείφθημεν.[6] – ᴗ –

[1] see *Proc. Class. Assoc.* 1921 [2] Ahr.-Wil.: mss καγγονων (repeated after τίμια) [3] ll. 2–3 *E*; Τῖμας cf. 144: εἰς cf. *Il.* 15. 402. *Od.* 6. 175: τε = σε, cf. Hoff. *Gr. Dial.* 2. 13: mss πορφυρᾶ καταυταμενὰτατιμασεις ἔπ. Previous lines ran *e. g.* Νύκτι τᾷδε σύ μ' εἴσαο, | ὦ χρυσοστέφαν' Ἀφρόδιτ', | ὔναρ ἀθανάτω τέω πλέκοισα | κρᾶτος ἀμβροσίαν κόμαν, [4] mss -νῃ [5] *E*: mss τιμή: cf. Ὑρράδιος, Παλλάδιος [6] so *E*: εὖ ἐπ. cf. 100 ἔφλαξας = ἔφλεξας cf. Alc. 116, Theocr. 4. 35: τόσῳ = ὅσῳ: mss ἦλθες καὶ ἐπ. ἦλθες γὰρ δὴ καὶ ἀπὼν οἷς γράφεις· ἐγὼ δέ σε μὰ ὤμαν· ἂν δ' ἐφύλαξας ἐ. φ. καιομ. π. and later χαῖρε δὲ καὶ αὐτὸς ἡμῖν πολλά, καθάπερ ἡ καλὴ Σ. φησιν, καὶ οὐκ ἰσάριθμα μόνον τῷ χρόνῳ ὃν ἀλλήλων ἀπελείφθημεν, ἀλλὰ γὰρ καὶ ἀεὶ χαῖρε: metre cf. 82, 85

87 To Timas

Athenaeus *Doctors at Dinner*: And Sappho, when in the fifth Book of her Lyric Poems she says to Aphrodite:

. . . and hanging on either side thy face the purple handkerchief which Timas sent for thee from Phocaea, a precious gift from a precious giver; [1]

means the handkerchief as an adornment of the head, as is shown also by Hecataeus or the writer, whoever he was, of the book entitled *The Guide to Asia*, in the words 'And the women wear handkerchiefs on their heads.'

88

Hesychius *Glossary*: Timadia:

little Timas

89

Julian *Letter to Iamblichus*:

You are come; it is well; [2] I was longing for you, and now you have made my heart to flame up and burn with love. Bless you, I say, thrice bless you, and for just so long as you and I have been parted.[3]

[1] prob. the description of a dream, T. having sent the kerchief for S.'s statue of Aphrodite (cf. Rouse *Gk. Votive Offerings* 404, 275, *A.P.* 6. 270, 337, 340), and this being the letter of thanks; there is a pun on *Timas* and *timia* (precious); the previous lines were perh. to this effect (cf. *fr.* 123): 'Last night thou appearedst to me in a dream, O golden-wreathed Aphrodite, plaiting the ambrosial hair of thy immortal head.' [2] Jul. inserts 'for come you truly have in your letter, though you are far away' [3] the latter half of the fragment is preserved further on in this adaptation, 'Bless you also, I say, thrice over, as the beautiful S. says, and not only for just so long as you and I have been parted, but rather for ever'

90

Aristid. 1. 425 [μονῳδία ἐπὶ Σμύρνῃ]· . . . τὸ ὑπὲρ πάσης τῆς πόλεως ἑστηκὸς γάνος οὐ διαφθεῖρον τὰς ὄψεις, ὡς ἔφη Σαπφώ, ἀλλ᾽ αὖξον καὶ στέφον καὶ ἄρδον ἅμα εὐθυμίᾳ· ὑακινθίνῳ μὲν ἄνθει[1] οὐδαμῶς ὅμοιον, ἀλλ᾽ οἷον οὐδὲν πώποτε γῆ καὶ ἥλιος ἀνθρώποις ἔφηναν.

e. g. ζάφθερον ταὶς ὄψιας γάνος – ⏓ [2]

91

Arist. *Rhet.* 2. 23 . . . ἢ ὥσπερ Σαπφώ, ὅτι τὸ ἀποθνήσκειν κακόν· οἱ θεοὶ γὰρ οὕτω κεκρίκασιν· ἀπέθνῃσκον γὰρ ἄν.

e. g. τὸ θναίσκην κάκον· οἱ θέοι γὰρ οὕτω
| κεκρίκαισι· θάνον κε γάρ.[3]

92

Eust. *Op.* 345. 52 τούτους σου τοὺς κατασκόπους οὐ πόρνη κατὰ τὴν ὑμνουμένην Ἱεριχουντίαν ἐκείνην τῷ τοῦ ἐμοῦ τόπου καλῷ παρενέρριψε, φιλία τις δηλαδὴ πολυρέμβαστος καὶ καλὸν δοκοῦσα, εἴποι ἂν ἡ Σαπφώ, δημόσιον, ἀλλὰ καὶ καθαρά, καὶ κατὰ τὴν παρ᾽ Ἡσιόδῳ Δίκην παρθένος, καὶ <τοῖς>[4] πολλοῖς ἀνομίλητος.

e. g. . . . . . . ᾆ
| πολυρέμβαστον φιλίαν μέμειξαι
| καὶ κάλον δόκεισαν τὸ δαμόσιον.[5]

93

Hdn. π.μ.λ. 2. 932. 29 Lentz (for fuller context see 51): ἐφυλαξάμην δὲ διαλέκτους διὰ τόδε· (51)· καί·

Ἄλλα, μὴ κάμπτε στέραν φρένα . . . .[6]

[1] from *Od.* 6. 231 [2] metre 82: ὄψιας cf. ἄκουαι 2. 12 [3] for metre cf. 86: Greg. adds εἴπερ ἦν καλὸν τὸ ἀποθνήσκειν, but the ellipse is idiomatic [4] *E* [5] metre 82 [6] *E*: στέραν = στερέαν: mss ἄλλαν (see 51) μὴ καμεστεραν φ. (τι over εσ meant to correct to κάμπτι, for wh. cf. Alc. 122. 10)

90

Aristides *Orations* [praise of Smyrna] . . . the glamour that is upon the whole city, not as Sappho said, blinding the eyes, but magnifying it and wreathing it and moreover watering it with joyfulness,—not indeed 'like a hyacinth flower,' but such as earth and sun never before have shown to men.

e.g. . . . a glamour blinding the eyes

91[1]

Aristotle *Rhetoric* . . . . Or, as Sappho says:

Death is an ill; the Gods at least think so,
Or else themselves had perished long ago.

92

Eustathius *Opuscula* [a letter]: These spies were introduced into my estate by no harlot like her of Jericho, a friendship I mean of a vagrant sort which deems, as Sappho would say, a public thing beautiful, but a pure one and as virgin as Hesiod's Justice, unapproachable to the many.

e.g. . . . with whom you are mingled in a vagrant | friendship which deems that beautiful which | any man may have for the asking.[2]

93

Herodian *Words without Parallel*: I made the above exception of dialects because of the following examples: (51): and this:

Foolish girl, do not try to bend a stubborn heart.

[1] also in Greg. on Hermog. *Rh. Gr.* 7. 1153 Walz [2] prob. ref. to Charaxus and Doricha

94

Demetr. *Eloc.* 142 (cf. on Sa. 149) πολλὰς δ' ἄν τις καὶ ἄλλας <τοιαύτας>[1] ἐκφέροι χάριτας. γίγνονται καὶ ἀπὸ λέξεως χάριτες ἢ ἐκ μεταφορᾶς, ὡς ἐπὶ τοῦ τέττιγος·

. . . . πτερύγων δ' ὑπακακχέει
λιγύραν ἀοίδαν, ὄποτα φλόγι
<ὁ θέ>ος κατέτᾳ <γάα>ν
ἐπι<πε>πτάμενος καταύγη . . .

ἢ ἐκ κ.τ.λ.[2]

95

Zenob. (*Paroem.* 1. 58)

Γέλλως παιδοφιλωτέρα·

ἐπὶ τῶν ἀώρως τελευτησάντων, ἤτοι ἐπὶ τῶν φιλοτέκνων μὲν τρυφῇ <δὲ> διαφθειρόντων αὐτά· Γελλὼ γάρ τις ἦν παρθένος· καὶ ἐπειδὴ ἀώρως ἐτελεύτησε, φασὶν οἱ Λέσβιοι αὐτῆς τὸ φάντασμα ἐπιφοιτᾶν ἐπὶ τὰ παιδία καὶ τοὺς τῶν ἀώρων θανάτους αὐτῇ ἀνατίθεασι· μέμνηται ταύτης Σαπφώ.

96

Hdn. π.μ.λ. 2. 932. 29 Lentz (after *fr.* 93, where see context) καί·

Ἄβρα δηὖτ' ἐπ' ἄγκ' ἆς πάλαι ἀλλόμαν.[3]

ἀντὶ τοῦ ἠλλόμην.

97

E.M. 822. 39 ᾠϊόν· δεῖ γινώσκειν ὅτι τὸ ᾠόν τὸ ι ἔχει, πρῶτον μὲν ὅτι εὕρηται τὸ ι κατὰ διάστασιν παρὰ τῇ Σαπφοῖ·

Φαῖσι δή ποτα Λήδαν ὐακίνθινον
πεπυκάδμενον ὤϊον
εὔρην[4] . . .

[1] Weil [2] *E*: καταύγη from καταύγημι cf. ὔρημι 2. 11: for metre of last line cf. Heph. 33: mss ὅ τι ποτ' ἂν φλόγιον καθέταν (καθέτως) ἐπιπτάμενον καταυδείη (ἢ Finckh) [3] *E*: ἄγκα = ἀγκύλας, cf. ἀγκάς, ἀγκάσι: ἀλλόμαν = ἠλεόμην: mss ἄβρα· δεῦτε πάγχης π. ἀ, [4] Neue: ποτα Neue: mss ποτέ, ποταμόν

94[1]

Demetrius *on Style*: And many similar instances of charm might be adduced. Charm comes also from a form of expression or from a metaphor, as of the cricket:

. . . . and pours down a sweet shrill song from beneath his wings, when the Sun-god illumines the earth with his down-shed[2] flame outspread:

or from, etc.

95[3]

Zenobius *Centuries of Proverbs*:

Fonder of children than Gello;

a saying used of those who die young, or of those who are lovers of children but spoil them; for Gello was a girl who died young, and of whom the Lesbians say that her ghost haunts little children, ascribing to her the death of such as die before they are grown up. It occurs in Sappho.

96

Herodian *Words without Parallel*: . . . . And:

Lo! to the soft arms of her whom I had shunned so long [I have come back again];[4]

ἀλλόμαν 'shunned' is for *ἠλλόμην*.

97[5]

Etymologicum Magnum: *ὠϊόν* 'egg'; it should be understood that this word has the *i*, first because the *i* is found as a separate syllable in Sappho:

They say that once upon a time Leda found hidden an egg of hyacinthine hue. . . .

[1] inserted by *B* in Alc. 39 (my 161), but cf. Wil. *Herm.* '05 124: metrical arrangement and emendation doubtful, but cf. 82 ff. [2] or perh. in the later sense 'perpendicular' [3] cf. Suid, *E.M.* 795. 9 (Γελῶ), Hesych. Γελώ and Γελλώ [4] reading doubtful [5] cf. Ath. 2. 57 d, Eust. *Od.* 1686. 49

98

Ath. 1. 21 b ἔμελε δ' αὐτοῖς καὶ τοῦ κοσμίως ἀναλαμβάνειν τὴν ἐσθῆτα καὶ τοὺς μὴ τοῦτο ποιοῦντας ἔσκωπτον. Πλάτων. . . . Σαπφὼ περὶ Ἀνδρομέδας σκώπτει·

. . . . τίς δὲ
ἀγροίωτις ἄγροίωτιν ἐπεμμένα
σπόλαν <τέον> θαλύει νόον,
οὐκ ἐπισταμένα τὰ βράκε' ἕλκην ἐπὶ τῶν σφύρων;[1]

99

Stob. *Fl.* 71. 4 [ὅτι ἐν τοῖς γάμοις τὰς τῶν συναπτομένων ἡλικίας χρὴ σκοπεῖν]· Σαπφοῦς·[2]

. . . ἀλλ' ἔων φίλος ἄμμιν
λέχος ἄρνὔσο νεώτερον·[3]
οὐ γὰρ τλάσομ' ἔγω συνοί-
κην νέῳ ἔσσα[4] γεραιτέρα.

100

Sch. Pind. *O.* 2. 96 [ὁ μὰν πλοῦτος ἀρεταῖς δεδαιδαλμένος | φέρει τῶν τε καὶ τῶν | καιρόν]· ὁ νοῦς· ὁ δὲ πλοῦτος οὐ μόνος ὢν καθ' ἑαυτόν, ἀλλὰ καὶ ἀρετῇ κεκοσμημένος, καιρίως τῶν τε ἑαυτοῦ ἀγαθῶν καὶ τῆς ἀρετῆς ἀπολαύει, συνετὴν ἔχων τὴν φροντίδα πρὸς τὸ ἀγρεύειν τὰ καλά. τούτων γὰρ τὸ ἕτερον καθ' ἑαυτὸ οὐχ ἡδύ· ὡς καὶ Καλλίμαχος (*H. in Jov.* 95), καὶ ἡ Σαπφώ·

[1] *E*: cf. *A.P.* 7. 411 ἀγροιῶτιν ὕλαν, *Od.* 22. 184 σάκος γέρον, Hesych. θαλύεσθαι· φλέγεσθαι, θαλυσσόμενος· φλεγόμενος: mss Ath., Eust. τίς δ' ἀγροιῶτις (-ώτατον) θέλγει νόον οὐκ κ.τ.λ., Max. τίς δὲ ἀγροιωτειν ἐπεμμένα στολήν: Eust. paraphr. ποία γυνὴ χωριτική, ἐζωσμένη ἀγροικικώτερον (-τατον?) ἐφέλκεται ἐραστήν; [2] so arr. Weir-Smyth: metre Catull. 61 [3] cf. νῶν = νόον 86 [4] mss ἔσσα, οὖσα, νέ' οὖσα

98[1]

Athenaeus *Doctors at Dinner*: They took pains, too, to put on their clothes neatly, and made fun of those who failed to do so; compare Plato . . . Sappho jests about Andromeda in the words:

. . . And what countrified wench in countrified clothes fires your breast, though she knows not how to draw her gown over her ankles?[2]

99[3]

Stobaeus *Anthology* [That in marriage it is well to consider the ages of the parties concerned] . . . Sappho:

. . . But if you love me, choose yourself a younger wife; for I cannot submit to live with one that is younger than I.

100[4]

Scholiast on Pindar ['wealth adorned with virtues brings with it the opportunity for all manner of things']: The meaning is: wealth when it is not alone but decorated with virtue enjoys in season its own benefits and those of virtue, having a spirit naturally apt for the search after what is good. For neither of the two is desirable of itself. Compare Callimachus . . . , and Sappho:

[1] cf. Eust. *Od.* 1916. 49, Philem. 61, Max. Tyr. 24 (18). 9
[2] *i.e.* when she sits down [3] cf. *Paroem.* 2. 277 [4] cf. Plut. *Nobil.* 5, Sch. Pind. *P.* 5. 1: Plut. has 'high-birth' instead of 'wealth,' perh. rightly (S. was well-born, see p. 143)

. . . ὁ πλοῦτος<δ'> ἄνευ ἀρέτας
οὐκ ἀσίνης πάροικος·[1]
ἀ δὲ κρᾶσις ἀμφοτέρων[2]
δαιμονίαν ἄκραν ἔχει·[3]

τοῦτο προσεῖναι τῷ Θήρωνι μαρτυρεῖ.

101 εἰς τὰς Χάριτας καὶ τὰς Μούσας

Heph. 56 [π. χοριαμβικοῦ]· τὰ δὲ (περαιοῦται) εἰς τὸν ἀμφίβραχυν ἢ βακχεῖον· οἷον δίμετρα μὲν . . ., τρίμετρα δὲ . . ., τετράμετρα δέ, ἃ καὶ συνεχέστερά ἐστιν, οἷα ταυτὶ τὰ Σαπφοῦς·

Δεῦτέ νῦν ἄβραι Χάριτες καλλίκομοί τε Μοῖσαι.

102

At. Fort. 359 *De Metris Hor.* (6. 301 Keil) ad Hor. *Od.* i. 8: Apud Anacreontem (est metrum choriambicum dimetrum catalecticum); . . ., Sappho;

. . . . . . πάρθενον ἀδύφωνον

103

Heph. 64 [π. ἀντισπαστικοῦ]· τῶν δὲ τετραμέτρων τὸ μὲν καταληκτικὸν καθαρόν ἐστι τὸ τοιοῦτον·

κατθναίσκει, Κυθέρη', ἄβρος Ἄδωνις· τί κε θεῖμεν;
καττύπτεσθε, κόραι, καὶ κατερείκεσθε χίτωνας.[4]

104

Paus. 9. 29. 8 Πάμφως δὲ ὃς Ἀθηναίοις τῶν ὕμνων ἐποίησε τοὺς ἀρχαιοτάτους, οὗτος ἀκμάζοντος ἐπὶ τῷ Λίνῳ τοῦ πένθους Οἰτολίνον ἐκάλεσεν αὐτόν· Σαπφὼ δὲ ἡ Λεσβία τοῦ Οἰτολίνου τὸ ὄνομα ἐκ τῶν ἐπῶν τῶν Πάμφω μαθοῦσα, Ἄδωνιν ὁμοῦ καὶ Οἰτολίνον ᾖσε.

[1] cf. 89. 1: mss Sch. *O.* πλοῦτος, *P.* ὁ πλ., Plut. εὐγένεια: mss Sch. *O.* also ἀγαθὸς σύνοικ. [2] *E*: mss ἡ δὲ ἐξ ἀμφοτέρων κρᾶσις [3] *E*, cf. Hesych. δαιμονίαν ἄκραν· μακαρίαν θειοτάτην (so read): mss εὐδαιμονίας ἔχει τὸ ἄκρον· (Plut. om. τό) [4] κατερείκ. Pauw: mss -ερύκ.

Wealth without worth is no harmless housemate;
but the blending of the two is the top of fortune.

This Pindar declares to be the lot of Theron.

101[1] To the Graces and the Muses

Hephaestion *Handbook of Metre* [on the choriambic]: Some on the other hand end with an amphibrach or a bacchius, for example the dimeter . . . . , the trimeter . . . . , and the tetrameter—which is used in longer sequences—, such as the lines of Sappho beginning

O hither, soft Graces and lovely-tressèd Muses.

102

Atilius Fortunatianus *On the Metres of Horace* [Horace's *Lydia, dic per omnes*]: In Anacreon we find it (the choriambic dimeter catalectic): . . . . , and in Sappho:

a sweet-voicèd maiden

103[2]

Hephaestion *Ibid*: Of the (antispastic) tetrameter the pure catalectic is like this:

The delicate Adonis is dying, Cytherea; what can we do?
Beat your breasts, maidens, and rend your garments.

104

Pausanias *Description of Greece*: Pamphōs, who composed the oldest Athenian hymns, called Linus 'Oetolinus' or 'Linus Dead' at the climax of the mourning for him. And Sappho of Lesbos, having learnt the name of 'Linus Dead' from the lines of Pamphos, sang of 'Adonis' and 'Linus Dead' both together.

[1] cf. At. Fort. 259 who read νῦν [2] ascription based on Paus. 9. 29. 8 (see below); one of the chorus seems to have played the Goddess

105

Poll. 7. 73 [π. λινῶν ἐσθήτων καὶ ἀμοργίνων]· ἐν δὲ τῷ πέμπτῳ τῶν Σαπφοῦς Μελῶν ἔστιν εὑρεῖν·

ἀμφὶ δ' ἄβροις λασίοισ' εὖ Ϝ' ἐπύκασσε . . .[1]

καὶ φασὶν εἶναι ταῦτα σινδόνια ἐπεστραμμένα.

106

Diogen. (*Paroem.* 1. 279):

Μήτ' ἔμοι μέλι μήτε μελίσσαις·[2]

ἐπὶ τῶν μὴ βουλομένων παθεῖν τι φαῦλον μετὰ ἀγαθῶν.

107

Clearch. ap. Ath. 12. 554b [διὰ τί μετὰ χεῖρας ἄνθη . . . φέρομεν;]· . . . ἢ πάντες οἱ ἐρῶντες οἷον ἐκτρυφῶντες ὑπὸ τοῦ πάθους καὶ ὡριαινόμενοι τοῖς ὡραίοις ἁβρύνονται. φυσικὸν γὰρ δή τι τὸ τοὺς οἰομένους εἶναι καλοὺς καὶ ὡραίους ἀνθολογεῖν. ὅθεν αἵ τε περὶ τὴν Περσεφόνην ἀνθολογεῖν λέγονται, καὶ Σαπφώ φησιν ἰδεῖν ἄνθε' ἀμέργουσαν παῖδ' ἄγαν ἁπαλάν.

e.g. Εὔιδόν ποτ' ἄνθε' ἀμέρ-
| γοισαν παῖδ' ἄγαν ἀπάλαν ἔγω.

108 πρὸς τὴν θυγατέρα

Max. Tyr. 18. 9 [τίς ἡ Σωκράτους ἐρωτική;]· ἀναίθεται (ὁ Σωκράτης) τῇ Ξανθίππῃ ὀδυρομένῃ ὅτε[3] ἀπέθνῃσκεν, ἡ δὲ Σαπφὼ τῇ θυγατρί·

οὐ γὰρ θέμις ἐν μοισοπόλῳ οἰκίᾳ
θρῆνον θέμεν· οὐκ ἄμμι πρέπει τάδε.[4]

[1] *B*: mss λασσίοις εὖ ἐπύκασε [2] mss Diog. μηδὲ μ. μηδὲ μέλισσα (or -σας), others add ἐμοί [3] ms ὅτι [4] μοισοπόλῳ Neue: mss μουσοπόλων; θέμεν *E*, cf. *Od.* 9. 235: mss εἶναι (correction of θέμις from above)

105

Pollux *Vocabulary* [on clothes of Amorgine and other linen]: In the fifth Book of Sappho's Lyric Poems we find:

And wrapped her all about with soft cambric;[1]

and they say that this means pieces of close-woven[2] linen.

106

Diogenian *Centuries of Proverbs*:

I will have neither honey nor bees;[3]

proverbial of those who will not take the sour with the sweet.

107

Clearchus in Athenaeus *Doctors at Dinner* [why we carry flowers in our hands]: . . . . Or else it is that all lovers, waxing wanton with their passion, are melted by the sight of what is ripe and blooming. For it is certainly a thing quite natural that those who believe themselves beautiful and blooming should gather flowers. And that is why Persephone and her companions are described as flower-gathering, and Sappho says that she saw a very beautiful little girl culling flowers.

e. g. I saw one day a-gathering flowers
The daintiest little maid.

108 To Her Daughter

Maximus of Tyre *Dissertations* [what was the nature of Socrates' love-affairs]: Socrates chides Xanthippe for weeping when he is about to die, and so does Sappho chide her daughter:

No house that serves the Muse hath room, I wis,
For grief; and so it ill beseemeth this.

[1] *or* him [2] *or* twisted? [3] *i. e.* if I can't have the honey without a sting, I won't have either: cf. *Paroem.* 2. 527, Tryph. *Rhet. Gr.* 8. 760 (Walz), who ascribes it to Sappho

109

Paus. 8. 18. 5 [π. Στυγός]· κεράτινα δὲ καὶ ὀστέϊνα, σίδηρός τε καὶ χαλκὸς, ἔτι δὲ μόλιβδος καὶ κασσίτερος καὶ ἄργυρος καὶ τὸ ἤλεκτρον ὑπὸ τούτου σήπεται τοῦ ὕδατος· τὸ δὲ αὐτὸ μετάλλοις[1] τοῖς πᾶσι καὶ ὁ χρυσὸς πέπονθε· καίτοι γε καθαρεύειν γε τὸν χρυσὸν τοῦ ἰοῦ,[2] ἥ τε ποιητρία μάρτυς ἐστὶν ἡ Λεσβιά καὶ αὐτὸς ὁ χρυσὸς ἐπιδείκνυσιν. ἔδωκε δ' ἄρα ὁ θεὸς τοῖς μάλιστα ἀπερριμμένοις κρατεῖν τῶν ὑπερηρκότων τῇ δόξῃ.

e. g. κόθαρος γὰρ ὁ χρῦσος ἴω.[3]

110

Sch. Pind. *P.* 4. 410 [ἄφθιτον στρωμνάν]· ἄφθιτον δὲ αὐτὸ εἶπε καθὸ χρυσοῦν ἦν· ὁ δὲ χρυσὸς ἄφθαρτος· καὶ ἡ Σαπφὼ ὅτι· Διὸς παῖς ὁ χρυσός, κεῖνον οὐ σὴς οὐδὲ κὶς δάπτει, βροτεᾶν † φρένα κράτιστον φρενῶν. †

e. g. Διὸς γὰρ πάϊς ἔστ' ὁ χρύσος·
κῆνον οὐ σέες οὐδὲ κῖς
δαρδάπτοισ'· ὁ δὲ δάμναται
καὶ φρένων βροτέαν κράτιστον.[4]

ϛ'

111

Heph. 70 [π. ἰωνικοῦ τοῦ ἀπὸ μείζονος]· ἐνίοτε δὲ ἐναλλὰξ τὰς ἰωνικὰς ταῖς τροχαϊκαῖς παραλαμβάνουσιν, ἀντὶ μὲν τῶν ἰωνικῶν ἔσθ' ὅτε τὰς δευτέρας παιωνικὰς παραλαμβάνοντες, ἀντὶ δὲ τῶν ἑξασήμων τροχαϊκῶν ἔσθ' ὅτε τὰς ἑπτασήμους τροχαϊκάς, οἷον·

[1] mss ἐν μ. [2] *E*: mss ὑπὸ τοῦ ἰοῦ [3] metre cf. Heph. 33
[4] *E*, cf. Sch. Hes. below: κῖς = κῖες cf. πόλῖς Hfm. 541: φρένα incorp. correction of φρένων, βροτέαν being thought accus.: mss δάπτει due to κῖς being thought sing.: metre cf. 109: some edd. supposing Sappho-citation lost and comparing Sch. Hes. *Op.* 428 (τοῦτο καὶ Πίνδαρον οὕτω καλεῖν περὶ

109

Pausanias *Description of Greece* [the Styx]: Things of horn and of bone, iron and copper, lead and tin and silver and electrum, all are corroded by the water; and gold suffers like the other metals. And yet, that gold remains pure of rust is both declared by the Lesbian poetess and proved by our own experience. It seems that God has given the least-considered of things power over those that are deemed to be of great price.

e.g. For gold is pure of rust.

110

Scholiast on Pindar [‘that immortal coverlet,’ *i.e.* the Golden Fleece]: He calls it immortal because it was golden; and gold is indestructible; compare Sappho:

e.g. Gold is a child of Zeus; no moth nor worm devours it, and it overcomes the strongest of mortal hearts.[1]

Book VI

111[2]

Hephaestion *Handbook of Metre* [The *Ionicum a majore*]: Sometimes they use ionics alternately with trochaics, in some lines substituting the second paeon for an ionic, and in some employing seven-‘time’ trochaics instead of six-‘time,’ as:

[1] the Scholiast on Hesiod ascribes this to Pindar [2] cf. *Paroem. Gr.* 2. 363 (Σαπφοῦς)

τοῦ χρυσοῦ λέγοντα· κεῖνον σῆς οὐ κὶς δάμναται, ὡς ἄσηπτον κὶς δάπτει, βροτέαν) ascribe Διὸς κ.τ.λ. to Pind. (*fr.* 222 Bgk.), perh. rightly

Δέδυκε μὲν ἀ σέλαννα
καὶ Πληΐαδες, μέσαι δὲ
νύκτες, παρὰ δ' ἔρχετ' ὤρα,
ἔγω δὲ μόνα κατεύδω.

112

Heph. 68 [π. ἰωνικοῦ τοῦ ἀπὸ μείζονος]· καὶ τρίμετρα βραχυκατάληκτα τὰ καλούμενα Πραξίλλεια, ἃ τὴν μὲν πρώτην ἔχει ἰωνικήν, τὴν δὲ δευτέραν τροχαϊκήν, οἷά ἐστι τὰ τοιαῦτα Σαπφοῦς·

πλήρης μὲν ἐφαίνετ' ἀ σέλαννα,
αἰ δ' ὠς περὶ βῶμον ἐστάθησαν . . .

113 A and B

Ox. Pap. 220. 9 [π. Ἀνακρεοντείου]· ἑπομέ]νως δὲ καὶ παραπλησίως καὶ τοῦ Πραξιλλείου στίχου τεμών τις δύο τὰς πρώτας συλλαβὰς ποιήσει τὸ Ἀνακρεόντειον· καθόλου δὲ κἀπὶ τούτου πάσας ἀφελών τις τὰς ἐκ τῆς πρώτης χώρας παρὰ μίαν βραχεῖαν ἀποτελέσει τὸ μέτρον ὁμοίως· σκόπει γοῦν τάδε καταλελοιπότα τὰς πρώτας συλλαβάς· μεν εφαινεθ α σελανα (112)· ονιαν τε και υγειαν· σα φυγοιμι παιδες ηβα.

[Εὐδαιμ]ονίαν τε κὐγίειαν[1]

[Γῆρας] ζαφύγοιμι, παῖδες· ἤβα[1]

114

Heph. 68 [π. ἰωνικοῦ τοῦ ἀπὸ μείζονος]· τὰ δὲ τρίμετρα ἀκατάληκτα διχῶς συνέθεσαν οἱ Αἰολεῖς· τὰ μὲν γὰρ ἐκ δύο ἰωνικῶν καὶ τροχαϊκῆς ἐποίησαν, οἷον·

[1] *E*: all three are prob. first lines

The Moon is gone
And the Pleiads set,
  Midnight is nigh;
Time passes on,
And passes; yet
  Alone I lie.[1]

112

Hephaestion *Handbook of Metre* [The *Ionicum a majore*]: And there are brachycatalectic trimeters, namely what are called Praxilleans, which have the first meter ionic and the second trochaic, such as the following lines of Sappho:

The Moon rose full, and the maidens, taking their stand about the altar . . .[2]

113 A and B

From a Papyrus of about A.D. 100 [on the Anacreontic metre]: Similarly with the Praxillean, if you cut off its first two syllables you will make the Anacreontic; or putting it generally as in the preceding case (of the Phalaecian), you will make it in like manner if you remove all the first foot[3] except one short. Consider the following lines when docked of their first syllables (—*fr.* 112 *then*—):

Both happiness and health . . .

I pray I may escape [old age], my children; youth[4] . . .

114

Hephaestion *Handbook of Metre* [the *Ionicum a majore*]: The Aeolic poets made acatalectic trimeters in two ways, first, of two ionics and a trochaic, as:

[1] Heph. arranges as 2 lines [2] S. wrote much in this metre; cf. *fr.* 113 and Trich. 7 (Heph. 392 Cons.) [3] presumably – – ᴗ [4] the words 'happiness' and 'old age' were in the part cut off, and so are not quite certain

Κρῆσσαί νύ ποτ' ὧδ' ἐμμελέως πόδεσσιν
ὤρχηντ' ἀπάλοισ' ἀμφ' ἐρόεντα βῶμον,
πόας τέρεν ἄνθος μάλακον ματεῖσαι.[1]

115 πρὸς Μνησιδίκην

Heph. 69 [π. ἰωνικοῦ τοῦ ἀπὸ μείζονος]· καὶ τετράμετρα δὲ ἀκατάληκτα διαφόρως συνέθεσαν· ἢ γὰρ τρισὶν ἰωνικαῖς μίαν τροχαϊκὴν τὴν τελευταίαν ἐπήγαγον—καλεῖται δὲ Αἰολικόν, ὅτι Σαπφὼ πολλῷ αὐτῷ ἐχρήσατο—οἷον·

Εὐμορφοτέρα Μνασιδίκα τᾶς ἀπάλας Γυρίννως

116 εἰς Εἰρήνην

Ibid.

Ἀσαροτέρας οὐδαμά ποι Εἴρηνα σέθεν τύχοισα . . .[2]

117 πρὸς Μνησιδίκην

Ath. 15. 674 d [π. στεφάνων]· Αἰσχύλος δὲ . . . σαφῶς φησιν ὅτι ἐπὶ τιμῇ τοῦ Προμηθέως τὸν στέφανον περιτίθεμεν τῇ κεφαλῇ, ἀντίποινα τοῦ ἐκείνου δεσμοῦ . . . Σαπφὼ δ' ἁπλούστερον τὴν αἰτίαν ἀποδίδωσιν τοῦ στεφανοῦσθαι ἡμᾶς, λέγουσα τάδε·

σὺ δὲ στεφάνοις, ὦ Δίκα, πέρθεσσ' ἐράταις
φόβαισιν
ὄρπακας ἀνήτοιο συνέρραισ' ἀπάλαισι χέρσιν·[3]

[1] cf. Alc. 76. 2, Hesych. (after μανῶν) ματεῖ· πατεῖ, Theocr. 29. 15 [2] οὐδ. π. Εἰ.: so Hfm. -E: or πα ὦ Εἰρ. ? Choer. ad loc. paraphr. βλαβερωτέρας οὐδαμῶς πού ποτε, Εἰρήνη, σοῦ ἐπιτυχοῦσα (or -αν) and vouches for εἴρηνᾰ: mss Ch. -άπα εἰρήνα, ἀπώρανα, Heph. ἀ. πώρανα, -απ' ὤρανα: Blf. -ά πω, 'ραννα (name): τύχοισα: mss also -σαν [3] περθεσσ(ο) E: mss παρθεσθ'

Thus of old did the dainty feet of Cretan maidens dance pat to the music beside some lovely altar, pressing the soft smooth bloom of the grass.[1]

115[2] To Mnesidicé

Hephaestion *Handbook of Metre* [the *Ionicum a majore*]: Moreover they composed acatalectic tetrameters of various kinds; for either they added a single final trochaic to three ionics—and this is called Aeolic because Sappho often used it—as:

Mnasidica, of fairer form than the dainty Gyrinno

116[3] To Peace

The Same: And this:

Having never, methinks, found thee more irksome, O Peace[4] . . .

117[5] To Mnesidicé

Athenaeus *Doctors at Dinner* [on garlands]: Aeschylus . . . says clearly that our object in putting wreaths on our heads is to do honour to Prometheus by a sort of requital of his bonds. . . . But Sappho gives a simpler reason, saying:

. . . But do you, Dica, let your dainty fingers twine a wreath of anise-sprays and bind your lovely locks; for it may well be that the blessed Graces,

[1] l. 3 placed here by Santenius from Heph. 70 [2] cf. Longin. *Prol.* Heph. 3, *Thes. Corn.* Ald. 268 b, *E.M.* 243. 51, Max. Tyr. 24 (18). 9 [3] cf. *Dikaiomata* (Halle Pap.) 182 [4] perh. a name cf. Clem. Al. 4. 19. 122, but reading doubtful without sequel [5] cf. Sch. Theocr. 7. 63, Poll. 6. 107

εὐάνθεα γὰρ <παρ>πέλεται καὶ Χάριτας μάκαιρα<ς>
μᾶλλον προτόρην·[1] ἀστεφανώτοισι δ' ἀπυστρέφονται.

ὡς <τὸ> εὐανθέστερον γὰρ καὶ κεχαρισμένον μᾶλλον <ὂν> τοῖς θεοῖς, παραγγέλλει στεφανοῦσθαι τοὺς θύοντας.

118

Ath. 15. 687 a ὑμεῖς δὲ οἴεσθε τὴν ἁβρότητα χωρὶς ἀρετῆς ἔχειν τι τερπνόν[2]; καίτοι Σαπφώ, γυνὴ μὲν πρὸς ἀλήθειαν οὖσα καὶ ποιητρία, ὅμως ᾐδέσθη τὸ καλὸν τῆς ἁβρότητος ἀφελεῖν, λέγουσα ὧδε·

. . . . ἔγω δὲ
φίλημ' ἀβροσύναν, καί μοι τὸ λάμπρον
ἔρος ἀελίω καὶ τὸ κάλον λέλογχε·

φανερὸν ποιοῦσα πᾶσιν ὡς ἡ τοῦ ζῆν ἐπιθυμία τὸ λαμπρὸν καὶ τὸ καλὸν εἶχεν αὐτῇ· ταῦτα δέ ἐστιν οἰκεῖα τῆς ἀρετῆς.

119 πρὸς Ἀλκαῖον

Arist. *Rhet.* 1. 9 τὰ γὰρ αἰσχρὰ αἰσχύνονται καὶ λέγοντες καὶ ποιοῦντες καὶ μέλλοντες, ὥσπερ καὶ Σαπφὼ πεποίηκεν εἰπόντος τοῦ Ἀλκαίου· 'θέλω τι Ϝείπην ἀλλά με κωλύει αἴδως·'[3]

αἰ δ' ἦχες ἔσλων ἴμμερον ἢ κάλων
καὶ μή τι Ϝείπην γλῶσσ' ἐκύκα κάκον,
αἴδως κεν οὐκί σ' ἦχεν ὄππατ',[4]
ἀλλ' ἔλεγες περὶ τῶ δικαίως.[5]

[1] *E* (or keep μάκ. as voc.): παρπ. = πάρεστι cf. Soph. *Ant.* 478: mss εὐάνθεα γ. πέλεται κ. Χάριτες μάκαιρα: Fick εὐάνθεα γ. κ. Μέλεται ('Muses') κ. Χάριτες, μάκαιρα: προτόρην Seid. = προσορᾶν cf. προτί Alc. 156: mss προτέρην: Fick προσόρηντ' [2] *E*, see context: mss τρυφερόν from above [3] Alc. *fr.* 124 [4] *E*: mss α. κ. σε οὐκ εἶχεν [5] *B* = ᾧ ἐδικαίους: mss τῶ (ὧ, ᾧ) δικαίω

too, are more apt to look with favour on that which is adorned with flowers, whereas they turn away from all that goes ungarlanded;

for she urges the makers of the sacrifice to wreathe their heads on the plea that that which is the more adorned with flowers is the more pleasing to the Gods.

118

Athenaeus *Doctors at Dinner*: Do you think that delicacy or refinement without virtue is a thing to be desired? Why, Sappho, who was a woman out and out and a poetess, too, hesitated nevertheless to separate refinement from honour, for she says:

. . . But I love delicacy, and the bright and the beautiful belong for me to the desire of the sunlight;[1]

making it clear that the desire to live comprehended for her the bright or famous and the beautiful or honourable; and these belong to virtue.

119[2] To Alcaeus

Aristotle *Rhetoric*: For we are ashamed of what is shameful, whether in word or deed or intention; compare Sappho's answer when Alcaeus said, 'I fain would tell you something, but shame restrains me:'

If your desire were of things good or fair, and your tongue were not mixing a draught of ill words, then would not shame possess your eye, but you would make your plea outright.

[1] *pace* Athenaeus, S. probably means physical brightness and beauty; without them life would not be worth living
[2] cf. Cram. *A.P.* 1. 266. 25 (takes this and Alc. 124 as from an amoeboeic poem of S.)

120

Ath. 13. 564 d [π. ὄμματα τὰ τῶν ἐρωμένων]· καὶ ἡ Σαπφὼ δὲ πρὸς τὸν ὑπερβαλλόντως θαυμαζόμενον τὴν μορφὴν καὶ καλὸν εἶναι νομιζόμενόν φησιν·

ὄσταθι κἄντα <θᾶ με φίλαν> φίλος [1]
καὶ τὰν ἐπ' ὄσσοισ' ὀμπέτασον χάριν.

121

Max. Tyr. 24 (18). 9 καὶ ὅτιπερ Σωκράτει οἱ ἀντίτεχνοι, Πρόδικος καὶ Γοργίας καὶ Θρασύμαχος, τοῦτο τῇ Σαπφοῖ Γοργὼ καὶ Ἀνδρομέδα· νῦν μὲν ἐπιτιμᾷ ταύταις, νῦν δὲ ἐλέγχει καὶ εἰρωνεύεται αὐτὰ ἐκεῖνα τὰ Σωκράτους. 'Τὸν Ἴωνα χαίρειν' φησὶν ὁ Σωκράτης·

. . . . . πόλλα μοι τὰν
πολλυανάκτιδα παῖδα χαίρην· [2]

Σαπφὼ λέγει.

122

Heph. 72 [π. τοῦ ἀπ' ἐλάσσονος ἰωνικοῦ]· καὶ ὅλα μὲν οὖν ᾄσματα γέγραπται ἰωνικά, ὥσπερ Ἀλκμᾶνι . . ., Σαπφοῖ δέ·

Τί με Πανδίονις ὄρραννα χελίδω . . . [3];

[1] ὔσταθι = ἀνάστηθι *E*, cf. Hesych. ὔστασαν : mss στᾶθι : suppl. *E*, cf. 66. 10 and Ath. 460 d for loss of words in Ath.'s quotations [2] πολλυ. *E* (λλ Hfm.): mss πολυανάκτιδα: the word-order shows it is an epithet: edd. Πολ., Πωλ. [3] *E*: = οὐρανία cf. Hesych. (so read) ὠράνα χελίδω· <οὐρανία χελίδων | ὤροφος·> ὀροφὴ (*i. e* ἡ ὀρ.) and κόννα· σποδός (*i. e.* κόνια): mss ὠράνα χελίδων : next line *E e.g.* ὀνίαι (vb.) νέαν πάλιν ὤραν ἐπάγοισα;

120

Athenaeus *Doctors at Dinner* [on the eyes of lovers]: And Sappho, too, says to the man exceedingly admired for his good looks:

Stand up, look me in the face as friend to friend, and unveil the charm that is in your eyes.

121

Maximus of Tyre *Dissertations*: And what his rivals Prodicus and Gorgias and Thrasymachus were to Socrates, that were Gorgo and Andromeda to Sappho. At one time she chides these rivals, at another she refutes them in argument and uses the very same forms of irony that Socrates does. For instance, Socrates [as an opening to a discussion in which he refutes him] says 'A very good day to Master Ion,'[1] and Sappho [in similar circumstances] begins:

A very good day to a daughter of very many kings.

122

Hephaestion *Handbook of Metre* [the *Ionicum a minore*]: And indeed whole poems have been written in ionics, for instance Alcman's . . ., and Sappho's:

Why does the heavenly swallow, daughter of Pandion [vex] me . . .?[2]

[1] Plat. *Ion* 530 a: the syntax suggests formality [2] l. 2 ran perh. thus: 'by bringing in the new season?' S. wrote much in this metre, cf. Trich. 8 (Heph. 395 Cons.)

123

Heph. 74 [π. τοῦ ἀπ' ἐλάσσονος ἰωνικοῦ]· τῶν δε τριμέτρων τὸ μὲν ἀκατάληκτον·

Διελεξάμαν ὄναρ Κυπρογενήᾳ·[1]

παρὰ τῇ Σαπφοῖ . . .

124

Apoll. *Pron.* 66. 3 ἐμέθεν· πυκνῶς αἱ χρήσεις παρὰ Αἰολεῦσιν·

. . . . . ἔμεθεν δ' ἔχεισθα λάθαν.

125, 126

Heph. 87 [π. τοῦ ἀπ' ἐλάσσονος ἰωνικοῦ]· ἀνακλωμένου δὲ ὄντος αὐτοῦ, προταχθεῖσα ἰαμβικὴ ἑξάσημος ἢ ἑπτάσημος ποιεῖ τὸ τοιοῦτον, οἷον παρὰ Σαπφοῖ·

Ἔχει μὲν Ἀνδρομέδα κάλαν ἀμοίβαν . . .

Ψάπφοι, τί τὰν πολύολβον Ἀφροδίταν
[ἀτίμασας ; . . . . . .][2]

Ζ'

127

Ibid. 89 [π. ἀσυναρτήτων]· δύναται δὲ καὶ εἰς τρίπουν ἀναπαιστικὸν[3] διαιρεῖσθαι, εἰ ἀπὸ σπονδείου ἄρχοιτο, οἷον τὸ Σαπφοῦς·

αὐτὰ δὲ σύ, Καλλιόπα ⏓ – ⏑ – ⏑ – ⏓,

τοῦ προσοδιακοῦ ὂν καὶ τοῦτο εἶδος.

[1] *E*: mss ζαελ., προσελ., the former a metrical emendation of a hyper-aeolising ζαλ. (ζά and διά were both Aeol.): Ahr. ζὰ δ' ἐλ: (but δέ is out of place in an obvious first line)
[2] *E, e.g.* [3] Hense: mss τρίτον ἀνάπαιστον

123[1]

Hephaestion *Handbook of Metre* [the *Ionicum a minore*]: Of the trimeters the acatalectic is exemplified by:

I dreamt that I talked with the Cyprus-born;

in Sappho.

124

Apollonius *Pronouns*: ἐμέθεν 'of me'; it occurs frequently in the Aeolic writers; compare

. . . and forgettest me.

125, 126

Hephaestion *Handbook of Metre*: But when the ionic is 'broken' or 'impure,'[2] an iambic meter of six or seven 'times' precedes it giving the following result, as in Sappho:

Andromeda has driven a fine bargain;

and:

Why, Sappho, [do you disdain] Aphrodite of the many blessings?

Book VII

127

The Same [metres combining two 'heterogeneous' parts]: And it (the earlier half of a certain 'heterogeneous' line) can also be divided as a three-foot anapaestic, if it begins with a spondee, as in Sappho's:

And thou thyself, Calliope . . .,

this, too, being a form of the prosodiac.

[1] cf. Sch. Heph. [2] *e. g.* πολύολβον below

128

Et. Mag. 250. 10 δαύω· τὸ κοιμῶμαι· Σαπφώ·

Δαύοις ἀπάλας ἐτάρας ἐν στήθεσιν ⏑ – ⏓ [1]

λέγει δὲ Ἡρωδιανός, ὅτι ἅπαξ κεῖται ἡ λέξις παρὰ Σαπφοῖ.

129 εἰς τὰς Μούσας

Heph. 106 [π. ἀσυναρτήτων]· καὶ τὸ ἐξ ἰθυφαλλικῶν δύο ἡ Σαπφὼ πεποίηκε·

Δεῦρο δηὖτε, Μοῖσαι, χρύσιον λίποισαι
[δῶμα] [2] . . . .

130 πρὸς Κλῆϊν

Ibid. 98 ἄλλο ἀσυνάρτητον ὁμοίως κατὰ τὴν πρώτην ἀντιπάθειαν, ἐκ τροχαϊκοῦ διμέτρου ἀκαταλήκτου καὶ ἰαμβικοῦ ἑφθημιμεροῦς, ὅπερ ἐὰν παραλλάξῃ τὴν τομήν, γίγνεται τροχαϊκὸν προκαταληκτικόν·

Ἔστι μοι κάλα πάϊς χρυσίοισιν ἀνθέμοισιν
ἐμφέρην ἔχοισα μόρφαν, Κλεῦις ἀγαπάτα, [3]
ἀντὶ τᾶς ἔγω οὐδὲ Λυδίαν παῖσαν οὐδ᾽ ἐράνναν
[Λέσβον ἀγρέην κε] [4] . . . . . .

τούτων δὲ τὸ μὲν δεύτερον δῆλόν ἐστιν ἀπὸ τῆς τομῆς ὅτι οὕτως συγκεῖται ὡς προείρηται, ἐκ τοῦ τροχαϊκοῦ διμέτρου ἀκατα ήκτου καὶ τοῦ ἑφθημιμεροῦς ἰαμβικοῦ, τὸ δὲ πρῶτον, διὰ τὸ πρὸ συλλαβῆς ἔχειν τὴν τομήν, ἐγένετο προκαταληκτικόν, ἐκ τροχαϊκοῦ ἑφθημιμεροῦς, 'ἔστι μοι κάλα πάϊς,' καὶ διμέτρου ἀκαταλήκτου τοῦ 'χρυσίοισιν ἀνθέμοισιν·' τὸ δὲ τρίτον ἐξ ὑπερκαταλήκτου, 'ἀντὶ τᾶς ἔγω οὐδὲ Λυδίαν,' καὶ βραχυκαταλήκτου, 'πᾶσαν οὐδ᾽ ἐράνναν.'

[1] δαύοισ(α)? *B* [2] *E*, *e.g.* [3] mss Κλεΐς, but H. apparently read Κλέευις or Κλέειϊς: prob. abbrev. for some compound of κλέος with alternative form Κλέϊς or Κλεΐϊς (so 82) [4] Λέσ. *B*, cf. Mosch. 3. 89: ἀγ. *E e.g.*, opt. of ἄγρημι, cf. Eur. *H.F.* 643

128

Etymologicum Magnum: δαύω 'I sleep'; Sappho:

May you sleep in the bosom of a tender comrade . . .

And Herodian says that the word occurs once in Sappho.

129 To the Muses

Hephaestion *Handbook of Metre* [on 'unconnectable' metres]: And the line which is composed of two ithyphallics is used by Sappho:

O come hither, ye Muses, from your golden [house] . . .

130[1] To Cleïs

The Same: Another kind of 'unconnectable' line which similarly involves the first 'antipathy,' is formed from a trochaic dimeter acatalectic and an iambic of three feet and a half which by a shifting of the caesura becomes a trochaic procatalectic:

I have a pretty little daughter who looks like a golden flower, my darling Cleïs, for whom I would not take all Lydia, nay nor lovely [Lesbos].

Of these lines, the second is shown by the caesura to be composed, as I have said, of the trochaic dimeter acatalectic and the iambic of three feet and a half; the first, having the caesura a syllable earlier, becomes procatalectic, composed of a trochaic of three feet and a half, 'ἔστι μοι κάλα παῖς,' and a dimeter acatalectic, 'χρυσίοισιν ἀνθέμοισιν'; while the third consists of a hypercatalectic trochaic, 'ἀντὶ τᾶς ἔγω οὐδὲ Λυδίαν,' and a brachycatalectic, 'πᾶσαν οὐδ' ἐράνναν.'

[1] cf. Sch. Heph: the ancient metrists made Κλ. ⏑ – ⏑, reading 8 stresses with 'rests' after πάϊς, μόρφαν, and Λυδίαν; edd. who suppose them wrong read 7 stresses and no rests, taking χρ. as 3 syll., Κλεῦις and Λύδ. as 2

131

Sch. Ar. *Plut.* 729 ἡμιτύβιον· ἀντὶ τοῦ σουδάριον, ῥάκος ἡμιτριβὲς λινοῦν τι οἷον ἐκμαγεῖον, καὶ Σαπφώ·

ἡμιτύβιον στέλασσον·[1]

ἢ δίκροσσον φακίολιον.

132

E.M. 759. 35 οἱ μέντοι Αἰολεῖς φασὶ

Τίοισιν ὀφθάλμοισιν . . . ;

ὡς παρὰ Σαπφοῖ.

133

Dem. *Eloc.* 164 τὸ μὲν γὰρ εὔχαρι μετὰ κόσμου ἐκφέρεται καὶ δι' ὀνομάτων καλῶν ἃ μάλιστα ποιεῖ τὰς χάριτας, οἷον τό·

Ποικίλλεται μὲν γαῖα πολυστέφανος.

134

Arist. *Eth. Nic.* 1149 b 15 ἡ δ' ἐπιθυμία, καθάπερ τὴν Ἀφροδίτην φασί·

δολοπλόκας γὰρ Κυπρογένεος πρόπολον[2]

[1] Hemst.-*E* (cf. 17): mss σταλάσσων [2] δολοπλόκας: cf. l. 2: Κυπρογένεος πρόπολον *B* from Hesych. Κ. π.· προαγωγόν: mss Κυπρογενοῦς without πρόπολον

131

Scholiast on Aristophanes ἡμιτύβιον: equivalent to *sudarium*, a half-worn linen cloth like a dishclout, compare Sappho:

. . . a dripping clout;

or a two-fringed bandage.

132

Etymologicum Magnum: The Aeolic writers, however, (using τίοις for τίσι) say:

With what eyes . . .? [1]

as it is in Sappho.

133

Demetrius *On Style*: Charm is produced along with ornament and by means of beautiful words most conducive to that effect; compare:

The many-garlanded earth puts on her broidery.

134

Aristotle *Nicomachean Ethics*: But desire is cunning, as they say of Aphrodite:

for the servant of the wile-weaving Cyprus-born . . . [2]

[1] *e. g.* 'with what eyes will you look at me?' *i. e.* 'how will you be able to look me in the face?' [2] Persuasion; cf. *fr.* 33: this and the previous frag. prob. from the same poem are claimed for S. by Wil.

135

Heph. 65 [π. ἀντισπαστικοῦ]· ἔστι δὲ πυκνὸν καὶ τὸ τὴν δευτέραν μόνην ἀντισπαστικὴν ἔχον (τετράμετρον), ᾧ μέτρῳ ἔγραψαν ᾄσματα· καὶ Σαπφὼ[1] ἐπὶ τέλους τοῦ ἑβδόμου·

Γλύκηα μᾶτερ, οὔ τοι δύναμαι κρέκην τὸν ἴστον
πόθῳ δάμεισα παῖδος βραδίνω δι' Ἀφροδίταν.[2]

Η'

136

Mar. Plot. *de Metr.* (6. 517 Keil): Hymenaicum dimetrum dactylicum Sapphicum monoschematistum est; semper enim duobus dactylis constat:

τεσσεραμήνιον[3]
ὦ τὸν Ἀδώνιον.[4]

137

Plut. *de Coh. Ira* 7 καὶ παρὰ πότον μὲν ὁ σιωπῶν ἐπαχθὴς τοῖς συνοῦσι καὶ φορτικός, ἐν ὀργῇ δὲ σεμνότερον οὐδὲν ἡσυχίας, ὡς ἡ Σαπφὼ παραινεῖ·

σκιδναμένας ἐν στήθεσιν ὄργας
γλῶσσαν μαψυλάκαν πεφύλαχθε.[5]

138

Sch. Soph. *El.* 149 (= Suid. ἀηδών)· τὸ δὲ Διὸς ἄγγελος (ἡ ἀηδὼν) ὅτι τὸ ἔαρ σημαίνει, καὶ Σαπφώ·

ἦρος ἄγγελος ἰμμερόφωνος ἀήδω[6]

[1] *E*: mss ἔγραψεν ᾄσματα καὶ Σ. τέλους τ. *B*: mss τῆς τοῦ, τε του, τοῦ, τῆς [2] βραδίνω *B*, cf. Theocr. 10. 24: mss -αν [3] reading doubtful, but context shows lines belong together: *E*, cf. τεσσαράβοιος: mss indicate τεσσερυμήνᾰον 'four times wedded' or 'to whom we cry Hymenaeus four times' but?: mss νεσζερυμηνιον, νεσσερυιαηνιον [4] cf. Bek. *An.* 346 [5] Volg. -*B*, cf. Pind. *N.* 7. 105: mss πεφυλάχθαι (Plut.'s adaptation) γ. μαψυλάκταν [6] *E* (or voc. as Sapphic?): mss -δών, cf. Sch. Soph. *Ai.* 628, Küster on Suid.

135[1]

Hephaestion *Handbook of Metre* [on the antispast]: A frequent type (of tetrameter) has only its second meter antispastic, a measure in which they wrote whole poems; for instance Sappho at the end of her Seventh Book:

Sweet mother, I truly cannot weave my web; for I am o'erwhelmed through Aphrodite with love of a slender youth.

Book VIII[2]

136

Marius Plotius *Metre*: The hymenaic dactylic dimeter of Sappho is monoschematist (*i. e.* all lines scan alike); for it always consists of two dactyls:

Woe for him of the four months' sojourn, woe for Adonis![3]

137

Plutarch *on Restraining Anger*: A man who is silent over his wine is a burden to the company and a boor, whereas in anger there is nothing more dignified than tranquillity; compare the advice of Sappho:

When anger swells in the heart, restrain the idly-barking tongue.

138

Scholiast on Sophocles: The phrase 'messenger of Zeus' is used (of the nightingale) because she is a sign of the spring; compare Sappho:

the lovely-voiced harbinger of Spring, the nightingale.[4]

[1] cf. *E.M.* 506. 1, *E.G.* 316. 35, Zonar. 1190 [2] for S.'s dactylic hexameters cf. Terent. Maur. 2157 [3] A. lived 4 months of the year alone, 4 with Persephone, and 4 with Aphrodite [4] in Soph. ἄγγελος means 'messenger sent by' Zeus, in Sappho 'announcer of' Spring

139

Ath. 2. 54 f ἐρέβινθοι· . . . Σαπφώ·

χρύσειοι <δ’> ἐρέβινθοι ἐπ’ ἀϊόνων ἐφύοντο.

140

Ibid. 13. 571 d: (*fr.* 12) καὶ ἔτι·

Λάτω καὶ Νιόβα μάλα μὲν φίλαι ἦσαν ἔταιραι . . .[1]

141

Apoll. *Pron.* 99. 17 καὶ σὺν τῷ α λέγεται (ἡ σφίν) παρ’ Αἰολεῦσιν·

. . . . . ὄτα πάννυχος ἄσφι κατάγρει
[ὄππατ’ ἄωρος][2] . . . . . .

141 A

Et. Mag. 117. 14 ὦρος καὶ ἄωρος, κατὰ πλεονασμὸν τοῦ α μηδὲν πλέον σημαίνοντος· ὦρος γὰρ ὁ ὕπνος· Καλλίμαχος· . . . καὶ Σαπφώ·

. . . ὀφθάλμοις δὲ μέλαις χύτο νύκτος ἄωρος.[3]

142

Hdn. 2. 187. 16 (= *E.M.* 662. 32) πέπταμαι· ἐκ τοῦ ἴπτημι γίνεται ὁ παθητικὸς παρακείμενος ἔπταμαι ἔπτασαι ἔπταται καὶ πλεονασμῷ τοῦ π πέπταμαι Αἰολικῶς. οἱ γὰρ Αἰολεῖς εἰώθασι προστιθέναι σύμφωνον, ὥσπερ τὸ ἐπτερύγωμαι πεπτερύγωμαι οἷον·

ὠς δὲ πάϊς πεδὰ μάτερα πεπτερύγωμαι.

[1] cf. 168 [2] *E*, cf. 141 A and καθαιρέω [3] mss χύτ’ ἄ., νυκτὸς ἄ. (Cod. Aug. καὶ Σ. νυκτὸς ἄωρον)

139 [1]

Athenaeus *Doctors at Dinner* [among instances of ἐρέβινθος 'pulse']: Compare Sappho:

And golden pulses grew upon the shore.

140

The Same: (*fr.* 12) and again:

Though Leto and Niobe were very dear comrades, . . .[2]

141

Apollonius *Pronouns*: And σφίν 'to them' is used in Aeolic with *a* before it; compare

. . . . . when night-long [sleep] closes their [eyes]

141 A [3]

Etymologicum Magnum: ὦρος and, with pleonastic *a*, ἄωρος; for ὦρος means 'sleep'; compare Callimachus: . . . . ; and Sappho:

and night's black slumber was shed upon [their] eyes.

142

Herodian *On Inflexions* πέπταμαι 'I have flown': the verb ἵπτημι has a perfect passive ἔπταμαι ἔπτασαι ἔπταται, and with a pleonastic π in Aeolic πέπταμαι. For the Aeolians add a consonant, as πεπτερύγωμαι for ἐπτερύγωμαι; compare

and I have flown [to you] like a child to its mother.[4]

[1] cf. Eust. 948. 44 [2] prob. sarcastic [3] cf. Cod. Aug. *ap.* Tittm. Zonar. cxxiv [4] cf. Sch. *ad loc*, Zon. 1540, Greg. Cor. 638

143[1] εἰς παῖδα ἀνώνυμον

Anth. Pal. 6. 269 ὡς Σαπφοῦς·[1]

Παῖς ἔτ' ἄφωνος ἔοισα τόρ' ἐννέπω αἴ τις
ἔρηται[2]
φώναν ἀκαμάταν κατθεμένα πρὸ πόδων·
Αἰθοπίᾳ με κόρᾳ Λάτως ὀνέθηκεν Ἀρίστω[3]
Ἑρμοκλειταία τῷ Σαϋναϊάδα[4]
5 σὰ πρόπολος, δέσποινα γυναίκων· ᾇ σὺ χάρεισα
πρόφρων ἀμμετέραν εὐκλέϊσον γενίαν.

144 εἰς Τιμάδα

Ibid. 7. 489 (*Plan.* p. 229)· Σαπφοῦς· εἰς Τιμάδα ὁμοίως πρὸ γάμου τελευτήσασαν·

Τίμαδος ἅδε κόνις,[5] τὰν δὴ πρὸ γάμοιο θάνοισαν
δέξατο Φερσεφόνας κυάνιος θάλαμος,
ἇς καὶ ἀπυφθιμένας[6] παῖσαι νεόθαγι σιδάρῳ[7]
ἄλικες ἰμμέρταν κρᾶτος ἔθεντο κόμαν.

145[8] εἰς Πελάγωνα

Ibid. 7. 505 (*Plan.* p. 196)· εἰς Πελάγωνα Σαπφοῦς·

Τῷ γρίππει Πελάγωνι πάτηρ ἐπέθηκε Μένισκος
κύρτον καὶ κώπαν, μνᾶμα κακοζοΐας.[9]

[1] Schol. εἰς τὸ ἀντιβόλον οὐ κεῖται τοῦ κυροῦ Μιχαηλοῦ πόθεν οὖν ἐγράφη οὐκ οἶδα [2] παῖς ἔτ' d'Orv. : ms παῖδες : τορ(ά) Paton : ms τετ' : d'Orv. τάδ' [3] Bent. : ms Ἀριστα (Paus. 1. 29. 2 apparently read wrongly Ἀρίστᾳ, unless we read there with Wel. -*B* ἔπη τὰ Πάμφω for ἐ. τ. Σαπφοῦς, cf. Paus. 8. 35. 8) [4] d'Orv. -*B*, cf. Hfm 588 : ms ἑρμοκλείταο τῶσ αὖν αϊάδα [5] perh. Τιμαδί' *E*, cf. 88 and *Proc. Class. Assoc.* 1921 [6] perh. ἄπυθι φθ. *E*, cf. 87 and Hesych. ἄποθεν, but see *Il.* 5. 62 : mss καὶ ἀπὸ φθ. [7] *Plan.* 2nd hand νεοθηγέϊ χάλκῳ, but cf. *A.P.* 7. 181 [8] cf. *Od.* 12. 14 [9] Scal. : mss κακοζωᾶς

143 On a Nameless Infant

Palatine Anthology: Ascribed to Sappho:[1]

I am a little maid who cannot talk, but yet, if I am asked a question, I say plain enough with the voice that never wearies of speech at my feet: 'I was dedicated to the Aethopian Child of Leto by Aristo daughter of Hermocleitus son of Saunaïdas, a ministrant, thou Lady of women, of thine; to whom in gratitude bound be thou gracious, and give our family good fame.'

144 On Timas

The Same: Sappho, on Timas who in li[illegible]nner died before her marriage:

This is the dust of Timas,[2] who [illegible]eceived into Persephone's black chamber all [illegible], and for whose death[3] all her fair companions took knife and shore the lovely hair of their heads.

145[4] On Pelagon

The Same: on Pelagon, Sappho:

To the fisherman Pelagon his father Meniscus has put up a fishing-basket and an oar as a memorial of his hard life.

[1] ascription doubtful; note in the ms 'not in Michael's copy, so I do not know its origin'; inscribed on the base of a statue of a nameless baby-girl dedicated to Artemis as a thank-offering for her birth by her mother a priestess of Artemis [2] perh. 'this dust is little Timas' [3] or perh. 'though she died so far away' (at Phocaea?) cf. 87 [4] ascription doubtful

Θ′

ΕΠΙΘΑΛΑΜΙΑ

146

Ath. 10. 425 c (cf. 11. 475 a)· τοῖς δὲ θεοῖς οἰνοχοοῦσάν τινες ἱστοροῦσι τὴν Ἁρμονίαν. . . . Ἀλκαῖος δὲ καὶ τὸν Ἑρμῆν εἰσάγει αὐτῶν οἰνοχόον (Alc. 5), ὡς καὶ Σαπφὼ λέγουσα·[1]

κῆ δ' ἀμβροσίας μὲν κράτηρ ἐκέκρατο,
Ἔρμαις δ' ἔλεν ὄλπιν[2] θέοισ' οἰνοχόησαι.
κῆνοι δ' ἄρα πάντες καρχήσι' ὄνηχον[3]
κἄλειβον, ἀράσαντο δὲ πάμπαν ἔσλα γάμβρῳ.[4]

147[5]

Him. *Or.* 1. 20 εἰ δὲ καὶ ᾠδῆς ἐδέησεν, ἔδωκα ἂν καὶ μέλος τοιόνδε· Νύμφα ῥοδέων ἐρώτων βρύουσα, νύμφα Παφίης ἄγαλμα κάλλιστον, ἴθι πρὸς εὐνήν, ἴθι πρὸς λέχος, μείλιχα παίζουσα, γλυκεῖα νυμφίῳ. Ἕσπερός σ' ἑκοῦσαν ἄγοι, ἀργυρόθρονον ζυγίαν Ἥραν θαυμάζουσαν.

e. g. Ὦ βρύοισ' ἔρων βροδίων
νύμφα, τᾶς Παφίας ἀνάσσ-
ας ἄγαλμα κάλιστον,

πρὸς εὔναν ἴθι, πρὸς λέχος,
ὦτε μέλλιχα παίσεαι
παῖγνα γλύκηα γάμβρῳ.
Ἔσπερος δ' ἔκοισαν ἄγοι σ'
ἀργυρόθρονον ζυγίαν
Ἦραν θαυμανέοισαν.

[1] ll. 3, 4 ap. Ath. 11 μνημονεύει δὲ τῶν καρχησίων καὶ Σαπφὼ

Book IX

EPITHALAMIES[1]

146

Athenaeus *Doctors at Dinner*: According to some accounts the wine-bearer of the Gods was Harmonia. . . . But Alcaeus makes Hermes also their wine-bearer, as indeed Sappho does in the following passage:

There stood a mixing-bowl of ambrosia ready mixed, and Hermes took the wine-jug to pour out for the Gods. And then they all took up the beakers, and pouring a libation wished all manner of good luck to the bridegroom.[2]

147

Himerius *Epithalamy of Severus*: And if an ode were needed I should give such a song as this: Bride that teemest with rosy desires, bride the fairest ornament of the Queen of Paphos, hie thee to bed, hie thee to the couch whereon thou must sweetly sport in gentle wise with thy bridegroom. And may the Star of Eve lead thee full willingly to the place where thou shalt marvel at the silver-thronèd Lady of Wedlock.[3]

[1] in grouping these here regardless of metre we perh. confuse two ancient editions; cf. 162 and on 48 [2] ll. 3, 4 (not quite certainly to be joined directly to 2) from Ath. 'Sappho, too, mentions this kind of cup in the lines: And then' etc.: cf. Macr. 5. 21. 6, Ath. 2. 39 a, 5. 192 c, Eust. *Od.* 1633. 1, *Il.* 1205. 18 [3] the context points to Sappho as H.'s original

---

ἐν τούτοις· κῆνοι κ.τ.λ. [2] mss also ἕρπιν [3] ὤνηχον Hfm. -*E*: mss ἔχον, ἔσχον [4] mss τῷ γ. [5] *E e.g.*: the voc. form νύμφα, and the metre of H.'s last sentence show that we are very near S.'s own words: παῖγνα i.e. παίγνια cf. χρυσότερα: θαυμ. fut. of θαυμαίνω: metre Catull. 61

148[1]

Demetr. *Eloc.* 148, 146 ἔστι δέ τις ἰδίως χάρις Σαπφικὴ ἐκ μεταβολῆς, ὅταν τι εἰποῦσα μεταβάλληται καὶ ὥσπερ μετανοήσῃ· οἷον·

Ἴψοι δὴ τὸ μέλαθρον[2]
Ὑμήνăον,
ἄερρατε, τέκτονες ἄνδρες,
Ὑμήναον·
5 γάμβρος Ϝίσσος Ἄρευϊ,[3]
<Ὑμήναον,>
ἄνδρος μεγάλω πόλυ μείζων,
<Ὑμήναον,>
πέρροχος ὡς ὄτ' ἄοιδος
10 <Ὑμήναον,>
ὀ Λέσβιος ἀλλοδάποισιν,
<Ὑμήναον·>

ὥσπερ ἐπιλαμβανομένη ἑαυτῆς ὅτι ἀδυνάτῳ ἐχρήσατο ὑπερβολῇ καὶ ὅτι οὐδεὶς τῷ Ἄρηϊ ἴσος ἐστί.

149[4]

Ibid. 141 χαριεντίζεται δέ ποτε (ἡ Σαπφώ) καὶ ἐξ ἀναφορᾶς, ὡς ἐπὶ τοῦ Ἑσπέρου·

Ἔσπερε πάντα φέρων,[5] ὄσα φαίνολις ἐσκέδασ'
αὔως,

[1] 9–11 placed here from Demetr. *El.* 146 ἐκ δὲ παραβολῆς καὶ ἐπὶ τοῦ ἐξέχοντος ἄνδρος ἡ Σ. φησι· Περρ. κ.τ.λ. ἐνταῦθα γὰρ χάριν ἐποίησεν ἡ παραβολὴ μᾶλλον ἢ μέγεθος Bent. -*E.*
[2] (1–8) cf. Heph. 132 where read μεσυμνικόν [3] so Hfm.: mss γ. ἔρχεται (εἰσέρχεται) ἴσ. Ἀ. [4] so arranged by Wil.
[5] mss also φέρεις

148

Demetrius *On Style*: And there is a charm peculiarly Sapphic in metabole or change, when having said something she turns round and, as it were, changes her mind, for instance:

> Up with the rafters high,
> *Ho for the wedding!* [1]
> Raise them high, ye joiners,
> *Ho for the wedding!*
> The bridegroom 's as tall as Ares,
> *Ho for the wedding!*
> Far taller than a tall man,
> *Ho for the wedding!*
> Towering as the Lesbian poet
> *Ho for the wedding!*
> Over the poets of other lands,
> *Ho for the wedding!*

as it were interrupting herself because she has used an impossible hyperbole, no one really being as tall as Ares.

149 [2]

The Same: Sometimes, too, Sappho derives charm from anaphora or repetition, as in this passage, of the Evening Star:

Evening Star that bringest back all that lightsome Dawn hath scattered afar, thou bringest the sheep,

[1] the refrain, omitted by Dem., occurs in Heph., who quotes ll. 1–5 to illustrate the 'intervening' refrain: ll. 9–11 from Dem. *El.* 146 'by comparison, moreover, S. says of the very tall man "Towering, etc."; for the comparison there conveys charm rather than a sense of size' [2] cf. *E.M. Vet.* 129, *E.M.* 174. 43, *E.G.* 212. 43, 446. 3, Sch. Eur. *Or.* 1260, Cram. *A.O.* 2. 444. 17

φέρεις ὄϊν,
φέρεις αἶγα, φέρεις ἀπὺ Ϝὸν μάτερι παῖδα.[1]

καὶ γὰρ ἐνταῦθα ἡ χάρις ἐστὶν ἐκ τῆς λέξεως τῆς φέρεις ἐπὶ τὸ αὐτὸ ἀναφερομένης.

150

Sch. Hermog. π. ἰδεῶν 1. 1. *Rhet. Gr.* (7. 883 Walz)· αἱ μὲν γὰρ τῶν ἰδεῶν μονοειδεῖς ἔχουσι τὰς ἐννοίας, ὡς ἡ καθαρότης, αἱ δὲ καὶ μέχρι τριῶν καὶ τεττάρων προέρχονται τρόπων, ὡς ἡ σεμνότης καὶ εἴ τινες ἕτεραι ταύτῃ ὅμοιαι, ὡς αἱ ἱστορικαί· καὶ γὰρ αὗται διὰ τὸν χρόνον πλησιάζουσι ταῖς μυθικαῖς, ὡς καὶ Θουκυδίδης φησί· καὶ ὅσαι τὰ ταῖς αἰσθήσεσιν ἡδέα ἐκφράζουσιν, ὄψει, ἀκοῇ, ὀσφρήσει, γεύσει, ἁφῇ, ὡς Ὅμηρος· (*Il.* 8. 377–8)· καὶ Σαπφώ· (4)· καί·

οἶον τὸ γλυκύμαλον ἐρεύθεται ἄκρῳ ἐπ' ὔσδῳ
ἄκρον ἐπ' ἀκροτάτῳ, λελάθοντο δὲ μαλοδρόπηες.
οὐ μὰν ἐκλελάθοντ', ἀλλ' οὐκ ἐδύναντ' ἐπί-
κεσθαι·

καὶ Θεόκριτος· (8. 78) καί· (3. 54).

151

Demetr. *Eloc.* 106 τὸ δὲ ἐπιφώνημα καλούμενον ὁρίζοιτο μὲν ἄν τις λέξιν ἐπικοσμοῦσαν· ἔστι δὲ τὸ μεγαλοπρεπέστατον ἐν τοῖς λόγοις· τῆς γὰρ λέξεως ἡ μὲν ὑπηρετεῖ, ἡ δὲ ἐπικοσμεῖ. ὑπηρετεῖ μὲν ἡ τοιάδε· οἴαν . . . καταστείβοισι· ἐπικοσμεῖ δὲ τὸ ἐπιφερόμενον τό· χάμαι . . . ἄνθη. ἐπενήνεγκται τοῦτο τοῖς προλελεγμένοις[2] κόσμος σαφῶς καὶ κάλλος . . . καὶ καθόλου τὸ ἐπιφώνημα τοῖς τῶν πλουσίων ἔοικεν ἐπιδείγμασιν, γείσοις λέγω καὶ τριγλύφοις καὶ πορφύραις πλατείαις· οἶον γάρ τι καὶ αὐτὸ τοῦ ἐν λόγοις πλούτου σημεῖόν ἐστιν.

[1] ἀπὺ Ϝὸν *E* (or print ϜϜὸν?) cf. Theocr. 12. 33, *Ad.* 32, Hom. ἀπὸ ἕθεν, ἀπὸ ἕο, πόσεϊ ᾧ, and for metre Alc. 112 B: mss ἄποιον (Dem. om.) [2] Finckh : mss προενηνεγ.

---

[1] the sequel was prob. 'Even so to-night bring thou home

thou bringest the goat, thou bringest her child home to the mother;[1]

here the charm lies in the repetition of the word 'bringest.'

150

Scholiast on Hermogenes *Kinds of Style*: For some kinds of style express but one sort of idea, for instance the pure or simple kind; others two, three, or even four, for instance the noble and those which resemble it, such as the kinds used by historians—which, indeed, as Thucydides says, approximate to those employed by mythographers because they are concerned with chronology—, or such as give pleasure to the senses, sight, hearing, smell, taste, touch, as Homer: (*Iliad* 347 f); or Sappho: (4); and:

Like the pippin blushing high
On the tree-top beneath the sky,
Where the pickers forgot it—nay,
Could not reach it so far away;[2]

or Theocritus: (8. 78) and: (3. 54).

151

Demetrius *On Style*: The so-called epiphoneme may be defined as a phrase which adds adornment, and it is supreme as an elevator of style. It should be remembered that a phrase either aids the sense or adorns it. For instance, the sense is aided by such a phrase as 'Like the hyacinth' etc. while it is adorned by the words which follow, 'and it still blooms' etc. The addition thus made to the foregoing sentence is clearly an adornment or embellishment. . . . In general the epiphoneme is like the shows or displays of the rich, such as the cornices and triglyphs of their houses and the purple borders of their robes. For it is essentially a mark of wealth in words.

the bride to the bridegroom'   [2] cf. Sch. Theocr. 11. 39: see also Long. *Past.* 3. 33: descriptive of the bride, cf. Himer. 1. 16

οἷαν τὰν ὑάκινθον ἐν ὄρρεσι ποίμενες ἄνδρες
πόσσι καταστείβοισι, χάμαι δ' ἔτι πορφύρα
ἄνθη.[1]

152

Cram. *A.O.* 1. 71. 19 ἀεί . . . ὁ δ' Αἰολεὺς τριχῶς· <ἀΐ>·

. . ἀϊπάρθενος ἔσσομαι·[2]

καὶ αἰεί καὶ αἰέν.

153

Ibid. 1. 190. 19 ἦσι·

Δώσομεν, ἦσι πάτηρ,[3]

φησὶν ἡ Σαπφώ, ἠτί δὲ λέγει 'Αλκμὰν ἀντὶ τοῦ ἦσι.

154

Heph. 45 [π. δακτυλικοῦ]· τὸ δὲ τετράμετρον (Αἰολικὸν καταληκτικόν)·

Θυρώρω πόδες ἐπτορόγυιοι,
τὰ δὲ σάμβαλα πεμπεβόηα
πέσσυγγοι δὲ δέκ' ἐξεπόνασαν·
e. g. κὠ πάτηρ τὰ μὲν ἄλλα μέτερρος
5 ὐπὲρ δ' εὐγενίας βίον ἀμφισβάτεις τῷ Κέκροπι ζατέλεσσεν.[4]

[1] *E*, cf. Long. *Past.* 4. 8: ἄνθη vb.: for ᾱ bef. ᾰ cf. κλέα ἄνδρων *Il.* 9. 189: mss χ. δέ τε (so apparently Demetr.) πόρφυρον ἄνθος [2] for the compound cf. Cram. *A.P.* 3. 321, Hdn. *Epim.* 184 Boiss. [3] mss ἠσὶ δώσομεν· ἠ. π. [4] ll. 4–6

Like the hyacinth which the shepherd tramples underfoot on the mountain, and it still blooms purple on the ground.[1]

152

Cramer *Inedita* (Oxford): ἀεί 'ever' . . . . and in Aeolic it has three forms—ἀΐ, for instance:

I shall be ever-maiden;

αἰεί, and αἰέν.

153

Ibid. ἦσι 'quoth':

'We will give,' quoth the father,

says Sappho; and Alcman uses ἠτί for ἠσί.

154

Hephaestion *Handbook of Metre* [on dactylics]: The Aeolic catalectic tetrameter:

The doorkeeper's feet are seven fathoms long, and his sandals five hides to the pair—it took ten shoemakers to make them; [and his father lived in other ways an honest life, but claimed to be better born than Cecrops himself.][2]

[1] Demetrius perh. read δέ τε 'and,' Longus δ' ἔτι 'and still' [2] see p. 291

E e.g., see p. 290: μέτερρος *E.M.* 587. 12, ἀμφισβάτεις (partcp.) Hfm. 282: cf. Luc. *Tim.* 23 εὐγενέστερον τοῦ Κέκροπος ἢ Κόδρου

Demetr. *Eloc.* 167 (cf. Sa. 165): ἄλλως δὲ σκώπτει (ἡ Σαπφώ) τὸν ἄγροικον νυμφίον καὶ τὸν θυρωρὸν τὸν ἐν τοῖς γάμοις εὐτελέστατα καὶ ἐν τοῖς πέζοις ὀνόμασι μᾶλλον ἢ ἐν ποιητικοῖς. ὥστε αὐτῆς μᾶλλόν ἐστι τὰ ποιήματα ταῦτα διαλέγεσθαι ἢ ᾄδειν, οὐδ' ἂν ἁρμόσαι πρὸς τὸν χόρον ἢ πρὸς τὴν λύραν, εἰ μή τις εἴη χόρος διαλεκτικός.

Synes. *Ep.* 3. 158 d ὁ δὲ ἀδικούμενος Ἁρμόνιός ἐστιν ὁ τοῦ θυρωροῦ πατήρ, ὡς ἂν εἴποι Σαπφώ· τὰ μὲν ἄλλα σώφρων καὶ μέτριος ἐν τῷ καθ' ἑαυτὸν βίῳ γενόμενος, ἀλλ' ὑπὲρ εὐγενείας ἀμφισβητῶν τῷ Κέκροπι διετέλεσεν.

155, 156

Heph. 107 [π. ἀσυναρτήτων]· καὶ τὸ ἐκ χοριαμβικῶν ἑφθημιμερῶν τῶν εἰς τὴν ἰαμβικὴν κατάκλειδα ἡ αὐτὴ ποιήτρια (Σαπφώ)·

Ὄλβιε γάμβρε, σοὶ μὲν δὴ γάμος, ὡς ἄρᾱο
ἐκτετέλεστ', ἔχεις δὲ πάρθενον, ἂν ἄραο·

κἄσθ' ὅπου[1] συνῆψε τὴν λέξιν·

μελλίχιος[2] δ' ἐπ' ἰμμέρτῳ κέχυται προσώπῳ . . .

157

Him. *Or.* 1 φέρε οὖν εἴσω τοῦ θαλάμου παραγαγόντες αὐτὸν (τὸν λόγον) ἐντυχεῖν τῷ κάλλει τῆς νύμφης πείσομεν· ὦ καλὴ ὦ χαρίεσσα· πρέπει γάρ σοι τὰ τῆς Λεσβίας ἐγκώμια. σοὶ μὲν γὰρ ῥοδόσφυροι χάριτες χρυσῆ τ' Ἀφροδίτη συμπαίζουσιν, Ὧρα δὲ λειμῶνας βρύουσι κ.τ.λ.

[1] Thiemann: mss καὶ ὁ ποῦς or om.—λέξιν [2] Herm: mss μελλίχροος, μελίχρος, -χρως, -χρονος

---

[1] prob. only Sappho's fun; mocking the bridegroom was part of the ceremony [2] the halting effect of the metre is

Demetrius *On Style*: Very different is the style in which she (Sappho) mocks the boorish[1] bridegroom and the keeper of the wedding-door. It is quite commonplace, and the words are better suited to prose than to poetry. Indeed these poems of hers can be better spoken than sung, and would not be fitting for the dance or the lyre, unless for a sort of speaking-dance.[2]

Synesius *Letters*: The name which is wronged by the ill-behaviour (of a certain bride at her uncle's funeral) is that of Harmonius, Master Doorkeeper's father, who, as Sappho would say, in other respects lived a decent and honest life, but claimed to be better born than Cecrops himself.

155, 156

Hephaestion *Handbook of Metre* [on 'unconnectable' metres]: And the same poetess (Sappho) uses the choriambic of three feet and a half with the iambic close:

Happy bridegroom, the marriage is accomplished as you prayed it should be, and the maiden you prayed for is yours;

and in some places she lets a word overlap into the second part of the line:

and soft and gentle is shed over her delightsome face. . . .[3]

157

Himerius *Epithalamy of Severus*: Come then, let us take this discourse of ours into the chamber and introduce it to the beauty of the bride. 'O beauteous one, etc. . . . (for thou deservest the praise of the Lesbian poetess), thine it is, etc.'[4]

due to the licence regularly allowed in the 1st foot (cf. Heph. 44): according to the Scholiast Thyrōrus ('Doorkeeper') was the name of a brother of the deceased (who was son of Syn.'s friend H. and uncle of the bride) [3] probably from the same poem; the subject of the verb is probably 'love' [4] metre Catull. 61

e.g. Ὦ κάλ', ὦ χαρίεσσα, σοὶ
αἰ βροδόσφυροι Χάριτες
χρύσια τ' Ἀφρόδιτα
συμπαίζοισι . . . . .[1]

158

Choric. ap. Graux *Textes Grecs* 97 ἐγὼ οὖν τὴν νύμφην, ἵνα σοι πάλιν χαρίσωμαι, Σαπφικῇ μελῳδίᾳ κοσμήσω·

. . . σοὶ χάριεν μὲν εἶδος
κὤππατα μελλιχόχροα
<νύμφ',> ἔρος δὲ <τέῳ> κάλῳ
περκέχυται προσώπῳ,
5 καί σε τέτικεν ἐξόχως
Ἀφρόδιτα – ∪ ∪ –[2]

159

Apoll. *Coni.* 223. 25 ἑξῆς ῥητέον περὶ τῶν διαπορητικῶν· ἆρα· οὗτος κατὰ πᾶσαν διάλεκτον ὑπεσταλμένης τῆς κοινῆς καὶ Ἀττικῆς ἦρα λέγεται·

ἦρ' ἔτι παρθενίας ἐπιβάλλομαι;[3]

Σαπφώ.

160

Heph. 27 [π. ἀποθέσεως μέτρων]· καταληκτικὰ δὲ (καλεῖται μέτρα), ὅσα μεμειωμένον ἔχει τὸν τελευταῖον πόδα, οἷον ἐπὶ ἰαμβικοῦ·

χαίροι τ' ἄ νύμφᾰ, χαιρέτω τ' ὀ γάμβρος·[4]

ἐνταῦθα γὰρ ἡ βρος τελευταία συλλαβὴ ἀντὶ ὅλου ποδὸς ἰαμβικοῦ κεῖται.

[1] *E. e. g.* [2] *E*: or μελλικόχροα? mss καὶ ὄμματα μελιχρὰ, περικέχ., and καὶ σὲ τετίμηκεν ἐ. [3] mss Ap. παρθενίης, Dion. -ικὰς [4] *E*: mss χαίροις ἀνύμφα (ἄν.) χ. δ': Aeol. confused nom. and voc.

e.g. O beauteous one, O lovely one, thine it is to sport with the rose-ankled Graces and Aphrodite the golden . . .

158

Choricius *Epithalamy of Zachary*: And so, to give you pleasure once again, I will adorn the bride with a Sapphic song:

Thy form, O bride, is all delight; thy eyes are of a gentle hue; thy fair face is overspread with love; Aphrodite hath done thee exceeding honour.

159[1]

Apollonius *Conjunctions*: We must now take the conjunctions expressing hesitation. ἆρα: this conjunction takes the form ἦρα in every dialect except the Koine or Common, and Attic;

Can it be that I still long for my virginity?

Sappho.

160

Hephaestion *Handbook* [on 'rests' in metre]: And metres are called catalectic when their last foot is shortened, as in the iambic:

Farewell the bride, farewell the bridegroom![2]

where the last syllable stands instead of a whole iambus.

[1] cf. Sch. Dion. Thr. *Gram. Gr.* 3. 290 Schneid. [2] *or* 'Hail to the bride,' etc.

161

Heph. 44 [π. δακτυλικοῦ]· πεντάμετρα δὲ (Αἰολικά) καταληκτικὰ εἰς δισύλλαβον·

Τίῳ σ', ὦ φίλε γάμβρε, κάλως ἐϊκάσδω;
ὄρπακι βραδίνῳ σε κάλιστ' ἐϊκάσδω.[1]

162

Serv. Verg. *G.* 1. 31: Generum vero pro maritum positum multi accipiunt iuxta Sappho, quae in libro quae inscribitur Ἐπιθαλάμια ait:

. . . . χαῖρε, νύμφα,
χαῖρε, τίμιε γάμβρε, πόλλα.[2]

163

Dionys. *Comp.* 25 τὸ συμπλεκόμενον τούτῳ πάλιν κῶλον ἐκ δυοῖν συνέστηκε μετρῶν· 'μήτε μικρὸν ὁρῶντά τι καὶ φαῦλον ἁμάρτημα, ἑτοίμως οὕτως ἐπὶ τούτῳ.' εἴ γε τοι <τὸ> Σαπφικόν τις ἐπιθαλάμιον τουτί·

οὐ γὰρ ἦν ἀτέρα πάϊς, ὦ γάμβρε, τοαύτα·[3]

καὶ τοῦ κωμικοῦ τετραμέτρου λεγομένου δὲ Ἀριστοφανείου τουδί· 'ὅτ' ἐγὼ τὰ δίκαια λέγων ἤνθουν καὶ σωφροσύνη 'νενόμιστο.' τούς τε τελευταίους πόδας τρεῖς καὶ τὴν κατάληξιν, <ἀπόθεσιν>[4] ἐμβαλὼν, συνάψειε τοῦτον τὸν τρόπον· 'οὐ γὰρ ἦν ἑτέρα πάϊς ὦ γάμβρε τοαύτα καὶ σωφροσύνη 'νενόμιστο·' οὐδὲν διοίσει τοῦ· 'μήτε μικρὸν . . . τούτῳ.'

164

Demetr. *Eloc.* 140 αἱ δὲ ἀπὸ τῶν σχημάτων χάριτες δῆλαί εἰσι καὶ πλεῖσται παρὰ Σαπφοῖ· οἷον ἐκ τῆς ἀναδιπλώσεως, ὅπου νύμφη πρὸς τὴν παρθενίαν φησί·

[1] κάλιστ' *B*: mss μάλ. [2] metre cf. Heph. 62 [3] Blf.-*B* from context: mss ο. γ. ἑτέρα ἦν (or νῦν) παῖς κ.τ.λ. [4] *E*

161

Hephaestion *Handbook* [on dactylics]: And the Aeolic dactylic pentameter catalectic with a disyllable:

To what, dear bridegroom, may I well liken thee?
To a slender sapling do I best liken thee.

162

Servius on Vergil: Many commentators hold that *son-in-law* is here used for *husband*, as it is by Sappho, who in the Book entitled *Epithalamies* says:

Farewell, bride, and farewell, honoured bridegroom![1]

163

Dionysius *On Literary Composition* [on Demosthenes *Against Aristocrates* 1]: The clause which follows this consists of two metres put together: 'μήτε μικρὸν ὁρῶντά τι καὶ φαῦλον ἁμάρτημ' ἑτοίμως οὕτως ἐπὶ τούτῳ.' Now if we take this line of a wedding-song of Sappho's:

For never, bridegroom, was there another maiden such as this;

and after inserting a 'rest' join it with the last three feet and the incomplete final foot of the comic tetrameter—known as the Aristophanean—in the following way: οὐ γὰρ ἦν ἀτέρα πάϊς ὦ γάμβρε τοαύτα [rest] καὶ σωφροσύνη 'νενόμιστο, we shall find the resulting metre the same as that of 'μήτε μικρὸν' κ.τ.λ.

164

Demetrius *On Style*: The charm which comes from the use of figures of speech is obvious and manifold in Sappho; for instance, from repetition, where a bride says to her virginity:

[1] γαμβρός 'one connected by marriage' is used by some Greek poets to mean bridegroom

Παρθενία, παρθενία, ποῖ με λίποισ' ἀποίχῃ;[1]

ἡ δὲ ἀποκρίνεται πρὸς αὐτὴν τῷ αὐτῷ σχήματι·

Οὐκέτι, νύμφα, προτὶ σ' ἴξω, προτὶ σ' οὐκέτ' ἴξω.[2]

πλείων γὰρ χάρις ἐμφαίνεται ἢ εἴπερ ἅπαξ ἐλέχθη καὶ ἄνευ τοῦ σχήματος. καίτοι ἡ ἀναδίπλωσις πρὸς δεινότητας μᾶλλον δοκεῖ εὑρῆσθαι, ἡ δὲ καὶ τοῖς δεινοτάτοις καταχρῆται ἐπιχαρίτως.[3]

165

Demetr. *Eloc.* 166 διὸ καὶ ἡ Σαπφὼ περὶ μὲν κάλλους ᾄδουσα καλλιεπής ἐστι καὶ ἡδεῖα, καὶ περὶ ἐρώτων δὲ καὶ ἔαρος καὶ περὶ ἁλκυόνος, καὶ ἅπαν καλὸν ὄνομα ἐνύφανται αὐτῆς τῇ ποιήσει, τὰ δὲ καὶ αὐτὴ εἰργάσατο.

166

Strab. 13. 615 Κάναι δὲ πολίχνιον Λοκρῶν τῶν ἐκ Κύνου, κατὰ τὰ ἄκρα τῆς Λέσβου τὰ νοτιώτατα, κείμενον ἐν τῇ Καναίᾳ. αὕτη δὲ μέχρι τῶν Ἀργινουσσῶν διήκει καὶ τῆς ὑπερκειμένης ἄκρας, ἣν Αἶγά τινες ὀνομάζουσιν ὁμωνύμως τῷ ζῴῳ· δεῖ δὲ μακρῶς τὴν δευτέραν συλλαβὴν ἐκφέρειν Αἰγάν ὡς ἀκτάν καὶ ἀρχάν· οὕτω καὶ τὸ ὄρος ὅλον ὠνομάζετο, ὃ νῦν Κάνην καὶ Κάνας λέγουσιν. . . . ὕστερον δὲ αὐτὸ τὸ ἀκρωτήριον Αἰγὰ κεκλῆσθαι <δοκεῖ>,[4] ὡς Σαπφώ φησι, τὸ δὲ λοιπὸν Κάνη καὶ Κάναι.

167

Sch. Ap. Rh. 4. 57 [οὐκ ἄρ' ἐγὼ μούνη μετὰ Λάτμιον ἄντρον ἀλύσκω]· . . . περὶ δὲ τοῦ τῆς Σελήνης ἔρωτος ἱστοροῦσι Σαπφὼ καὶ Νίκανδρος ἐν δευτέρῳ Εὐρώπης· λέγεται δὲ κατέρχεσθαι ἐς τοῦτο τὸ ἄντρον τὴν Σελήνην πρὸς Ἐνδυμίωνα.

[1] Blf: mss λιποῦσα οἴχῃ [2] so Seid. -*B* (cf. Alc. 156. 9): mss οὐκ ἔτι ἥξω πρὸς σέ, ο. ἐ. ἥ. [3] Finckh: mss ἐπὶ χάριτος [4] Mein.

Maidenhead, maidenhead, whither away?

and it replies in the same figure:

Where I must stay, bride, where I must stay.

For there is more charm in it put thus than if the figure were not employed and it were said but once. Now repetition would seem to have been invented more with a view to an effect of energy or force,[1] but Sappho employs even what is most forceful in a charming way.

165

Demetrius *On Style*: And that is why when Sappho sings of beauty her words are full of beauty and sweetness, and the same when she sings of love and springtime and the halcyon, and the pattern of her poetry is inwoven with every beautiful word there is, some of them made by herself.

166[2]

Strabo *Geography*: Canae is a little town of the Locrians of Cynus opposite the southernmost Cape of Lesbos, situated in Canaea, a district which extends as far as the islands of Arginusae and the cape which lies near them. This cape is called by some writers Aiga 'the goat,' after the animal; but the second syllable ought rather to be made long, Aigā, like ἀκτά and ἀρχά; for that is the name of the whole mountain which is now called Cane or Canae; . . . later the actual promontory seems to have been known as Aigā, as Sappho gives it, and eventually as Cane or Canae.

167

Scholiast on Apollonius of Rhodes *Argonautica* ['So I am not the only visitant of the Latmian cave']: . . . The love of the Moon-goddess is told of by Sappho, and by Nicander in the 2nd Book of the *Europa*; and it is said that the Moon comes down to Endymion in this cave.

[1] cf. Rhys Roberts *ad loc.*   [2] cf. Steph. Byz. αἰγά

168

Gell. 20. 7 [de Niobae liberis] : Nam Homerus pueros puellasque eius bis senos dicit fuisse, Euripides bis septenos, Sappho bis novenos, Bacchylides et Pindarus bis denos.

169

Serv. Verg. *Aen.* 6. 21 ['septena quot annis | corpora natorum']: quidam septem pueros et septem puellas accipi volunt, quod et Plato dicit in Phaedone et Sappho in Lyricis . . . quos liberavit Theseus.

170

Id. *Ecl.* 6. 42 ['furtumque Promethei']: Prometheus . . . post factos a se homines dicitur auxilio Minervae caelum ascendisse et adhibita facula ad rotam solis ignem furatus, quem hominibus indicavit. ob quam causam irati dii duo mala immiserunt terris, febres[1] et morbos, sicut et Sappho et Hesiodus memorant.

171

Philostr. *Ep.* 51 ἡ Σαπφὼ τοῦ ῥόδου ἐρᾷ καὶ στεφανοῖ αὐτὸ ἀεί τινι ἐγκωμίῳ, τὰς καλὰς τῶν παρθένων ἐκείνῳ ὁμοιοῦσα, ὁμοιοῖ δὲ αὐτὸ καὶ τοῖς τῶν Χαρίτων πήχεσιν ἐπειδὰν ἀποδύσωσι[2] σφῶν τὰς ὠλένας.

172

Himer. *Or.* 13. 7 τὰ δὲ σὰ νῦν δέον καὶ αὐτῷ τῷ Μουσαγέτῃ εἰκάζεσθαι, οἷον αὐτὸν καὶ Σαπφὼ καὶ Πίνδαρος ἐν ᾠδῇ κόμῃ τε χρυσῇ καὶ λύρᾳ[3] κοσμήσαντες κύκνοις ἔποχον εἰς Ἑλικῶνα πέμπουσιν, Μούσαις Χάρισί τε ὁμοῦ συγχορεύσοντα,[4] ἢ οἷον τὸν Βακχειώτην (οὕτω γὰρ αὐτὸν ἡ λύρα καλεῖ, τὸν Διόνυσον λέγουσα) ἦρος ἄρτι τὸ πρῶτον ἐκλάμψαντος, ἄνθεσί τ' εἰαρινοῖσι[5] καὶ κίσσου κορύμβοις Μούσαις κατοχοὶ ποιηταὶ στέψαντες, νῦν μὲν ἐπ' ἄκρας κορυφὰς Καυκάσου καὶ Λυδίας τέμπῃ, νῦν δ' ἐπὶ Παρνάσου σκοπέλους καὶ Δελφίδα πέτραν ἄγουσι. . . .

[1] corrupt: *B* sugg. *feminas*: if *duo* is right the Hesiod citation which follows (*Op.* 100–1) is inadequate, perh. a gloss
[2] mss -σῃ [3] Herw: mss λύραις [4] mss συγχορεύσαντα
[5] mss ἠρίνοισι

168

Gellius *Attic Nights* [on Niobe's children]: For Homer says that she had six of either sex, Euripides seven, Sappho nine, and Bacchylides and Pindar ten.[1]

169

Servius on Vergil *Aeneid* ['seven of their children every year']: Some commentators take this to mean that seven boys and seven girls, as Plato says in the *Phaedo* and Sappho in her *Lyric Poems* . . . , were set free by Theseus.

170

Id. *Eclogues* ['and the theft of Prometheus']: Prometheus . . . after he had created man, is said to have ascended with Minerva's help into heaven, and there lighting a torch at the wheel of the Sun, to have stolen fire and revealed it to man. Angered at the theft, the Gods sent two ills upon earth, fever[2] and disease, as we are told by Sappho and Hesiod.

171

Philostratus *Letters*: Sappho loves the rose, and always crowns it with a meed of praise, likening beautiful maidens to it; and she compares it to the bared fore-arms of the Graces.

172

Himerius *Orations*: Your case is now to be likened to the choir-leader of the Muses himself, such as he is when both Sappho and Pindar send him in a poem, adorned with golden hair and with a lyre and drawn by swans, to dance with the Muses and Graces on Mount Helicon; or such again as is the Great Reveller—as the lyre calls Dionysus—when the Muse-inspired poets lead him in the first dawn of Spring, crowned 'with Springtime blossoms' and ivy-clusters, now to the topmost heights of Caucasus and the valleys of Lydia, now to the crags of Parnassus and the Rock of Delphi. . . .[3]

[1] Sappho probably in 140
[2] *B* suggests *woman*
[3] some of H.'s phrases are borrowed, *e.g.* 'springtime blossoms' from *Il.* 2. 89

173

Phot. (Reitz.) p. 57

ἄκακος·

ὁ κακοῦ μὴ πεπειράμενος, οὐχ ὁ χρηστοήθης· οὕτω Σαπφώ.

174

Et. Mag. 77. 1 ἀμαμαξύς· ἡ ἀναδενδράς . . . Σαπφὼ διὰ τοῦ δ

ἀμαμάξυδες

λέγει.

175

Orion 3. 12

ἀμάρα·

. . . παρὰ τὸ τῇ ἄμῃ[1] αἵρεσθαι καὶ ὀρύττεσθαι· οὕτως ἐν ὑπομνήματι Σαπφοῦς.

176

Apoll. *Adv.* 182. 22 ὃν τρόπον καὶ ἐπ' ὀνομάτων μεταπλασμοὶ γίνονται, καθάπερ τὸ ἐρυσάρματες, τὸ λῖτα, τὸ παρὰ Σαπφοῖ

αὖα [2]

Et Mag. 174. 38 αὔω· . . . εἴρηται παρὰ τὸ αὖα Αἰολικῶς τὸ ἡμέραν·[3] [τὴν γὰρ ἠῶ οἱ Αἰολεῖς αὔαν φασί.][4]

[1] mss *E.M.* and *E. Gud.*, which add ἄμη δέ ἐστιν ἐργαλεῖον οἰκοδομικόν or the like: mss Or. ἄμεν [2] mss Ap. αὐα [3] *E*: mss π. τὴν αὔαν A. τὴν ἡμέραν [4] τὴν γὰρ κ.τ.λ. incorrect, probably a gloss; the nom. was αὔως with metaplastic acc. αὖα cf. Hom. ἠῶ δῖαν (= ᾱϜόα)

173

Photius *Lexicon*: ἄκακος:

ingenuous

'without experience in evil,' not 'good-natured.' So Sappho.

174[1]

Etymologicum Magnum: ἀμαμαξύς: . . .

the tree-climber vines;

Sappho uses the form with *d* in the plural.

175

Orion *Etymologicum*: ἀμάρα,

conduit,

from its being raised (αἴρεσθαι) or thrown up by means of a spade (ἄμη). So the *Notes on Sappho*.[2]

176

Apollonius *Adverbs*: The way in which metaplasms are found in nouns, for instance ἐρυσάρματες 'drawing chariots,' λῖτα 'linen cloth,' and Sappho's αὖα,

dawn

Etymologicum Magnum: The Aeolic for ἡμέραν 'day' is αὖα; [for the Aeolic writers use αὔα for ἠῷ 'dawn'].

[1] cf. Choer. 1. 357, Suid. ἀμάμυξις, ἀναδενδράδα [2] prob. Chamaeleon's tract *On Sappho* Ath. 13. 599 c

177

Et. Mag. 174. 42 αὔως· ἡ ἠώς, τουτέστιν ἡ ἡμέρα· οὕτω λέγεται παρὰ τοῖς Αἰολεῦσι· Σαπφώ

Πότνι' αὔως . . .

178

Ath. 4. 182 e [π. μάγαδιν]· Εὐφοριὼν δὲ ὁ ἐποποιὸς ἐν τῷ Περὶ Ἰσθμίων 'οἱ νῦν' φησιν 'καλούμενοι ναβλισταὶ καὶ πανδουρισταὶ καὶ σαμβυκισταὶ καινῷ μὲν οὐδενὶ χρῶνται ὀργάνῳ.' τὸν γὰρ βάρωμον καὶ βάρβιτον, ὧν Σαπφὼ καὶ Ἀνακρέων μνημονεύουσι, καὶ τὴν μάγαδιν καὶ τὰ τρίγωνα καὶ τὰς σαμβύκας ἀρχαῖα εἶναι.

179

Poll. 7. 49.

βεῦδος,

ὡς Σαπφώ, κιμβερικόν, ἔστι δὲ τὸ κιμβερικὸν διαφανής τις χιτωνίσκος.

180

Phryn. Bek. *An.* 1. 34. 2 Σαπφὼ δὲ

γρύταν

καλεῖ τὴν μύρων καὶ γυναικείων τινῶν θήκην.[1]

181

Hesych. ἕκτορες· πάσσαλοι ἐν ῥυμῷ, Σαπφὼ δὲ τὸν Δία, Λεωνίδης τὸν κροκύφαντον.

182

Cram. *A.O.* 4. 325. 28 καὶ ἀνώπαλιν παρὰ τοῖς Αἰολεῦσιν ἀντὶ τοῦ δ ζ παραλαμβάνεται, ὡς ὅταν τὸ διάβατον ἡ Σαπφώ

ζάβατον

λέγῃ.

[1] cf. 82. 6 : mss γρύτην

177

Etymologicum Magnum αὔως ; 'dawn,' that is 'day'; this form was used in Aeolic ; compare Sappho :

The queenly Dawn. . . .

178

Athenaeus *Doctors at Dinner* [on the word *magadis*]: the epic writer Euphorion, in his book *The Isthmian Festival*, says that those who are now called players of the *nabla* or the *pandoura* or the *sambūca* are not players of new instruments. For the *barōmos* and *barbitos* mentioned by Sappho and Anacreon, and the *magadis*, *trigōnon*, and *sambūca*, are all ancient.[1]

179

Pollux *Vocabulary*: Sappho's word *beudos*,

shift,

is equivalent to κιμβερικόν, which is a transparent vest.

180

Phrynichus *Introduction to Learning*: Sappho calls by the name of *grutè*,

hutch,

the chest in which unguents and women's articles are kept.

181

Hesychius *Glossary*: ἕκτορες 'holders,' the pegs on a carriage-pole ; but Sappho calls Zeus 'the Holder,' and Leonidas uses 'holder' to mean a hair-net.

182

Cramer *Inedita* (*Oxford*): And conversely the Aeolic writers use ζ for δ, as when Sappho says ζάβατον for διάβατον,

fordable

[1] cf. Ath. 14. 636 c, *E.M.* 188. 21

183

Sch. *Il.* 14. 241 [ἐπισχοίης]· τῷ δὲ χαράκτηρι γενόμενον ὅμοιον τῷ ἰοίην καὶ

ἀγαγοίην

παρὰ Σαπφοῖ . . . εἰκότως ἐβαρυτονήθη τὸ ἐπισχοίης.

184

Choer. *Gram. Gr.* 4. 1. 270 Lentz [π. τῶν εἰς υν ληγόντων]· . . . κίνδυν, κίνδυνος, κίνδυνα· οὕτως δὲ ἔφη Σαπφὼ τὸ κίνδυνος· ὁ γοῦν Ἀλκαῖος τὴν δοτικὴν ἔφη τὸ κίνδυνι.[1]

185

Joh. Alex. *Gram. Gr.* 4. 30 Dind. ἡ ὀξεῖα ἢ ἐν τέλει τίθεται ἢ πρὸ μιᾶς τοῦ τέλους ἢ πρὸ δύο, πρὸ τριῶν δ' οὐκέτι· τὸ γὰρ

Μήδεϊα

παρὰ Σαπφοῖ πεπονθὸς παραιτούμεθα, ὅτι τὴν ει δίφθογγον διεῖλεν.

186

Cram. *A.O.* 1. 278. 17 καὶ ἡ γενικὴ τῶν πληθυντικῶν Μωσάων παρὰ Λάκωσι, παρὰ δὲ Σαπφοῖ

Μοισάων

187

Phryn. 273 (361 Ruth.)

νίτρον·

τοῦτο Αἰολεὺς μὲν ἂν εἴποι, ὥσπερ οὖν καὶ ἡ Σαπφώ, διὰ τοῦ ν, Ἀθηναῖος δὲ διὰ τοῦ λ λίτρον.

[1] *E*: mss κ. κ. κ. ὡς καὶ Σ. ἔφη τὸν κίνδυνα (or κίνδυν κίνδυνος οὕτως δὲ ἔφη Σ. τὸν κίνδυνον) . . . τῷ κίνδυνι

SAPPHO

183

Scholiast on the *Iliad* [ἐπισχοίης πόδας 'mightest set thy feet upon']: Resembling in type the forms ἰοίην 'I might go' and ἀγαγοίην,

I might lead,

in Sappho . . ., the word ἐπισχοίης was rightly accented paroxytone.

184

Choeroboscus *On the Canons of Theodosius* [on nouns in -υν]: κίνδυν 'danger,' genitive κίνδυνος, accusative κίνδυνα; Sappho thus declined the noun κίνδυνος; Alcaeus used the dative κίνδυνι.

185

John of Alexandria: The acute accent falls on the last syllable or on the penultimate or on the antepenultimate, but not further back; for I do not count the form Μήδεϊα,

Medea,

which is found in Sappho, because she has separated the vowels of the diphthong *ei*.

186

Cramer *Inedita* (*Oxford*): And the genitive plural of Μοῦσα is Μωσάων in Laconian, and Μοισάων,

of the Muses,

in Sappho.

187

Phrynichus *The Atticist*: *nitron*,

soda:

this word would be pronounced by an Aeolian, as Sappho writes it, with an *n*, but by an Athenian with an *l*.

188

Sch. *Il.* 3. 219 [ἀΐδρεϊ]· . . . ἄϊδρις· ταύτης δὲ τῆς εὐθείας ὀφείλει γενικὴ ἐκπίπτειν ἀΐδρεος, καὶ ἀΐδρεϊ. οὐ γὰρ δή γε διὰ τοῦ δ, οὐ γάρ ἐστι παρώνυμον μακρᾷ παραληγόμενον, ἀλλ' ὡς τὸ ἔχις, πόσις, ὄφις, οὕτως ὀφείλει κλίνεσθαι· ὥστε ἐκ τοῦ ἐναντίου ἁμάρτημα τὸ παρὰ τῇ Σαπφοι τὸ

πολυΐδριδι,

εἰ μὴ ἄρα ὁμοίως τοῖς Ἀττικοῖς ἐκλίθη· ὁ γὰρ Σοφοκλῆς ἴδριδα ἔφη τὴν αἰτιατικήν, ὅ τε Φρύνιχος τὴν εὐθεῖαν ἴδριδες.

189

Sch. Theocr. 2. 88 [καί μευ χρὼς μὲν ὅμοιος ἐγίνετο πολλάκι θάψῳ]· χλωρὸς ἢ ξανθός· θάψος δέ ἐστιν εἶδος ξύλου ὃ καλεῖται σκυθάριον, ὥς φησι Σαπφώ· τούτῳ δὲ τὰ ἔρια βάπτουσι. τινὲς τὸ Σκυθικὸν ξύλον.

σκύθαρρον.[1]

190

Orion 28. 15 ὡς παρὰ Σαπφοῖ χελώνη χελύνη.

χέλυννα [2]

191

Poll. 6. 98 μεσόμφαλοι δὲ φιάλαι καὶ βαλανειόμφαλοι [3] τὸ σχῆμα προσηγορίαν ἔχουσι, χρυσόμφαλοι δὲ τὴν ὕλην, ὡς αἱ Σαπφοῦς χρυσαστράγαλοι.

e.g. . . . χρυσαστράγαλοι φίαλαι . . .

[1] *E*; ⏑ ⏑ ⏑ not found in Lesbian poetry: mss σκυθάριον [2] cf. *fr.* 80, Lachm. Babr. 115. 4 where mss χέλυμνα, and Cram. *A.O.* 2 101. 5 [3] cf. Mein. on Cratin. Δραπ. 9, Ath. 11. 501 d, Hesych.; there was perh. confusion betw. βαλανίομφ. 'acorn-bossed' and βαλανειόμφ. 'bath-stopper'

188

Scholiast on *Iliad* [ἀΐδρεϊ 'unknowing, ignorant']: The genitive to the nominative ἄϊδρις ought to be ἀΐδρεος and the dative ἀΐδρει; for it ought not to have a δ in it, since it is not a derivative with a long vowel in the penultimate syllable, but ought to be declined like ἔχις, πόσις, and ὄφις; and therefore the form πολυΐδριδι,

learned,

used by Sappho is wrong; unless indeed this was declined as it was in Attic, for Sophocles used the accusative ἴδριδα and Phrynichus the nominative plural ἴδριδες.

189[1]

Scholiast on Theocritus ['my skin went often the colour of boxwood']: 'Green' or 'yellow'; θάψος is a kind of wood which is called, according to Sappho,

scytharium-wood;

it is used for dyeing; some call it Scythian-wood.

190

Orion *Etymologicum*: . . . as in Sappho χελύνη for χελώνη tortoise or

lyre.

191

Pollux *Vocabulary*: Mid-bossed cups and bath-stopper cups get their names from their shape, but the gold-bossed from the substance of which they are made, like Sappho's

. . . gold-knuckle cups . . .[2]

[1] cf. Phot. θάψος and another schol. on this passage, who ascribe the term 'Scythian-wood' to S. [2] *i.e.* a gold cup with the bottom round like one end of a 'knuckle-bone' or die

ΑΛΚΑΙΟΥ

Βίος

Str. 13. 617 ἔχει δὲ ἡ Μυτιλήνη λίμενας δύο, ὧν ὁ νότιος κλειστὸς τριηρικὸς ναυσὶ πεντήκοντα, ὁ δὲ βόρειος μέγας καὶ βαθύς, χώματι σκεπαζόμενος· προκεῖται δ᾽ ἀμφοῖν νησίον μέρος τῆς πόλεως ἔχον αὐτόθι συνοικούμενον· κατεσκεύασται δὲ τοῖς πᾶσι καλῶς. ἄνδρας δ᾽ ἔσχεν ἐνδόξους τὸ παλαιὸν μὲν Πιττακόν, ἕνα τῶν ἕπτα σοφῶν, καὶ τὸν ποιητὴν Ἀλκαῖον καὶ τὸν ἀδελφὸν Ἀντιμενίδαν . . . ἐτυραννήθη δὲ ἡ πόλις κατὰ τοὺς χρόνους τούτους ὑπὸ πλειόνων διὰ τὰς διχοστασίας, καὶ τὰ Στασιωτικὰ καλούμενα τοῦ Ἀλκαίου ποιήματα περὶ τούτων ἐστίν· ἐν δὲ τοῖς τυράννοις καὶ ὁ Πιττακὸς ἐγένετο. Ἀλκαῖος μὲν οὖν ὁμοίως ἐλοιδορεῖτο καὶ τούτῳ καὶ τοῖς ἄλλοις, Μυρσίλῳ καὶ Μελάγχρῳ καὶ τοῖς Κλεανακτίδαις καὶ ἄλλοις τισίν, οὐδ᾽ αὐτὸς καθαρεύων τῶν τοιούτων νεωτερισμῶν. Πιττακὸς δὲ εἰς μὲν τὴν τῶν δυναστειῶν κατάλυσιν ἐχρήσατο τῇ μοναρχίᾳ καὶ αὐτός, καταλύσας δὲ ἀπέδωκε τὴν αὐτονομίαν τῇ πόλει.

Diog. Laert. 1. 74 [π. Πιττακοῦ]· οὗτος μετὰ τῶν Ἀλκαίου γένομενος ἀδελφῶν Μέλαγχρον καθεῖλε τὸν τῆς Λέσβου τύραννον· καὶ περὶ τῆς

---

[1] see on Sappho, p. 143 [2] see also *fr.* 121, 161 and Arist. *Pol.* 1311 b [3] of Mytilene according to Suidas s. *Pittacus*,

ALCAEUS

LIFE

Strabo *Geography*: Mytilene has two harbours, of which the southern is landlocked and affords anchorage for fifty triremes, and the northern spacious and deep and protected by a breakwater. Both are flanked by a small island upon which part of the city is built. This city is well equipped with every convenience. Among famous Mytileneans of more ancient times are Pittacus, one of the Seven Sages, and the poet Alcaeus and his brother Antimenidas[1] . . . In those days, as the result of dissensions, the city was ruled from time to time by tyrants, who form the theme of the *Political Songs*, as they are called, of Alcaeus. The aforesaid Pittacus, being one of their number, did not escape the abuse of Alcaeus any more than the rest, Myrsilus, Melanchrus, the Cleanactids and others, although the poet was not free himself of the imputation of playing the revolutionary, while Pittacus made use of the monarchy only as a means of overthrowing arbitrary power and gave the city back its self-government as soon as his object was achieved.[2]

Diogenes Laertius *Lives of the Philosophers* [on Pittacus]: This man was associated with the brothers of Alcaeus in the overthrow of Melanchrus despot of Lesbos.[3] In the war between Mytilene and

who gives the date as Ol. 42 (B.C. 612–609); A. himself was too young, cf. *fr.* 75

Ἀχιλλείτιδος χώρας μαχομένων Ἀθηναίων καὶ Μυτιληναίων ἐστρατήγει μὲν αὐτός, Ἀθηναίων δὲ Φρύνων παγκρατιαστὴς Ὀλυμπιονίκης. συνέθετο δὴ μονομαχῆσαι πρὸς αὐτόν· καὶ δίκτυον ἔχων ὑπὸ τὴν ἀσπίδα, λαθραίως περιέβαλε τὸν Φρύνωνα καὶ κτείνας ἀνεσώσατο τὸ χωρίον. ὕστερον μέντοι φησὶν Ἀπολλόδωρος ἐν τοῖς Χρονικοῖς διαδικασθῆναι τοὺς Ἀθηναίους περὶ τοῦ χωρίου πρὸς τοὺς Μυτιληναίους, ἀκούοντος τῆς δίκης Περιάνδρου, ὃν καὶ τοῖς Ἀθηναίοις προσκρῖναι. τότε δ' οὖν τὸν Πιττακὸν ἰσχυρῶς ἐτίμησαν οἱ Μυτιληναῖοι, καὶ τὴν ἀρχὴν ἐνεχείρησαν αὐτῷ. ὁ δὲ δέκα ἔτη κατασχὼν καὶ εἰς τάξιν ἀγαγὼν τὸ πολίτευμα κατέθετο τὴν ἀρχήν, καὶ δέκα ἐπεβίω ἄλλα.

Diog. Laert. 75 Ἡράκλειτος δέ φησιν Ἀλκαῖον ὑποχείριον λαβόντα καὶ ἀπολύσαντα φάναι 'Συγγνώμη τιμωρίας κρείσσων.'

Ibid. 77 ἐτελεύτησε δ' (ὁ Πιττακὸς) ἐπὶ Ἀριστομένους τῷ τρίτῳ ἔτει τῆς πεντηκόστης δευτέρας Ὀλυμπιάδος, βιοὺς ὑπὲρ ἔτη ἑβδομήκοντα.[1]

Euseb. Ol. 46. 2: Sappho et Alcaeus poetae cognoscebantur.

Ath. 15. 694 a [π. σκολίων] . . . ὡς Ἀριστοφάνης παρίστησιν ἐν Δαιταλεῦσιν λέγων οὕτως·

Ἆσον δή μοι σκόλιόν τι λαβὼν Ἀλκαίου κ' Ἀνακρέοντος.

[1] mss add ἤδη γηραιός an old variant

Athens for the possession of the Achilleïd (or district of Sigeum in the Troad), he was in command on the one side and the Olympian champion Phrynon on the other. The two generals coming to single combat, Pittacus enveloped his antagonist unawares in a net which he carried under his shield, and killed him, thus saving the district for Mytilene. Later, however, if we may believe the *Chronicles* of Apollodorus, it became the subject of arbitration between the two cities, and Periander, who acted as judge, awarded it to Athens. However that may be, Pittacus was highly honoured thereafter by his countrymen, and made head of the state. After holding office ten years, during which he brought order into the administration, he resigned it and lived for ten years more as a private citizen.[1]

Diogenes Laertius *Lives of the Philosophers*: According to Heracleitus, when Alcaeus fell into his hands Pittacus set him at liberty with the words 'Forgiveness is better than punishment.'

The Same: Pittacus . . . died in the archonship of Aristomenes, the third year of the 52nd Olympiad (B.C. 570), at the age of over seventy.

Eusebius *Chronicle*: Olympiad 46. 2 (B.C. 595): Flourished the poets Sappho and Alcaeus.[2]

Athenaeus *Doctors at Dinner* [on drinking-songs]: Compare what Aristophanes says in the *Banqueters*, 'Take and sing me a drinking-song of Alcaeus or Anacreon.'

[1] see below on *fr*. 160 [2] cf. Suid. on Sappho (p. 145)

Cic. *Tusc. Disp.* 4. 71 Fortis vir in sua republica cognitus quae de iuvenum amore scribit Alcaeus!

Hor. *Od.* 1. 32. 3 . . . age dic Latinum,
barbite, carmen,
Lesbio primum modulate civi,
qui ferox bello, tamen inter arma
sive iactatam religarat udo
litore navim,
Liberum et Musas Veneremque et illi
semper haerentem puerum canebat
et Lycum nigris oculis nigroque
crine decorum.

Ibid. 2. 13. 26 . . . et te sonantem plenius aureo,
Alcaee, plectro dura navis,
dura fugae mala, dura belli.

Dion. Hal. 5. 421 Reiske: Ἀλκαίου δὲ σκόπει τὸ μεγαλοφυὲς καὶ βραχὺ καὶ ἡδὺ ὅσον αὐτῆς μὴ τῇ διαλέκτῳ τι κεκάκωται· καὶ πρὸ ἁπάντων τὸ τῶν Πολιτικῶν ᾀσμάτων[1] ἦθος. πολλαχοῦ γοῦν τὸ μέτρον τις εἰ περιέλοι ῥητορικὴν ἂν εὕροι πολιτικήν.[2]

Quint. *Inst.* 10. 1 Alcaeus in parte operis aureo plectro merito donatur, qua tyrannos insectatur; multum etiam moribus confert; in eloquendo quoque brevis et magnificus et diligens, et plurimum Homero similis; sed in lusus et amores descendit, maioribus tamen aptior.

[1] mss πραγμάτων [2] mss πολιτείαν

[1] cf. Cic. *N.D.* 1. 21 [2] ref. perh. to the civil strife and

LIFE OF ALCAEUS

Cicero *Tusculan Disputations*: Alcaeus was a brave man and eminent in the state to which he belonged, and yet what extravagant things he says of the love of youths![1]

Horace *Odes*: . . . Come sing me a Latin song, thou lyre first played by a citizen of Lesbos, a gallant warrior who, alike amid the very fight or when his storm-tossed ship was moored to the wet shore,[2] sang of Bacchus and the Muses, of Venus and her inseparable boy, and of the beautiful Lycus so dark of eye and hair.

The Same: . . . and thee, Alcaeus, chanting with fuller note unto thy golden quill the toils of the sea, the toils of exile, and the toils of war.[3]

Dionysius of Halicarnassus *Critique of the Ancient Writers*: only look at the nobility of Alcaeus, his conciseness, his sweetness—so far as they are not impaired by his dialect—, and above all the moral tone of his *Political Poems*. Often if the reader could but remove the metre he would find political rhetoric.[4]

Quintilian *Principles of Oratory*: Alcaeus is rightly awarded the 'golden quill' in that part of his works where he assails the tyrants; his ethical value too is great, and his style is concise, lofty, exact, and very like Homer's; but he stoops to jesting and love-making though better fitted for higher themes.

the ship of state [3] cf. Hor. *Od.* 4. 9. 7, *Ep.* 1. 19–29, 2. 2. 99, Porph. and Acr. *ad loc.*, and Jul. *Mis.* p. 433 H. [4] cf. *Comp.* 24, Synes. *Somn.* 156.

Heph. π. Σημείων 138 καὶ μάλιστα εἴωθεν ὁ ἀστερίσκος τίθεσθαι ἐὰν ἑτερόμετρον ᾖ τὸ ᾆσμα τὸ ἑξῆς· ὃ καὶ μᾶλλον ἐπὶ τῶν ποιημάτων <τῶν κατὰ περικοπὴν ἢ>[1] τῶν μονοστροφικῶν γίνεται <τῶν> Σαπφοῦς τε καὶ Ἀνακρέοντος καὶ Ἀλκαίου· ἐπὶ δὲ τῶν Ἀλκαίου[2] ἰδίως κατὰ μὲν τὴν Ἀριστοφάνειον ἔκδοσιν ἀστερίσκος ἐπὶ ἑτερομετρίας ἐτίθετο μόνης, κατὰ δὲ τὴν νῦν τὴν Ἀριστάρχειον καὶ ἐπὶ ποιημάτων μεταβολῆς.

Ath. 10. 429 f ἐγὼ δ' ἐπεὶ παρεξέβην περὶ τῶν ἀρχαίων κράσεων διαλεγόμενος, ἐπαναλήψομαι τὸν λόγον τὰ ὑπὸ Ἀλκαίου τοῦ μελοποιοῦ λεχθέντα ἐπὶ νοῦν βαλλόμενος· φησὶ γάρ που οὗτος· 'Ἔγχεε κέρναις ἕνα καὶ δύο.' ἐν τούτοις γάρ τινες οὐ τὴν κρᾶσιν οἴονται λέγειν αὐτόν, ἀλλὰ σωφρονικὸν ὄντα καθ' ἕνα κύαθον ἄκρατον πίνειν καὶ πάλιν κατὰ δύο. τοῦτο δὲ ὁ Ποντικὸς Χαμαιλέων ἐκδέδεκται τῆς Ἀλκαίου φιλοινίας ἀπείρως ἔχων.

Ibid. 15. 668 e [π. κοττάβου]· ὅτι δὲ ἐσπούδαστο παρὰ Σικελιώταις ὁ κότταβος, δῆλον ἐκ τοῦ καὶ οἰκήματα ἐπιτήδεια τῇ παιδιᾷ κατασκευάζεσθαι ὡς ἱστορεῖ Δικαίαρχος ἐν τῷ Περὶ Ἀλκαίου.

Str. 13. 618 [π. Λέσβου]· . . . καὶ Ἑλλάνικος δὲ Λέσβιος ὁ συγγραφεὺς καὶ Καλλίας ὁ τὴν Σαπφὼ καὶ τὸν Ἀλκαῖον ἐξηγησάμενος.

[1] Consbruch -*E* [2] ἐπὶ δὲ τούτων *i.e.* all three? *E*

LIFE OF ALCAEUS

Hephaestion *On Graphical Signs*: The asterisk is usually employed if the poem which follows is in a different metre. This is more often the case with those composed in triads than with the monostrophic poems of Sappho, Anacreon, and Alcaeus. The poems of Alcaeus are peculiar in this, that in the Aristophanic edition the asterisk was used only to mark a change of metre, but in the now current edition of Aristarchus it marks a fresh poem whatever the metre.

Athenaeus *Doctors at Dinner*: Having completed my digression on ancient methods of mixing wine, I will resume my theme and consider what the lyric poet Alcaeus means by the phrase 'Mix ere you pour it one and two.' Some authorities hold that he does not refer to the proportion of wine to water but, being a temperate man, would have us drink first one ladleful of unmixed wine and then two, and no more. This is the interpretation of Chamaeleon of Pontus, but he does not realise how fond of the bottle Alcaeus was.[1]

The Same [on the *cottabos*]: The love of the Sicilians for this game is proved by the fact that they went so far as to build special rooms to play it in, as we are told by Dicaearchus in his tract *On Alcaeus*.[2]

Strabo *Geography* [on Lesbos]: the historian Hellanicus, too, was a Lesbian, and Callias the commentator on Sappho and Alcaeus.[3]

[1] cf. *fr*. 164 [2] cf. *fr*. 85 and Ath. 15. 666 b, 11. 460 f
[3] cf *fr*. 85

Suid. Δράκων Στρατονικεύς· γραμματικός. . . . Περὶ τῶν Πινδάρου Μελῶν, Περὶ τῶν Σαπφοῦς Μέτρων, Περὶ τῶν Ἀλκαίου Μελῶν.

Ibid. Ὡραπόλλων· . . . γραμματικὸς διδάξας ἐν Ἀλεξανδρείᾳ καὶ ἐν Αἰγύπτῳ, εἶτα ἐν Κωνσταντινουπόλει ἐπὶ Θεοδοσίου. ἔγραψε . . . Ὑπόμνημα Σοφοκλέους, Ἀλκαίου, εἰς Ὅμηρον.

Vide *A.P.* 9. 184, 571, Max. Tyr. 37, Ar. Byz. on Ar. *Thesm.* 162, Ath. 10. 429 a, Him. ap. Schenkl

ΑΛΚΑΙΟΥ ΜΕΛΩΝ

Α′

ΥΜΝΩΝ

1 εἰς Ἀπόλλωνα

Him. *Or.* 14. 10 ἐθέλω δὲ ὑμῖν καὶ Ἀλκαίου τινὰ λόγον εἰπεῖν ὃν ἐκεῖνος ᾖσεν ἐν μέλεσι παιᾶνα γράφων Ἀπόλλωνι. ἐρῶ δὲ ὑμῖν οὐ κατὰ τὰ μέλη τὰ Λέσβια, ἐπεὶ μηδὲ ποιητικός τις ἐγώ, ἀλλὰ τὸ μέτρον αὐτὸ λύσας εἰς λόγον τῆς λύρας. ὅτε Ἀπόλλων ἐγένετο, κοσμήσας αὐτὸν ὁ Ζεὺς μίτρᾳ τε χρυσῇ καὶ λύρᾳ, δούς τε ἐπὶ τούτοις ἅρμα ἐλαύνειν, κύκνοι δὲ ἦσαν τὸ ἅρμα, εἰς Δέλφους πέμπει καὶ Κασταλίας νάματα ἐκεῖθεν προφητεύσοντα δίκην καὶ θέμιν τοῖς Ἕλλησιν· ὁ δὲ ἐπιβὰς ἐπὶ τῶν ἁρμάτων ἐφῆκε τοὺς κύκνους εἰς Ὑπερβορέους πέτεσθαι. Δέλφοι μὲν οὖν, ὡς ᾔσθοντο, παιᾶνα συνθέντες καὶ μέλος καὶ χόρους ἠϊθέων περὶ τὸν τρίποδα

---

[1] cf. *fr.* 85 [2] he speaks of the inventory of a temple-treasury found at Delos containing θήκην τρίγωνον ἔχουσαν βιβλία Ἀλκαίου 'a three-cornered roll-box or book-case containing the Books of Alcaeus'; this shape would suit ten rolls, and the tenth is the highest numbered Book of

ALCAEUS

Suidas *Lexicon*: Dracon of Stratoniceia: A grammarian, writer of books . . . *On the Poems of Pindar, On the Metres of Sappho, On the Poems of Alcaeus.*[1]

The Same: Horapollo: . . . a grammarian who first taught at Alexandria and elsewhere in Egypt, and afterwards at Constantinople under Theodosius. He wrote . . . treatises *On Sophocles, On Alcaeus,* and *On Homer.*

Herm. 1911. 420, 421; Homolle *Mon. Grecs* i. 7. p. 49.[2]

THE POEMS OF ALCAEUS

Book I

HYMNS

1 To Apollo

Himerius *Orations*: I will tell you likewise one of Alcaeus' tales, a tale which he sang in lyric verse when he wrote a paean to Apollo. And I tell it you not according to the Lesbian verse—for I am not of poetic humour—but changing the actual metre of the lyric verse into prose. When Apollo was born, Zeus furnished him forth with a golden headband and a lyre, and giving him moreover a chariot to drive—and they were swans that drew it—, would have him go to Delphi and the spring of Castaly, thence to deliver justice and right in oracles to Greece. Nevertheless once he was mounted in the chariot, Apollo bade his swans fly to the land of the Hyperboreans. Now when the Delphians heard of it, they set a paean to a tune and held dances of youths about the

A. quoted; the date of the inscr. is not given, but it looks as if *fr.* 1 was to the Delian and not the Pythian Apollo.

στήσαντες, ἐκάλουν τὸν θεὸν ἐξ Ὑπερβορέων ἐλθεῖν· ὁ δὲ ἔτος ὅλον παρὰ τοῖς ἐκεῖ θεμιστεύσας ἀνθρώποις, ἐπειδὴ καιρὸν ἐνόμιζε καὶ τοὺς Δελφικοὺς ἠχῆσαι τρίποδας, αὖθις κελεύει τοῖς κύκνοις ἐξ Ὑπερβορέων ἀφίπτασθαι. ἦν μὲν οὖν θέρος καὶ τοῦ θέρους τὸ μέσον αὐτό, ὅτε ἐξ Ὑπερβορέων Ἀλκαῖος ἄγει τὸν Ἀπόλλωνα, ὅθεν δὴ θέρους ἐκλάμποντος καὶ ἐπιδημοῦντος Ἀπόλλωνος θερινόν τι καὶ ἡ λύρα περὶ τὸν θεὸν ἁβρύνεται· ᾄδουσι μὲν ἀηδόνες αὐτῷ, ὁποῖον εἰκὸς ᾆσαι παρ' Ἀλκαίῳ τὰς ὄρνιθας· ᾄδουσι δὲ καὶ χελιδόνες καὶ τέττιγες, οὐ τὴν ἑαυτῶν τύχην τὴν ἐν ἀνθρώπων ἀγγέλλουσαι, ἀλλὰ πάντα τὰ μέλη κατὰ θεοῦ φθεγγόμεναι· ῥεῖ καὶ ἀργοροῖς ἡ Κασταλία κατὰ ποίησιν νάμασι καὶ Κηφισσὸς μέγας αἴρεται πορφύρων τοῖς κύμασι, τὸν Ἐνιπέα τοῦ Ὁμήρου μιμούμενος. βιάζεται μὲν γὰρ Ἀλκαῖος ὁμοίως Ὁμήρῳ ποιῆσαι καὶ ὕδωρ θεῶν ἐπιδημίαν αἰσθέσθαι δυνάμενον.

Heph. 84 ἐπιωνικὸν δὲ ἀπὸ μείζονος τρίμετρον καταληκτικόν ἐστί, τὸ καλούμενον Ἀλκαϊκὸν ἑνδεκασύλλαβον . . . οἷον·

Ὦ 'ναξ Ἀπόλλων, παῖ μεγάλω Δίος,
e.g.[1] ὄν ἐξεκόσμη γιγνόμενον πάτηρ
μίτρᾳ τε χρύσᾳ καὶ χελύννᾳ[2]
δοίς τ' ἐπὶ τοίσδεσιν[3] ἄρμ' ἐλαύνην

5 κυκνόσσυτον,[4] Δέλφοις μὲν ἔπεμπε καὶ
Καφισσόδωρον Κασταλίας ὕδωρ[5]
δίκαν προφατεύσοντα κῆθα[6]
καὶ θέμιν Ἐλλάδεσιν· σὺ δ' ἔββαις

κύκνοις ἔπηκας πτέσθ' ἐπ' Ὑπερβόροις·
10 Δέλφοις δ' ἄρ', ὡς ᾄσθοντο, παάονα
αὔλοις[7] τε σύνθεντες χόροισι
πὲρ τρίποδ' ἀϊθέων κέλοντο

[1] ll. 2–24, *E* from Him. [2] χελ. Sa. 190 [3] see on Sa. 6
[4] cf. θεόσσυτος, αὐτόσσυτος and Sa. 172 [5] cf. Paus. 10. 8. 5. ἤκουσα . . . τὸ ὕδωρ τῇ Κασταλίᾳ ποταμοῦ δῶρον εἶναι τοῦ Κηφισσοῦ· τοῦτο ἐποίησε καὶ Ἀλκαῖος ἐν προοιμίῳ τῷ εἰς Ἀπόλλωνα
[6] Hdn. π. παθ. 2. 192, *fr.* 73 [7] cf. Plut. *Mus.* 14

tripod, and besought the God to come back thence. Yet Apollo dealt law among those of that country for a whole year. Then, when he thought it was time that the tripods of Delphi, too, should give sound, he bade the swans fly back again from the Hyperboreans. Now it is summer, and the very midst of summer, when Alcaeus brings Apollo back from that land, and therefore with the summer brightly shining and Apollo present, the lyre, too, puts on a summer wantonness concerning the God. Nightingales sing to him as birds might well sing in Alcaeus, swallows also sing and crickets, not announcing their own fortunes in the world but telling in all their tunes of the God. Castaly, in poetic style, flows with springs of silver, and great Cephissus lifts himself with his waves all shining, in imitation of the Enipeus of Homer. For Alcaeus, like Homer, perforce makes the water able to know that a God is present.

Hephaestion *Handbook of Metre*: The epionic trimeter *a majore* is acatalectic, the so-called Alcaic eleven-syllable . . . for instance:

O King Apollo, son of great Zeus,[1]

e. g. whom thy father did furnish forth at thy birth with golden headband and lyre of shell, and giving thee moreover a swan-drawn chariot to drive, would have thee go to Delphi and the water which is Cephissus' gift to Castaly,[2] there to deliver justice and right in oracles unto Greece; nevertheless, once mounted, thou badest thy swans fly to the land of the Hyperboreans; and although when the Delphians heard of it they set a pacan unto flutes and dances of youths around the tripod and besought thee to come

[1] cf. Sch. Heph. 84; and *fr.* 6: Heph. tells us this is Ode 1 of Book I [2] cf. Pausanias 'I have heard . . . that the water is a gift to Castalia from the Cephissus, and Alcaeus says this too in his prelude to Apollo'

e.g. Ὑπερβόρων σ' ἔλθην· σὺ δ' ὅλον Ϝέτος
κήθυι θεμιστεύσαις, ὄτα καῖρος ἦν
15 καὶ Δελφίκοις ἄχην τρίποσσιν,
αὖθι[1] κύκνοις ἐκέλω ἀππέτεσθαι.

ἦν μὰν θέρος καὶ τῶ θέρεος μέσον,
ὄτ' ἐξ Ὑπερβόρων πάλιν ἴκεο·
ᾆδόν τ' ἀήδω καὶ χελίδω
20 φθεγγομένα τε βρότοισι τέττιξ

τέαν τύχαν, καὶ Κασταλία ἀργύροις
ῥῆ νάμασιν καὶ πορφυροκύματος[2]
ἄρθη μέγαις Κάφισσος εὖ Ϝείδων θέον οὐκ ἀπόδαμον ἔντα[3] . . .

2–5 εἰς Ἑρμῆν

Heph. 83 ἐπιχοριαμβικὸν μὲν οὖν τὸ Σαπφικὸν καλούμενον ἐνδεκασύλλαβον οἷον· (Sa. 1) . . . ἔστι δὲ καὶ παρ' Ἀλκαίῳ—καὶ ἄδηλον ὁποτέρου ἐστὶν εὕρημα, εἰ καὶ Σαπφικὸν καλεῖται—, οἷον·

Χαῖρε Κυλλάνας ὁ μέδεις,[4] σὲ γάρ μοι
θῦμος ὔμνην, τὸν κορύφαισιν αὔϜαις[5]
Μαῖα γέννατο Κρονίδᾳ μάεισα[6]
παμβασίληι.

[1] cf. Thess. inscr. αὖθε Hfm. 48, Alc. 122. 10 ἄγι, Apoll. *Adv.* 163. 2, Hdn. 2. 932. 20 [2] cf. χρυσάρματος [3] Pind. *P.* 4. 5 [4] mss Choer. also μέδων: ll. 2–4 only in Choerob. on Heph. *l.c.* [5] some mss κορυφᾶσιν αὔϜαις = ἀϜίαις *E*, cf. ἄημι, Hesych. ἄος· πνεῦμα, Theocr. 30. 5 παραύϜαις (ms παραύλ.) = παρηΐαις: mss αὐγαῖς, ἄγναις: *B* αὔταις [6] μάεισα

e. g. thence, yet for a whole year dealtest thou law in that country; then when it was time for the tripods of Delphi, too, to give sound, thou badest the swans fly back thither. Now it was summer and the midst of summer when thou returnedst from the Hyperboreans; the nightingale sang and the swallow, the cricket sang also to tell mankind of thy fortunes, while Castaly flowed with springs of silver, and great Cephissus lifted his shining waves well knowing that a God was come home.

2–5 To Hermes

Hephaestion *Handbook of Metre*: As an epichoriambic type of this kind of verse we may compare the so-called Sapphic eleven-syllable, for instance: (Sa. 1) . . . ; it also occurs in Alcaeus—and it is uncertain which of the two poets invented it, though it is called Sapphic—, for instance: [1]

Hail, thou ruler of Cyllene! thee it is my will to sing, whom Maia bare upon the breezy heights unto the love of the omnipotent Son of Cronus.

[1] Heph. tells us this was Ode 2 of Book I: cf. Choer. on Heph., Apoll. *Synt.* 93 (*Gram. Gr.* 2. 2. 78) who discusses whether μέδεις is verb or partcp.: perh. cf. for the rest Philostr. *Vit. Ap.* 5. 15, *Im.* 1. 25

(δέδαα δαείς, μέμαα μαείς) 'desired, loved,' Michelangeli -*E* mss μαεία, μέγιστα: *B* μίγεισα

3

Men. *Encom. Rh. Gr.* 9. 149 Walz [π. γενεαλογικῶν]· ἀλλ' ἐπεὶ εὕρηται καὶ τοῦτο τὸ εἶδος τῶν ὕμνων παρὰ τοῖς ἀρχαίοις καὶ ἤδη τινὲς καὶ Διονύσου γονὰς ὕμνησαν καὶ Ἀπόλλωνος γονὰς ἕτεροι καὶ Ἀλκαῖος <καὶ> Ἡφαίστου καὶ πάλιν Ἑρμοῦ, καὶ τοῦτ' ἀποτετμήμεθα τὸ μέρος . . . ἔστι δὲ ποιητῇ μὲν[1] καθ' αὑτὸν[2] μόνον τὸ εἶδος χρήσιμον, συγγραφεῖ δὲ οὐδέποτε. ὁ μὲν γὰρ καὶ Χάριτας μαιευομένας καὶ Ὥρας ὑποδεχομένας καὶ τὰ τοιαῦτα πραγματεύεται, ὁ δ' ἐπ' ἀνάγκης ὅτι βραχύτατα ἐρεῖ.

4

Paus. 7. 20. 2 βουσὶ γὰρ χαίρειν μάλιστα Ἀπόλλωνα Ἀλκαῖός τε ἐδήλωσεν ἐν ὕμνῳ τῷ εἰς Ἑρμῆν, γράψας ὡς ὁ Ἑρμῆς βοῦς ὑφέλοιτο τοῦ Ἀπόλλωνος.

Porph. Hor. *Od.* 1. 10. 1 ['Mercuri facunde nepos Atlantis . . .']: Hymnus est in Mercurium ab Alcaeo lyrico poeta.

Id. 1. 10. 9 ('te boves olim nisi reddidisses | per dolum amotas, puerum minaci | voce dum terret, viduus pharetra | risit Apollo'): . . . fabula haec autem ab Alcaeo ficta et iterum Mercurius idcirco traditur furandi repertor, quia oratio, cuius inventor est, animos audientium fallit.

Sch. *Il.* 15. 256 [Ἀπόλλωνα χρυσάορον]· Ἑρμῆς ὁ Διὸς καὶ Μαίας τῆς Ἄτλαντος εὗρε λύραν, καὶ τοὺς Ἀπόλλωνος βόας κλέψας εὑρέθη ὑπὸ τοῦ θεοῦ διὰ τῆς μαντικῆς. ἀπειλοῦντος δὲ τοῦ Ἀπόλλωνος ἔκλεψεν αὐτοῦ καὶ τὰ ἐπὶ τῶν ὤμων τόξα· μειδιάσας δὲ ὁ θεὸς ἔδωκεν αὐτῷ τὴν μαντικὴν ῥάβδον, ἀφ' ἧς καὶ χρυσόρραπις ὁ Ἑρμῆς προσηγορεύθη· ἔλαβε δὲ παρ' αὐτοῦ τὴν λύραν ὅθεν καὶ χρυσάωρ ὠνομάσθη ἀπὸ τοῦ τῆς κιθάρας ἀορτῆρος.[3]

[1] mss ὡς π. μ. (from marginal correction of previous line)
[2] *E*: mss αὐτὸ [3] see p. 324

3

Menander *Declamations* [on genealogic hymns]. . . . But since this literary form is found among the ancients, and some ere this have sung of the birth of Dionysus and others of the birth of Apollo, and Alcaeus of that of Hephaestus also and again of that of Hermes, I have made it a separate class. . . . The form is useful only to the poet, never to the prose-writer; for the one deals with the midwifery of the Graces and the nursing of the Seasons and the like, whereas the other will of necessity express himself as briefly as possible.[1]

4

Pausanias *Description of Greece*: Apollo's delight in oxen is shown by Alcaeus in the *Hymn to Hermes*, where he says that Hermes stole oxen from Apollo.

Porphyrio on Horace Ode 1. 10 ['Mercury, thou eloquent son of Atlas' daughter']: A hymn to Mercury by the lyric poet Alcaeus.

The Same ['Thee it was, at whom once Apollo smiled when as a babe thou tookest his quiver while he sought to terrify thee with threats because of thy theft of his oxen']: This story (the theft of the quiver) originated with Alcaeus, and thus for the second time Mercury is made the discoverer of thieving because of the deception wrought by oratory, the art he invented.

Scholiast on *Iliad* ['Apollo wielder of gold']: Hermes, the son of Zeus and Maia daughter of Atlas, discovered the lyre, and having stolen the oxen of Apollo was found out by the God's power of divination. But when Apollo threatened him, he stole the very bow and arrows that were upon his shoulder. Whereat the God smiled, and gave him the divining-staff from which Hermes came to be called 'God of the golden wand,' and received from him the lyre which has given him the name of 'the wielder of gold' from the strap to which the lyre is fastened.[2]

[1] Men. seems to imply that A. did not write a hymn to Dionysus, but cf. 174 [2] see next page *footnote*

e. g.[1] κὤτ' Ἀπόλλωνος βόας ἐξέκλεψας
εὖρε μέν σφε μάντις ἄναξ, ἐπεὶ δὲ
δεῖνά σ' ἀπείλη, τότα δὴ σὺ καὶ τάπ-
ομμάδι' αὔτω
5 ἐξέκλεψας τόξ'·[2] ὀ δὲ μειδιάσαις
μαντίκαν σοι ῥάβδον ἔδωκ', ἀπ' ἆς τὺ
καὶ κλύεις χρυσόρραπις ἐν βρότοισι,
κἄλαβεν αὖτος
ἆπ σέθεν χέλυν, τόθεν ὠνύμασται
10 χρυσάωρ . . .

5

Ath. 10. 425 c [π. οἰνοχοῶν]· τοῖς δὲ θεοῖς οἰνοχοοῦσάν τινες ἱστοροῦσι τὴν Ἁρμονίαν . . . Ἀλκαῖος δὲ καὶ τὸν Ἑρμῆν εἰσάγει αὐτῶν οἰνοχόον ὡς καὶ Σαπφὼ λέγουσα· (Sa. 146).

---

6 εἰς Ἀθηνᾶν

Strab. 9. 411 [π. Κορωνείας]· κρατήσαντες δὲ (οἱ Βοιωτοί) τῆς Κορωνείας ἐν τῷ πρὸ αὐτῆς πεδίῳ τὸ τῆς Ἰτωνίας Ἀθηνᾶς ἱερὸν ἱδρύσαντο ὁμώνυμον τῷ Θεσσαλικῷ καὶ τὸν παραρρέοντα ποταμὸν Κουάριον προσηγόρευσαν ὁμοφώνως τῷ ἐκεῖ· Ἀλκαῖος δὲ καλεῖ ΚωϜάλιον[3] λέγων·

Ὦ 'νασσ' Ἀθανάα πολε[μάδοκε],[4]
ἄ ποι Κορωνείας ἐπιϜείδεο
ναύω πάροιθεν ἀμφι[κλύστω][5]
ΚωϜαλίω[3] ποτάμω παρ' ὔχθοις . . .

ἐνταῦθα δὲ καὶ τὰ Παμβοιώτια συνετέλουν.

[1] *E* from Sch. *Il.* [2] cf. Theocr. 29. 29. [3] *E*, cf. κῶας: mss Κωρ.: Call. *Pall.* 5. 63 Κουρ. [4] Wel.-Ahr.: mss λέγων ἄσσ' ἀθάνα ἀπολε . . . [5] ἄ ποι Κορ. Wel: mss ἀπὸ Κοιρωνίας:

e.g. And when thou stolest away the oxen of Apollo, 'tis true he found them, being Lord of divination; but when he threatened thee full direly, then thou stolest away the very bow and arrows that were upon his shoulder: whereat he smiled, and gave thee the divining-staff from which men know thee to this day as 'God of the golden wand,' and himself received from thee the lyre whence he is called 'Wielder of gold.'

5

Athenaeus *Doctors at Dinner* [on winebearers]: According to some writers the winebearer of the Gods was Harmonia . . . Alcaeus makes Hermes bear their wine and so does Sappho (146).

---

6 To Athena

Strabo *Geography*: When they conquered Coronea, the Boeotians built in the plain which lies before it the temple of Itonian Athena, calling it after the Thessalian one, and named the river which flows beside it Cuarius after the river in Thessaly. But Alcaeus calls it Coälius, saying:

O Queen Athena, upholder of War, who standest, we know, watching over Coronea before a stream-flanked temple on the banks of the Coälius . . .

And it is here that they used to hold the Pan-Boeotian festival.

ἐπιϜείδεο *E*, cf. for gen. προοράω: *B* ἐπὶ πισέων: ναύω Wel: mss ἐπιδεων' αυω: ἀμφικλ. *E* (in a bend of the river): Wel. ἀμφιβαίνεις: mss ἀμφὶ . . .

7

Strab. 9. 412 [π. Ὀγχηστοῦ]· οὐκ εὖ δ' ὁ Ἀλκαῖος, ὥσπερ τὸ τοῦ ποταμοῦ ὄνομα παρέτρεψε τοῦ Κουαρίου, οὕτω καὶ τοῦ Ὀγχηστοῦ κατέψευσται, πρὸς ταῖς ἐσχατιαῖς τοῦ Ἑλικῶνος αὐτὸν τιθείς· ὁ δ' ἐστὶν ἄπωθεν ἱκανῶς τούτου τοῦ ὄρους.

8

Apoll. *Pron.* 76. 32 σαφὲς ὅτι καὶ τὸ Αἰολικὸν δίγαμμα ταῖς κατὰ τὸ τρίτον πρόσωπον προσνέμεται, καθὸ καὶ αἱ ἀπὸ φωνήεντος ἀρχόμεναι δασύνονται. Ἀλκαῖος·

. . . . . ὤστε θέων μήδεν' Ὀλυμπίων

λῦσ' ἄτερ Ϝέθεν[1] . . . . .

9 εἰς Ἥφαιστον

[*Vide* 3]

10 εἰς Ἄρη

Cram. *A.O.* 3. 237. 1 ζητοῦμεν καὶ τὴν τοῦ Ἄρης, Ἄρεος γενικήν, πῶς εὕρηται διὰ διφθόγγου· λέγομεν Ἄρευος, Ἄρευι· (24)· ἡ κλητική·

. . . . Ἄρευ, δι' ὦ φόβος δαΐκτηρ[2] . . .

11 [εἰς Ἀφροδίτην]

Ox. Pap. 1233. 12. 5–9

[. . . . . τέ]μενος λάχοισ[α]
[. . . . . . . κ]ορύφαν πόληος
[. . . . .]ν Ἀφρόδιτα
[. . . . .]

[1] Bek. (but λῦσαι ἄτερ): mss λυσεατερ γεθεν [2] Cram: mss διακ.

7[1]

Strabo *Geography* [on Onchestus]: And Alcaeus, who changed the name of the river Cuarius, has done ill in his misstatement concerning Onchestus in the passage where he places it at the foot of Helicon, whereas it really lies a considerable distance from that mountain.

8

Apollonius *Pronouns*: It is clear moreover that the Aeolic digamma [*w*] is prefixed to the pronouns of the third person, just as those that begin with a vowel are [ordinarily] aspirated. Compare Alcaeus:

. . . so that [he] could loose none of the Olympians without his aid.[2]

9 To Hephaestus

[*See* 3]

10 To Ares

Cramer *Inedita* (*Oxford*): We are enquiring also how Ἄρεος the genitive of Ἄρης 'War' is found with a diphthong, Ἄρευος, [and the dative] Ἄρευι; compare: (24); and for the corresponding vocative:

. . . O War, through whom murderous Fear . . .

11 [To Aphrodite]

From a Second-Century Papyrus:

. . . who possessest a precinct . . . summit of the city . . . Aphrodite . . .

[1] perh. from the same hymn [2] prob. Hephaestus' aid; cf. *Od.* 8. 266 ff

12

Apoll. *Pron.* 395 A ἡ τεός Δωρικὴ τῇ σός ὁμωνυμεῖ . . . καὶ παρ' Αἰολεῦσιν· Ἀλκαῖος ἐν πρώτῳ·

τὸ δ' ἔργον ἀγήσαιτο τέα κόρα [1]

13 [εἰς Ἔρωτα?]

Et. Gud. 278. 17 τὰ γὰρ ἄνθη λέγεται ἥμερα [2] ἐπεὶ ἐν τῷ ἔαρι φύονται ὅτε καὶ τὰ ἐρωτικὰ θερμότερά ἐστι. τούτου χάριν καὶ ὁ Ἀλκαῖος Ζεφύρου καὶ Ἴριδος τὸν Ἔρωτά φησιν.

Plut. *Amator.* 20 τὰ μὲν οὖν πολλὰ ποιηταὶ προσπαίζοντες ἐοίκασι τῷ θεῷ γράφειν περὶ αὐτοῦ καὶ ᾄδειν ἐπικωμάζοντες, ὀλίγα δὲ εἴρηται μετὰ σπουδῆς αὐτοῖς, εἴτε κατὰ νοῦν καὶ λογισμὸν εἴτε σὺν θεῷ τῆς ἀληθείας ἁψαμένοις· ὧν ἕν ἐστι καὶ περὶ τῆς γενέσεως·

. . . . . . δεινότατον θεῶν
<τὸν> γέννατ' εὐπέδιλλος Ἶρις
χρυσοκόμᾳ Ζεφύρῳ μίγεισα· [3]

εἰ μή τι καὶ ὑμᾶς ἀναπεπείκασιν οἱ γραμματικοὶ λέγοντες πρὸς τὸ ποικίλον τοῦ πάθους καὶ τὸ ἀνθηρὸν γεγονέναι τὴν εἰκασίαν.

14 εἰς Διοσκούρους

Ox. Pap. 1233. 4

[Δεῦτ' Ὄλυμπον ἀστέρ]οπο[ν] λίποντε[ς]
[παῖδες ἴφθ]ιμοι Δίος ἠδὲ Λήδας [4]
[ἰλλάῳ] θύμῳ προ[φά]νητε Κάστορ
καὶ Πολύδευκες,

5 οἳ κατ' εὔρηαν χθόνα καὶ θάλασσαν
παῖσαν ἔρχ[εσθ'] ὠ[κυπό]δων ἐπ' ἴππων,
ρῆα δ' ἀνθρώ[ποις] θανάτω ρύεσθε
δακρυόεντος [5]

12

Apollonius *Pronouns*: The pronoun τεός is Doric for σός 'thy' . . . and occurs in the Aeolic writers; compare Alcaeus Book I:

. . . and may thy daughter lead the enterprise[1]

13[2] [To Love?]

Etymologicum Gudianum: For flowers are called gentle [that is, cultivated as opposed to wild,] because they grow in the Spring which is the particular season of love. And that is why Alcaeus calls Love the child of Zephyr or the West-Wind and Iris or the Rainbow.

Plutarch *Amatorius*: Although the poets generally seem to write and sing praise of Love in a jesting mood, sometimes, whether of their own choice and reflexion or by the grace of God, they get at the truth and treat of him seriously, as for instance in the matter of his birth:

. . . awfullest of Gods, whom sandalled Iris bore to Zephyr of the golden hair

—unless indeed you follow the grammarians in holding that the description is aimed at the motley and various nature of the passion.

14 To the Dioscuri

From a Second-Century Papyrus:

Come ye hither from star-bright Olympus, ye stalwart children of Zeus and Leda, and shine forth in propitious wise, O Castor and Polydeuces, who go on swift-footed horses over broad earth and all the sea, and do so easily save men from lamentable death

[1] prob. Persuasion, cf. Sa. 33 [2] cf. *E.M.* 470. 28, Theocr. 13 *Arg.* (Ἔριδος for Ἴριδος), Eust. *Il.* 391. 24, 555. 30

[1] ἀγήσαιτο Bast: mss -ατο [2] mss ἵμερα [3] γέννατ' *B*: mss γείνατ': μίγεισα Pors: mss μιχθεῖσα [4] ll. 1–3 Hunt-Wil. [5] P ζακρ. hyperaeol. ? Wil. keeps as compd. of κρυόεις

εὐσδύ[γ]ων[1] θρῴσκοντ[ες ὂν] ἄκρα νάων
10 [π]ήλοθεν λάμπροι προτό[νοισ' ἴσο]ντες[2]
ἀργαλέα δ' ἐν νύκτι φ[άος φέ]ροντες
νᾶϊ μελαίνᾳ. . . .

15 εἰς Ἀχιλλέα

Eust. ad Dion. Perieg. 306 ἄλλοι δέ φασιν ἕτερον εἶναι τοῦτον Ἀχιλλέα παρὰ Σκύθαις βασιλέα τῶν τόπων, ὃς ἠράσθη τε τῆς Ἰφιγενείας καὶ πεμφθεῖσαν ἐκεῖσε ἔμεινεν ἐπιδιώξας,[3] ἐξ οὗ ὁ τόπος Ἀχίλλειον. οἱ δὲ τοῦτο λέγοντες παραφέρουσι μάρτυρα τὸν Ἀλκαῖον λέγοντα·

Ὦ 'ναξ Ἀχίλλευ ὃς γᾶς Σκυθίκας μέδεις . . .[4]

16 εἰς τὰς Νύμφας

Heph. 66 [π. ἀντισπαστικοῦ]· τὸ δὲ ἀκατάληκτον (τετράμετρον) καλεῖται Σαπφικὸν ἑκκαιδεκασύλλαβον, ᾧ τὸ τρίτον ὅλον Σαπφοῦς γέγραπται, πολλὰ δὲ καὶ Ἀλκαίου ᾄσματα·

Νύμφαι,[5] ταὶς Δίος ἐξ αἰγιόχω φαῖσι τετυγμέναις . . .

17 [εἰς Ἥλιον ?]

Ox. Pap. 1233. 3. 8–11[6]

[Πάντροφ'] Ἆλι', ὃς ποτάμων παρ' ἄ[κταις]
[ἦλθες ἢ πὰρ] πορφυρίαν θάλασσαν
[ᾇ κλύδων ἐρ]ευγόμενος ζαλαίαν
[ᾄονα τ]ύ[πτε]ι·

[1] cf. *C.R.* 1916. 103 [2] Hunt -*E* (*l.c.*) [3] *E*: mss Ἰφ. πεμφθείσης ἐκεῖ καὶ ἐμ. ἐπιδιώκων [4] ὦ 'ναξ *E*: mss om. (intermediate stage ὢν ἀχ.): γᾶς *B*: mss τᾶς [5] *E* (like all H.'s citations where possible, the line is the first of a poem): mss -αις [6] Hunt -*E* (*C.R.* 1916, 103)

by leaping to the high-top of benchèd barks, there to sit far-seen upon the forestays, and so lighting the midnight path of the black ship[1] . . .

15 To Achilles

Eustathius on Dionysius the Geographer: Others say that this is another Achilles, king of the district among the Scythians, who had fallen in love with Iphigeneia and remained there after following her when she was sent thither. The commentators who hold this view call Alcaeus to witness where he says:

O King Achilles, who rulest the land of Scythia . . .

16 To the Nymphs

Hephaestion *Handbook of Metre* [on the antispastic]: The acatalectic tetrameter is called the Sapphic sixteen-syllable, and the whole of Sappho's third Book is written in it, as well as many poems of Alcaeus, such as:

O Nymphs, who they say are sprung from the Aegis-Bearer . . .

17 [To the Sun?][2]

From a Second-Century Papyrus:

All-nurturing Sun, who hast come by river-banks or by the purple sea where the gushing wave beats on the surfy shore, while many maids stand in a

[1] *i. e.* St. Elmo's fire [2] If l. 1 is rightly restored this poem *may* be connected with the eclipse of May 28, 585 B.C., but one would perh. expect a ref. to it earlier than the 3rd stanza

5 [κἄνθα] πόλλαι παρθένικαι πέρ[εσταν]
[καὶ κά]λων μήρων ἀπάλαισι χέρ[σι]
[δέρμ]α θέλγονται τόθεν ὡς ἄλει[φαρ]
[ἤπιο]ν ὕδωρ

[κακχέοισαι . . . .]

18 εἰς Πενίαν

Stob. *Fl.* 96. 17 [πενίας ψόγος]· Ἀλκαίου ποιητοῦ·

Ἀργάλεον Πενία κάκον ἄσχετον, ἃ μέγαν
δάμναις λᾶον Ἀμαχανίᾳ σὺν ἀδελφίᾳ[1] . . .

B′

ΠΟΛΕΜΙΚΩΝ

19

Ath. 14. 627 a [π. μουσικῆς]· τὸ δ' ἀρχαῖον ἡ μουσικὴ ἐπ' ἀνδρείαν προτροπὴ ἦν. Ἀλκαῖος γοῦν ὁ ποιητής, εἰ τις καὶ ἄλλος μουσικώτατος γενόμενος, πρότερα τῶν κατὰ ποιητικὴν τὰ κατὰ τὴν ἀνδρείαν τίθεται, μᾶλλον τοῦ δέοντος πολεμικὸς γενόμενος. διὸ καὶ ἐπὶ τοῖς τοιούτοις σεμνυνόμενός φησιν·

. . . .

μαρμαίρει δὲ μέγας δόμος χάλκῳ· παῖσα δ' Ἄρῃ κεκόσμηται στέγα
λάμπραισιν[2] κυνίαισι, κὰτ τᾶν λεῦκοι κατύπερθεν ἴππιοι λόφοι
νεύοισιν κεφάλαισιν ἄνδρων ἀγάλματα· χάλκιαι δὲ πασσάλοις

[1] ἀργάλεον Blass: μέγαν: mss also μέγα: δάμναις *B*: mss -νησι [2] mss λάμπρασι(ν)

ring and rub with dainty hands the flesh of their fair thighs, taking and pouring the gentle water over themselves even as an unguent . . . [1]

18 To Poverty

Stobaeus *Anthology*: From the poet Alcaeus:

O Poverty, thou grievous and resistless ill, who with thy sister Helplessness overwhelmest a great people . . .

Book II

WAR-SONGS

19 [2]

Athenaeus *Doctors at Dinner* [on music]: In ancient times music was used as an incitement to courage. For instance, the poet Alcaeus, who was a very great musician, became over-warlike and puts the claims of courage before those of poetry, and therefore prides himself on things of war in the following words:

. . . .

The great house is all agleam with bronze. War has bedecked the whole roof with bright helmets, from which hang waving horse-hair plumes to make adornment for the heads of men; the pegs are

[1] for bathing as a sign of warmer weather, cf. Long. *Past.* 3. 24 [2] cf. Eust. *Il.* 1319. 67

κρύπτοισιν περικείμεναι λάμπραι κνάμιδες,
ἄρκος ἰσχύρω βέλεος,[1]
5 θόρρακές τε νέω λίνω κοῦιλαί[2] τε κατ' ἄσπιδες
βεβλήμεναι,
πὰρ δὲ Χαλκίδικαι σπάθαι, πὰρ δὲ ζώμματα[3]
πόλλα καὶ κυπάσσιδες·
τῶν οὐκ ἔστι λάθεσθ', ἐπειδὴ πρώτιστ' ὑπὰ
Ϝέργον ἔσταμεν[4] τόδε.

καίτοι μᾶλλον ἴσως ἥρμοττε τὴν οἰκίαν πλήρη εἶναι μουσικῶν ὀργάνων. ἀλλ' οἱ παλαιοὶ τὴν ἀνδρείαν ὑπελάμβανον εἶναι μεγίστην τῶν πολιτικῶν ἀρετῶν κ.τ.λ.

20

Strab. 14. 661 [π. Καρῶν]· τοῦ δὲ περὶ τὰ στρατιωτικὰ ζήλου τά τε ὄχανα ποιοῦνται τεκμήρια καὶ τὰ ἐπίσημα καὶ τοὺς λόφους· ἅπαντα γὰρ λέγεται Καρικά· . . . ὁ δὲ Ἀλκαῖος·

λόφον τε σείων Κάρικον . . . . .

21

Hdn. π.μ.λ. 2. 929. 15 Lentz παρῃτησάμεθα δὲ Αἰολίδα διάλεκτον διὰ τὸ πτάζω·

ἔπταζον ὤστ' ὄρνιθες ὦκυν
αἴετον ἐξαπίνας φάνεντα.[5]

22, 23, 24

Choer. *Gram. Gr.* 4. 214. 20 ἀλλ' ἐπειδὴ τὰ εἰς ευς ἀποβάλλουσι τὸ υ κατὰ τὴν γενικήν . . . χωρὶς τοῦ Ἄρευς Ἄρευος· τοῦτο γὰρ ἐφύλαξε τὸ υ παρὰ τοῖς Αἰολεῦσιν, οἷον·

. . . . Ἄρευος στροτιωτέροις[6]

[1] mss ἰ. βέλευς, ἰσχυροβελὲς: ἄρκος: mss also ἔρκος [2] mss κοιλαι [3] mss ζώματα [4] subjunct. = ἐστάωμεν [5] *B*: mss ἔπταζον· ὡς τύ· and ἐξαπτήνας [6] mss στρατ.

hidden with bright brazen greaves to ward off the strong arrow, corslets of new linen cloth and hollow shields are piled upon the floor, and beside them stand swords of Chalcidian steel, and many a doublet, many a kilt. These we cannot forget, so soon as ever we undertake this task.

Whereas the house should rather, perhaps, have been full of instruments of music. But the ancients considered courage to be the greatest of the political virtues, etc.

20[1]

Strabo *Geography* [the Carians]: Their warlike proclivities are indicated by the shield-thong, shield-device, and helmet-plume, all of which are called Carian; compare . . . and Alcaeus

and tossing a Carian plume . . .

21

Herodian *Words without Parallel*: I excepted the Aeolic dialect because of πτάζω 'to cower'; compare

They cowered like birds at the sudden sight of a swift eagle.

22, 23, 24

Chocroboscus *On the Canons of Theodosius*: But since nouns in *-eus* lose the *u* in the genitive . . . except Ἄρευς Ἄρευος 'War,' for this has kept the *u* in Aeolic, as:

greater warriors than the War-God

[1] cf. Eust. *Il.* 367. 25.

καὶ πάλιν·

. . . . τὸ γὰρ
Ἄρευι κατθάνην κάλον . . . .

καὶ πάλιν·

μεῖξαν τ' ἐς ἀλλάλοις Ἄρευα.[1]

25 [2]

Hesych. ἐπιπνεύων·[3]. . . Ἀλκαῖος·

ἦ ποι σὺν ἄνδρων ἆγε <δε>δάσμενον
στρότον, νόμισμ' ἐπ' οἰ πνέοισα.[4]

26 [5]

Ox. Pap. 1233. 8. 3–5

[. . . .] εὖτέ με γῆρας τε[τόρη ἀλγάρεον, ἔνθ' ἔμοι]
[μὴ γένοι]το λάθε[σθ]αι χ[ά]ρ[ιτος τῶν προτέρον φίλων.]

27 [6] [εἰς Μυτιλήνην]

Ibid. 5–12

[Νῦν παί]δων ἀπάλων σ' ὐμν[έομεν γᾶ τρόφ', ὄσοι στίχι]
[τᾳ πρώ]τᾳ πολιάταν, ὄλιγον σφ[ῶν πεποήμμενοι]
[ἔξισαν·] τὸ γὰρ ἐμμόρμενον ὄρ[γον θέσαν ἄνδρεσι]

[1] mss also μίξαντες ἀλλήλοισιν Ἄρευι (Ἄρευα) [2] cf. *Camb. Philol. Soc. Proc.* 1916 [3] ms ὀπιπεύων, see Schmidt

and again:

for 'tis noble to die in war;

and again:

They mingled war one against another.[1]

25

Hesychius *ἐπιπνεύων* 'breathing upon, inspiring': . . . Alcaeus:

Verily she did join together a divided host of men by inspiring it with law and order.

26

From a Second-Century Papyrus:

. . . As for me, when grievous age wears me out, then be it not mine to forget the kindness of such as were my friends of old.

27 [To Mytilene]

From the Same:

Now is our song of thee, thou great Nurse of all those tender youths who recking so little of themselves took the field in the first rank of our people; for they have done the allotted task of men with the

[1] cf. Cram. *A.O.* 3. 237. 3

---

[4] *E l.c.*: ms *ἤπουσυναγανδρωνδάσμενον στρατὸν νομισμένοι πνέοισα* [5] *E*, *C.R.* 1916. 103 [6] so *E*, *l.c.*

[μὴ ἄλλ]αισ' ἄνδρεσι τοῖς γεινο[μένοις διανοΐαις.]
5 [αἰ πάντ]ᾱ σόφος ἦ καὶ φρέσι πύκνα[ις ἴκελος θέω,]
[οὐδὲ κ' ὦ]ς παρὰ μοῖραν Δίος οὐδὲ τρίχ' [ἐτιλλόμαν,]
[ἄνδρες τ'] ὄντες ἄσαις μει[χνύμεθ' ἀνδροπρέπεσιν βίον·]
[νέοισιν δ]ὲ φέρεσθαι βάθυ[ν ἐς πῶρον Ἀρηΐω]
e. g. [οὐκ ἔοικε κλόνω· οὖτοι δ', ὄτ' ἔπηλθεν δυσεπήβολος]
[στρότος τὰν πόλιν, οὐκ ἐξεφόβεντ', ἀλλὰ σὺν ἔντεσι]. . .

28 [1]

Aristid. 1. 821 δι' ἃ πάντα χρὴ καὶ τὸ συμβεβηκὸς ἐνεγκεῖν ὡς πρᾳότατα, καὶ τῶν δευτέρων ἐρρωμένως ἀντέχεσθαι, καὶ τὸν λόγον βεβαιῶσαι, ὅτι·

Οὐκ οἴκιαι κάλως τετεγάσμεναι
λίθοι τε τειχέων εὖ δεδομήμενοι [2]
οὐδὲ στένωποι καὶ νεώρι'
ἀ πόλις, ἀλλ' ἄνερες χράεσθαι
5 τοῖς αἶ πάρεισι δυννάμενοι . . .

29 [1]

Nicol. *Progymn.* 1. 277 Walz πρὸς ἃ δὴ βλέπων Ἀλκαῖος ὁ ποιητὴς οὐ ξύλα καὶ λίθους ἀλλ' ἄνδρας ἐφιλοσόφησε πόλεως σύστασιν.

[1] *E, Camb. Philol. Soc. Proc.* 1916 : mss . . . ἐστεγασμέναι . . . οὐδε λίθοι . . . στενωποί τε καὶ . . . ἄνδρες χρῆσθαι . . . ἀεὶ παρυῦσι δυνάμ. [2] or ἠὒ δεδμήμενοι?

same will as those who have grown to be men. Were I all-wise, were I like to a God in shrewdness of wit, even so I would not so much as pluck out a hair contrary to the decree of Zeus,[1] and being grown men our lives are mingled with troubles befitting our estate; but for youths to rush into the deep tumult of the battle mellay—that is not for them. [Yet these, when a host ill-conquerable came up against our city, laid fear aside and took arms and. . . .]

28 [2]

Aristides *Rhodian Oration*: For all these reasons we must bear our misfortune as gently as we can and stoutly reject the second place, and confirm the saying that

Not houses finely roofed or the stones of walls well-builded, nay nor canals and dockyards, make the city, but men able to use their opportunity.

29 [2]

Nicolaus *First Exercises in Oratory*: It was in reference to this that the poet Alcaeus made the profound statement that a city was composed not of timber and stones but of men.

[1] *i. e.* I am content to be a grown man as my beard shows me to be [2] cf. Aristid. 1. 791

Aristid. 2. 273 π. τῶν Τεττάρων· . . . τὸν λόγον ὃν πάλαι μὲν Ἀλκαῖος ὁ ποιητὴς εἶπεν, ὕστερον δὲ οἱ πολλοὶ παραλαβόντες ἐχρήσαντο ὡς ἄρα·

οὐ λίθοι ξύλα τ', οὐ τέχνα
τεκτόνων πόλις, ἀλλ' ὄπᾳ
ποττά κ' ἔωσιν ἄνδρες
αὔτοις σῴζην εἴδοτες, ἔν-
5 ταῦθα τείχεα καὶ πόλις.[1]

30[2]

Sch. Aesch. *Sept.* 398 [οὐδ' ἑλκοποιὰ γίγνεται τὰ σήματα]· ταῦτα παρ' Ἀλκαίου·

οὐ <γὰρ> τιτρῴσκει τἀπίσαμ' οὐδ'
αὖτα κατ' αὖτ' ἐδύναν ἔχοισιν
αἰ μὴ‿αὖτος ὤχων αἴ κε γέναιος ᾖ.[3]

31

Cram. *A.P.* 4. 61. 13 ἄρκος· οὐδέτερον, οὗ μέμνηται Ἀλκαῖος·

. . . . . . τῷ‿ἀχάλιννον[4]
ἄρκος ἔσῃ . . . .

32

Apoll. *Pron.* 101. 3 ἄσφε Αἰολεῖς·

. . . . ὄτ' ἄσφ' ἀπολλυμένοις σάως·[5]

Ἀλκαῖος δευτέρῳ.

[1] mss οὐδὲ ξύλα οὐδὲ τέχνη αἱ πόλεις εἶεν ἀλλ' ὅπου ποτ' ἂν ὦσιν . . . ἐντ. καὶ τείχη καὶ πόλεις [2] *E*, *Camb. Philol. Soc. Proc.* 1916 [3] mss . . . τὰ ἐπίσημα ὅπλα οὐδὲ αὐτὰ καθ' ἑαυτὰ δύναμιν ἔχει εἰ μὴ ἄρα ὁ φέρων αὐτὰ ἐὰν γενναῖος ᾖ: ἐδύναν = ὀδύνην [4] *E*, *i. e.* ἀχάλινον (the quotation must

Aristides *The Four Great Athenians*: . . . the saying which the poet Alcaeus said long ago, but which has since been used by all and sundry, that

Not stone and timber, nor the craft of the joiner, make the city; but wheresoever are men who know how to keep themselves safe, there are walls and there a city.

30

Scholiast on Aeschylus [Blazons make no wounds]: This comes from Alcaeus:

For blazons wound not nor of themselves carry pain, except he that wields them, if *he* be a noble man.

31

Cramer *Inedita* (*Paris*) ἄρκος 'defence': neuter; used by Alcaeus:

. . . to whom you shall be an unbridleable defence.[1]

32

Apollonius *Pronouns*: ἄσφε 'them' is Aeolic; compare Alcaeus, Book II:

. . . when thou savest them from destruction.

[1] *i. e.* irresistible

have proved ἀ. neuter): cf. χαλίννος *E.G.* 561. 4: mss τὸν χάλινον: metre 'Alcaic' [5] 2nd. pers. sing. of σάωμι (or σάῳς, of σαώω?) *E*

33

Cram. *A.O.* 1. 298. 17 Αἰολεῖς νάεσσι·[1]

κἀπιπλεύϝην νάεσσιν

Ἀλκαῖος.

34

Ibid. 4. 336. 6

Ἀρέως

ἀπὸ Ἄρευς. εὑρέθη δὲ παρὰ Ἀλκαίῳ.

35

Poll. 4. 169

κύπρον

δὲ τὸ οὕτω καλούμενον μέτρον εὕροις ἂν καὶ παρὰ Ἀλκαίῳ ἐν δευτέρῳ Μελῶν.

Γʹ καὶ Δʹ

ΣΤΑΣΙΩΤΙΚΩΝ

36

Apoll. *Adv.* 197. 12 τῇδε γὰρ ἔχει καὶ τὸ ἐπίρρημα παρ' Αἰολεῦσι τὸ μέσοι·

. . . γαίας καὶ νιφόεντος ὀρράνω μέσοι·

τῇδε ἔχει καὶ ἀπὸ τοῦ τήλοθι τὸ πήλοι.[2]

[1] νάεσσιν *Et*: mss. *A.O.* νέασσι: -πλεύϝην *E*, cf. on 2. 2: mss -πλεύσειν: *B* -πλεύσῃ [2] cf. Ibid. 177. 5 τὸ γὰρ παρὰ τοῖς περὶ τὸν Ἀλκαῖον μέσσοι . . . ὃν τρόπον παρὰ τὸ οἶκος τὸ οἴκοι ἐγένετο σημαῖνον τὸ ἐν οἴκῳ

33[1]

Cramer *Inedita (Oxford)*: The Aeolic form is νάεσσι ('in ships'); compare Alcaeus:

. . . and to sail thither in ships

34[2]

Ibid. Ἄρεως

of Ares

from Ἄρευς, which is found in Alcaeus.

35[3]

Pollux *Vocabulary*:

cyprus,

the measure so-named, you may find also in the second book of Alcaeus' *Lyric Poems*.

Books III and IV

POLITICAL POEMS

36

Apollonius *Adverbs*: For it is thus also in Aeolic with the adverb μέσοι 'amid' or 'between':

. . . between earth and snowy sky;

and it is the same with πήλοι from τήλοθι 'afar.'[4]

[1] cf. *E.M.* 605. 27 [2] cf. Eust. *Il.* 118. 35 [3] cf. Poll. 10. 113 [4] cf. the Same: For the word μέσσοι, used by Alcaeus . . . in the same way as οἴκοι 'at home,' comes from οἶκος and means 'in the house': perh. from the same poem as 37

37, 38, 39

Heracl. *Alleg. Hom.* 5 ἐν ἱκανοῖς δὲ καὶ τὸν Μυτιληναῖον μελοποιὸν εὑρήσομεν ἀλληγοροῦντα. τὰς γὰρ τυραννικὰς ταραχὰς ἐξ ἴσου χειμερίῳ προσεικάζει καταστήματι θαλάσσης·

Ἀσυννέτημι τῶν ἀνέμων στάσιν·[1]
τὸ μὲν γὰρ ἔνθεν κῦμα κυλίνδεται,
τὸ δ' ἔνθεν· ἄμμες δ' ὂν τὸ μέσσον
νᾶϊ φορήμεθα σὺν μελαίνᾳ

5 χείμωνι μόχθεντες μεγάλῳ μάλα·
πὲρ μὲν γὰρ ἄντλος ἰστοπέδαν ἔχει,
λαῖφος δὲ πὰν ζάδηλον ἤδη
καὶ λάκιδες μέγαλαι κατ' αὖτο,

χόλαισι δ' ἄγκονναι·[2]

τίς οὐκ ἂν εὐθὺς ἐκ τῆς προτρεχούσης περὶ τὸν πόντον εἰκασίας ἀνδρῶν πλωϊζομένων θαλάττιον εἶναι νομίσειε φόβον; ἀλλ' οὐχ οὕτως ἔχει. Μυρσίλος γὰρ ὁ δηλούμενός ἐστι καὶ τυραννικὴ κατὰ Μυτιληναίων ἐγειρομένη σύστασις. ὁμοίως δὲ τὰ ὑπὸ τούτου <πραττόμενα>[3] αἰνιττόμενος ἑτέρωθί που λέγει·

τὸ δηὖτε κῦμα τὸ προτιάνεμον[4]
στείχει, παρέξει δ' ἄμμι πόνον πόλυν
ἄντλην, ἐπεί κε νᾶος ἔββᾳ·[5]

κατακόρως ἐν ταῖς ἀλληγορίαις ὁ νησιώτης θαλασσεύει καὶ τὰ πλεῖστα τῶν διὰ τοὺς τυράννους ἐπεχόντων κακῶν πελαγίοις χειμῶσιν εἰκάζει.

Hesych.

. . . . τετραέλικτον ἄλμαν[6]

ἤγουν τρικυμίαν.

[1] mss ἀσυνέτην νῆ (καὶ) κ.τ.λ. [2] ἄγκονναι *B-E* i. e. ἀγκοῖναι cf. Hesych.: mss ἄγκυραι [3] *E* [4] i. e. προσήνεμον *E*, *Camb. Philol. Soc Proc.* 1916: mss τῷ προτέρω νέμω correction of τῷ πρώτῳ ἀνέμῳ [5] ἔββᾳ *E l.c.*: Seid. ἔμβᾳ: mss ἐμβαίνει

37, 38, 39

Heracleitus *Homeric Allegories*: We shall find the lyric poet of Mytilene using allegory in a considerable number of passages. He likens the disturbances caused by the tyrants very literally to stormy weather at sea:

I cannot tell the lie of the wind;[1] one wave rolls from this quarter, another from that, and we are carried in the midst with the black ship, labouring in an exceeding great storm. The water is up to the mast-hole, the sail lets daylight through with the great rents that are in it, and the halyards[2] are working loose.[3]

Who hearing this would not conclude immediately from the moving sea-imagery that the fear conveyed by the words is fear of the sea on the part of men aboard ship? Yet it is not so, for the poet means Myrsilus and a monarchical conspiracy hatching against the Mytileneans. And he similarly hints at Myrsilus' intrigues in another place:

Lo now! the wave that is to windward of us comes this way, and will give us sore labour to bale it out when it breaks over us.

In fact the islander almost overdoes the sea-going in his allegories, likening most of the prevailing tyrant-troubles to storms on the ocean.

Hesychius *Glossary*:

a four-times coilèd surge of brine

that is, the third or greatest wave.[4]

[1] or 'factious strife of the winds'; prob. the words have a double intention [2] the ropes that keep the yard in position [3] cf. Boiss. *A.G.* 3. 295, Hor. *Od.* 1. 14: prob. not from the same poem as 37 [4] as it was usually called

[6] doubtfully ascribed to A. by *B* on 152 (154 Bgk.): mss ἅλμαν: cf. Sch. Pind. *I.* 1. 52

40

Hdn. π.μ.λ. (2. 916. 12 Lentz) εἴρηται δὲ ὁ δαίμων παρ' Ἀλκαίου διὰ τοῦ α μένοντος τοῦ σ Ποσείδαν·

. . . . . . οὐδέ πω Ποσείδαν
ἄλμυρον ἐστυφέλιξε πόντον.

41[1] [εἰς τὴν Πατρίδα]

Berl. Klassikertexte 5. 2. 12 (*a*) and *Aberdeen Papyri*[1] (*b*)

(*a*) [Τίς γνώμα σ' ἐσέ]δυ καὶ διανοΐα
[ἂ τόσσον τετάρα]ξαι χρόνον, ὦ πά[τρι ;]
[θάρση· οὐ φᾶσε γ]ὰρ αὖτος Κρονίδα[ς χρέων]
[ἔμμεναί σ' Ἄρε' ὄπ]πᾳ κέ σ' ἔλη τρέ[μην,]
5 [οὐδ' ἀμφικτίον'] οὐδ'[2] οὖν ἄλα πήλ[ορον]
[ζαπλεύσαντ' ἐρ]έταν δῆ[θ'] ἐκατη[βόλω]
[τενέην δόρρος ἄε]θλον πολυπή[μονα,]
[αἰ μὴ πάντας ἀρ]ίστηας ἀπυκρ[ιν]έη[ς]
[αὖτα τῶν σέθεν ε]ἰς μάκρον ἀπει[μένα.]
10 ἄνδρες γὰρ πόλιος πύργος Ἀρεύιος·[3]
[νῦν δέ σ' οὖδεν ἔ]τ' ὡς κῆνος ἐβόλλετο
[δρᾶσαν ὤκεα δὴ] μοῖρα κατέσχ[εθε,]
[καὶ βρύτηρες ἐ]πεί σοι ἦμεν ἐπεί[μενοι]
[ἂπ σέθεν παράγ]ων Ζεῦς ὔπελ[εν πάλι]ν·
15 [βεβόλλευτο γὰρ] αὔτῳ· τά τ' ἔχεις [κάκ]ων
[νῦν ὄτις κε θέλη]σ' ἐβφερέτω λ[ύσιν.]
[τὸν ἐψησάμενον τοὶς] πυάν[οις δέει]
(*b*) [καὶ φάγην· τάδε δ' ἄμμ' ο]ὐ̣[κὶ] μ̣[έμηλ' ἔτι.]

[1] *E*, cf. *C.R.* 1917 33 ; (*a*) from phot. only [2] P ουτ' [3] cf. Sch. Aesch. *Pers.* 347, Sch. Soph. *O. T.* 56 (Ἀλκαῖος)

40

Herodian *Words without Parallel*: The God Poseidon has the *a* and the *s* in Alcaeus:

. . . nor had Poseidan yet roughened the salt sea.

41 [To his Country]

From a First-Century Papyrus:

What purpose or intent is in thee, my Country, that thou hast been so long time distraught? Be of good cheer; for the son of Cronus himself[1] did tell thee that thou hadst no need to fear warfare howsoever it should seize thee, nor should neighbour foeman, nay nor oarsman from over the far-bounded sea, maintain for long the woeful conflict of the far flung spear, unless thou shouldst of thyself send afar all the best of thy people, to sunder them from thee.[2] For 'tis men that are a city's tower in war. But alas! thou no longer doest the Father's will, and so a swift fate hath overtaken thee, and us that had been sent to help thee, Zeus—for so he had willed it—hath made to miscarry[3] and taken away from thee again. And let whoso will, bring thee assuagement of thy woes. He that hath made him pottage, he also must eat it;[4] these things are no longer a concern of ours. And whatsoever Fate it

[1] an oracle? [2] scholia ref. to the 'first banishment,' of Alcaeus, Sappho, Phanias, Antimenidas, and others, to Pyrrha in Lesbos for plotting against Myrsilus [3] ref. either to an attempt of the exiles to return by force of arms or rejection by M. of an offer of the exiles to return and combine with him against an external foe [4] *i. e.* you have made your bed and you must lie on it

[οὐδ' ἄεικες ἄρ' ἄτι]ς τόδ' ἔησι [κᾶρ]
20 [ἴησιν· Τενάγη]ς γὰρ τάδε σοι ἄ[ρχετ]ο
[Ἀολίων, ὃν ἄδε]λφος Μάκαρ ἔγχε[ϊ]
[κατέκτεννε π]άροιθεν βαρυλ[ει]ψάνῳ.
[τᾶς ἔγω πέρι το]ίσσουτον ἐπεύ[χ]ομαι,
[οὔτω μήκετ' ἴδ]εσθαι ἀελίω φάος [1]
25 [ὄλεσθαι δὲ τάχ', α]ἴ γε Κλεανακτίδαν
[ἢ τὸν χιρραπόδαν] ἢ 'ρχεανακτίδαν
[ζῶν ἔγω περίδω], τὸν μελιάδεα
[πόλις καὶ στάσις ὐμ]μάλικος ὤλεσαν. [2]

42

Ath. 10. 430 a κατὰ γὰρ πᾶσαν ὥραν καὶ πᾶσαν περίστασιν πίνων ὁ ποιητὴς οὗτος (Ἀλκαῖος) εὑρίσκεται· χειμῶνος μὲν ἐν τούτοις· (157)· . . . ἐν δὲ τοῖς συμπτώμασιν· (158)· . . . ἐν δὲ ταῖς εὐφροσύναις· [3]

Νῦν χρῆ μεθύσθην καί τινα πρὸς βίαν
πόνην, [4] ἐπειδὴ κάτθανε Μύρσιλος.

43, 44

Apoll. *Pron.* 97. 20 [ἄμμιν κ.τ.λ.]· τὰ γὰρ παρ' Αἰολεῦσιν ἕνεκα τῆς συντάξεως πολλάκις ἀποβάλλει τὸ ν διὰ εὐφωνίαν· (Sa. 42)·

αἰ δέ κ' ἄμμι Ζεῦς τελέσῃ νόημα·

Ἀλκαῖος. μένει τε ἐπὶ τοῦ·

. . . . . ἄμμιν ἀθάνατοι θέοι
νίκαν <ἔδωκαν>· [5]

Ἀλκαῖος τρίτῳ, καὶ ἐπ' ἄλλων πλειόνων.

[1] P]ησθ', *i. e.* ἴδησθε due to misinterpretation of elided diphthong [2] P prob. ο]μη: P]μηκιλος: cf. Theocr. 29 [3] Mein: mss εὐφρόναις [4] Ahr. πώνην 'drink,' but if τινα were subjt. of the 2nd vb. it would be subjt. of the 1st, and so could not follow καὶ: for this meaning cf.

is that sendeth this trouble, 'tis sent with good reason. These woes began for thee with Tenages, son of Aeolus, that was slain of yore by the sword of his brother Macar,[1] a sword that left sorrow behind it. And now I make this prayer concerning thee: that I may no longer see the daylight, if the son of Cleanax[2] or yonder Splitfoot[3] or the son of Archeanax be suffered yet to live by one whom his dear sweet native-land, and factious strife as old as itself, together have done away.

42

Athenaeus *Doctors at Dinner*: For at every time and on every occasion the poet Alcaeus is found drinking; in the winter, in these lines: (157): . . . ; in his misfortune, in these: (158): . . . ; and in his rejoicing, in these:

'Tis time for wine and time for women, now that Myrsilus is dead.

43, 44

Apollonius *Pronouns* (on ἄμμιν 'to us,' etc.): For the forms used by the Aeolic writers often discard the *n* for the sake of euphony in sentence-construction, compare (Sa. 42), and this:

and if Zeus will accomplish what is our intent;

Alcaeus. And the *n* remains in:

. . . the immortal Gods have given us the victory;

from Alcaeus' third Book, and in many more places.

[1] cf. Sch. *Il.* 24. 544: founder of the Greek colony of Lesbos [2] Myrsilus [3] Pittacus

Hesych. πονεῖν· ἐνεργεῖν *E*: mss πονεῖν, a very old reading, cf. Soph. *Fr.* 655 N [5] *E* (lost by haplogr.)

45

Harpocr. 1. 288 Dind. τετύφωμαι· . . . ἀντὶ τοῦ ἐμβεβρόντημαι, ἔξω τῶν φρενῶν γέγονα . . . καὶ γὰρ Ἀλκαῖός φησι·

πάμπαν δ' ἐτύφωσ' ἐκ δ' ἔλετο φρένας.[1]

46

Eust. *Il.* 603. 39 λέγει ὁ αὐτὸς (Ἀριστοφάνης ὁ γραμματικός) καὶ ὅτι τὸ συνεστραμμένον πνεῦμα καὶ κατάρασσον ἄνεμον

καταρη

λέγουσιν ὁ Ἀλκαῖος καὶ ἡ Σαπφὼ διὰ τὸ κατωφερῆ ὁρμὴν ἔχειν.

47

Heph. 84 ἐπιωνικὸν δὲ ἀπὸ μείζονος τρίμετρον καταληκτικόν ἐστι, τὸ καλούμενον Ἀλκαϊκὸν ἑνδεκασύλλαβον, . . . οἷον (*fr.* 1).

Μέλαγχρος, αἴδως ἄξιος εἶς πόλι[2]

48

Sch. Nic. *Ther.* 613 [καὶ μυρίκης λάζοιο νέον πανακαρπέα θάμνον | μάντιν ἐν αἰζηοῖσι γεράσμιον]· . . . καὶ ἐν Λέσβῳ δὲ ὁ Ἀπόλλων μυρίκης κλάδους ἔχει· ὅθεν καὶ μυρικαῖος καλεῖται. καὶ Ἀλκαῖός φησιν ἐν τοῖς περὶ Ἀρχεανακτίδην[3] καὶ τὸν πρὸς Ἐρυθραίους πόλεμον φανῆναι τὸν Ἀπόλλωνα καθ' ὕπνον ἔχοντα μυρικῆς κλῶνα.

e.g. ἔμοι γὰρ πολέμεντι πρὸς Ἐρυθράοις
Ἀπόλλων κατ' ὕπνον κλῶνα μυρίκινον
ἦλθ' ἔχων . . . .

[1] Pors: mss π. δὲ τύφως ἐκ δὲ λέγετο φ. [2] *E*, εἶς = ὤν: mss εἰς πόλιν [3] cf. 41. 26

45

Harpocration *Lexicon to the Attic Orators*: τετύφωμαι: . . . equivalent to ἐμβεβρόντημαι 'to be out of one's mind' . . . . ; compare Alcaeus:

He struck him mad altogether and took his wits away.

46[1]

Eustathius on the *Iliad*: Aristophanes the grammarian says that a whirlwind or downward-striking blast is called

a down-rushing wind

by Alcaeus and Sappho, because it has a downward motion.

47[2]

Hephaestion *On Poems*: The epionic trimeter *a majore* catalectic, the Alcaic eleven-syllable, as it is called, ... for instance (*fr.* 1); and:

Melanchros, being worthy of his country's respect

48

Scholiast on Nicander *Venomous Bites* [And thou shouldest take a young branch of tamarisk ere it bear fruit, a magician honoured among men]: . . . and in Lesbos Apollo holds branches of tamarisk, and so is called 'God of the tamarisk.' And Alcaeus, in the poems on the son of Archeanax and the Erythraean War, tells us that Apollo appeared in a dream with a branch of tamarisk in his hand.

e. g. For when I was fighting the Erythraeans, Apollo came unto me in my sleep with a tamarisk branch in his hand.

[1] cf. Sa. 54 [2] cf. Cram. *A.O.* 1. 208. 13 where read Μέλαγχρος αἰδῶς ἄξιος ἀντὶ τοῦ αἰδοῦς

49

Apoll. *Pron.* 100. 12 ὔμμε Αἰολεῖς·

τὸ γὰρ θέων ἰότατ' ὔμμε λάχον τῶν ἀϝάτων γέρας θήσει[1] . . . . .

50

Sch. Ar. *Vesp.* 1234 παρὰ τὰ 'Αλκαίου·

Ὤνηρ οὗτος ὁ μαιόμενος τὸ μέγα κρέτος[2]
ὀντρέψει τάχα τὰν πόλιν· ἀ δ' ἔχεται ῥόπας·[3]

ἀντὶ τοῦ ζητῶν μέγα κράτος· ἐκ τῶν 'Αλκαίου δὲ παρῳδεῖ εἰς Κλέωνα ὡς μαινόμενον.

51

Diog. Laert. 1. 81 τοῦτον (Πιττακόν) 'Αλκαῖος σαράποδα μὲν καὶ σάραπον ἀποκαλεῖ διὰ τὸ πλατύπουν εἶναι καὶ <σαίρειν καὶ>[4] ἐπισύρειν τὼ πόδε, χιρροπόδαν[5] δὲ διὰ τὰς ἐν τοῖς ποσὶν ῥαγάδας, ἃς χιράδας ἐκάλουν, γαύρακα[6] δὲ ὡς εἰκῇ γαυριῶντα, φύσκωνα δὲ καὶ γάστρωνα ὅτι παχὺς ἦν, ἀλλὰ μὲν καὶ ζοφοδορπίδαν[7] ὡς ἄλυχνον, ἀγάσυρτον δὲ ὡς ἐπισεσυρμένον καὶ ῥυπαρόν.

e.g. . . . οἱ σάραπον καὶ χιρροπόδαν τινά,
γαύρακα, φύσκωνα, ζοφοδορπίδαν,
κάλον μάλ' ἄνδρα κἀγάσυρτον,
θήκατ' ἔμας πόλιος μόναρχον.

[1] *E*, cf. *Il.* 23. 79, Pind. *P.* 2. 50: mss λαχόντων αφυτον θ. γ. [2] mss κράτος [3] mss ἀνατρέψει and ῥοπᾶς [4] *E* [5] mss χειροπόδην, cf. *E.M.* 810. 27 χεῖραι (read χῖραι)· αἱ ἐν τοῖς ποσὶ ῥαγάδες· καὶ χειρόποδες οἱ οὕτω τοὺς πόδας κατερρωγότες, Eust. *Il.* 194. 49 [6] Hfm. from Hesych. γαύρηξ· ὁ γαυριῶν: mss γαύρικα [7] cf. Hesych. ζοφοδερκίας· <ὁ ἐν σκότῳ βλέπων | ζοφοδορπίδας·> σκοτόδειπνος, λαθροφάγος (so read

49

Apollonius *Pronouns*: ὔμμε 'you,' Aeolic; compare

For the prerogative which belongs to you by grace of the Gods, he will make the prerogative of insatiate men.

50

Scholiast on Aristophanes *Wasps* [where it is parodied]: From Alcaeus:

This man with his longing for great power will quickly overturn his country; she is tottering now[1];

κρέτος 'power' instead of κράτος; he is parodying Alcaeus in reference to Cleon, as being a madman.[2]

51[3]

Diogenes Laertius *Life of Pittacus*: This is he whom Alcaeus calls *Drag-foot* because he was flat-footed and dragged or trailed his feet after him, *Splitfoot* because of the so-called chaps or cracks in the skin between his toes, *Prancer* because he bore himself proudly without reason, *Pudding-belly* or great-paunch because he was fat, *Sup-i'-the-dark* because he did not use lamps,[4] and *Swept-and-Garnished* because he was slovenly and dirty.

[1] the Gk. is 'near a swing-down' (of the scales and the like) [2] the scholiast implies that Ar. parodied μαιόμενος 'longing for' with μαινόμενος 'mad on' [3] cf. Suid. σαράπους, Poll. 2. 1715, Plut. *Qu. Conv.* 8. 6. 1 [4] the true explanation is more probably that he supped long and late; Hesych. however explains it as 'supping in the dark, eating in secret'

51 A

Eust. *Od.* 1687. 52 τὸν ἐφιάλτην

ἐπιάλταν

κατὰ παλαιὰν παρασημείωσιν ὁ Ἀλκαῖος λέγει.

52

Id. 314. 43 (*Il.* 2. 654) Ἀλκαῖος δέ, φασί, καὶ Ἀρχίλοχος

ἀγέρωχον

τὸν ἄκοσμον καὶ ἀλαζόνα οἶδε.

53 πρὸς Πιττακόν (?)

Heph. 68 [π. ἰωνικοῦ τοῦ ἀπὸ μείζονος]· ἔνια δὲ (τῶν τριμέτρων ἀκαταλήκτων) ἐκ μιᾶς ἰωνικῆς καὶ δύο τροχαϊκῶν οἷον·

Τριβόλλετερ·[1] οὐ γὰρ Ἀρκάδεσσι λώβα . . .

54

Artem. ὀνειρ. 2. 25 ταύτης γὰρ (τῆς δρυός) τὸν καρπὸν ἤσθιον οἱ Ἀρκάδες· καὶ ὁ Ἀλκαῖός φησι·

. . . Ἄρκαδες ἔσσαν βαλανήφαγοι.

55

Apoll. *Pron.* 105. 31 ἡ τεός Δωρικὴ τῇ σός ὁμωνυμεῖ . . .· καὶ παρ' Αἰολεῦσιν· Ἀλκαῖος ἐν πρώτῳ· (12)· καί·

οἴκῳ τε πὲρ σῷ καὶ πὲρ ἀτιμίαις . . .·

ὁ αὐτὸς κοινῷ ἔθει.

[1] mss Heph. τριβωλ., Choer. τριβολ. adding ἔστι δὲ εἶδος ἀκάνθης: if it were τρῐ. Heph. would have remarked it, cf. Ibid. 70: did τρῖβη = thorn?

51 A [1]

Eustathius on the *Odyssey*: According to the ancient marginal note Alcaeus says ἐπιάλτας

the nightmare

for ἐφιάλτης.

52

The Same on the *Iliad*: It is said that Alcaeus and Archilochus knew the unruly and insolent as ἀγέρωχοι or

overweening

53 To Pittacus (?)

Hephaestion *Handbook of Metre* [on the *Ionicum a majore*]: Some of the acatalectic trimeters are composed of one ionic and two trochaics thus:

O thou destroyer of hips and haws [2]—for 'tis no shame to an Arcadian [to be called that] . . .

54

Artemidorus *On Dreams*: The fruit of the oak was eaten by the Arcadians; compare Alcaeus:

The Arcadians were eaters of acorns.

55

Apollonius *Pronouns*: The possessive τεός 'thy' is equivalent in Doric to σός. . . . ; and also in Aeolic; compare Alcaeus Book i: (12); and:

Near to your house and near to your infamies . . . ;

in the latter passage the same poet uses the common form σός.

[1] cf. *E.M.* 434. 12 [2] *i. e.* eater of wild fruit, like a bird; Pittacus was of low birth, cf. 54: cf. Choer. *Ep.* 1, 272

56

Eust. *Od.* 1. 107. (1397. 32) [πεσσοῖσι . . . θυμὸν ἔτερπον]· τοὺς δὲ πεσσοὺς λέγει (ὁ τὰ Περὶ Ἑλληνικῆς Παιδιᾶς γράψας) ψήφους εἶναι πέντε αἷς ἐπὶ πέντε γραμμῶν ἔπαιζον ἑκατέρωθεν, ἵνα ἕκαστος τῶν πεττευόντων ἔχῃ τὰς καθ' ἑαυτόν . . . παρετείνετο δέ, φησί, δι' αὐτῶν καὶ μέση γράμμη, ἣν ἱερὰν ὠνόμαζον . . . ἐπεὶ ὁ νικώμενος ἐπ' ἐσχάτην ἵεται· ὅθεν καὶ παροιμία 'κινεῖν τὸν ἀφ' ἱερᾶς λίθον,' δηλαδὴ ἐπὶ τῶν ἀπεγνωσμένων καὶ ἐσχάτης βοηθείας δεομένων. Σώφρων . . . .· Ἀλκαῖος δέ φησιν ἐκ πλήρους·

. . . . . . νῦν δ' οὗτος ἐπικρέτει [1]
κινήσαις τὸν ἀπ' ἴρας πύκινος λίθον.[2]

57

Sch. Pind. *O.* 1. 91 [ἅταν ὑπέροπλον ἅν οἱ πατὴρ ὕπερ κρέμασε κάρτερον αὐτῷ λίθον]· περὶ μὲν τῆς τοῦ Ταντάλου κολάσεως ἕτεροι ἑτέρως λέγουσιν . . . καὶ Ἀλκαῖος δὲ καὶ Ἀλκμὰν λίθον φασὶν ἐπαιωρεῖσθαι τῷ Ταντάλῳ· <ὁ μὲν Ἀλκαῖος·

. . . . Ταντάλῳ>
κεῖτ' ὑπὲρ κεφάλας μέγας, ὦ Αἰσιμίδα, λίθος.[3]

ὁ δὲ Ἀλκμάν· (Alcm. 89).

58

Heph. 94 [π. ἀσυναρτήτων]· ἔνδοξόν ἐστιν ἐπισύνθετον καὶ τὸ διπενθημιμερὲς τὸ ἐγκωμιολογικὸν καλούμενον, ὅπερ ἐστὶν ἐκ δακτυλικοῦ πενθημιμεροῦς καὶ ἰαμβικοῦ τοῦ ἴσου, ᾧ κέχρηται μὲν καὶ Ἀλκαῖος ἐν ᾄσματι οὗ ἡ ἀρχή·

Ἦρ' ἔτι Διννομένῃ τῷ τ' Ὑρραδείῳ [4]
τἄρμενα λάμπρα κέαντ' ἐν μυρσινήῳ; [5]

[1] *B*: mss -κρέκει [2] ἀπ' ἴρας *B*: mss πήρας (πείρας) a corruption which Eust. (633. 61) wrongly supposes a playful substitution for ἱερᾶς: πύκινος *E*: mss -ον [3] κεῖτ' ὑπὲρ *E*: mss κεῖσθαι πὰρ (περὶ, παρὰ) through κεῖθ' ὑπέρ: Ahr. κεῖσθαι περ (= ὑπέρ) but this equation rests on a misunderstanding

56

Eust. on the *Odyssey* [they were diverting themselves at draughts]: The author of the treatise *On Greek Games* declares that the draughts were five pebbles with which they played upon five lines drawn on either side, so that each of the players had his own . . . And there was a line drawn in the middle which they called sacred . . . because the loser comes to the furthest line. Hence the proverb 'to move the piece on the sacred line,' used, of course, of those whom desperation drives to their last resource; compare Sophron: . . . . ; Alcaeus gives the phrase in full:

And now this fellow has prevailed, by moving the piece on the sacred line, the cunning man.

57

Scholiast on Pindar ['the overwhelming bane which his father hung over him, to wit a mighty stone']: The punishment of Tantalus is variously related . . . . ; Alcaeus and Alcman say that a stone was hung over him; compare Alcaeus:

Over Tantalus' head, O son of Aesimus, there hung a great stone;

and Alcman (Alcm. 89).

58

Hephaestion *Handbook of Metre* [on 'unconnectable' metres]: A well-known combination, too, is the double two-and-a-half-foot metre called the encomiologic, consisting of a two-and-a-half-foot dactylic and an iambic of equal length; it is used by Alcaeus in the poem which begins:

And are the weapons still lying bright and ready in the myrtle-grove for Dinnomenes and the son of Hyrrhas?[1]

[1] Pittacus

---

[4] Seid: cf. Cram. *A.O.* 4. 326. 30, Hfm. *Gr. Dial.* 2. 588: mss τῷ τυρρακήῳ [5] κέαντ' *B*: mss κέατ'

59 πρὸς Πιττακόν (?)

Ath. 11. 460 d [π. ποτηρίων]· καὶ Ἀλκαῖος·

. . . . . ἐκ δὲ ποτήρια[1]
πώνης Διννομένῃ παρίσδων.

60, 61

Sch. *Il.* 22. 68 [ῥεθέων]· . . . Αἰολεῖς δὲ τὸ πρόσωπον καὶ

ῥεθομαλίδας

τοὺς εὐπροσώπους φασί.

Eust. *Od.* 1571. 43 τὶς δὲ τῶν μεθ' Ὅμηρον τὸ μὲν μῆλον Δωρίσας εἰς μᾶλον, τὴν δὲ ὄψιν εἰς εἶδος μεταλαβὼν καὶ συνθεὶς[2] τὰς λέξεις—Ἀλκαῖος δ' ἦν ἐκεῖνος ὁ λυρικός[3]—,

Ϝιδομαλίδαν[4]

ἔφη σκωπτικῶς τινα, διὰ τὸ καλλωπίζεσθαι τὰ μῆλα τῆς ὄψεως, ἐρευθόμενον δηλαδὴ κορικώτερον.

62

Paroem. 2. 765

. . . . πάλιν ταὶς[5]
ὗς παρορίννει·

ἐπὶ τῶν παρακινούντων τινὰ εἰπεῖν καὶ ἄκοντα ἃ οὐ βούλεται. Ἀλκαίου ἡ παροιμία.

63

Apoll. *Pron.* 97. 11 καθάπερ γὰρ τῷ ταχεῖς παρακεῖται τὸ ταχέσιν οὕτω καὶ τὸ ἡμεῖς τὸ ἡμέσιν· τό τε ἐν τετάρτῳ Ἀλκαίου

ἄμμεσιν πεδάορον

οὕτω φέρεσθαι ἀπὸ τοῦ ἡμέσιν.

[1] *E*: mss -ων [2] συνθεὶς *E*: mss μεταθ. [3] mss κωμικός [4] mss εἰδομαλίδην: that this is not a corruption of ῥεθομ. appears from Hesych. ἰδομαλίαδαι (sic)· οἱ τὰς ὄψεις κοσμούμενοι and ἴδοι· ὀφθαλμοί (*B*) [5] ταὶς *E*: mss here ἡ (through ταῖς), elsewhere om.

59 To Pittacus (?)

Athenaeus *Doctors at Dinner* [on cups]: . . . and Alcaeus:

. . . and you drain goblets sitting beside Dinnomenes.

60, 61[1]

Scholiast on the *Iliad* [ῥεθέων 'limbs']: . . . . But the Aeolic writers use ῥέθος for the face, and call pretty persons

apple-faced

Eustathius on the *Odyssey*: One of the later poets Doricised the word μῆλον 'apple,' changed ὄψις 'face' into εἶδος, and putting the two together—the poet in question is the lyrist Alcaeus—called a person in jest

apple-cheeked,

because he prided himself on the apples of his cheeks, that is his rather maiden-like blushes.

62[2]

Greek Proverb-writers:

He's stirring up the pigs again;

used of those who urge an unwilling man to say what he would rather not. The proverb occurs in Alcaeus.

63

Apollonius *Pronouns*: For just as with ταχεῖς we have ταχέσιν so with ἡμεῖς 'we' we have ἡμέσιν 'to us,' and the form ἄμμεσιν 'to us,' used in the fourth Book of Alcaeus,

high above us

comes from ἡμέσιν.

[1] cf. Eust. *Od.* 1412. 32, Suet. Miller *Mél.* 415 [2] cf. Simp. ad Arist. *de Caelo* 35 b Ald., *Paroem.* 1. 318 (ἐπὶ τῶν βιαίων λέγεται καὶ ἐριστικῶν), Arsen. 460: metre 'Sapphic'

64

Ath. 7. 311 a [π. λαβράκων]· Ἀλκαῖος δὲ ὁ μελοποιὸς μετεωρόν φησιν αὐτὸν νήχεσθαι.

65

Aristid. 2. 155 [π. ῥητορικῆς]· εἰ δέ τινες καὶ ἄλλοι περιβοῶντες ῥητορικὴν ψέγουσι, μᾶλλον δὲ τονθορύζοντες ἐκ τοῦ ψέφως[1] <τε> τοξεύοντες κατὰ Ἀλκαῖον . . . τοσοῦτόν μοι πρὸς τούτους ἀποκεκρίσθω, ὅτι ῥητορικῇ παρὰ πόδας διδόασι τὴν δίκην.

e.g. . . . οἲ τονθόρυζον ἐκ ψέφαος τ' αἴ
| τόξευον ἀμμέων . . . .

66

Plut. *Def. Or.* 2 νεωστὶ δὲ γεγονὼς παρ' Ἄμμωνα, τὰ μὲν ἄλλα τῶν ἐκεῖ δῆλος ἦν μὴ πάνυ τεθαυμακώς, περὶ δὲ τοῦ λύχνου τοῦ ἀσβέστου διηγεῖτο λόγον ἄξιον σπουδῆς λεγόμενον ὑπὸ τῶν ἱερέων· ἀεὶ γὰρ ἔλαττον ἀναλίσκειν ἔλαιον ἔτους ἑκάστου, καὶ τοῦτο ποιεῖσθαι τεκμήριον ἐκείνους τῆς τῶν ἐνιαύτων ἀνωμαλίας, τὸν ἕτερον τοῦ προάγοντος ἀεὶ τῷ χρόνῳ βραχύτερον ποιούσης· εἰκὸς γὰρ ἐν ἐλάττονι χρόνῳ τὸ δαπανώμενον ἔλαττον εἶναι. θαυμασάντων δὲ τῶν παρόντων, τοῦ δὲ Δημητρίου καὶ γέλοιον φήσαντος εἶναι ἀπὸ μικρῶν πραγμάτων οὕτω μεγάλα θηρᾶν, οὐ κατ' Ἀλκαῖον ἐξ ὄνυχος τὸν λέοντα γράφοντες, ἀλλὰ θρυαλλίδι καὶ λύχνῳ τὸν οὐρανὸν ὁμοῦ τι σύμπαντα μεθίσταντας καὶ τὴν μαθηματικὴν ἄρδην ἀναιροῦντας . . .

e.g. ἐξ ὄνυχος δὲ λέοντα γράψαις

[1] ψέφως Lobeck -*E* cf. Gal. 8. 780, Hesych. ψεφαίαις: mss ψόφου, σκότου

64

Athenaeus *Doctors at Dinner* [on the greedy fish called labrax or bass]: The lyric poet Alcaeus says that the bass swims near the surface.[1]

65

Aristides [on rhetoric]: If any others go about declaiming against rhetoric, or rather muttering and shooting at it from the dark, as Alcaeus says . . . . , let so much be my answer:—even as they do it, rhetoric is taking its revenge.

e.g. . . . who muttered and kept shooting at us from the dark.

66

Plutarch *On the Cessation of Oracles*: On a recent visit to Ammon it was clear he had been particularly struck with the ever-burning lamp, about which he told us an interesting circumstance related to him by the priests. It seems that they use less oil for it every year, and since it is only reasonable to suppose that the less the oil consumed the shorter the time of burning, they believe this to be an indication that the length of the year is not constant, but that each is shorter than its predecessor. At this there was general astonishment, and Demetrius exclaimed that it was really absurd to pursue so great a quest with such tiny equipment, not, in Alcaeus' phrase,

painting a lion from the claw,

but changing the position of the entire heavens and throwing mathematics out of the window by means of a lamp and a lamp-wick.[2]

[1] he prob. compared the tyrant Pittacus to this fish, perh. in the poem to which 162 belongs [2] cf. *Paroem.* 2. 165

67

Sch. Soph. *O.C.* 954 [θυμοῦ γὰρ οὐδὲν γῆράς ἐστιν ἄλλο πλὴν | θανεῖν]· οἷον οὐκ ἔστι θυμοῦ κρατῆσαι ἄνθρωπον ὄντα· οὐ καταγηράσκει τὸ ὠμὸν τοῦ θυμοῦ, εἰ μὴ ἐξέλθοι τοῦ βίου ὁ ἄνθρωπος· ἀδύνατον γάρ ἐστι ζῶντα ἄνθρωπον μὴ θυμῷ χρήσασθαι· τοῦτο δὲ παροιμιακῶς λέγεται, ὅτι ὁ θυμὸς ἔσχατον γηράσκει· λέγεται δὲ διὰ τοὺς πρεσβυτέρους, ὅσῳ γὰρ γηράσκουσι, τὸν θυμὸν ἐρρωμενέστερον ἔχουσιν· καὶ Ἀλκαῖος, ὥς λέγομεν, οὕτω κατὰ κοινὸν[1] αὐτοῦ μιμνήσκεται.

e.g. θῦμον ἔσχατον λόγος ἐστὶ γήραν

68[2] [εἰς Δία]

Ox. Pap. 1234. 1 a

. . . οὔ[κὶ προ]ταίρει·[3]

π[όη Ϝεκ]άβολον, πάτερ, ἀπ[λάνην τε]
κα[ρδία]ν κήνω, πάτερ, ἀ[λλὰ πάντας]
το[ίς κεν] ὠναίσχυντος ἐπ[ιπνέησι]
5 μ[ῖ]σος ἄλιτρον.

69[4] εἰς Δία

Ibid. 1 b

Ζεῦ πάτερ, Λύδοι μὲν ἐπ' ἀ[λλοτέρραις]
συμφόραισι δισχελίοις στά[τηρας]
ἄμμ' ἔδωκαν αἴ κε δυναίμεθ' ἴρ[αν]
ἐς πόλιν ἔλθην,

[1] mss Sch. also ὡς λέγεται ο. κ. κοινοῦ, Suid. ὡς λεγομένου κατὰ τὸ κοινόν [2] Hunt -*E*, *C.R.* 1919. 108, *Ox. Pap.* xi [3] = προσαίρει [4] Hunt -Wil. -*E* ibid.

67 [1]

Scholiast on Sophocles ['for anger knows no old age but death']: That is, no mortal man can overcome anger. The fierceness of anger does not grow old unless the man dies, because it is impossible for a living man not to become angry. It is put proverbially in the words 'anger grows old last.' This is said because of the aged, since the older they grow the stronger grows their anger. Alcaeus gives the statement in general terms as we do.

e.g. 'Tis said that wrath is the last thing in a | man to grow old.

68 [To Zeus]

From a Second-Century Papyrus:

. . . he doth not take up. Make thou far-darting, Father, and unerring the heart of yonder man, Father, but all such as are inspired by the shameless one make thou a sinful thing of hate.

69 To Zeus

From the Same:

Father Zeus, though the Lydians, in other men's time of misfortune and having received no benefit at our hands and knowing us not at all, gave us

[1] cf. Suid. θυμὸς ἑπταβόειος

5 οὐ πάθοντες οὐδάμα πω 'σλον οὖδεν
οὐδὲ γινώσκοντες· ὁ δ' ὡς ἀλώπαξ
ποικιλόφρων εὐμάρεα προλέξαις
ἤλπετο λάσην
e.g.[1] μὴ 'κτελέσσαις τοῖσι Ϝέοις πολίταις.

70

Ox. Pap. 1234. 2. i. a

. . . τọ[ύ]τῳ τάδ' εἴπην· 'Ὁ δηὖτ[' ἐταρηΐα̣][2]
ἀείκει πεδέχων συμποσίων [κάκων]
βάσμος, φιλώνων πεδ' ἀλεμ[ατωτάτων]
εὐωχήμενος αὔτοισιν ἐπά[κρισε.']
5 κῆνος δὲ γαώθεις 'Ατρεΐδα[ν γάμῳ][3]
δαπτέτω πόλιν, ὡς καὶ πεδὰ Μυρσίλω,
θᾶς κ' ἄμμε βόλλητ' Ἄρευς ἐπιτεύχεας
τρόπην, ἐκ δὲ χόλω τῶδε λαθοιμεθα,[4]

χαλάσσομεν δὲ τᾶς θυμοβόρω δύας
10 ἐμφύλω τε μάχας, τάν τις 'Ολυμπίων
ἐνῶρσε, δᾶμον μὲν εἰς ἀϜάταν[5] ἄγων
Φιττάκῳ δὲ δίδοις κῦδος ἐπήρατον.

71

Ibid. 2. i. b[6]

Φίλος μὲν ἦσθα κἀπ' ἔριφον κάλην
καὶ χοῖρον· οὔτω τοῦτο νομίσδεται.

[1] *E* [2] ll. 1–4 *E*, *C.R.* 1916. 104 [3] Hunt from schol.
[4] Wil. λαθώμεθα and χαλάσσωμεν perh. rightly [5] P ανάταν
[6] see *C.R. l.c.*

---

[1] Mytilene; for the machinations of Croesus with M. cf. Diog. Laert. *Life of Pittacus* 1. 4. 74 'When C. offered him

two thousand staters in the hope we might reach the sacred city,[1] this fellow like a cunning-hearted fox made fair promises [to his own fellow-citizens] and then reckoned he would escape scotfree [if he failed to perform them].

70

From a Second-Century Papyrus:

. . . to say to him: 'He who shared evil revels with an unseemly crew, as a mere stone of the base, now, by making merry with good-fellows of the idlest and vainest, has become the headstone over them all.' And in the pride of his marriage with a daughter of Atreus[2] let him do despite to his countrymen as he did with Myrsilus, till Ares choose to turn our luck and we forget this our anger and have rest from the heart-devouring pain and internecine battle which one of the Olympians hath roused in us to bring destruction on the people and to give delightful glory unto Pittacus.

71[3]

From the Same:

You were friends enough with me once to be invited to sup on kid and pork; this is the way of the world.[4]

money he refused it' [2] the scholiast tells us that Pittacus married a sister of Dracon a descendant of Atreus, *i. e.* of the Atreid founders of Lesbos [3] an accusation of ingratitude [4] the scholiast says this became a proverb

72[1] [πρὸς Πιττακόν ?]

Ox. Pap. 1234. 2. ii

. . . [λά]βρως δὲ συσπέλλα[ις τὰ ϝὰ λ]αῖ'ἄπαν[2]
πίμπλεισιν ἀκράτω [δόμ' ἐ]π' ἀμέρᾳ
καὶ νύκτι, πλάφλασμ[οι τ'] ἔσαχθεν
5 ἔνθα νόμος θάμ' ἔωθ[ε φ]ώνην.

κῆνος δὲ τούτων οὐκ ἐπελάθετο
ὤνηρ ἐπειδὴ πρῶτον ὀνέτροπε,
παίσαις γὰρ ὀννώρινε[3] νύκτας,
τῶ δὲ πίθω πατάγεσκ' ὀ πύθμην.

10 σὺ δὴ τεαύτας[4] ἐκγεγόνων ἔχης
τὰν δόξαν οἴαν ἄνδρες ἐλεύθεροι
ἔσλων ἔοντες ἐκ τοκήων . . .

73[5]

Ibid. 3

. . . πὰν φόρτιον δ' ἔ[ρριψαν αὔτοις]
[δ'] ὄττι μάλιστα σάο[ισι ναῦται·]

καὶ κύματι πλάγεισ[α βαρυκτύπῳ]
ὄμβρῳ μάχεσθαι χε[ίματι τ' οὔκετι]
5 φαῖσ' οὖδεν ἰμμέρρη[ν, ἔκοισα]
[δ'] ἔρματι τυπτομ[ένα κε δύννην.]

κήνα μὲν ἐν τούτ[ῳ 'στίν· ἔγω δέ κε]
τούτων λελάθων, ὦ φ[ίλοι αὔιται,]

[1] connexion with 75 is impossible: restored by *E*, *C.R.* 1916. 77 (λάβρως Hunt) [2] = συστείλας *E* [3] = ἀνώρινε [4] = τοιαύτης [5] restored by Hunt, Wil., Hicks, *E*, *C.R.* 1914. 77

72 [To Pittacus?]

From a Second-Century Papyrus:

. . . and garnering his plunderous crop, fills the whole house both day and night with unmixed wine, and wassailings have been brought in unto the place where the law is wont to speak; and yon man forgot them not, so soon as he had overthrown him; for he set them a-going every night, and the bottom of the flagon rang and rang again.[1] Aye, you that come of such lineage[2] have the honour and glory enjoyed by the free sons of noble parents . . .

73

From the Same:

. . . The sailors have cast all their cargo overboard and are saving themselves as best they can. Meanwhile, beaten with the roaring wave, the ship[3] bethinks her that she no longer desires to fight with storm and tempest but would willingly strike a reef and go to the bottom. That is her plight; but as for me, dear comrades, I would forget these things

[1] when it was set down empty [2] sc. γενεᾶς: his father was a Thracian, his mother a Lesbian [3] of State

σύν τ' ὔμμι τέρπ[εσθ]α[ι θέλοιμι]
10 καὶ πεδὰ Βύκχιδος αὖθι [δαῖτος.]
τῶ [1] δ' ἄμμες ἐς τὰν ἆψ ἔρον ἄ[γρεμεν,]
αἴ καί τις ἄφ[ρων π]άντα τ[άραξέ ϝοι]
μείχνυντε[ς . . . . ;]

74 [2] [εἰς Μυτιλήνην]

Ox. Pap. 1234. 4. 6–17

. . . [οὐδ' αὖ σφρί]γαις ᾇ πὰν [τέ]κνον [ἀκλέων]
[σφρίγαι τοκ]ήων ἐς φαΐκροις [3] [δόμοις]
[στρώφασθ'] ἔδαπτέ σ'· ἐν [δ]' ἀσ[ά]μ[οισ']
[ὧν [4] ἔτι ϝοί]κεος ἦσκ' ὄνεκτον.
10 [ἀλλ' ὡς] προτ' [5] ὔβριν καὶ μεγάθε[ι] π[όθ]εις
[δραίη] τά τ' ἄνδρες δραῖσιν ἀτάσθαλοι,
[τούτω]ν κεν ἦσκ' ὄνεκτον [οὖ]δε[ν·]
[νῦν δ' ὄ]τα πόλλακις ἐσφάλημεν
[τύχαν ὀ]ν[ο]ρθώθημε[ν ἐπ' ἀρχάαν·]
15 [αἰ γὰρ] μέμεικται τῷ [ὀξυτέρῳ τάδε]
[τὰ ϝάδε', ἀ]λλά πᾳ τι δαί[μων]
e.g. [παῖσί μόρ' ἐνν ἄγαθοισι χέρρον.]

75 [6]

Ibid. 6. 7–13

. . . [κἄγω μὲν οὐ μέ]μναιμ'· ἔτι γὰρ πάϊς
[τρόφω 'πὶ γόνν]ῳ σμῖκρος ἐπίσδανον·
[πάτρος δ' ἀκούω]ν οἶδα τίμ[α]ν
10 [τὰν ἔλαβεν παρὰ] Πενθίλῃος

[1] *i.e.* τίῳ = τίνι 'for what?' [2] restored by Hunt, Wil., *E*, *C.R.* 1916. 106, 1919. 128 [3] letter-traces doubtful; cf. φαικός [4] εἶς? [5] P ποτ' [6] restored by Hunt, *E*, *C.R.* 1919. 129

and make merry here both with you and with Bacchus.[1] And yet why take we our love off our country, even though fools have thrown all she hath into confusion, mingling . . . ?

74 [To Mytilene]

From a Second-Century Papyrus:

. . . Nor yet did he harm thee in that he itched, as every child of unfamed parents itches, to go in and out of garish houses; for being still at home among the obscure, he was bearable as yet. But when he did the deeds of wicked men in wanton presumption and drunken with power, there was no bearing such things as those. And now after many a slip we stand upright in our ancient estate; [for though these sweets] are mingled with that [sour], still God, I ween, [decrees us something bad in everything that is good.[2]]

75

From the Same:

. . . And as for me, I remember it not; for I was still a little child sitting on his nurse's knee; but I know from my father the honour yon man had received of yore from the son of Penthilus;[3] and

[1] cf. *E.M.* 216. 48, *Ox. Pap.* 1360. 3 [2] *i. e.* our political position, though not ideal, is now bearable [3] Dracon, whose sister Pittacus married

[κῆνος πάροιθα·] νῦν δ' ὃ πεδέτρ[οπε]
[τυραννέοντα[1] τὸ]ν κακοπάτριδα
e.g. [Μελάγχροον καὖτος[2] τ]υράννευ-
[ων ἔλαθ' ἀμμετέρας πόληος.]

76[3] πρὸς Μυτιληναίους

Ox. Pap. 1360. 1

[. . . . . .] ὀ δὲ πλάτυ
[ὔμμαις ὑπερστείχων] κεφάλαις μάτει,
[ὔμμες δὲ σίγατ' ὦτε μύσται]
[τὸν κάλεσαν νέκυν εἰσίδο]ντες.
5 [ἀλλ', ὦ πόλιται, θᾶς ἔτι τ]ὸ ξύλον
[κάπνον παρ' ὔμμεσιν] προΐει μόνον,
[κασβέσσατ' ὡς τάχιστα, μή πα]
[λαμπρότερον τὸ φάος γένηται.]

77[4]

Ibid. 2, 9–13

Οὐ πάντ' ἦς ἀπ[άτηλο̄ς ∪ ∪ – ∪ ⏓]
οὐδ' ἀσύννετος, ἄμμεσσι[5] δ' ἀ[πομμόσαις][6]
βώμῳ Λατοΐδα τοῦτ' ἐφυλάξα[ο]
μή τις τῶν κακοπατρίδαν[7]
5 εἴσεται φανέρα[8] τοῖσιν ἀπ' ἀρχάω[. . .

[1] = τυραννέϝοντα [2] P prob. Μέλαγχρον αὖτος [3] restored by Hunt, *E* (*C.R.* 1919. 129) from scholia ὑμεῖς δὲ σιγᾶτε ὥσπερ νεκρῶν ἱεροὶ μύσται (these two words are doubtful) οὐδὲν δυνάμενοι ἀντιστῆναι τῷ τυράννῳ and ἀλλ', ὦ Μυτιληναῖοι, ἕως ἔτι κάπνον μόνον ἀφίησι τὸ ξύλον, τοῦτ' ἔστιν ἕως οὐδέπω τυραννεύει, κατάσβητε καὶ καταπαύσατε ταχέως μὴ

now he that overturned the despotism of the traitor [Melanchros, is himself, ere we knew it], become despot [of our city].

76 To the Mytileneans

From a Second-Century Papyrus:

. . . But he goes striding wide over your heads, and you hold your tongues like initiates when they behold the dead they have called up. Nay rather, my fellow-countrymen, up and quench the log while it but smoulders among you, lest the light thereof come to a brighter flame.[1]

77

From the Same:

You were not altogether a knave . . ., . . .,[2] nor yet a fool, but kept the oath you swore to us by the altar of the Son of Leto, that none of the Children of Treason should know truly who it was to whom in the beginning . . .

[1] restored from Scholia [2] the gap prob. contained an adv. of time (*e. g.* ποτά or πέρυσιν), and a voc.

λαμπρότερον τὸ φῶς γένηται [4] *E, C.R. l.c.* [5] P αμμοισι [6] = ἀπομόσας [7] mock-patronymic? a substitution for Ἀτρεΐδαν, founders of Lesbos, to whom P.'s wife belonged [8] adv. cf. λάθρα

78

Apoll. *Pron.* 95. 14 [ἡ ἁμῶν παρὰ Δωριεῦσι]· . . . ἀμέων· ὁμοίως Αἰολεῖς· Ἀλκαῖος·

μηδ' ὀνίαις τοῖς πλέασ' ἀμμέων[1] παρέχην. . . .

79

Ibid. 96. 1 Αἰολεῖς ὑμμέων. Ἀλκαῖος·

. . . . . . ὄττινες ἔσλοι
ὑμμέων τε καὶ ἀμμέων.

80

Zenob. (*Paroem.* 2. 145) Πιτάνη εἰμί· αὕτη παρ' Ἀλκαίῳ κεῖται· λέγεται δὲ κατὰ τῶν πυκναῖς συμφοραῖς περιπιπτόντων ἅμα καὶ εὐπραγίαις· παρ' ὅσον καὶ τῇ Πιτάνῃ τοιαῦτα συνέβη πράγματα, ὧν καὶ Ἑλλάνικος μέμνηται· φησὶ γὰρ αὐτὴν ὑπὸ Πελασγῶν ἀνδραποδισθῆναι καὶ πάλιν ὑπὸ Ἐρυθραίων ἐλευθερωθῆναι.

e.g. . . . . Πιτάνα δ' ἔμμι . . .

Ε′

. . . .

S′

81

Sch. Pind. *I.* 2. 17 [τὸ τ' Ὠργείου φυλάξαι | ῥῆμ' ἀλαθείας ἐτᾶς ἄγχιστα βαῖνον, | 'Χρήματα χρήματ' ἀνήρ' ὃς φᾶ κτεάνων θ' ἅμα λειφθεὶς καὶ φίλων]· τοῦτο ἀναγράφεται μὲν εἰς τὰς Παροιμίας ὑπ' ἐνίων, ἀπόφθεγμα δέ ἐστιν Ἀριστοδήμου καθάπερ φησὶ Χρύσιππος

[1] *E*: = πλείοσι cf. πλέας (acc.) *Il.* 2. 129, Mytil. Inscr. Collitz *Gr. Dial.* 213. 9–11 : mss τοι σπλεας ὑμεων : Hase τοῖς πέλας ἀ.

78

Apollonius *Pronouns* [the form ἀμῶν 'of us' in Doric]: . . . ἀμέων. Similarly in Aeolic; compare Alcaeus:

. . . nor make troubles for those who are more than we.

79

The Same: The Aeolic form is ὐμμέων 'of you'; compare Alcaeus:

. . . whoever of you and us are good men.[1]

80[2]

Zenobius *Proverbs*:

I am Pitanè;

this proverb is in Alcaeus; it is used of those who get frequent good and bad fortune, because this was the lot of the city of Pitanè, as indeed we learn from Hellanicus, according to whom it was captured by the Pelasgians and set free again by the Erythraeans.

Book V

. . . . . .

Book VI[3]

81

Scholiast on Pindar [' To keep the saying that goes nearest to the real truth, "Money, money is the man," the saying of the Argive who had lost both his goods and his friends']: This is ascribed by some commentators to the *Proverbs*, but it is really an apophthegm of Aristodemus, as Chrysippus tells

[1] metre Hor. *Od*. 1. 5 [2] cf. Phot 2. 91, Suid. Πιτάνη
[3] the subject of this Book being unknown, I have placed here unclassifiable fragments of a general type

ἐν τῷ περὶ Παροιμιῶν· τοῦτον δὲ τὸν Ἀριστόδημον Πίνδαρος μὲν οὐ τίθησιν ἐξ ὀνόματος, ὡς δήλου ὄντος ὅς ἐστιν ὁ τοῦτο εἰπών, μόνον δὲ ἐσημειώσατο τὴν πατρίδα, ὅτι Ἀργεῖος· Ἀλκαῖος δὲ καὶ τὸ ὄνομα καὶ τὴν πατρίδα τίθησιν, οὐκ Ἄργος ἀλλὰ Σπάρτην·

ὠς γὰρ δήποτ' Ἀριστόδαμον
φαῖσ' οὐκ ἀπάλαμνον ἐν Σπάρτᾳ λόγον
εἴπην, χρήματ' ἄνηρ, πένιχρος
δ' οὔδεις πέλετ' ἔσλος οὐδὲ τίμιος.[1]

82[2]

Demetr. π. ποιημάτων (*Vol. Hercul. Oxon.* 1. 122)

. . . ἐδόκ]η δ' ἄρεσ[το]ν ἔμμεναι
πώνην· τῷ δέ κεν ἦσι[3] τ[όσσο]ς
πὲρ ταὶς φρένας οἶνος, οὐ δίω τόος·[4]
κάτω γὰρ κεφάλαν κατίσχει[5]
5 τὸν Ϝον θάμα θῦμον αἰτιάμενος[6]
πεδά τ' ούόμενος[7] τά κεν θῆ,
τὸ δ' οὐκέτι Ϝά[νδα]νεν πεπαιτάτῳ.

καὶ τοιαῦτα καὶ Ἴβυκο[ς.]

83

Heph. 66 [π. ἀντισπαστικοῦ]· ὁ δὲ Ἀλκαῖος καὶ πενταμέτρῳ ἀκαταλήκτῳ ἐχρήσατο·

Κρονίδα βασίληος γένος Αἶαν, τὸν ἄριστον πεδ'
Ἀχιλλέα

[1] Diogenes' word-order, so *B*: Sch. and Suid. both differ [2] *E* from phot. cf. *Camb. Philol. Soc. Proc.*, 1916; cf. Vogliano *Stud. It. Fil. Cl.* 1910. 285 (Bursian 1920) [3] P ηι [4] P περι: δίω = ζῷ *i.e.* ζώει, or ζῶ 3rd pers. sing. of ζῶμι, cf. σάως 32 and ἐνδεδίωκε Inscr. Heracl. (read δίως = διώῃς for ζόῃς Theocr. 29. 19) [5] P κατισχε from Ϝάνδανεν below

us in his treatise *On Proverbs*; Aristodemus is not named by Pindar, as though it were obvious who the author is; he merely indicates that the place of his birth was Argos. Alcaeus on the other hand gives both name and birthplace, making the latter Sparta, not Argos:

. . . For even as once on a day 'tis told Aristodemus said at Sparta—and 'twas no bad thing—, the money is the man, and no poor man is either good or honourable.[1]

82

From a Papyrus of the First Century B.C. found at Herculaneum, Demetrius *on Poems*:

. . . And to drink seemed to him a pleasant thing; but one that hath so much wine as that about his wits, such an one lives no life at all; for he hangs his head, chiding oft his own heart and repenting him of what he hath done. And so it ceased to please him when he came to his ripest.

And we find the same sort of sentiment in Ibycus.

83[2]

Hephaestion *Handbook of Metre* [on the antispastic]: Alcaeus also used an acatalectic pentameter:

Sprung from the royal son of Cronus, Ajax second in valour to Achilles . . .

[1] cf. Diog. Laert. 1. 31, Suid. χρήματα, Arsen. 476, *Paroem.* 2. 129 [2] cf. Choer. *Gram. Gr.* 4. 123. 25

---

6 P -μενας 7 = μετοιόμενός τε: Hesych. πεδαλευόμενος records old variant

84

Vet. Et. Mag. σείω· ἔστι γὰρ σεεύς[1] παρ' Ἀλκαίῳ, οἷον·

. . . . γᾶς γὰρ πέλεται σέευς·[2]

καὶ ἐκ τούτου γίνεται σέω καὶ σείω, ὡς πλέω πλείω καὶ πνέω πνείω. . .

85

Ath. 3. 85 f [π. ὀστρακοδέρμων]· . . . Ἀριστοφάνης ὁ γραμματικὸς . . . ὁμοίας φησὶν εἶναι τὰς λεπάδας ταῖς καλουμέναις τελλίναις. Καλλίας δ' ὁ Μυτιληναῖος ἐν τῷ περὶ τῆς παρ' Ἀλκαίῳ Λεπάδος φησὶν εἶναι ᾠδὴν ἧς ἡ ἀρχή·

Πέτρας καὶ πολίας θαλάσσας
τέκνον . . . . ,

ἧς ἐπὶ τέλει γεγράφθαι·

. . . . . ἐκ δὲ παίσας[3]
χαύνοις φρένας, ἀ θαλασσία λέπας.

ὁ δὲ Ἀριστοφάνης γράφει ἀντὶ τοῦ λεπὰς χέλυς, καί φησιν οὐκ εὖ Δικαίαρχον ἐκδεξάμενον λέγειν τὸ λεπάς,[4] τὰ παιδάρια δὲ ἡνίκ' ἂν εἰς τὸ στόμα λάβωσιν αὐλεῖν ἐν ταύταις καὶ παίζειν, καθάπερ καὶ παρ' ἡμῖν τὰ σπερμολόγα τῶν παιδαρίων ταῖς καλουμέναις τελλίναις.

86

Heph. 72 [π. τ. ἀπ' ἐλάσσονος ἰωνικοῦ]· καὶ ὅλα μὲν οὖν ᾄσματα γέγραπται ἰωνικά, ὥσπερ . . . , Ἀλκαίῳ δὲ πολλά, ὥσπερ καὶ τόδε·

ἔμε δεῖλαν, ἔμε παῖσαν κακότατα πεδέχοισαν

[1] *E*, cf. σεεὶ δύο *Pap. Ber.* 953. 5: mss σέω (σέος) ὡς
[2] σέευς *E*: mss σέῳ and σέως (from above)
[3] *E*: mss ἐκ λεπάδων through corruption ἐκ δὲ παῖδας (-ων): Ahr. ἐκ δὲ παίδων misunderstanding the whole passage, and if ἐκ is in tmesi a genitive is unlikely
[4] *E*: mss λέγ. τὰς λεπάδας from corruption in 3

84

Old Etymologicum Magnum: σείω 'to shake'; there is a word σεεύς 'shaker' in Alcaeus, for instance:

For he is the shaker of the earth;

and from this comes σέω or σείω; compare πλέω πλείω and πνέω πνείω . . .

85

Athenaeus *Doctors at Dinner* [on shellfish]: . . . Aristophanes the grammarian . . . declares the *lepas* to resemble what is called the *tellina*. But Callias of Mytilene, in his tract *On the* Lepas *of Alcaeus*, says that there is a song in Alcaeus beginning:

Child of the rock and the grey sea

and ending:

. . . and thou fillest all hearts with pride, thou *lepas* of the sea.[1]

Instead of *lepas*, however, Aristophanes reads *chelys*, 'tortoise[2] or turtle,' and says that Dicaearchus[3] reads *lepas* without understanding what a *lepas* was, namely a shell which playing children used to put in their mouths to make a whistle, as our guttersnipes do with what is called the *tellina*.

86 [4]

Hephaestion *Handbook of Metre* [on the *ionicum a minore*]: And whole poems are written in ionics, for instance . . ., and many by Alcaeus, as:

Me a woman miserable, me a sharer in all misfortune

[1] metre as 81 [2] the same word means lyre, the earliest lyres having been made of tortoiseshell; the poem was apparently an address to the trumpet (see L. and S. σάλπιγξ) which Ar. altered into an address to the lyre [3] in his tract *On Alcaeus* Ath. 15. 668 e [4] cf. Heph. 123–4, who implies that the stanzas each contained 10 feet like Hor. 3. 12, and Gram. ap. Hermann *El. Metr.* 472, Gram. ap. Gais. Heph. 332

87

Et. Gud. 162. 31 ἤνασσεν, Fάνασσεν·

. . . καὶ πλείστοισι Fάνασσε λάοις·[1]

Ἀλκαῖος.

88

Heph. 47 [π. δακτυλικοῦ]· ἔστι δέ τινα καὶ λογαοιδικὰ καλούμενα δακτυλικά, ἅπερ ἐν μὲν ταῖς ἄλλαις χώραις δακτύλους ἔχει, τελευταίαν δὲ τροχαϊκὴν συζυγίαν. ἔστι δὲ αὐτῶν ἐπισημότατα τό τε πρὸς δύο δακτύλους ἔχον τροχαϊκὴν συζυγίαν, καλούμενον δὲ Ἀλκαϊκὸν δεκασύλλαβον·

καί τις ἐπ' ἐσχατίαισιν οἴκεις[2]

89[3]

Zon. μάλευρον· τὸ ἄλευρον καὶ πλεονασμῷ τοῦ μ μάλευρον·

μίγδα μάλευρον

90

Comm. Arat. *Phaen.* Iriarte *Reg. Bibl. Matr. Codd. Gr.* 239

. . . . καὶ τάδ'
ὡς λόγος ἐκ πατέρων ὄρωρε·

κατ' Ἀλκαῖον.

91

Vet. Et. Mag. Miller 94 and *E.M.* 290. 42 δυσί· . . . ἔστι δὲ εἰπεῖν ὅτι πολλάκις αἱ διάλεκτοι κλίνουσι ταῦτα, ὡς παρὰ Ἀλκαίῳ·

. . . . εἷς τῶν δυοκαιδέκων

[1] Bek. -*E*; Aeol. rarely fails to distinguish dat. and acc. pl.: mss *Et.* πλείστοις ἐάν., *A.O.* πλ. ἔν. corrected to ἄν.: mss *A.O.* λεοῖς perh. indicating λᾶοις [2] mss οἴκοις, οἰκεῖς : cf. *A.O.* [3] Phot. μάλευρον· τὸ ἄλευρον Ἀλκαῖος (so *B* : mss Ἀχαιὸς)

87

Etymologicum Gudianum: ἤνασσεν 'ruled' is found in the form Ϝάνασσεν; compare Alcaeus:

. . . and ruled over full many peoples.

88

Hephaestion *Handbook of Metre* [on dactylics]: There are dactylics called logaoedic, which have dactyls in their earlier part but a trochaic dipody at the end. The best-known of them is the line which has two dactyls before the trochaic dipody and is called the ten-syllable Alcaic; compare:—

and one that dwelt on the outskirts[1]

89[2]

Zonaras *Lexicon*: μάλευρον 'wheat flour'; the same as *alcuron* with a pleonastic *m*; compare

wheat flour mingled

90

Commentator on Aratus *Phaenomena*: As Alcaeus says:

These things began, 'tis said, with our fathers.

91[3]

Old Etymologicum Magnum: δυσί 'to two' . . . I may add that these numerals are often declined in the dialects; compare Alcaeus:

one of the twelve

[1] cf. Sch. Heph., Cram. *A.O.* 1. 327. 4 which proves οἴκεις partcp. [2] cf. Phot. 1. 404 who gives the author's name (mss 'Αχαιός) [3] cf. *E.M.* 290. 49

92

Sch. Soph. *O.T.* 153 [ἐκτέταμαι φοβερὰν φρένα]· ἐκπέπληγμαι, φοβερὰν δὲ τὴν περίφοβον. καὶ Ἀλκαῖος·

ἐλάφω δὲ βρόμος ἐν στήθεσι φυίει φόβερος·[1]

ἀντὶ τοῦ περίφοβος.

92 A

Str. 13. 606 τὴν δὲ Ἄντανδρον Ἀλκαῖος μὲν καλεῖ Λελέγων πόλιν·

Πρώτα μὲν Ἄντανδρος Λελέγων πόλις

93

Sch. Theocr. 7. 112 [Ἕβρον πὰρ ποταμὸν]· Ἀλκαῖός φησιν ὅτι Ἕβρος κάλλιστος ποταμῶν.

e.g. . . . . . ποτάμων ἀπάντων
| Ἔβρε κάλιστε

94

Zenob. (*Paroem.* 1. 36) αἲξ Σκυρία· Χρύσιππός φησιν ἐπὶ τῶν τὰς εὐεργεσίας ἀνατρεπόντων τετάχθαι τὴν παροιμίαν, ἐπειδὴ πολλάκις τὰ ἀγγεῖα ἀνατρέπει ἡ αἴξ· ἄλλοι δέ φασιν ἐπὶ τῶν ὀνησιφόρων λέγεσθαι, διὰ τὸ πολὺ γάλα φέρειν τὰς Σκυρίας αἶγας. μέμνηται Πίνδαρος καὶ Ἀλκαῖος.

95

Sch. Ap. Rh. 1. 957 [κρήνῃ ὑπ' Ἀρτακίῃ]· Ἀρτακία κρήνη περὶ Κύζικον, ἧς καὶ Ἀλκαῖος μέμνηται καὶ Καλλίμαχος ὅτι τῆς Δολιονίας ἐστιν.

e.g. Κύζικον Δολῑονίαν . . . .

[1] βρόμος: Blf. τρόμος: *B* τέτρομος for δὲ βρ. cf. Apoll. *Pron.* 334 (2. 1. 1. 58 Lentz)

92

Scholiast on Sophocles ['my fearful heart is tortured']: that is, 'panic-stricken,' and 'fearful' means 'terrified'; compare Alcaeus:

and a fearful madness springs up in the breast of the hart;[1]

where 'fearful' means 'terrified.'

92 A

Strabo *Geography*: Antandros is called by Alcaeus a city of the Leleges; compare:

Antandros, first city of the Leleges

93

Scholiast on Theocritus ['beside the banks of Hebrus']: Alcaeus says that Hebrus is the fairest of rivers[2]

e.g. . . . O Hebrus, fairest of all rivers

94

Zenobius *Proverbs*: The she-goat of Scyros: Chrysippus says that the proverb is used of those who upset the doing of kindness, because the goat often upsets the pail. Others hold that it is used of those who bring benefits, because the goats of Scyros give so much milk. The saying occurs in Pindar and Alcaeus.

95

Scholiast on Apollonius of Rhodes ['by the Artacian spring']: This spring is near Cyzicus, which both Alcaeus and Callimachus speak of as being situated in Dolionia.

e.g. . . . Dolionian Cyzicus

[1] metre Heph. 72 [2] perh. in connexion with the death of Orpheus and the carrying of his head by the current to Lesbos Verg. *Geo.* 4

96

Sch. Ap. Rh. 4. 992 [αἵματος Οὐρανίοιο γένος Φαίηκες ἔασι]· . . . καὶ Ἀλκαῖος δὲ κατὰ τὰ αὐτὰ Ἀκουσιλάῳ λέγει τοὺς Φαίακας ἔχειν τὸ γένος ἐκ τῶν σταγόνων τοῦ Οὐράνου.

e.g. Φαίακες ὀρράννων σταγόνων γένος [1]

97

Sch. Hes. *Theog.* 313 [τὸ τρίτον Ὕδρην αὖτις ἐγείνατο]· τὴν Ὕδραν δὲ Ἀλκαῖος μὲν ἐννεακέφαλόν φησί, Σιμωνίδης δὲ πεντηκοντακέφαλον.

e.g. . . . Ὕδραν ἐννεακέπφαλον *or* . . . ἐννακέφαλλος Ὕδρα [2]

98

Phot. 7. 15

ἄγωνος·

κατὰ σχηματισμὸν ἀντὶ τοῦ ὁ ἀγών· ἀπὸ δὲ γενικῆς ἐσχηματίσθη. οὕτως Ἀλκαῖος ὁ λυρικὸς πολλάκις ἐχρήσαο.

99

Hesych. ἀλιβάπτοις· <πορφυροῖς |

ἀλίβαπτον·>

πορφυρᾶν ὄρνιν. Ἀλκαῖος καὶ Ἀλκμάν.[3]

100

Et. Mag. 76. 51

ἀμάνδαλον

τὸ ἀφανὲς παρὰ Ἀλκαίῳ· ἀμαλδύνω, <ἀμαλδῦνον καὶ>[4] ἀμάλδανον τὸ ἀφανὲς καὶ ἀφανιζόμενον· καὶ ὑπερθέσει ἀμάνδαλον.

[1] ὀρράννων = οὐρανίων *E*, cf. Sa. 122 [2] *i. e.* with ictus-lengthening *E*, cf. ὀγκρέμμασαν 121, ὀννώρινε 72, Sa. 121, τρικέφᾱλον Hes. *Th.* 287 (◡ ◡ ◡ ◡ not found in Lesbian) [3] *B*: mss Ἀχαιὸς κ. ἀλμ.άς [4] *E*

96

Scholiast on Apollonius of Rhodes ['The Phaeacians are sprung from the blood of Heaven']: . . . and moreover Alcaeus agrees with Acusilaüs in saying that the Phaeacians take their descent from the drops that fell from Uranus or Heaven.[1]

e.g. . . . The Phaeacians, sprung from drops | celestial

97

Scholiast on Hesiod ['And for a third bore she Hydra']: Alcaeus calls the

Hydra nine-headed

Simonides 'fifty-headed.'

98

Photius *Lexicon*: ἄγωνος

conflict:

by 'adaptation' for ἀγών; it is 'adapted' from the genitive; it is often used thus by the lyric poet Alcaeus.

99

Hesychius *Glossary*: ἁλιβάπτοις, purple. | ἁλίβαπτον

sea-dipt

a purple bird; Alcaeus and Alcman.

100[2]

Etymologicum Magnum: ἀμάνδαλον; used in the sense of

unseen

by Alcaeus. From ἀμαλδύνω 'to destroy'; ἀμαλδῦνον or ἀμάλδανον 'that which is unseen or disappearing'; and by transposition ἀμάνδαλον.

[1] *i. e.* when he was mutilated [2] cf. Cram. *A.P.* 4. 8. 16

101

Hesych.

αὔϝολλαι·[1]

ἄελλαι· παρὰ Ἀλκαίῳ.[2]

102

Cram. *A.O.* 1. 253. 20: ζητοῦμεν οὖν καὶ τὸ τοῖσδεσσι πῶς εἴρηται· καὶ ἄμεινον λέγειν ἐπέκτασιν· τοῦτο μιμούμενος Ἀλκαῖός φησι

τῶνδέων

103

Eust. *Od.* 1759. 27 [ἦα]· λέγει δὲ (Ἡρακλείδης) καὶ χρῆσιν εἶναι τοῦ

ἔον

παρὰ Ἀλκαίῳ.

104

Et. Mag. 377. 19 ἔρρεντι· παρὰ Ἀλκαίῳ· ἀπὸ τοῦ ἔρρω ἢ ἐρρῶ περισπωμένου, ἡ μετοχὴ ἐρρείς ἐρρέντος, καὶ ὡς παρὰ τὸ ἐθέλοντος ἐθελοντί, οὕτω καὶ παρὰ τὸ ἐρρέντος

ἔρρεντι[3]

105

Ibid. 385. 9 ἐσυνῆκεν· Ἀλκαῖος

ἐσύνηκεν

καὶ Ἀνακρέων ἐξυνῆκεν πλεονασμῷ.

[1] *E*, = ἀϝέολλαι cf. σπολέω and στελῶ, ἀόλλης and ἀέλλης, Αἴολος = ἄϝιολος for ἀϝέολος: for υϝ cf. 33: mss αὐεοῦλλαι
[2] Ahr: mss ἄκλω [3] mss ἐρρεντί bis

101

Hesychius *Glossary*: αὔϜολλαι: for ἄελλαι

storms

found in Alcaeus.

102

Cramer *Inedita* (*Oxford*): We inquire therefore how it is that we find the form τοῖσδεσσι 'to these.' It is best to call it 'lengthening.' On this pattern Alcaeus says τῶνδεων

of these

103 [1]

Eustathius on the *Odyssey*: Heracleides says that there is an occurrence of the form ἔον

I was

in Alcaeus.

104 [2]

Etymologicum Magnum: The word ἔρρεντι is used by Alcaeus; it is from ἔρρω or ἐρρῶ 'to go,' 'to go slowly' or 'to perish,' participle ἐρρείς ἐρρέντος, and from ἐρρέντος the adverb ἔρρεντι [3] like ἐθελοντί 'willingly' from ἐθέλοντος 'willing.'

105

The Same: ἐσυνῆκεν: Alcaeus uses the form ἐσύνηκεν

he understood

and Anacreon ἐξυνῆκε, with the pleonastic augment.

[1] cf. Fav. 222 [2] cf. *E.M. Vet.* 127 [3] meaning doubtful; perh. 'haltingly or 'hesitatingly'

106

Choer. *Gram. Gr.* 4. 1. 131 Lentz τὸ

ὦ Εὐρυδάμαν [1]

παρὰ τῷ 'Αλκαίῳ, μετὰ τοῦ ν λεγόμενον κατὰ τὴν κλητικήν.

107

Et. Mag. 319. 30. ἔθηκε· σημαίνει δύο, τὸ προκατέθηκεν ἢ ἐποίησεν· . . . ἀφ' οὗ καὶ

θέσις

ἡ ποίησις παρὰ 'Αλκαίῳ.

108

Cram. *A.P.* 3. 278. 9 . . . οἷόν ἐστι παρὰ τῷ 'Αλκαίῳ τὸ

κάλιον

ἀντὶ τοῦ κάλλιον.

108 A

Sch. *Od.* 11. 521 [Κήτειοι]· . . . ἦν γὰρ ὁ Τήλεφος Μυσίας βασιλεύς, καὶ 'Αλκαῖος δέ φησι τὸν

Κήτειον

ἀντὶ τοῦ Μυσόν.

109

Choer. *Gram. Gr.* 4. 1. 27 a Lentz [π. τῶν εἰς υν ληγόντων]· κίνδυν κίνδυνος, κίνδυνα· οὕτως δὲ ἔφη Σαπφὼ τὸ κίνδυνος. ὁ γοῦν 'Αλκαῖος τὴν δοτικὴν ἔφη τὸ

κίνδυνι [2]

[1] Const. L. Πολυδάμαν [2] for mss reading cf. Sa. 184

106[1]

Choeroboscus on Theodosius:

O Eurydaman

is found in Alcaeus for *O Eurydamas*, ending with *n* in the vocative.

107

Etymologicum Magnum: ἔθηκε has two meanings, 'he placed' and 'he did' . . .; hence Alcaeus uses the noun θέσις for ποίησις

doing *or* making

108

Cramer *Inedita* (*Paris*) . . . Compare Alcaeus' use of κάλιον for κάλλιον

more beautiful

108 A

Scholiast on the *Odyssey* ['Ceteians']: . . . For Telephus was king of Mysia, and Alcaeus moreover uses

Ceteian

for 'Mysian.'

109

Choeroboscus [On nouns ending in -υν]: κίνδυν 'danger,' genitive κίνδυνος, accusative κίνδυνα; Sappho thus declined the noun κίνδυνος. Alcaeus used the dative κίνδυνι

by danger

[1] cf. Constant. Lascar. *Nom. et Verb.* 116 b

110

Eust. *Od.* 1648. 6 καὶ ἐκ τοῦ κτείνω

κταίνω

Δωρικώτερον παρὰ Ἀλκαίῳ.

111 [1]

Phot.

μετρῆσαι

ἐπὶ τοῦ ἀριθμῆσαι· Ἀλκαῖος

112

Et. Mag. 344. 6 ἔννεον· ἔστ τὸ ῥῆμα νέω· Ἀλκαῖος·

αὖταρ ἐπεὶ χέρρεσσι νέον . . . [2]

ὁ παρατατικὸς ἔνεον καὶ πλεονασμῷ τοῦ ν ἔννεον.

112 A

Ox. Pap. 221. 11. 9 Schol. *Il.* 21. 219 οὐδέ τί πῃ δύναμαι προχέειν ῥόον εἰς ἅλα δῖαν | στεινόμενος νεκύεσσι· στενοχωρούμενος· παρὰ ταῦτα Ἀλκαῖος·

στένω μὰν Ξάνθω ῥόος ἐς θάλασσαν ἴκανε. [3]

113

Hdn. π.μ.λ. (2. 930. 20 Lentz) οἱ γὰρ περὶ Ἀλκαῖον

ὄϊδα

λέγουσι τρισυλλάβως.

[1] cf. Theocr. 16. 60, 30. 25 [2] *E*: some mss om. Ἀλκ.—νέον: mss *E.M.* αὐτῆς ἐπεὶ χείρεσσι, *Vet.* αὐτὰρ ἐπῆν χείρεσι: ἔννεον apparently from *Il.* 21. 11: *B* ascr. to *Od.* 5. 344, thinking the quotation from A. is lost [3] metre cf. Sa. 149. 3

110

Eustathius on the *Odyssey*: And from κτείνω comes the rather Doric form κταίνω

to kill

in Alcaeus.

111

Photius *Lexicon*:

to measure

in the sense of 'to count'; Alcaeus.

112 [1]

Etymologicum Magnum: ἔννεον they swam: the verb is νέω 'to swim'; compare Alcaeus:

but when they swam with their hands . . . ;

the imperfect is ἔνεον or with pleonastic *n* ἔννεον.

112 A

From a Papyrus of the Second Century containing Scholia on the *Iliad*: 'Nor can I pour forth my stream into the great sea, because I am straitened with dead bodies': that is 'cramped'; whence comes Alcaeus' line:

Verily 'twas the stream of a narrow Xanthus that came to the sea.

113

Herodian *Words without Parallel*: For Alcaeus pronounces οἶδα

I know

as three syllables.

[1] cf. *E.M. Vet.* Miller 114

114 [1]

Sch. Ar. *Av.* 1648 [διαβάλλεταί σ' ὁ θεῖος]· ἐπὶ τοῦ ἐξαπατᾶν . . . παρόμοιον δὲ καὶ τὸ Ὁμηρικόν . . .· καὶ παρ' Ἀλκαίῳ·

παραβάλλεταί σε

115

Cram. *A.O.* 1. 366. 22 . . . ἢ ἀπὸ τοῦ πέφυγα ἡ μετοχὴ πεφυγώς· ὁ γοῦν Ἀλκαῖος μετατιθεὶς τὸ σῖγμα εἰς τὸ ν κατὰ πλεονασμὸν ἑτέρου γ φησὶ

πεφύγγων

116

Hdn. π.μ.λ. (2. 949. 23 Lentz) πιέζω· τὰ εἰς -ζω λήγοντα ῥήματα ὑπὲρ δυὸ συλλαβὰς βαρύτονα οὐδέποτε τῷ ε παραλήγεσθαι θέλει . . . σημειῶδες ἄρα παρ' Ἀττικοῖς καὶ τοῖς Ἴωσι λεγόμενον διὰ τοῦ ε τὸ πιέζω, ὥσπερ καὶ παρὰ τῷ ποιητῇ . . . προσέθηκα δὲ καὶ τὰς διαλέκτους, ἐπεὶ παρ' Ἀλκαίῳ διχῶς λέγεται, παρὰ δὲ Ἀλκμᾶνι διὰ τοῦ α.

117

Tryphon πάθη λέξεων 11 (*Mus. Crit. Cant.* 1. 34) [π. προσθέσεως]· ἅπαξ δὲ παρ' Ἀλκαίῳ τὸ ῥῆξις

Ϝρᾶξις [2]

λέγεται.

118

Cram. *A.O.* 1. 342. 1 ἀπὸ τῶν εἰς -ος τὴν

τεμένηος

παρὰ Ἀλκαίῳ ἅπαξ χρησαμένῳ.

[1] cf. Hesych. ζαβάλλειν· ἐξαπατᾶν (*B*): perh. the comic poet Alcaeus (Mein.) [2] mss οὔρηξις

114

Scholiast on Aristophanes ['Your uncle imposes on you']: that is 'deceives' . . . ; similarly in Homer . . . ; and in Alcaeus:

he cheats you

115[1]

Cramer *Inedita* (*Oxford*) . . . Or the form πέφυγα 'I have fled' has the participle πεφυγώς. Alcaeus, at any rate, changing the *s* to an *n* and doubling the *g*, says πεφύγγων

having fled

116

Herodian *Words without Parallel*: πιέζω 'to press': verbs ending in -ζω which are paroxytone and of more than two syllables never have epsilon in the penultimate. . . . We should note therefore as remarkable the epsilon-form πιέζω used in Attic and Ionic as well as in Homer. . . . I have added the dialects because both forms, πιέζω and πιάζω, occur in Alcaeus, and Alcman uses πιάζω.

117[2]

Tryphon *Changes in Words* [prefixing of letters]: In one place in Alcaeus ῥῆξις

breaking

appears as Fρᾶξις.

118

Cramer *Inedita* (*Oxford*): From the nouns in *-os* Alcaeus once uses the genitive τεμένηος for τεμένεος

of the precinct

[1] cf. Eust. *Od.* 1596. 5, Fav. 357, Cram. *A.O.* 1. 325. 30
[2] cf. Lascar. *Op. Gram.* 133 v. where Fρήξεις ἀντὶ ῥήξεις

119

Eust. *Il.* 1155. 40 τείρεα δὲ ἢ παρὰ τὸ εἴρειν . . . ἢ . . . παρὰ τὸ τείρειν, καθὰ καὶ τοῦτο ἐν τοῖς τοῦ Γεωργίου κεῖται. πολλοὶ γάρ, φησίν, ἐκ τῶν ἀστέρων καταπονοῦνται . . . ἐφανέρωσε δέ, φησί, τὸ ε Ἀλκαῖος εἰπὼν

τερέων

δίχα τοῦ ι.

119 A

Prisc. *Inst. Gram.* 7. 7 (*Gram. Lat.* Keil) [de vocativo]: . . . in femininis etiam Alcaeus

Νήρῃ

pro Νηρηΐ[1] posuit, et Theopompus Χάρῃ pro Χάρης.

120[2]

Ox. Pap. 1233. 2. ii.

. . . ὠς λόγος κάκων ἀ[πύφυιε Fέργων]
Περράμῳ καὶ παῖσ[ι Τρόεσσιν ἄλμα[3]]
ἐκ Fέθεν πίκρον·[4] π[ερὶ δ' ἔλλατο φλόξ]
Ἴλιον ἴραν.

5 οὐ τεαύταν[5] Αἰακίδ[αις πόθεννον]
πάντας ἐς γάμον μάκ[αρας καλέσσαις]
ἄγετ' ἐκ Νήρηος ἔλων [μελάθρων]
πάρθενον ἄβραν

[1] mss νερη pro νερης [2] restored by Hunt, Wil., and *E*,

119[1]

Eustathius on the *Iliad*: τείρεα 'constellations' comes either from εἴρειν 'to string' . . . or from τείρειν 'to rub or wear out,'—on which point the following occurs in the writings of Georgius[2]: 'Many of the stars get exhausted . . . and it is clear that the word should be spelt with *ei* (and not *i*) because Alcaeus uses the genitive τειρέων

of the constellations

without the ι.'

119 A

Priscian *Grammar* [on the Vocative]: . . . Even in a feminine noun Alcaeus uses Νήρη

O daughter of Nereus

for Νηρηΐ, while Theopompus makes the vocative of Χάρης 'Chares,' Χάρη.

120

From a Second-Century Papyrus:

. . . Through Helen 'tis said there sprang from evil deeds a branch bitter unto Priam and all the Trojans, and a flame rolled around sacred Ilium. Not such was the dainty maiden whom the son of Aeacus, with all the Gods gathered at his longed-for espousals, took from the palace of Nereus and

[1] cf. Cram. *A.P.* 4. 192. 10 [2] Choeroboscus

C.R. 1914. 76, 1919. 127 [3] = κλάδος cf. *E.M.* 69. 27 [4] ἐκ Fέθεν *E*: P εξ (corr. to εκ) σεθεν ἔλλατο: cf. ἔλσα, ἤλσατο, Hfm. *Gr. Dial.* 2. 486 [5] = τοιαύταν

ἐς δόμον Χέρρωνος· ἔλ[υσε δ' ἄγνᾳ]
10 ζῶμμα πάρθενῳ φιλό[τας ἀγαύω]
Πήλεος καὶ Νηρεΐδων ἀρίστ[ας,]
ἐς δ' ἐνίαυτον

παῖδα γέννατ' αἰμιθέων [κράτιστον]
ὄλβιον ξάνθαν ἐλάτη[ρα πώλων·]
15 οἰ δ' ἀπώλοντ' ἀμφ' Ἐ[λένᾳ Τρόες τε]
καὶ πόλις αὔτων.

Ζ'

ΕΡΩΤΙΚΩΝ

121 πρὸς Μελάνιππον

Hdt. 5. 95 πολεμεόντων δέ σφεων (Μυτιληναίων καὶ Ἀθηναίων) . . . Ἀλκαῖος ὁ ποιητὴς συμβολῆς γενομένης καὶ νικώντων Ἀθηναίων αὐτὸς μὲν φεύγων ἐκφεύγει· τὰ δέ οἱ ὅπλα ἴσχουσι Ἀθηναῖοι καί σφεα ἀνεκρέμασαν πρὸς τὸ Ἀθήναιον τὸ ἐν Σιγείῳ· ταῦτα δὲ Ἀλκαῖος ἐν μέλεϊ ποιήσας ἐπιτιθεῖ ἐς Μυτιλήνην, ἐξαγγελλόμενος τὸ ἑωυτοῦ πάθος Μελανίππῳ ἀνδρὶ ἑταίρῳ.

Strabo 13. 600 Πίττακος δὲ ὁ Μυτιληναῖος πλεύσας ἐπὶ τὸν Φρύνωνα στρατηγὸν (τῶν Ἀθηναίων) διεπολέμει τέως, διατιθεὶς καὶ πάσχων κακῶς· ὅτε καὶ Ἀλκαῖός φησιν ὁ ποιητὴς ἑαυτὸν ἔν τινι ἀγῶνι κακῶς φερόμενον τὰ ὅπλα ῥίψαντα φυγεῖν· λέγει δὲ πρός τινα κήρυκα κελεύσας ἀγγεῖλαι τοῖς ἐν οἴκῳ Ἀλκαῖος σῶς κ.τ.λ.

---

[1] Thetis [2] Achilles [3] a letter

led home to the house of Cheiron, where the love that was betwixt the noble Peleus and the best of all the Nereids[1] loosed the girdle of a pure virgin, and bore them a year afterwards a son that was mightiest of demigods, a victorious driver of bay steeds[2]; but the Trojans and their city were destroyed because of Helen.

Book VII

LOVE POEMS

121 To Melanippus[3]

Herodotus *Histories*: During the war between Mytilene and Athens . . . when a battle took place which left the Athenians victorious, the poet Alcaeus made good his escape, but his arms fell into the hands of the Athenians, who hung them up as an offering in the temple of Athena at Sigeum. This is told by Alcaeus in a poem which he sent to his friend Melanippus at Mytilene saying what had happened to him.

Strabo *Geography*: Pittacus of Mytilene sailed against the Athenian general Phrynon and carried on war against him for some time with ill success. It was during this campaign that the poet Alcaeus tells us how, being hard pressed, he threw away his arms and took to flight; and he addresses the following words to a herald whom he bids take tidings to his friends at home:

e.g.[1] [Κᾶρυξ, εἰς Μυτιλάνναν ἐράταν συθεὶς
φιλτάτῳ Μελανίππῳ φάθ' ὄτ'] Ἄλκαος
σάος ἄρ' οἰ ἔντεα δ' οὔ· κῦτον ἀληκτόϝιν [2]
εἰς Γλαυκώπιον ὀγκρέμμασαν Ἄττικοι.[3]

122 [4] πρὸς Μελάνιππον

Ox. Pap. 1233. 1. ii. 8–20

Τί ὦν ἔ[μμεν ἄρᾱ] Μελάνιππ', ἄμ' ἔμοι; τί [δὲ]
δινν·άεντ' ὄτα κ' [εἰς] Ἀχέροντα [5] μ' ἔη[σι κᾶρ]
ζάβαι[ς ἀ]ελίω κόθαρον φάος [ἐλπίσω]
ὄψεσθ'; ἀλλ' ἄγι, μὴ μεγάλων ἐπ[ιβάλλεο.]
5 καὶ γὰρ Σίσυφος Αἰολίδαις βασίλευς [ἔφα]
ἄνδρων πλεῖστα νοησάμενος [θάνατον φύγην·]
ἀλλὰ καὶ πολύϊδρις ἔων ὐπὰ κᾶρι [δὶς]
[διν]νάεντ' Ἀχέροντ' ἐπέραισε· μ[όρεν δέ ϝοι]
[κάτ]ω μ[όχ]θον ἔχην Κρονίδαις βά[ρυν ἔξοχα]
10 [μέ]λαίνας χθόνος. ἀλλ' ἄγι, μὴ τά[δ' ὀδύρρεο·]
[ἄσ]σα [6] βάσομεν αἴ ποτα κἄλλοτα ν[ῦν μάται.]
[ἀλλ'] ἦν ὄττινα τῶνδε πάθην τα[λασιφρόνως]
[πρόσηκ'· ὄττ' ἄνε]μος βορίαις ἐπι[τέλλεται,]
e.g. [οὐ σόφων ὀνάγην σκάφος εὔρεαν εἰς ἄλα.]

[1] *E* [2] σάος Hfm., ἄρ' οἰ *E*: mss σόος ἄροι, σῶς ἄρει, σοσαροι: ἔντεα δ' Wel: mss ἐνθάδ', ἐνθάδε, ἔνθα δὲ: οὔ· κῦτον

[Speed thee, herald, to lovely Mytilene and say to my dearest Melanippus :] ‘Your Alcaeus is safe as you see,[1] but not his arms; that shield of everlasting might[2] the Athenians have hung up in the temple of the Grey-Eyed Goddess.’

122 To Melanippus[3]

From a Second-Century Papyrus:

O why, Melanippus, do you pray you might be with me? or why, when once Fate has sent me to eddying Acheron, shall I hope to re-cross it and see again the pure light of the sun? Nay, set not your desire on things too great. King Sisyphus son of Aeolus, he thought with a craft unsurpassed to have escaped death; but for all his cunning he crossed the eddying Acheron in fate the second time, and the Son of Cronus ordained that he should have below a toil the woefullest in all the world. So I pray you bewail not these things. If ever cries were unavailing, our cries are unavailing now. Assuredly some of these things were to be suffered with an enduring heart. When the wind rises in the north[4] [no skilful pilot puts out into the wide sea.]

[1] the Greek is ‘say that his Alcaeus etc.’ [2] the epithet, like the use of the word ‘herald,’ has a humorous intention [3] letter from exile [4] Pittacus, who banished him, was of low birth and Thracian extraction

---

E (= *σκῦτον* cf. Hom. *ἐκέδασσε* for *ἐσκέδ.*, *κάπετος* from *σκάπτω*, and Arch. *ἐγκῦτι*, Lat. *cŭtis*) : mss *οὐκυτόν*, *οὐχυτον*, *οὐκ αὐτὸν*, *οὐ κεῖται* : *ἀληκτόϜιν* *E* : mss *-ρὶν*, *-ρὴν* [3] *E* (Γλ. Dind.) : for *-κρέμμ.* cf. Hfm. 296, *ὀννώριvε* 72 : mss *ἐς γλαυκωπὸν ἱερὸν ὃν ἐκρέμασαν* Ἄ. [4] restored by Hunt, Wil., *E*, *C.R.* 1914. 75 [5] P *οταμε* . . . *δινναενταχεροντα* against metre [6] P]*τα* *i. e.* *ἅττα*

123 πρὸς Μένωνα

Heph. 44 [π. δακτυλικοῦ]· τὸ μὲν οὖν Αἰολικὸν ἔπος τὸ καταληκτικὸν τοιοῦτόν ἐστι·

Κέλομαί τινα τὸν χαρίεντα Μένωνα κάλεσσαι,
αἰ χρῆ συμποσίας ἐπόνασιν ἔμοι Ϝε γένεσθαι.[1]

124

Ibid. [π. ἐπιωνικοῦ τοῦ ἀπὸ μείζονος]· τρίμετρον δὲ ἀκατάληκτον τὸ τούτου [i. e. *fr.* 47] περιττεῦον συλλαβῇ τῇ τελευταίᾳ, καλούμενον δὲ Ἀλκαϊκὸν δωδεκασύλλαβον, οἷον·

Ἰόπλοκ' ἄγνα μελλιχόμειδε Σάπφοι,
θέλω τι Ϝείπην ἀλλά με κωλύει αἴδως.[2]

125

Ibid. 32 [π. ἰαμβικοῦ]· ἔστι δὲ ἐπίσημα ἐν αὐτῷ ἀκατάληκτα μὲν δίμετρα οἷον . ., τετράμετρον δὲ οἷον τὸ Ἀλκαίου·

Δέξαι με κωμάζοντα, δέξαι, λίσσομαί σε, λίσσομαι.

126

Sch. Plat. *Symp.* 217 e 'οἶνος καὶ ἀλήθεια,' ἐπὶ τῶν ἐν μέθῃ τὴν ἀλήθειαν λεγόντων· ἔστι δὲ ᾄσματος Ἀλκαίου ἀρχή·

Οἶνος, ὦ φίλε παῖ, καὶ ἀλάθεα [3]

καὶ Θεόκριτος.

[1] *E*: mss γεγενῆσθαι: Fick γε γένεσθαι [2] l. 2 only in Arist: Ϝείπην Herm: mss τ' εἰπῆν [3] (so Theocr.) Matthiae: mss ἀλάθεια

123 To Menon [1]

Hephaestion *Handbook of Metre* [on dactylics]: The catalectic Aeolic line is as follows:

I bid them call the pretty Menon, if I may have him for an added joy at my drinking-bout.

124

The Same [on the *epionicum a majore*]: The acatalectic trimeter, which exceeds this by the first syllable and is called the Alcaic twelve-syllable, is like this:

Pure Sappho of the violet tresses and the gentle smile, I would fain tell you something, did not shame prevent me.[2]

125 [3]

The Same [on the iambic]: The best-known acatalectic types of it are dimeters like . ., and tetrameters like this of Alcaeus:

Pray, pray receive, receive your serenader.

126

Scholiast on Plato *Symposium*: 'Wine and truth,' a saying used of those who speak the truth when drunk; and it is the beginning of a song of Alcaeus:

Wine, my dear boy, and truth . . .

and it occurs in Theocritus.[4]

[1] an invitation [2] l. 2 from Arist. *Rhet.* 1. 9 (see Sa. 119); cf. Cram. *A.P.* 1. 266. 25 [3] cf. Sch. Heph., Sch. Ar. *Plut.* 302, *Paroem.* 2. 363 [4] 29. 1

127

Sch. Pind. *O.* 11. 15 [Ζεφυρίων Λόκρων γενεὰν ἀλέγων]· ἀλέγων· μεριμνῶν.[1] καὶ Ἀλκαῖος·

. . . . οὐ <γὰρ> ἔγω Λύκον
ἐν Μοίσαισ' ἀλέγω·

παρὰ τὸ ἀλέγειν καὶ φροντίδα ποιεῖν.

128[2]

Ox. Pap. 1233. 33. 5–7

Ἔπετον Κυπρογενήας παλάμαισιν
e. g.[3] [δολομήδεσσι τύπεις·] ὄπποσέ κ[εν γὰρ]
[ἄλος ἢ γᾶς προφύγω, κῆσ]ε πόλω[ν[4] με]
[κίχεν Ὦρος . . . .]

129

Cram. *A.O.* 1. 413. 23 ζητεῖται <τὸ>[3] παρὰ τῷ Ἀλκαίῳ θηλυκόν

τερένας ἄνθος ὀπώρας

πῶς ἡ τέρενα εἴρηκεν, καὶ ἔστιν εἰπεῖν ὅτι ἀπὸ τοῦ τέρην ἡ γενικὴ τέρενος· καὶ μετάγεται ἡ γενικὴ εἰς εὐθεῖαν ὁ τέρενος· ἀπὸ τούτου θηλυκὸν τερένη, τερένης, καὶ Αἰολικῶς <τερένας>·[3] τερένας κ.τ.λ.

130, 131

Apoll. *Pron.* 80. 17 . . . καὶ ἔτι ὁμοίως (ἐν συνθέσει) παρὰ τῷ αὐτῷ Ἀλκαίῳ ἐν ἑβδόμῳ·

. . . . σὺ δὲ σαύτῳ τομίας ἔσῃ.[5]

. . . . ἀλλὰ σαύτῳ πεδέχων ἄϜως
πρὸς πόσιν[6] . . . . .

[1] mss ὕμνων [2] line 1 from Cram. *A.O.* 1. 144–5 [3] *E*
[4] πόλεις ? [5] τομίας Bast : mss το . μαις [6] ἀλλὰ σὺ σαύτῳ? ἄϜως *E* = αὔως (gen.) : or ἄϜας from αὖα (new nom. from acc. αὖα cf. Sa. 176) cf. ἄας Zenod. *Il.* 8. 470 : mss αβας

127

Scholiast on Pindar ['bearing in mind the Locrians of the West']: ἀλέγων: 'caring for,' 'thinking of'; compare Alcaeus:

. . . for I do not reckon Lycus among the Muses;[1]

ἀλέγω from ἀλέγειν 'to think about.'[2]

128[3]

From a Second-Century Papyrus:

I am thrown by the wily arts of the Cyprus-born; for whithersoever [on sea or land I flee, thither] ranging [hath Love overtaken me.]

129

Cramer *Inedita* (*Oxford*): It is asked with regard to the feminine found in Alcaeus

the soft smooth bloom of the fruiting-time

how he has come to use the form τέρενα 'soft, smooth'; and the answer is that the genitive of τέρην is τέρενος, and the genitive is transferred to the nominative which thus becomes τέρενος with a feminine τερένη, of which the genitive is τερένης, Aeolic τερένας, as above.

130, 131

Apollonius *Pronouns* [ἑαυτῷ 'to himself,' etc.]: . . . and similarly, moreover, as a single word in the seventh Book of the same Alcaeus

. . . and you will be your own steward.[4]

and:

. . . but sharing the morn with yourself a-drinking[5]

[1] cf. Hor. 1. 32. 9, who mentions Lycus, and, for the tone Cic. *N.D.* 1. 28 *naevus in articulo pueri delectat Alcaeus* etc.
[2] the quotation illustrates a different meaning [3] cf. Cram. *A.O.* 1. 144. 5, *E.M.* 666. 51, Fav. 354 [4] *i. e.* eat and drink whatever you like? [5] *i. e.* alone

132

Heph. 14 [π. κοινῆς]· ἐὰν μέντοι ἐν τῇ προτέρᾳ συλλαβῇ τελικὸν ᾖ τὸ ἄφωνον, τῆς δὲ δευτέρας ἀρκτικὸν τὸ ὑγρόν, οὐκέτι γίνεται κοινὴ <ἡ> συλλαβή, ἀλλὰ ἄντικρυς μάκρα, ὡς παρὰ Ἀλκαίῳ·

Ἔκ μ' ἔλᾱσας ἀλγέων . . . .

Η'

ΕΠΑΙΝΗΣΙΩΝ[1]

133[2] πρὸς Ἀντιμενίδαν

Strabo 13. 617 ἄνδρας δ' ἔσχεν (ἡ Μιτυλήνη) ἐνδόξους τὸ παλαιὸν μὲν Πιττακόν, ἕνα τῶν Ἑπτὰ Σοφῶν, καὶ τὸν ποιητὴν Ἀλκαῖον καὶ τὸν ἀδελφὸν Ἀντιμενίδαν, ὅν φησιν Ἀλκαῖος Βαβυλωνίοις συμμαχοῦντα τελέσαι μέγαν ἆθλον καὶ ἐκ πόνων αὐτοὺς ῥύσασθαι κτείναντα ἄνδρα μαχαίταν βασιληΐων παλαιστάν, ὥς φησι, κ.τ.λ.

Heph. 63 [π. ἀντισπαστικοῦ]· τὸ δὲ ἀκατάληκτον (τῶν τριμέτρων) τὸ μόνην τὴν τελευταίαν ἔχον ἰαμβικὴν καλεῖται Ἀσκληπιάδειον, οἷον τὸ Ἀλκαίου·

Ἦλθες ἐκ περάτων γᾶς ἐλεφαντίναν
λάβαν τῶ ξίφεος χρυσοδέταν ἔχων,

[1] this title, being founded on an emendation of *fr.* 138, is uncertain; if right, the Aeolic form with η would seem to point either to A. himself or some early Lesbian as first collector of the poems [2] ll. 1–2 Heph., 3–7 *E e. g.*, 8–10 O. Müller, 3 and 5–10 from Str., who shows that the name was in the poem (and without ictus-lengthening it is im-

132

Hephaestion *Handbook of Metre* [on 'common' syllables]: If, however, the mute is the final sound of the first syllable,[1] and the liquid the initial sound of the second, the first syllable is not then, as in the previous case, 'common' or doubtful, but altogether long; compare Alcaeus:

You have made me forget all my sorrows

Book VIII[2]

ENCOMIA

133[3] To Antimenidas

Strabo *Geography*: Mytilene has had many famous citizens. In ancient times there was Pittacus, one of the Seven Sages, and the poet Alcaeus and his brother Antimenidas, of whom Alcaeus tells that while fighting for the Babylonians he performed a mighty deed and saved them from troubles by slaying a warrior, as he says, etc.

Hephaestion *Handbook of Metre* [on the antispastic]: The acatalectic trimeter which has the last 'meter' iambic is called the Asclepiad, for instance Alcaeus:

You have come from the ends of the earth, [dear

[1] in the example ἐκ; cf. Atil. Fort. 302 K. who says Hor. took the metre of *Non ebur nec aureum*, *Od.* 2. 18, from Alc. who often used it [2] I have placed here unclassifiable fragments of a personal type [3] cf. Liban. 1. 406

possible in any Lesbian metre), 4–5 from Hesych. (= *B* 153) τετραμαρήων· πλίνθων· τετρα. πλ. κατὰ τέγματα· Ἀλκαῖος (so *B-E*, cf. τετεγάσμενοι 28: mss τετραβαρ. πλ. καὶ τάγματα)

e.g. [φίλ' Ἀντιμμενίδα, τῷ ποτὰ χράμενος][1]
τοῖσι τετραμαρήων κατὰ τέγματα
5 πλίνθων ναιετάοισιν Βαβυλωνίοις
συμμάχεις ἐτέλεσσας μέγαν αὔεθλον
κἀκ πόλλαν ὀνίαν ἄσφε[2] Ϝερύσσαο
κτένναις ἄνδρα μαχαίταν βασιληΐων[3]
παλαίσταν ἀπυλείποντα μόναν ἴαν[4]
10 παχέων ἀπὺ πέμπων . . . .

134

Ox. Pap. 1233. 11. 10–11

. . . .]Βαβύλωνος ἴρας
. . . .]ν Ἀσκάλωνα

135

Harpocr. 168 Σκυθικαί· . . . εἶδός τι ὑποδήματός εἰσιν αἱ Σκυθικαί· καὶ Ἀλκαῖος ἐν η΄.[5]

καὶ Σκυθίκαις ὐπαδησάμενος

136

Et. Mag. 513. 33

Κῖκις[6]

σημαίνει τὸν ἀδελφὸν τοῦ Ἀλκαίου· γίνεται παρὰ τὸ κῖκυς ὃ σημαίνει τὴν ἰσχύν.

[1] Ἀντιμμ. cf. ὀγκρέμμασαν 121, ὀννώρινε 72: τῷ relative supplying needed epithet to τῶ ξίφεος [2] necessary to the syntax [3] *B*: mss -ηων [4] μόναν ἴαν Ahr: mss μόνον μίαν [5] mss also ἐν νή, ἐν κ' [6] prob. dimin. of *e.g.* Κίκερμος Fick: mss κίκις . . . κίκυς

Antimenidas,] with the gold-bound ivory heft of the sword [with which, fighting for the Babylonians who dwell in houses of bricks four hands long,[1] you performed a mighty deed and saved them all from grievous troubles] by slaying a warrior who wanted but one palm's breadth of five royal cubits of stature.

134

From a Second-Century Papyrus:

. . . of sacred Babylon . . . Ascalon . . .[2]

135[3]

Harpocration *Lexicon to the Attic Orators*: Σκυθικαί . . . 'Scythians' are a kind of shoe; compare Alcaeus Book viii:

and shod with Scythians

136

Etymologicum Magnum:

Cîcis

is the brother of Alcaeus; from κῖκυς, meaning 'strength.'

[1] the usual size of a Babylonian brick *temp.* Nebuchadnezzar is about 12 × 12 × 3½ in.; these bricks often bear his name, cf. Layard *Nineveh*, p. 296; the palm's breadth or hand was rather over 3 in. [2] prob. ref. to Antimenidas' service with Nebuchadnezzar in Palestine [3] cf. Suid.

137 A and B

Apoll. *Pron.* 80. 14 [ἑαυτόν κ.τ.λ.]· καὶ παρὰ τοῖς Αἰολικοῖς δὲ ὡς ἐν παραθέσει ἀνεγνώσθη· (Sa. 15)·

ἔμ' αὔτῳ παλαμάσομαι

ἀλλὰ μάχεται [1] τό·

. . . . νόον δὲ Ϝαύτω
πάμπαν ἀέρρει.[2]

ἅπερ ἀσύνηθες ἐν ἁπλότητι μὴ οὐχὶ τὸ ε προσλαμβάνειν, καὶ ἔτι ὁμοίως παρὰ τῷ αὐτῷ Ἀλκαίῳ (130)

138

Hesych. ἐπαίνους· τὰς κρίσεις καὶ τὰς συμβουλίας καὶ τὰς ἀρχ<αιρ>εσίας. Σοφοκλῆς Θυέστῃ Σικυωνίῳ καὶ Ἀλκαῖος ταῖς Ἐπαινήσεσιν.[3]

139

Vet. Et. Mag. Miller 57 ἀχνάσδημι, ὡς παρ' Ἀλκαίῳ·

Ἀχνάσδημι κάλως· οὔτι γὰρ οἰ φίλοι.[4]

140

Procl. Hes. *Op.* 719 [εἰ δὲ κάκον εἴπῃς, τάχα κ' αὐτὸς μεῖζον ἀκούσαις]· Ἀλκαῖος·

. . . . αἰ Ϝείποις τὰ θέλῃς, ἀκούσαις
τά κ' οὐ θέλῃς.[5]

[1] mss ἐμάχετο [2] νόον Bast: mss νόῳ: δὲ Ϝαύτω Ahr: mss δ' ἑαύτω: Ap. read δὲ αὔτω [3] *E* 'in the *Encomia*' (see p. 402 n. 1): mss ἀλκέοι ταῖς ἐπαινήταισιν (ται corr. to τε) [4] *E*, cf. Plat. *Symp.* 194 a εὖ καὶ μάλ' ἂν φόβοιο, *Theaet.* 156 a μάλ' εὖ ἄμουσοι, *Dead Adonis* 32: mss κακῶς: οὔτι *E.M.*: *Vet. E.M.* οὔτε [5] (subjunctive) *E* bis: mss θέλεις

137 A[1] and B

Apollonius *Pronouns* [on reflexives]: And in Aeolic the reflexive is read as two words, as (Sa. 15) and

I shall contrive for myself

but the following is contrary:

and he heartens himself altogether;

which is unusual in having the simple form without the *e*; and moreover similarly in the same Alcaeus: (*fr.* 130).

138

Hesychius ἐπαίνους 'praises': decisions, recommendations, elections; Sophocles in the *Thyestes Sicyonius;* and Alcaeus in the *Encomia.*

139[2]

Old Etymologicum Magnum: ἀχνάσδημι 'to mourn' as in Alcaeus:

Deeply do I mourn, for my friends are nothing worth.

140[3]

Proclus on Hesiod *Works and Days* [If thou sayest an ill thing, soon shalt thou hear a greater thyself]: compare Alcaeus:

If you say what you choose, you will hear what you choose not.

[1] also in Cram. *A.P.* 4. 35. 16, Cyrill. 185. 3, Suid. [2] cf. *E.M.* 181. 44 [3] cf. *Paroem.* 1. p. 285: metre as 124

141

Sch. Ar. *Av.* 1410 [ὄρνιθες τίνες οἵδ' οὐδὲν ἔχοντες πτεροποικίλοι, τανυσίπτερε ποικίλα χελιδοῖ;]· τινὲς παρὰ τὸ Ἀλκαίου·

Ὄρνιθες τίνες οἵδ' ὠκεάνω γᾶς τ' ἀπὺ περράτων
ἦλθον πανέλοπες ποικιλόδερροι τανυσίπτεροι;[1]

142

Hdn. π.μ.λ. (2. 933. 14 Lentz) ὁ γοῦν Ἀλκαῖος κείνοθεν ἐστὶν ὅπου ἀποφήνατο αὐτό·

αἰ γὰρ κἄλλοθεν ἔλθη αἶ δὲ φάη κήνοθεν
ἔμμεναι[2]

143

Sch. *Il.* 21. 319 (Nicole 1. 203): χέραδος· Ἀπολλόδωρος τὸ πλῆθος τῶν θαλαττίων καὶ ποταμίων λίθων, οὓς ἡμεῖς τροχάλους· οἱ δὲ χεράδια[3] καλοῦσιν ὄντας χειροπληθεῖς· ἔστι δὲ ἡ λέξις παρὰ Ἀλκαίῳ·

αἰ δὴ μὰν χέραδος μὴ εὖ βεβάωτ' ἐργάσιμον
λίθον
κίνης,[4] καί κε Ϝίσως τὰν κεφάλαν ἀργαλίαν
ἔχοις.

144

Sch. *Od.* 21. 71 [ἐπισχεσίην]· καὶ Ἀλκαῖος·

οὐδέ τι μυννάμενος ἄλλυι τὸ νόημα . . .[5]

ἀντὶ τοῦ προφασιζόμενος, ἀλλαχοῦ ἀποτρέπων τὸ ἑαυτοῦ νόημα.

[1] γᾶς τ' Heck.-Blf.: mss γὰρ: ἦλθον: mss also ἦνθον
[2] αἶ δὲ φάη (opt.) *E*, αἶ = ἀεί, δέ in apod.: mss δὲ φοι: *B* τόδε φαῖ (= φαίη) [3] ms χερμάδια [4] *E* (or μὴ βεβάωτ'? cf. Hesych. βεβάως· βεβηκώς, ἱστάμενος): mss μὴ βεβάως κ.τ.λ: ἔχοις: ms ἔχοι [5] μύνν. pres. partcp. μυνάομαι Hfm.: mss μυν.: ἄλλυι Seid.: mss Sch. ἄλλα, Eust. ἄλλο

141

Scholiast on Aristophanes *Birds* [What birds are these that have nothing at all, birds motley-winged, O motley swallow of widespread wing?[1]]: Some commentators say this is from Alcaeus' lines:

What birds are these which have come from the ends of the earth and the ocean, wildgeese of motley neck and widespread wing?

142

Herodian *Words without Parallel*: Alcaeus sometimes actually uses the form κείνοθεν 'thence'; compare:

For even if he comes from another place, he can always say that he is come from that.[2]

143

Scholiast on *Iliad*: χέραδος 'stone-heap': according to Apollodorus this means a quantity of stones from the sea or from a river, which we call pebbles; others call them χεράδια or 'hand-stones' because one of them just fills the hand. The word occurs in Alcaeus:

If you move from a stone-heap a block of stone that is not firm set, then 'tis like you will get a sore head.

144[3]

Scholiast on *Odyssey* ['pretext, prevarication']: compare Alcaeus:

. . . nor prevaricating his intent at all;

that is, excusing or cloaking, turning his intention elsewhither.

[1] called a σκόλιον or drinking-song in l. 1416, but this may not be technically accurate for the original [2] emendation and translation uncertain [3] cf. Eust. *Od.* 1901. 52, *E.M.* 594. 55, Matr. *An.* 389

145

Vet. Et. Mag. Reitz. δήω· σημαίνει τὸ εὑρίσκω ἀπὸ τοῦ δέω, ὃ σημαίνει τὸ εὑρίσκειν, οὗ μέμνηται Ἀλκαῖος·

ἔγω μὲν οὐ δέω τάδε μαρτύρεντας·[1]

κατ' ἔκτασιν δήω.

146

Hdn. π.μ.λ. (2. 941. 28 Lentz) . . . μάθος. Ἀλκαῖος·

ἀπ πατέρων μάθος[2]

147, 148

Apoll. *Pron.* 95. 14 [ἀμέων]· ὁμοιῶς Αἰολεῖς· Ἀλκαῖος· (78)· ἐπὶ δὲ τῆς συνάρθρου·

πατέρων ἄμμων

καὶ τῇ ἐντελεστέρᾳ·

ἀμμετέρων ἀχέων[3]

149

Strabo 1. 37 [π. Νείλου]· τὸ δὲ πλείοσι στόμασιν ἐκδιδόναι κοινὸν καὶ πλειόνων, ὥστ' οὐκ ἄξιον μνήμης ὑπέλαβε (ὁ Ὅμηρος), καὶ ταῦτα πρὸς εἰδότας· καθάπερ οὐδ' Ἀλκαῖος, καίτοι φήσας ἀφῖχθαι καὶ αὐτὸς εἰς Αἴγυπτον.

150[4]

Plut. *Div. Am.* 5 χάριεν γὰρ ἅμα ταῖς ἡδοναῖς συνεκλιπεῖν τὰς ἐπιθυμίας, ἃς μήτε ἄνδρα φησὶν Ἀλκαῖος διαφυγεῖν μήτε γυναῖκα.

e.g. . . . . ὤν ἐπιθυμίαις
| οὔτ' ἄνηρ ζαπέφυγγ' οὔτε γύνα ποτά.

[1] mss also μέν κ' οὐ and ταῦτα; Hesych. expl. δήεις and

145 [1]

Old Etymologicum Magnum: δήω· this means 'I find,' from δέω with the same meaning used by Alcaeus:

For my part I find no witnesses of this; [2]

lengthened to δήω.

146

Herodian *Words without Parallel*: μάθος 'learning'; compare Alcaeus:

We learn from our fathers. [3]

147, 148

Apollonius *Pronouns* [ἀμεῶν 'of us']: Similarly in Aeolic: compare Alcaeus (78); and in the adjectival form ἄμμων; compare:

of our fathers

and the fuller form ἀμμετέρων; compare

of our troubles

149

Strabo *Geography* [on the Nile]: Its entering the sea by several mouths, however, is a characteristic it shares with other rivers, so that Homer did not consider it worthy of mention, particularly as it was well-known to his audience. Nor is Alcaeus more communicative, although he declares that he had been in Egypt himself.

150

Plutarch *Love of Riches*: For it is a good thing that we leave behind along with the pleasures (of love) the desires that belong to them, desires which according to Alcaeus are escaped neither by man nor woman.

[1] cf. *E.M.* 264. 19 [2] *or* 'I shall find' [3] *or* perh. 'We learn by suffering'

δήετε as futures in sense [2] Nauck ἀπ παθέων μ. cf. proverb πάθος μάθος [3] mss ἀχαιῶν [4] cf. 115: ζαπ. = διαπέφευγε

151

Ath. 3. 73 e [π. σικύου]· Ἀττικοὶ μὲν οὖν ἀεὶ τρισυλλάβως, Ἀλκαῖος δέ·

. . . . δάκη τῶν σίκυων·[1]

φησίν, ἀπὸ εὐθείας τῆς σίκυς, ὡς στάχυς στάχυος.

152

Hesych. τετράϜων· ὄρνεόν τι· Ἀλκαῖος·

τετράϜωσιν ἀήδονας[2]

153[3]

Vet. Et. Mag. Reitz. σισύρνας καὶ σισύρας· τὰ δασέα δέρματα τὰ τετριχωμένα· καὶ Ἀλκαῖος ὁ μελοποιός·

ἔνδυς σισύρναν

154[4]

Zenob. *Paroem.* 1. 31 (cf. 2. 61)

ἀντὶ κάκω κύνος ὖν ἀπαίτεις·[5]

ἐπὶ τῶν κακὰ[6] ἀντὶ τῶν κακῶν ἀπαιτούντων.

155[4]

Apostol. *Paroem.* 2. 669 (cf. 2. 525)

φεύγων τέφραν εἰς ἀνθρακίαν πέτεν·[7]

ἐπὶ τῶν ἀπὸ ἡττόνων χείροσι περιπεσόντων κακοῖς.

[1] mss δάκη φησί τ. σικύων: σίκυων *E* or the example would not prove Ath.'s statement; cf. Sa. 87 [2] *B-E*: mss τετράδων· ὁ. τι· Ἀ. | τετράδυσιν· ἀήδονας [3] added by Hfm.

151

Athenaeus *Doctors at Dinner* [on cucumbers]: In the Attic dialect the word is always of three syllables, but Alcaeus says:

. . . takes bites of the cucumbers;

σίκυων being from a nominative *σίκυς*, as *στάχυς* 'ear of corn,' genitive *στάχυος*.

152

Hesychius *Glossary*: Pheasant: A kind of bird; Alcaeus:

[compare] nightingales to pheasants [in song]

153

Old Etymologicum Magnum: *σισύρνα* and *σισύρα*: thick skins covered with hair; compare the lyric poet Alcaeus:

clad in a skin

154

Zenobius *Proverbs*:

Asking for a pig in place of a bad dog;[1]

a saying used of those who ask for a bad thing to replace a bad thing.

155

Apostolius *Proverbs*:

In fleeing the ashes he's fallen into the coals;

a saying used of those who fall from less into greater misfortune.

[1] ref. perh. to one of the tyrants

---

[4] added by *E*; metre 'Alcaic' [5] mss *κακοῦ*, *κακῆς* and *ἀπαιτεῖς* [6] mss also *καλὰ* [7] mss *τ. φ.* and *ἔπεσεν*

Θ΄ καὶ Ι΄

ΣΚΟΛΙΩΝ

156[1]

Berliner Klassikertexte 5. 2. 9810

'. . [πᾷ χρῆ]ν ἀρύστηρ' ἐσκέραμεν μέγαν;
[τί τόσσ]α μόχθης, τοῦτ' ἔμεθεν σύνεις
[ὡς οὔ τι] μὴ τὤξαυος[2] ἄλλως
[ἄμμαρ ἔ]μοι μεθύων ἀείσῃς;

5 [τί δὴ θα]λάσσας φειδόμεθ', ὡς κάρον
[χειμω]νοείδην αἶθρον ἐπήμενοι;
[αἰ δ' ἐνσ]τάθεντες ὡς τάχιστα
[τάν τε χ]άδαν[3] καμάκων ἔλοντες

[ἄπ νᾶα] λύσαμεν, προτ' ἐνώπια
10 [κέρα τρό]ποντες, καί κ' ἰθαρώτεροι
[φυίημ]εν ἰλλάεντι θύμῳ
[κἄτε κ' ἀ]μύστιδος ἔργον εἴη.'

[νώθην] δ'[4] ὀνάρταις χέρρα σύ μοι ἐμμάτων
['Ὁ παῖς,' ἔφαισ]θ', 'ἔμῳ φ[ερέ]τω κάρᾳ
e.g. [γνόφαλλον· οὐ γὰρ] εἰστίθησιν
[εἰς τὸ πλοῖον μ' ὄ]δε τᾷδ' ἀοίδᾳ·

[οὔτοι σὺ τὸν νῶν,] ἄγρι' ἄϋτά, μοι
[κίνῃς, ὅ γε βρύχων] ἄτε πῦρ μέγα
[οὐ βρατέραν ἔλαν[5]] τίθησθα
20 [τάνδε φέρην, χαλεπωτέραν δέ.']

[1] restored by *E*, *C.R.* 1909. 72, 1917. 9 [2] adj. [3] handle,

Books IX and X

DRINKING SONGS

156

From a Second-Century Papyrus:

'... What need to have mixed in the great bowl? Why labour so, when I tell you that I will never have you to waste the livelong day in wassailing and song? O why spare we to use the sea, suffering the winter-cool freshness of the morning to pass like a drunken sleep? If we had but gone quickly aboard, taken hold of the tiller, and loosed the ship from her moorings the while we turned the sailyard to front the breeze, then merrier should we be and light of heart, and it would be as easy work as a long draught of wine.' But hanging a [listless] arm upon my sleeve you cried, '[The lad] may bring [a cushion] for my head; for this fellow's song doth not put me [in his boat. Never think you disturb my mind,] you wild clamourer, [though with your roaring] like a great fire you make it [harder rather than easier to bear this heat.']

---

tiller, cf. χανδάνω, λαβή λαμβάνω [4] δ': P τ [5] ἔλαν = εἴλην, cf. Hesych. γέλαν (i. e. Ϝέλαν)

157

Ath. 10. 430 a κατὰ γὰρ πᾶσαν ὥραν καὶ πᾶσαν περίστασιν πίνων ὁ ποιητὴς οὗτος (Ἀλκαῖος) εὑρίσκεται· χειμῶνος μὲν ἐν τούτοις·

Νεύει μὲν ὁ Ζεῦς, ἐν δ' ὀράνῳ μέγας
χείμων, πεπάγαισιν δ' ὐδάτων ῥόαι·[1]
. . . .
. . . .
5 κάββαλλε τὸν χείμων', ἐπὶ μὲν τίθεις
πῦρ, ἐν δὲ κέρναις οἶνον ἀφειδέως
μέλιχρον, αὐτὰρ ἀμφὶ κόρσᾳ
μάλθακον ἀμφιδύω[2] γνόφαλλον.

158

Ibid. . . . ἐν δὲ τοῖς συμπτώμασιν·

Οὐ χρῆ κάκοισι θῦμον ἐπιτρέπην·[3]
προκόψομεν γὰρ οὖδεν, ἀσάμενοι
σ',[4] ὦ Βύκχι· φάρμακον δ' ἄριστον
οἶνον ἐνικαμένοις μεθύσθην.

159[5]

Ibid. 15. 674 c ἐκάλουν δὲ καὶ οἷς περιεδέοντο τὸν τράχηλον στεφάνους ὑποθυμίδας, ὡς Ἀλκαῖος ἐν τούτοις·

ἀλλ' ἀνήτω μὲν περὶ ταῖς δέραισι
περθέτω πλέκταις ὐπαθύμιδάς τις,
κὰδ δὲ χευάτω μύρον ἆδυ κὰτ τῶ
στήθεος ἄμμι.

[1] νεύει *E*, cf. Anacr. 6, Hor. *Epod*. 13. 1 : mss ὕει, but rain is incompatible with frost : Heck. νίφει : mss also ἐκ δ'
[2] imp. mid. *E* : mss ἀμφι, ἀμφὶ from above
[3] θῦμον Steph : mss μῦθον
[4] ἀσάμενοι σ(οὶ) ὦ *E* : mss ασαμενοι ὦ,

157[1]

Athenaeus *Doctors at Dinner*: For the poet Alcaeus is found drinking at every time and on every occasion; in the winter in these lines:

The Sky-God bows himself; there is a great storm in the heavens, the streams of water are frozen fast. . . . Defy the storm with a good fire and a bountiful mixing of honey-sweet wine, and then put a soft cushion on either side your brow.

158

The Same: . . . and in his misfortune, in this passage:

It is ill yielding the heart to mischance; for we shall make no advance if we weary of thee, O Bacchus, and the best medicine is to call for wine and drink deep.

159[2]

The Same: They called the garlands which they used to tie round their necks *hypothymides*; compare Alcaeus:

But let them put garlands woven of anise about our necks and pour sweet myrrh over our bosoms.[3]

[1] cf. Hdn. π.μ.λ. 7. 27 Lentz, Long. *Past.* 3. 3 [2] cf. Poll. 6. 107, Sch. Theocr. 7. 63, Ath. 678 d [3] ll. 3–4 put here by *B* from Ath. 687 d 'and that bravest and moreover most warlike of poets, Alcaeus, says "And pour, etc."'

ἀσάμενος ὦ [5] ll. 1–2 here, 3–4 Ibid. 687 d καὶ ὁ ἀνδρειότατος δὲ προσέτι δὲ καὶ πολεμικ<ώτατ>ος ποιητὴς Ἀλκαῖος ἔφη 'κὰδ κ.τ.λ.

160

Arist. *Pol.* 1285 a 33 ἦρχον δ' οἱ μὲν (τῶν αἰσυμνητῶν) διὰ βίου τὴν ἀρχὴν ταύτην, οἱ δὲ μέχρι τινῶν ὡρισμένων χρόνων ἢ πράξεων, οἷον εἵλοντό ποτε Μυτιληναῖοι Πιττακὸν πρὸς τοὺς φυγάδας ὧν προειστήκεσαν Ἀντιμενίδης καὶ Ἀλκαῖος ὁ ποιητής. δηλοῖ δ' Ἀλκαῖος ὅτι τύραννον εἵλοντο τὸν Πιττακὸν ἔν τινι τῶν Σκολιῶν Μελῶν· ἐπιτιμᾷ γὰρ ὅτι·

. . . . φώνᾳ δ' ἀθρόᾳ[1] τὸν κακοπάτριδα
Φίττακον[2] πόλιος τᾶς ἀχόλω καὶ βαρυδαίμονος
ἐστάσαντο τύραννον μέγ' ἐπαίνεντες[3] ἀόλλεες.

161[4]

Procl. Hes. *Op.* 584 [ἦμος δὲ σκόλυμός τ' ἀνθεῖ καὶ ἠχέτα τέττιξ | δενδρέῳ ἐφεζόμενος λιγυρὴν καταχεύατ' ἀοιδὴν | πυκνὸν ὑπὸ πτερύγων, θέρεος καματώδεος ὥρῃ, τῆμος πιόταταί τ' αἶγες καὶ οἶνος ἄριστος, | μαχλόταται δὲ γυναῖκες, ἀφαυρότατοι δέ τοι ἄνδρες | εἰσίν, ἐπεὶ κεφαλὴν καὶ γούνατα Σείριος ἄζει]· τοιαῦτα δὲ καὶ τὸν Ἀλκαῖον ᾄδειν·

Τέγγε πλεύμονας οἴνῳ· τὸ γὰρ ἄστρον περιτέλλεται,
ἀ δ' ὤρα χαλέπα, πάντα δὲ δίψαισ' ὐπὰ καύματος,
ἄχη δ' ἐκ πετάλων Ϝάδεα τέττιξ <ἐπιδενδρίων>[5]
ἄνθη δὲ σκόλυμος· νῦν δὲ γύναικες μιαρώταται[6]
5 λέπτοι δ' ἄνδρες ἐπεὶ καὶ κεφάλαν καὶ γόνα Σείριος
ἄζει[7] . . . .

[1] Reis.-*E* from Plut. where the form φωναὶ, i.e. φώνᾳ, shows that ἀ. φ. is not his rendering of ἀόλλεες: not in Arist. [2] *E*, so Sch. 41, Lesb. coin Mion. *Sup.* 6. p. 64, cf. Poll. 2. 175 where mss Ψιττακόν: mss here Πιττ. [3] ἀχόλω Schn. 'restless,' cf. χαλάω and Hesych. χαλιά· ἡσυχία: ἐπαίνεντες Ahr: mss -νέοντες [4] πάντα κ.τ.λ. only in Ath. [5] Ϝάδεα Graevius-Seid: mss τάδε ἂν: ἐπιδενδρίων *E*, cf. Jul. *Ep.* 24:

160[1]

Aristotle *Politics*: Some aesymnetes ruled for life, others only for definite periods or till they had accomplished definite tasks, as the Mytileneans chose Pittacus to deal with the exiles under Antimenidas and the poet Alcaeus. Now Alcaeus shows that Pittacus was elected tyrant in one of his *Drinking-songs*, where he chides his fellow-countrymen saying:

With one voice they have set up the base-born Pittacus to be tyrant of their spiritless and ill-starred country, shouting his praise by their thousands.[2]

161[3]

Proclus on Hesiod *Works and Days* ['When the artichoke flowers and the singing cricket sits upon the tree pouring down a sweet shrill song continually from beneath his wings, in the time when summer is wearisome, then are goats fattest and wine at its best, then are women most wanton, but men at their weakest; for Sirius parches head and knees']: Alcaeus sings in like strain:

Soak your throttle in wine;[4] for the star is coming round again,[5] the season is hard to bear with the world athirst because of the heat; the cricket sounds sweetly from the leaves of the tree-top, and lo! the artichoke is blowing; now are women at their sauciest, but men lean and weak because Sirius[5] parches both the head and the knees.

[1] cf. Dion. Hal. 5. 73, Plut. *Amat.* 18 [2] cf. Plut. *Erot.* 18 [3] cf. Ath. 10. 430 b, 1. 22 e, Gell. 17. 11. 1, Macrob. *Sat.* 7. 15. 13, Plut. *Symp.* 7. 1, Eust. *Od.* 1612. 14, Il. 890. 47, Plut. *Stoic. repug.* 29, Plin. *N.H.* 22. 43 [4] throttle: the Greek is 'lungs' [5] *i. e.* the dog-days are coming

---

for 2½ ll. read here by *B* see Sa. 94 [6] mss ἀνθεῖ δὲ καὶ σ. and μιαρ. γυν. [7] mss λεπ. δέ τοι: ἐπεὶ καὶ: mss ἐπεὶ: γόνα *B*, cf. Steph. Byz. s. γόννος: mss γόνατα

162

Ath. 1. 22 f (after 161. 1–2) . . . καὶ ἀλλαχοῦ·

Πώνωμεν,[1] τὸ γὰρ ἄστρον περιτέλλεται.

163

Ibid. 10. 430 c πῶς οὖν ἔμελλεν ὁ ἐπὶ τοσοῦτον φιλοπότης (Ἀλκαῖος) νηφάλιος εἶναι καὶ καθ' ἕνα καὶ δύο κυάθους πίνειν; αὐτὸ γοῦν τὸ ποιημάτιον, φησὶ Σέλευκος, ἀντιμαρτυρεῖ τοῖς οὕτως ἐνδεχομένοις· φησὶ γάρ·

Πώνωμεν·[1] τί τὰ λύχν' ὀμμένομεν; δάκτυλος ἀμέρα.
κὰδ δ' ἄερρε κυλίχναις μεγάλαις, ἄϊτ', ἀπ' οἴκιδος·[2]
οἶνον γὰρ Σεμέλας καὶ Δίος υἶος λαθικάδεα
ἀνθρώποισιν ἔδωκ'· ἔγχεε κέρναις ἕνα καὶ δύο
5 πλήαις κὰκ κεφάλας, ἀ δ' ἀτέρα τὰν ἀτέραν κύλιξ
ὠθήτω· . . . . .

ἕνα πρὸς δύο ῥητῶς κιρνάναι κελεύων.

164[3]

Ox. Pap. 1233. 32

Κὰτ τᾶς πόλλα π[αθοίσας κεφάλας κάκχεε μοι μύρον]
καὶ κὰτ τῶ πολ[ίω στήθεος· αἰ γάρ τισί κ' ἄλγος ἦ,]

[1] Mein: mss πίν. [2] *E*, cf. δοκίς dimin. of δοκός and *E.M.* 216. 48 Βύκχις· ὄνομα Αἰολικὸν παρὰ τὸ Βάκχος . . . ὡς ἵππος ἵππις καὶ οἶκος οἰκίς: mss αἰ τὰ ποικίλα (ποικίλλις): edd. ἄϊτα,

162

Athenaeus *Doctors at Dinner* (after *fr.* 161. 1–2) : . . . and in another place :

Let us drink, for the star is coming round.[1]

163

The Same : How then was such a lover of drink (as Alcaeus) to be sober and take only one or two cups at a time (as Chamaeleon of Pontus interprets the phrase) ? At any rate the actual song in which it occurs, testifies, as Seleucus points out, against this interpretation :

Let us drink ; why wait for the lamp-lighting ? the day has but a finger's breadth to go. Take down the great cups, beloved friend, from the cupboard ; for the Son of Semele and Zeus gave wine to make us forget our cares. Pour bumpers in a mixture of one and two,[2] and let cup chase cup around hotfoot ; [3]

thus bidding them expressly to mix the wine in a proportion of one to two.

164

From a Second-Century Papyrus :

Over my long-suffering head, over my hoary breast, pour me the unguent. If any man be in

[1] cf. p. 419 n. 5 [2] *i. e.* one of wine to two of water
[3] cf. Ath. 10. 430 a, and 11. 481 a

ποικίλαις [3] 1–2 *B-E* (*C.R.* 1914. 77) from Plut. *Qu. Conv.* 3. 1. 3 (= 42 Bergk), 3–6 *E e.g.*

e.g. πωνόντων. κάκα [δὴ παῖσι βρότοις ἔστ' ὄτ' Ὀλύμπιοι]
ἔδοσαν, πέδα δ' ἄλλω[ν τόδε μοι κωὐκὶ μόνῳ πάθος]
5 ἀνθρώπων. ὀ δὲ μὴ φ[αὶς ἄγαθον πώνεμεν ἔμμεναι]
[κ]ήν[ῳ] φαῖσθ' ‘Ἀπόλ[οι'· οὐ γὰρ ἴσαισθ' ὤγαθον οὐδ' ὃ μή.']

165

Sch. *Il.* 8. 177 [τείχεα ἀβληχρά]· ἄλλως δὲ ἤδη αὐτὸ τὸ βληχρός σημαίνει ὡς ἐπὶ τὸ πλεῖστον μᾶλλον τὸ ἀσθενές· Ἀλκαῖος θ'·

. . . . βλήχρων ἀνέμων ἀχείμαντοι πνόαι

166

Ath. 10. 430 b (after *fr.* 39. 1–2) . . . τοῦ δ' ἔαρος·

Ἦρος ἀνθεμόεντος ἐπάϊον ἀρχομένοιο·

καὶ προελθών·

ἐν δὲ κέρνατε τῶ μελιάδεος ὄττι τάχιστα
κράτηρα . . . . . .

167

Ibid. 10. 430 c (after *fr.* 42) . . . καὶ καθόλου δὲ συμβουλεύων φησίν·

Μῆδεν ἄλλο φυτεύσῃς πρότερον δένδριον ἀμπέλω.[1]

[1] δένδριον Ahr : mss δένδρον

pain, then let him drink. [To all men soon or late the Olympians] give misfortune, [and this woe of mine I share] with other men. And as for him that [says there is] no [good in drinking], you may say to him 'Be hanged with you! [you know not good from bad.']

165[1]

Scholiast on the *Iliad* ['weak walls']: The meaning of the simple form βληχρός without the *a* is usually 'weak' or 'light'; compare Alcaeus Book IX:

. . . the stormless breath of light winds

166

Athenaeus *Doctors at Dinner* [following *fr*. 39. 1–2] . . . and in the spring he says:

I heard the flowery Spring beginning;

and, a little further on:

make haste and mix a bowl of the honey-sweet.

167

The Same [following *fr*. 42] . . . and indeed he gives the following general advice:

Plant no tree sooner than the vine.

[1] cf. Cram. *A.O.* 1. 95. 15, Eust. 705. 62

168

Ath. 2. 38 e [π. μέθης]· ἀπὸ τοῦ κατὰ μέθην δὲ καταστήματος καὶ ταύρῳ παρεικάζουσι τὸν Διόνυσον . . . καὶ παρδάλει διὰ τὸ πρὸς βίαν τρέπεσθαι τοὺς ἐξοινωθέντας. Ἀλκαῖος·

ἄλλοτα μὲν μελιάδεος, ἄλλοτα
δ' ὀξυτέρω τριβόλων ἀρυτήμενοι·

εἰσὶ δ' οἳ καὶ θυμικοὶ γίνονται· τοιοῦτος δὲ ὁ ταῦρος· Εὐριπίδης (*Bacch.* 743). διὰ δὲ τὸ μάχιμον καὶ θηριώδεις ἔνιοι γίνονται· ὅθεν καὶ τὸ παρδαλῶδες.

169

Tzetzes ad Lycophr. 212 οἱ οἰνωθέντες τὰ τοῦ λογισμοῦ ἀπόρρητα ἐκφαίνουσιν· ὅθεν καὶ Ἀλκαῖός φησιν·

οἶνος γὰρ ἀνθρώποισι δίοπτρον . . .[1]

170, 171

Vet. Et. Mag. Miller 258 πῶ· . . . ἔστι δὲ καὶ ῥῆμα προστακτικὸν παρὰ Αἰολεῦσιν οἷον·

Χαῖρε καὶ πῶ τάνδε·

ὅπερ λέγεται ἐν ἑτέρῳ σύμπωθι[2] . . . οἷον·

Δεῦρο σύμπωθι.[3]

172[4]

Ath. 11. 481 a [π. κυλίκων] . . . καὶ ἐν τῷ δεκάτῳ·

Λάταγες ποτέονται κυλίχναν ἀπὺ Τηΐαν·

ὡς διαφόρων γινομένων καὶ ἐν Τέῳ κυλίκων.

[1] ἀνθρώποισι Fick, metre as 124 or, reading δ̯ιόπτρον as disyll., 3rd line of 'Alcaic': mss -ποις [2] mss *Vet.* ἑτέροις σύμποθι [3] *E.M.* om. δεῦρο adding ἀντὶ τοῦ σύμποθι ἢ ἐκ τοῦ πῶ τὸ πῶθι [4] cf. Ath. 5. 666 b, 668 d

168 [1]

Athenaeus *Doctors at Dinner* [on drunkenness]: It is from the condition of drunkenness that Dionysus is likened to a bull, and, through his making drunken persons violent, to a leopard. Compare Alcaeus:

drawing it sometimes honey-sweet, and sometimes as bitter as burdocks

Some men become angry; this is like the bull; compare Euripides (*Bacchae* 743). And some through quarrelsomeness become like wild beasts; whence the comparison to a leopard.

169

Tzetzes on Lycophron: Drunken people disclose the secrets of the mind; and this is why Alcaeus says:

for wine is a spying-hole unto man.[2]

170,[3] 171

Old Etymologicum Magnum: πῶ (the adverb) . . . and it is also imperative of a verb in Aeolic; compare:

Hail, and drink this!

which is equivalent to σύμπωθι in another passage; . . . compare:

Hither, and drink with me.

172

Athenaeus *Doctors at Dinner* [on cups, following *fr.* 164] . . . and in the tenth Book:

The heeltaps fly from Teian cups;[4]

thus showing that a particular kind of cup was made at Teos.

[1] cf. Eust. *Od.* 1910. 18 [2] or like κάτοπτρον, 'mirror'?
[3] cf. *E.M.* 698. 51 [4] *i. e.* in the game of cottabus

173

Et. Mag. 639. 17 οὐδείς· ἰστέον ὅτι τοῦ[1] οὐδείς ὅτε ἰσοδυναμεῖ τῷ οὔτις δύο μέρη λόγου εἰσί, τό τε οὔ καὶ τὸ δείς· οὐδὲ γάρ ἐστι σύνθετον· εἰ γὰρ ἦν σύνθετον ἤμελλε πρὸ μιᾶς ἔχειν τὸν τόνον . . . αὐτοῦ δὲ τοῦ δείς[2] τὸ οὐδέτερον δέν χωρὶς τῆς ου παραθέσεως ἔχομεν παρὰ Ἀλκαίῳ ἐν τῷ ἐνάτῳ·

καί κ' οὖδεν ἐκ δένος γένοιτο·

Ζηνόβιος.

174

Cram. *A.P.* 3. 121. 5 *Il.* 1. 39 [ἔρεψα]· μηδεὶς δὲ ἡμᾶς νεμεσητοὺς ἀποφήνειεν, ὡς εἰκῇ τὸ εἰραφιώτης γράψαντας· οὐ γάρ ἐστι τοῦ ποιητοῦ, ἀλλ' Ἀλκαίου·

Ἐρραφεώτας γὰρ ἄναξ . . . .[3]

175

Hdn. π.μ.λ. (2. 941. 15 Lentz) τὰ εἰς -ος λήγοντα οὐδέτερα δισύλλαβα, εἰ ἔχοι πρὸ τέλους τὸ α, συνεσταλμένον πάντως αὐτὸ ἔχει, εἰ μὴ κατὰ διάλεκτον εἴη, ὥσπερ τὸ πᾶρος·

ἐπὶ γὰρ πᾶρος ὀνίαρον ἴκνηται·

Ἀλκαῖός φησι.

176[4]

Poll. 6. 107 Ἀνακρέων . . . στεφανοῦσθαί φησι καὶ ἀνήτῳ, ὡς καὶ Σαπφὼ καὶ Ἀλκαῖος· οὗτοι δ' ἄρα καὶ σελίνοις.

Acro ad Hor. *Od.* 4. 11. 3 ['nectendis apium coronis']: vel quia Alcaeus frequenter se dicit apio coronari.

[1] *E*: mss τὸ [2] *E*: mss οὐδείς [3] Ἐρραφεώτας *E*: mss -του from οὐ γὰρ above [4] cf. 159

---

[1] cf. *Gram. Gr.* 3. 301, Bek. *A.* 3. 1362 [2] this epithet

173 [1]

Etymologicum Magnum [on the word οὐδείς 'nobody']: It should be noted that when it is equivalent to οὔτις there are two parts of the word οὐδείς 'nobody,' namely οὔ and δείς; it is not a compound. If it were, it would have the accent on the syllable before . . . The neuter of the actual word δείς ('any man') is found used apart from the οὐ ('not') in the 9th Book of Alcaeus:

and nothing will come of anything;

Zenobius.

174

Cramer *Inedita* (*Paris*) on the *Iliad* ['I roofed']: Let no one blame us for writing εἰραφιώτης without due consideration; for it is not Homer's word but Alcaeus'; compare

for the Lord Eirapheotes [2]

175

Herodian *Words without Parallel*: Disyllabic neuters ending in -*ος*, if they have alpha in the penultimate always have it short, unless it be in dialect, as πᾶρος 'decrepitude' in Alcaeus; compare:

for woeful decrepitude is coming.[3]

176

Pollux *Vocabulary*: Anacreon . . . says that he crowned himself with anise, and so say Sappho and Alcaeus; these two poets also speak in this connexion of celery (or parsley).

Acro on Horace ['parsley for weaving garlands'] . . . or else because Alcaeus often speaks of his being crowned with parsley.

of Bacchus was variously explained, *e. g.* because after his premature birth he was 'stitched up' (ἐρράφθαι) in the thigh of Zeus [3] metre 86

177

Ath. 11. 478 b [π. ποτηρίων]· τὰ μόνωτα ποτήρια

κότυλοι,

ὧν καὶ Ἀλκαῖος μνημονεύει.

177

Athenaeus *Doctors at Dinner* [on drinking-cups]: One-handled drinking-cups were called *κότυλοι*

goblets

and are mentioned by Alcaeus.

TABLES

COMPARING THE NUMERATION ADOPTED IN THIS EDITION (*E*) WITH THOSE FOLLOWED BY BERGK IN HIS 'POETAE LYRICI GRAECI' OF 1882 (BGK.) AND HILLER-CRUSIUS IN THEIR 'ANTHOLOGIA LYRICA' OF 1913 (HIL.)

ALCMAN

Bgk.	*E*	Bgk.	*E*	Bgk.	*E*	Bgk.	*E*
1	8	26	26	51	21	75	141
2	9	27	27	52	132	76	137
3	10	28	28	53	52	77	78
4	12	29	31	54	30	78	79
5	11	30	32	55	133	79	134
6	13	31	33	56A	59	80	135
7	14	32	35	56B	60	81	142
8	15	33	46	57	63	82	80
9	2B	34	47	58	64	83	85
10	2C	35	62	59	50	84	86
11	29	36 }	130	60	36	85A	81
12	3	37 }		61	65	85B	82
13	{ 5	38	131	62	66	86	58
	{ 6	39	61	63	67	87	89
14	7	40	53	64	68	88	90
15	1	41	54	65	69	89	91
16	16	42	55	66	37	90	136
17	18	43	56	67	70	91	143
18	19	44	57	68	71	92	144
19	22	45	43	69	72	93	92
20	23	46	44	70	73	94	93
21	24	47	45	71	74	95	94
22	87	48	48	72	75	96	95
23	1	49	Anacr.	73	76	97	38
24	2A		44	74A	77	98	20
25	25	50	51	74B	138	99	145

Bgk.	*E*	Bgk.	*E*	Bgk.	*E*	Bgk.	*E*
100	88	115	146	129	120	144	157
101A	39	116	107	130	148	145	124
101B	96	117	139	131	121	146A	40
102	83	118	108	132	149	146B	158
103	84		109	133	161	147A	159
104	97	119	110	134	122	147B	127
105	98	120	111	135	150	148	34
106	99	121	112	136A	123	149	128
107	101	122	113	136B	151	150	23
108	102	123	147	137	152	151	129
109	100	124	114	138	153	152	41
110	4	125	115	139	154	153	160
111	103	126	116	140	125	p. 78	42
112	104	127	117	141	155		162
113	105	128A	118	142	126		163
114	106	128B	119	143	156		

Hil.	*E*	Hil.	*E*	Hil.	*E*	Hil.	*E*
1	8	17	46	35	72	54	22
	12	18	47	36	73	55	23
	13	19	44	37	74	56	131
2	2B	20	45	38	71	57	81
3	9	21	69	39	75	58	82
4	16	22	*Adesp.*	40	76	59	25
5	1	23	31	41	77	60	62
6	29	24	19	42	2C	61	130
7	2A	25	Anacr.	43	14	62	48
7a	18		44	44	130	63	64
8	26	26	52	45	138	64	50
9	27	27	60	46	141	65	36
10	53	28	10	47	142	66	66
11	54	29	*Adesp.*	48	78	67	37
12	55	30	28	49	137	68	70
13	*Adesp.*	31	32	50	79	69	58
14	21	32	87	51	134	70	89
15	61	33	56	52	135	71	59
16	43	34	24	53	*Adesp.*	72	57

Hil.	*E*	Hil.	*E*	Hil.	*E*	Hil.	*E*
73	15	82	67	90	144	99	39
74	33	83	68	91	92	100	*Adesp.*
75	35	84	80	92	93	101	*Ad.*
76	51	85	85	93	94	102	*Ad.*
77	132	86	86	94	95	103	*Ad.*
78	30	87	91	95	38	104	*Ad.*
79	133	88	136	96	20	105	*Ad.*
80	63	88a	162	97	145		
81	65	89	143	98	88		

E	Bgk.	Hil.	*E*	Bgk.	Hil.	*E*	Bgk.	Hil.
1	23	5	24	21	34	50	59	64
2A	24	7	25	25	59	51	50	76
2B	9	2	26	26	8	52	53	26
2C	10	42	27	27	9	53	40	10
3	12	—	28	28	30	54	41	11
4	110	—	29	11	6	55	42	12
5 }	13	—	30	54	78	56	43	33
6 }			31	29	23	57	44	72
7	14	—	32	30	31	58	86	69
8	1	1	33	31	74	59	56A	71
9	2	3	34	148	—	60	56B	27
10	3	28	35	32	75	61	39	15
11	5	—	36	60	65	62	35	60
12	4	} 1	37	66	67	63	57	80
13	6	}	38	97	48	64	58	63
14	7	43	39	101A	99	65	61	81
15	8	73	40	146A	—	66	62	66
16	16	4	41	152	—	67	63	82
17	*Adesp.*	*Ad.*	42	p. 78	—	68	64	83
	46B	13	43	45	16	69	65	21
18	17	7a	44	46	19	70	67	68
19	18	24	45	47	20	71	68	38
20	98	96	46	33	17	72	69	35
21	51	14	47	34	18	73	70	36
22	19	54	48	48	62	74	71	37
23	20	55	49	48n	—	75	72	39

E	Bgk.	Hil.	*E*	Bgk.	Hil.	*E*	Bgk.	Hil.
76	73	40	106	114	—	135	80	52
77	74A	41	107	116	—	136	90	88
78	77	48	108	118	—	137	76	49
79	78	50	109			138	74B	45
80	82	84	110	119	—	139	117	—
81	85A	57	111	120	—	140	74Bn	—
82	85B	58	112	121	—	141	75	46
83	102	—	113	122	—	142	81	47
84	103	—	114	124	—	143	91	89
85	83	85	115	125	—	144	92	90
86	84	86	116	126	—	145	99	97
87	22	32	117	127	—	146	115	—
88	100	98	118	128A	—	147	123	—
89	87	70	119	128B	—	148	130	—
90	88	—	120	129	—	149	132	—
91	89	87	121	131	—	150	135	—
92	93	91	122	134	—	151	136B	—
93	94	92	123	136A	—	152	137	—
94	95	93	124	145	—	153	138	—
95	96	94	125	140	—	154	139	—
96	101B	—	126	142	—	155	141	—
97	104	—	127	147B	—	156	143	—
98	105	—	128	149	—	157	144	—
99	106	—	129	151	—	158	146B	—
100	109	—	130	36	44	159	147A	—
101	107	—		37		160	153	—
102	108	—	131	38	56	161	133	—
103	111	—	132	52	77	162	26n	88a
104	112	—	133	55	79			
105	113	—	134	79	51			

SAPPHO

Bgk.	*E*	Bgk.	*E*	Bgk.	*E*	Bgk.	*E*
1	1	6	5	11	12	16	16
2	2	7	7	12	13	17	17
3	3	8	8	13	38		18
4	4	9	9	14	14	18	19
5	6	10	10	15	15	19	20

Bgk.	*E*
20	21
21	124
22	22
23	23
24	49
25	50
27	137
28	119
29	120
30	139
31	140
32	76
33, 34	48
35	51
36	52
37	53
38	142
39	138
40, 41	81
42	54, 160
43	140
44	87
45	80
46	83
47	95
48	55
49	83
50	56
51	146
52	111
53	112
54	114
55	96
56	97
57	141
57A	24
58	125
59	126
60	101
61	102
62	103
63	25
64	69
65	68
66	70
67	66
68	71
69	72
70	98
71	73
72	74
73	67
74	75
75	99
76	115
77	116
78	117
79	118
80	100
81	57
82	127
83	128
84	129
85	130
86	121
87	123
88	122
89	105
90	135
91, 92	148
93	150
94	151
95	149
96	152
97	153
98	154
99	155
100	156
101	58
102	159
103	160
104	161
105	162
106	163
107, 108	136
109	164
110	93
111	26
112	62
113	106
114	78
115	27
116	131
117	79
118	143
119	144
120	145
121	107
122, 123	59, 60, 61
124	165
125	28
126	29
127	90
128	64
129	30
130	84A
131	166
132	31
133	32, 147
134	167
135	33
136	108
137	91
138	p. 148
139	p. 142
140	p. 153n
141	109
142	110
143	168
144	169
145	170
146	171
147	172
148	92
149	173
150	174
151	175
152	176
153	177
154	178
155	179
156	180
157	181
158	182
159	183
160	54
161	184
162	185
163	63
164	186
165	187
166	188
167	189
168	132
169	190
170	142

Hil.	*E*	Hil.	*E*	Hil.	*E*	Hil.	*E*
1	1	30	51	58	125	86	122
2	2	31	52	59	126	87	105
3	3	32	58	60	124	88	135
4	4	33	56	61	101	89 }	148
5	6	34	66	62	102	90 }	
6	5	35	54	63	103	91	150
7	7	36	142	64	25	92	151
8	9	37	138	65	97	93	149
9	10	38 }	81	66	69	94	153
10	12	39 }		67	68	95	154
11	13	40	140	68	70	96	155
12	14	41	87	69	71	97	156
13	16	42	80	70	72	98	159
14	17	43	83	71	98	99	160
15	18	44	95	72	73	100	161
16	19	45	55	73	74	101	162
17	20	46	83	74	75	102	163
18	21	47	99	75	115	103	164
19	32	48 }	146	76	116	103a	152
20	22	49 }		77	117	— b	53
22	137	50	111	78	118	— c	96
23	119	51	112	79	100	— d	62
24	121	52 }	114	80	57	— e	106
25	139	53 }		81	127	— f	78
26	140	54	67	82	128	— g	27
27	76	55	141	83	129	— h	131
28 }	48	56	24	84	130	— i	79
29 }		57	120	85	123	— k	108

E	Bgk.	Hil.	*E*	Bgk.	Hil.	*E*	Bgk.	Hil.
1	1	1	8	8	—	15	15	—
2	2	2	9	9	8	16	16	13
3	3	3	10	10	9	17	17	14
4	4	4	11	68n	—	18	17	15
5	6	6	12	11	10	19	18	16
6	5	5	13	12	11	20	19	17
7	7	7	14	14	12	21	20	18

E	Bgk.	Hil.
22	22	20
23	23	—
24	57A	56
25	63	64
26	111	—
27	115	103g
28	125	—
29	126	—
30	129	—
31	132	—
32	133	—
33	135	—
34, 35	*Adesp.* 56	—
38	13	—
48	33, 34	28
49	24	—
50	25	—
51	35	30
52	36	31
53	37	103b
54	42	35
55	48	45
56	50	33
57	81	80
58	101	32
59, 60, 61	122, 123	—, —
62	112	103d
63	163	—
64	128	—
66	67	34
67	73	54
68	65	67
69	64	66
70	66	68

E	Bgk.	Hil.
71	68	69
72	69	70
73	71	72
74	72	73
75	74	74
76	32	27
77	76n	—f
78	114	103i
79	117	103
80	45	42
81	40, 41	38, 39
83	46, 49	43, —
84A	130	—
87	44	41
88	119n	—
90	127	—
91	137	—
92	148	—
93	110	—
94	Alc. 39	Alc. 43
95	47	44
96	55	103c
97	56	65
98	70	71
99	75	47
100	80	79
101	60	61
102	61	62
103	62	63
104	62n	—
105	89	87
106	113	103e
107	121	—
108	136	103k
109	141	—

E	Bgk.	Hil.
110	142	—
111	52	50
112	53	51
114	54	52, 53
115	76	75
116	77	76
117	78	77
118	79	78
119	28	23
120	29	57
121	86	24
122	88	86
123	87	85
124	21	60
125	58	58
126	59	59
127	82	81
128	83	82
129	84	83
130	85	84
131	116	103h
132	168	—
133	*Adesp.* 104	*Ad.* 55
134	*Ad.* 129	—
135	90	88
136	107, 108	—, —
137	27	22
138	39	37
139	30	25
140	31	26
141	43	40
141A	57	—
142	38	36
143	118	104
144	119	105

E	Bgk.	Hil.	*E*	Bgk.	Hil.	*E*	Bgk.	Hil.
145	120	106	160	103	99	176	152	—
146	51	{ 48	161	104	100	177	153	—
		49	162	105	101	178	154	—
147	133B	—	163	106	102	179	155	—
148	91	89	164	109	103	180	156	—
149	95	93	165	124	—	181	157	—
150	93	91	166	131	—	182	158	—
151	94	92	167	134	—	183	159	—
152	96	103a	168	143	—	184	161	—
153	97	94	169	144	—	185	162	—
154	98	95	170	145	—	186	164	—
155	99	96	171	146	—	187	165	—
156	100	97	172	147	—	188	166	—
157	93n	—	173	149	—	189	167	—
158	—	97	174	150	—	190	169	—
159	102	98	175	151	—	191	170	—

ALCAEUS

Bgk.	*E*	Bgk.	*E*	Bgk.	*E*	Bgk.	*E*
1 }	1	18	37	35	158	50	82
2 }		19	38	36	159	51	85
3	1n	20	42	37A	160	52	59
4	1	21	47	37B	51	53	169
5	2	22	20	38	53	54A	170
6	3	23	41	39	{ 161	54B	171
7	4	24	30		Sa. 94	55	124
8	5	25	50	40	162	56	125
9	6	26	{ 40	41	163	57	126
10	7		84	42	164	58	127
11	8	27	21	43	172	59	86
12	9	28	10	44	167	60	128
13A	49	29	22	45	166	61	129
13B	13	30	23	46	123	62	*Adesp.*
14	12	31	24	47	168	63	Sa. 42
15	19	32	121	48A	83	64	87
16	165	33	133	48B	15	65	92A
17	36	34	157	49	81	66	25

Bgk.	*E*	Bgk.	*E*	Bgk.	*E*	Bgk.	*E*
67	31	90	174	112	65	135	46
68	45	91	54	113	66	136	108A
69	88	92	18	114	80	137	136
70	89	93	57	115	95	138	109
71	90	94	58	116	96	139	177
72	137A	95	132	117	67	140	110
73	32	96	79	118	97	141	35
74	55	97	92	119	48	142	111
75	91	98	175	120	52	143	112
76	173	99	62	121	98	144	119A
77	44	100	63	122	99	145	113
78	137B	101	131	123	100	146	114
79	33	102	145	124	34	147	115
80	43	103	135	125	101	148	116
81	139	104	146	126	102	149	117
82	56	105A	147	127	103	150	{61
83	140	105B	148	128	138		{60
84	141	106	149	129	51A	151	151
85	16	107	64	130	104	152	118
86	142	108	150	131	105	153	133
87	130	109	93	132	106	154	152
88	78	110	94	133	107	155	119
89	144	111	176	134	108		

Hil.	*E*	Hil.	*E*	Hil.	*E*	Hil.	*E*
1	1	12	21	24	55	36}	133
2	2	13	10	25	173	37}	
3	6	14	23	26	33	38	162
4	12	15	24	27	32	39	139
4a	25	16	157	28}	159	40	56
5	13	17	158	29}		41	49
6	37	18	169	30	Sa. 42	42	160
7	38	19	125	31	170	42a	143
8	42	20	92A	32	44	43	161
9	47	21	45	33	137B	44	163
10	20	22	88	34	124	45	164
11	40	23	90	35	41	46	167

Hil.	*E*	Hil.	*E*	Hil.	*E*	Hil.	*E*
47	140	60	85	73	18	86	131
48	141	61	87	74	50	87	125
49	16	62	8	75	15	88	58
50	142	63	83	76	57	89	132
51	84	64	43	77	168	90	63
52	91	65	172	78	135	91	145
53	130	66	79	79	126	92	144
54	78	67	22	80	86	93	146
55	174	68	137A	81	128	94	151
56	19	69	59	82	129	95	153
57	165	70	*Adesp.*	83	92		
58	36	71	166	84	175		
59	81	72	123	85	62		

E	Bgk.	Hil.	*E*	Bgk.	Hil.	*E*	Bgk.	Hil.
1	1	1	24	31	15	48	119	—
	2	—	25	66	4a	49	13A	41
	4	—	28	23n	—	50	25	74
2	5	2	29			51	37B	—
3	6	—	30	24	—	52	120	—
4	7	—	31	67	—	53	38	—
5	8	—	32	73	27	54	91	—
6	9	3	33	79	26	55	74	24
7	10	—	34	124	—	56	82	40
8	11	62	35	141	—	57	93	76
9	12	—	36	17	58	58	94	88
10	28	13	37	18	6	59	52	69
12	14	4	38	19	7	60	150	—
13	13B	5	39	154	—	61		
15	48B	75	40	26	11	62	99	85
16	85	49	41	23	35	63	100	90
18	92	73	42	20	8	64	107	—
19	15	56	43	80	64	65	112	—
20	22	10	44	77	32	66	113	—
21	27	12	45	68	21	67	117	—
22	29	67	46	135	—	78	88	54
23	30	14	47	21	9	79	96	66

E	Bgk.	Hil.
80	114	—
81	49	59
82	50	—
83	48A	63
84	26	51
85	51	60
86	59	80
87	64	61
88	69	22
89	70	—
90	71	23
91	75	52
92	97	83
92A	65	20
93	109	—
94	110	—
95	115	—
96	116	—
97	118	—
98	121	—
99	122	—
100	123	—
101	125	—
102	126	—
103	127	—
104	130	—
105	131	—
106	132	—
107	133	—
108	134	—
109	138	—
110	140	—
111	142	—

E	Bgk.	Hil.
112	143	—
113	145	—
114	146	—
115	147	—
116	148	—
117	149	—
118	152	—
119	155	—
119A	144	—
121	32	—
123	46	72
124	55	{19, 34
125	56	87
126	57	79
127	58	—
128	60	81
129	61	82
130	87	53
131	101	86
132	95	89
133	{33	36
	153	37
135	103	78
136	137	—
137A	72	68
137B	78	33
138	128	—
139	81	39
140	83	47
141	84	48
142	86	50
143	—	42a

E	Bgk.	Hil.
144	89	92
145	102	91
146	104	93
147	105A	—
148	105B	—
149	106	—
150	108	—
151	151	94
152	154	—
153	—	95
157	34	16
158	35	17
159	36	{28, 29
160	37A	42
161	39	43
162	40	38
163	41	44
164	42	45
165	16	57
166	45	71
167	44	46
168	47	77
169	53	18
170	54A	31
171	54B	—
172	43	65
173	76	25
174	90	55
175	98	84
176	111	—
177	139	—

LIST OF NEW FRAGMENTS

Fragments not included in Bergk's Edition of 1882

ALCMAN

163
164

SAPPHO

1A
35†
36
37
38
39
40
41
42
43
44
45
46
47
65
66
82
83†
84
85
86
89
113A
113B
158*

ALCAEUS

11
14
17
26
27
68
69
70
71
72
73
74
75
76
77
120
122
128†
134
143*
153*
154
155
156

Fragments newly restored *exempli gratia* from Paraphrases

ALCMAN

14
139

SAPPHO

11
24
29
30
31
33
48†
64
77
89
90
91
92
100†
107
109
110
142
147
154†
157

ALCAEUS

1
4
28
29
30
48
51
65
66
67
80
93
95
96
97
121
133†
150

* Included by Hiller-Crusius   † Partly 'new'

INDEX OF AUTHORS *

* The dates are those of the *floruit*, *i. e.* about the 40th year

INDEX OF AUTHORS

INDEX OF AUTHORS

INDEX OF AUTHORS

INDEX OF AUTHORS

INDEX OF AUTHORS

INDEX OF AUTHORS

INDEX OF AUTHORS

GENERAL INDEX

GENERAL INDEX

GENERAL INDEX

GENERAL INDEX

GENERAL INDEX

GENERAL INDEX

PRINTED IN GREAT BRITAIN BY
RICHARD CLAY & SONS, LIMITED,
BUNGAY, SUFFOLK.

THE LOEB CLASSICAL LIBRARY.

VOLUMES ALREADY PUBLISHED

Latin Authors.

APULEIUS. The Golden Ass (Metamorphoses). Trans. by W. Adlington (1566). Revised by S. Gaselee. (*2nd Impression.*)

AUSONIUS. Trans. by H. G. Evelyn White. 2 Vols.

BOETHIUS: TRACTS AND DE CONSOLATIONE PHILOSOPHIAE. Trans. by Rev. H. F. Stewart and E. K. Rand.

CAESAR: CIVIL WARS. Trans. by A. G. Peskett. (*2nd Impression.*)

CAESAR: GALLIC WAR. Trans. by H. J. Edwards. (*2nd Impression.*)

CATULLUS. Trans. by F. W. Cornish; TIBULLUS. Trans. by J. P. Postgate; and PERVIGILIUM VENERIS. Trans. by J. W. Mackail. (*5th Impression.*)

CICERO: DE FINIBUS. Trans. by H. Rackham. (*2nd Impression.*)

CICERO: DE OFFICIIS. Trans. by Walter Miller. (*2nd Impression.*)

CICERO: LETTERS TO ATTICUS. Trans. by E. O. Winstedt. 3 Vols. (Vol. I *3rd Impression.* Vol. II *2nd Impression.*)

CONFESSIONS OF ST. AUGUSTINE. Trans. by W. Watts (1631). 2 Vols. (*2nd Impression.*)

FRONTO: CORRESPONDENCE. Trans. by C. R. Haines. 2 Vols.

HORACE: ODES AND EPODES. Trans. by C. E. Bennett. (*4th Impression.*)

JUVENAL AND PERSIUS. Trans. by G. G. Ramsay. (*2nd Impression.*)

LIVY. Trans. by B. O. Foster. 13 Vols. Vol. I.

MARTIAL. Trans. by W. C. Ker. 2 Vols.

OVID: HEROIDES AND AMORES. Trans. by Grant Showerman. (*2nd Impression.*)

OVID: METAMORPHOSES. Trans. by F. J. Miller. 2 Vols. (Vol. I *2nd Edition.*)

PETRONIUS. Trans. by M. Heseltine; SENECA: APOCOLOCYNTOSIS. Trans. by W. H. D. Rouse. (*3rd Impression.*)

PLAUTUS. Trans. by Paul Nixon. 5 Vols. Vols. I and II. (Vol. I *2nd Impression.*)

PLINY: LETTERS. Melmoth's Translation revised by W. M. L. Hutchinson. 2 Vols.

PROPERTIUS. Trans. by H. E. Butler. (*2nd Impression.*)

QUINTILIAN. Trans. by H. E. Butler. 4 Vols.

SALLUST. Trans. by J. C. Rolfe.

SCRIPTORES HISTORIAE AUGUSTAE. Trans. by D. Magie. 4 Vols. Vol. 1.

SENECA: EPISTULAE MORALES. Trans. by R. M. Gummere. 3 Vols. Vols. I and II.

SENECA: TRAGEDIES. Trans. by F. J. Miller. 2 Vols.

SUETONIUS. Trans. by J. C. Rolfe. 2 Vols. (*2nd Impression.*)

TACITUS: DIALOGUS. Trans. by Sir Wm. Peterson; and AGRICOLA AND GERMANIA. Trans. by Maurice Hutton. (*2nd Impression.*)

TERENCE. Trans. by John Sargeaunt. 2 Vols. (*3rd Impression.*)

VIRGIL. Trans. by H. R. Fairclough. 2 Vols. (Vol. I *2nd Impression.*)

Greek Authors.

ACHILLES TATIUS. Trans. by S. Gaselee.
AESCHINES. Trans. by C. D. Adams.
APOLLODORUS. Trans. by Sir James G. Frazer. 2 Vols.
APOLLONIUS RHODIUS. Trans. by R. C. Seaton. (*2nd Impression.*)
THE APOSTOLIC FATHERS. Trans. by Kirsopp Lake. 2 Vols. (Vol. I *3rd Impression.* Vol. II *2nd Impression.*)
APPIAN'S ROMAN HISTORY. Trans. by Horace White. 4 Vols.
CALLIMACHUS AND LYCOPHRON, trans. by A. W. Mair, and ARATUS, trans. by G. R. Mair.
CLEMENT OF ALEXANDRIA. Trans. by Rev. G. W. Butterworth.
DAPHNIS AND CHLOE. Thornley's Translation revised by J. M. Edmonds; and PARTHENIUS. Trans. by S. Gaselee.
DIO CASSIUS: ROMAN HISTORY. Trans. by E. Cary. 9 Vols. Vols. I to VI.
EURIPIDES. Trans. by A. S. Way. 4 Vols. (Vols. I and II *3rd Impression.* Vols. III and IV *2nd Impression.*)
GALEN: ON THE NATURAL FACULTIES. Trans. by A. J. Brock.
THE GREEK ANTHOLOGY. Trans. by W. R. Paton. 5 Vols. (Vols. I and II *2nd Impression.*)
THE GREEK BUCOLIC POETS (THEOCRITUS, BION, MOSCHUS). Trans. by J. M. Edmonds. (*3rd Impression.*)
HERODOTUS. Trans. by A. G. Godley. 4 Vols. Vols. I and II.
HESIOD AND THE HOMERIC HYMNS. Trans. by H. G. Evelyn White. (*2nd Impression.*)
HOMER: ODYSSEY. Trans. by A. T. Murray. 2 Vols.
JULIAN. Trans. by Wilmer Cave Wright. 3 Vols. Vols. I and II.
LUCIAN. Trans. by A. M. Harmon. 8 Vols. Vols. I to III. (Vols. I and II *2nd Impression.*)
MARCUS AURELIUS. Trans. by C. R. Haines.
MENANDER. Trans. by F. G. Allinson.
PAUSANIAS: DESCRIPTION OF GREECE. Trans. by W. H. S. Jones. 5 Vols. and Companion Vol. Vol. I.
PHILOSTRATUS: THE LIFE OF APOLLONIUS OF TYANA. Trans. by F. C. Conybeare. 2 Vols. (*2nd Impression.*)
PHILOSTRATUS AND EUNAPIUS, LIVES OF THE SOPHISTS, Trans. by Wilmer Cave Wright.
PINDAR. Trans. by Sir J. E. Sandys. (*2nd Edition.*)
PLATO: EUTHYPHRO, APOLOGY, CRITO, PHAEDO, PHAEDRUS. Trans. by H. N. Fowler. (*3rd Impression.*)
PLATO: THEAETETUS AND SOPHIST. Trans. by H. N. Fowler.
PLUTARCH: THE PARALLEL LIVES. Trans. by B. Perrin. 11 Vols. Vols. I to X.
PROCOPIUS: HISTORY OF THE WARS. Trans. by H. B. Dewing. 7 Vols. Vols. I to III.
QUINTUS SMYRNAEUS. Trans. by A. S. Way.
SOPHOCLES. Trans. by F. Storr. 2 Vols. (Vol. I *3rd Impression.* Vol. II *2nd Impression.*)
ST. JOHN DAMASCENE: BARLAAM AND IOASAPH. Trans. by the Rev. G. R. Woodward and Harold Mattingly.
STRABO: GEOGRAPHY. Trans. by Horace L. Jones. 8 Vols. Vol. I.
THEOPHRASTUS: ENQUIRY INTO PLANTS. Trans. by Sir Arthur Hort, Bart. 2 Vols.
THUCYDIDES. Trans. by C. F. Smith. 4 Vols. Vols. I to III.
XENOPHON: CYROPAEDIA. Trans. by Walter Miller. 2 Vols.
XENOPHON: HELLENICA, ANABASIS, APOLOGY, AND SYMPOSIUM. Trans. by C. L. Brownson and O. J. Todd. 3 Vols. Vols. I and II.

IN PREPARATION

Greek Authors.

AENEAS TACTICUS, ASCLEPIODOTUS AND ONESANDER, The Illinois Club.
AESCHYLUS, H. W. Smyth.
ARISTOTLE, ECONOMICS, St. George Stock.
ARISTOTLE, ORGANON, St. George Stock.
ARISTOTLE, POETICS, AND LONGINUS, W. Hamilton Fyfe.
ARISTOTLE, POLITICS AND ATHENIAN CONSTITUTION, Edward Capps.
ATHENAEUS, C. B. Gulick.
DEMOSTHENES, DE CORONA AND MIDIAS, C. A. Vince and J. H. Vince.
DEMOSTHENES, PRIVATE ORATIONS, G. M. Calhoun.
DIO CHRYSOSTOM, W. E. Waters.
DIOGENES LAERTIUS, W. L. Hicks.
EPICTETUS, W. A. Oldfather.
EUSEBIUS, Kirsopp Lake.
GREEK IAMBIC AND ELEGIAC POETS, E. D. Perry.
GREEK LYRIC POETS, J. M. Edmonds.
HIPPOCRATES, W. H. S. Jones.
HOMER, ILIAD, A. T. Murray.
ISOCRATES, G. Norlin.
MANETHO, S. de Ricci.
PAPYRI, A. S. Hunt.
PHILOSTRATUS, IMAGINES, Arthur Fairbanks.
PLATO, ALCIBIADES, HIPPARCHUS, ERASTAI, THEAGES, CHARMIDES, LACHES, LYSIS, EUTHYDEMUS, W. R. M. Lamb.
PLATO, LAWS, R. G. Bury.
PLATO, PARMENIDES, PHILEBUS AND CRATYLUS, H. N. Fowler.
PLATO, PROTAGORAS, GORGIAS, MENO, W. R. M. Lamb.
PLATO, REPUBLIC, Paul Shorey.
PLATO, SYMPOSIUM, W. R. M. Lamb.
PLATO, POLITICUS, H. N. Fowler.
PLUTARCH, MORALIA, F. C. Babbitt.
POLYBIUS, W. R. Paton.
ST. BASIL, LETTERS, Prof. Van Den Ven.
XENOPHON, MEMORABILIA AND OECONOMICUS, E. C. Marchant.
XENOPHON, SCRIPTA MINORA, E. C. Marchant.

Latin Authors.

AMMIANUS, C. U. Clark.
AULUS GELLIUS, J. C. Rolfe.
BEDE, ECCLESIASTICAL HISTORY, Rev. H. F. Stewart.
CICERO, AD FAMILIARES, E. O. Winstedt.
CICERO, DE NATURA DEORUM, H. Rackham.
CICERO, DE ORATORE, ORATOR, BRUTUS, Charles Stuttaford.
CICERO, DE REPUBLICA AND DE LEGIBUS, Clinton Keyes.
CICERO, DE SENECTUTE, DE AMICITIA, DE DIVINATIONE, W. A. Falconer.
CICERO, CATILINE ORATIONS, Vol. V. B. L. Ullman.
CICERO, SPEECHES, Vol. VI. H. N. Watts.
CLAUDIAN, M. Platnauer.
FRONTINUS, DE AQUIS AND STRATEGEMATA, C. E. Bennett.
LUCAN, S. Reinach.
LUCRETIUS, W. H. D. Rouse.
OVID, TRISTIA AND EX PONTO, A. L. Wheeler.
ST. AUGUSTINE, MINOR WORKS, Rev. P. Wicksteed.
SENECA, MORAL ESSAYS, J. W. Basore.
STATIUS, H. G. Evelyn White.
TACITUS, ANNALS, John Jackson.
TACITUS, HISTORIES, C. H. Moore.
VALERIUS FLACCUS, A. F. Scholfield.
VELLEIUS PATERCULUS AND RES GESTAE DIVI AUGUSTI, F. W. Shipley.

DESCRIPTIVE PROSPECTUS ON APPLICATION

London - - WILLIAM HEINEMANN
New York - - G. P. PUTNAM'S SONS